Dominion or Decline

Dominion or Decline

Anglo-American Naval Relations on the Pacific, 1937–1941

Ian Cowman

BERG

Oxford · Washington, D.C.

First published in 1996 by
Berg
Editorial offices:
150 Cowley Road, Oxford, OX4 1JJ, UK
22883 Quicksilver Drive, Dulles, VA 20166, USA

Berg is an imprint of Oxford International Publishers Ltd.

Library of Congress Cataloging-in-Publication Data

Cowman, Ian.
 Dominion or decline: Anglo-American naval relations on the Pacific,
1937–1941 / Ian Cowman.
  p. cm.
 Includes bibliographical references and index.
 ISBN 1-85973-111-2 (alk. paper). --ISBN 1-85973-116-3 (pbk. : alk.
paper)
  1. United States--Military relations--Great Britain.   2. Great Britain--
Military relations--United States.   3. United States. Navy--History--20th
century.   4. Great Britain. Royal Navy--History--20th century.
5. Pacific Area--Strategic aspects.   I. Title.
VA50.C68 1996
940.54´5941--dc20   96-22984
                                                                                          CIP

British Library Cataloguing-in-Publication Data

A catalogue record for this book is available from the British Library.

ISBN 1 85973 111 2 (Cloth)
    1 85973 116 3 (Paper)

Typeset by JS Typesetting, Wellingborough, Northants.
Printed in the United Kingdom by WBC Book Manufacturers, Bridgend,
Mid Glamorgan.

Contents

Contents

Acknowledgements

I would like to thank the staff of the Public Records Office, the British Museum, the Imperial War Museum, the Greenwich Maritime Museum, Kings College Archives and Churchill College Cambridge, the staff of the National Archives, the Federal Records Centre, the Operational Naval Archives (in particular Martha and Cal), the Library of Congress, the Franklin Delano Roosevelt Library, and the Nimitz Library at Annapolis for all their help and assistance.

I would also like to thank Professor D. Cameron Watt and Dr. Peter Nailor for their valuable criticisms and, of course, Dr. Mike Dockrill, whose understanding and patience was truly monumental.

Abbreviations

ABCD	American-British-Chinese-Dutch
ABD	American-British-Dutch
ACNS	Assistant Chief of Naval Staff
AD of P	Assistant Director of Plans
AFC	Anglo-French Conference
ADM	Admiralty
BAD	British Admiralty Delegation (Washington)
BUS	British-United States
C-in-C China Station	Commander in Chief China Station
CAAF	Chief of the Army Air Forces
CAS	Chief of Air Staff
CGAFCC	Commanding General Air Forces Central
CID	Committee of Imperial Defence
CIGS	Chief of the Imperial General Staff
CINCAF	Commander in Chief Asiatic Fleet
CINCATL	Commander in Chief Atlantic
CINCPAC	Commander in Chief Pacific Fleet
CINCUS	Commander in Chief U.S. Fleet
CNO	Chief of Naval Operations/Office of the Chief of Naval Operations
CNS	Chief of Naval Staff
COS	Chiefs of Staff
CAB	Cabinet
Com Nav Eu	Commander Naval Forces Europe Command
D of P	Director of Plans
D of S	Director of Supply
DCNS	Deputy Chief of Naval Staff
DMO and P	Director of Military Operations and Plans
DNI	Director of Naval Intelligence
DO	Defence Committee
DOD	Director of Dockyards
DP (P)	Director of Policy and Plans Committee
DPR	Defence Policy Requirements Committee
DRC	Defence Requirements Committee
Eastfar	Far Eastern Command

FO	Foreign Office
GB	General Board
GHQ	General Headquarters
GOC	General Officer Commanding
JPC	Joint Planning Committee
JPS	Joint Planning Staff
LNC	London Naval Conference for 1935
Ltr	Letter
MM	Military Mission Washington
MNDBO	Mobile Naval Base Defence Organisation
Mtg	Meeting
OCAS	Officer Commanding Air Staff
OCMH	Office of the Chief of Military History
OCS	Office of the Chief of Staff of the Army
ODC	Overseas Defence Committee
OPC	Operational Planning Committee
OPD	Operational Plans Division of the Army
OPNAV	Operations Division Navy
PAS	Parliamentary Admiralty Secretary
Rad	Radiogram
RG	Record Group
SO	Senior Officer
Sec. Nav.	Secretary of the Navy
Sec. War	Secretary of War
SPENAVO	Special Naval Operations Division
TAG	Adjutant General of the Army
Tel.	Telegram
USAFFE	United States Army Forces, Far East
USFIP	United States Forces in the Philippines
VCNS	Vice Chief of Naval Staff
WO	War Office
WPD	War Plans Division

Introduction

The wartime alliance between the United States and Great Britain has proved to be of endless fascination to historians. One of the most enduring images surrounding the origins of that alliance has been the idea of the existence of a 'special relationship', traceable back to a turn of the century ethos and set of ideals. According to this image, the two most powerful representatives of the English speaking world enjoyed almost a familial relationship. Historical opinion has been divided between those seeing the alliance as a fundamental political expression of an underlying cultural unity,[1] and those seeing it as a marriage of convenience fraught with hostility and suspicion.[2] Thanks to research over the last decade a more balanced view has emerged, admitting that there were indeed certain features that made the wartime alliance unique, yet also recognising that considerable rivalry for advantage and leadership occurred.

To a large extent the origin and nature of the Anglo-American relationship – indeed the very balance between cooperation and conflict – has depended on the area under investigation. There have been detailed analyses of the diplomatic arena in the 1930s, in particular of British and American attempts to coordinate international opposition to the Axis. Other writers have looked at economic policies in the 1920s and 1930s and their influence on politics, and a third group has examined areas such as grand strategy and decolonisation.[3] Recent works have concentrated on how the United States came to supplant Britain as the pre-eminent world power. For example, Professor D. Cameron Watt has investigated in detail how mutual perceptions influenced policy, while David Reynolds has attempted to blend political, military and economic elements, referring to the relationship as having both a competitive and a cooperative foundation[4]. Yet in the period 1937 to 1941 strategic considerations underpinned diplomatic relations; the origins of the alliance were always essentially military. Those dealing with such matters have tended to approach the problem on a national, that is, on a single country basis.

Even less attention has been devoted to the role of the Royal Navy and the US Navy Department, despite the fact that it was they and not the politicians who played a fundamental if not crucial role in its formation.[5] James R. Leutze deals with Anglo-American naval relations from 1937 to 1941, but tries to encompass both main theatres of operation. Yet for the United States it was in the Pacific where war broke out, and the attitudes exhibited towards collaboration in the Atlantic were fundamentally different from those exhibited towards the Pacific; it is thus necessary to distinguish between the two operating areas.

In any case Leutze devotes little space to the most crucial period, the nine months preceding Pearl Harbor. Those authors who have analysed British Far Eastern strategy have tended to leap from the ABC-1 Conference in January, to August 1941 when Prime Minister Winston Churchill discussed with the Admiralty the possibility of despatching an Eastern Fleet. Professor Arthur Marder deals more specifically with Anglo-American naval relations in the region, but, like Leutze, his material is uneven: the bulk of his research deals with Anglo-Japanese naval relations.[6]

This work breaks new ground in three main areas. By concentrating on Anglo-American naval relations in the Pacific from 1937 to 1941, with the first two chapters contributing to a very necessary understanding of the background to this period, it is hoped that a gap in the historical literature will be filled. Secondly, in his two-volume work dealing with British naval policy, Stephen Roskill has characterized the 1920s as 'the period of Anglo-American antagonism' but suggests that in the 1930s this antagonism was overtaken by a spirit of cooperation. This account investigates whether that view was an accurate picture of conditions in the Pacific, and whether this cooperation was a genuine alliance of interests between the two navies or was foisted on both powers by the pressure of events as a marriage of convenience. For Britain, it became very much a choice whether she would exercise dominion over the United States in matters of strategy or suffer inevitable decline as a Pacific power.

This work also analyses the place of both navy plans divisions in the formulation of naval policy, and within each respective navy, as well as the place of each navy in that nation's military planning process. Very often war planning exerted an influence out of all proportion to the personnel involved; very often too, the naval view was in direct contrast to those of the other military services and government institutions. It was their mutual strategic vision and how the navies felt about each other that decided both the parameters if not the limits of British and American strategic naval cooperation in the Far East in event of war.

Finally, to place the discussions that took place in the late 1930s into their proper perspective, considerable emphasis has been placed on the emergence in the 1920s of the Admiralty's Far Eastern Naval War

Memorandum and the US Navy Department's War Plan 'Orange', and the changes that ensued in these strategic visions during the 1930s. For example, the relief of Singapore has been – understandably – the main focal point for British historical investigation. The fall of the base in early 1942 was, after all, the greatest military disaster suffered by British arms. Since its fall, an average of two books a year have been published about the Malayan campaign. W.D. McIntyre, for example, cites some seventy–four titles between 1942 and 1977, and the area was a major focal point for historical investigation in the late 1970s and early 1980s.[7] One might have imagined that there was nothing left that was new to say. However, this work attempts to show that there were strong Admiralty interests in the area north of the Malay Barrier during the inter–war period that very much determined policies in 1941; indeed, in Admiralty eyes Hong Kong was regarded as the equal of Singapore in importance.

From the investigation, four point have emerged that require amplification and definition. Each influenced the direction of naval policy and directly affected naval power in the Pacific. From the beginning, a differentiation must be made between fuelling points (that is, naval anchorages large enough and deep enough for a full fleet with sheltered water suitable for replenishment of fuel oil and supplies, but with a minimum of facilities) and naval bases. Major Harry Stark, an officer in the US Coast Artillery, has provided a good working definition of what constituted a naval base:

> A Naval Base is a navy yard on a fortified harbour containing wharves, docks, storehouses, and machine shops for the supply, equipment and repairing of naval vessels. The best naval bases are those at or near large commercial ports where they are comparatively free from attack and have at hand large accumulations of supplies needed for the service of the fleet.[8]

From a strategic standpoint base possession has always been seen as extremely important, and naval bases continue today to fulfil a necessary logistical role, although the need for such sites to be within easy sailing distance of each other has become less crucial in the nuclear age where the capability and radius of action of ships have increased dramatically. In the 1930s base facilities were seen as vital for the operation of all naval forces in distant waters: they provided for refurbishment, rest, refuelling and repair, and their strategic location was of paramount concern to all navies.

It is also necessary to define the kind of naval forces the Royal Navy and the US Navy Department intended to despatch to eastern waters, and in particular the difference between a capital ship force – which was composed of battleships with minimal auxiliary support – and a fleet, which consisted not only of battleships but also cruisers, destroyers, fleet tankers and supply ships together with considerable paraphernalia.

Fleet concentration, line of battle and the massing of firepower had been traditional concepts since the early days of sail. A historical doctrine aiming at command of the sea had been generally accepted by the middle of the nineteenth century, a philosophy mirrored by the leading seafaring nation, Great Britain, and seen in the design and construction of the early Royal Sovereign class in 1891, then the world's largest battleships. These, along with the earlier Warrior and Devastation designs, were forerunners of the modern capital ship. This is not to argue that battleship philosophy remained unchallenged; for example, the French school of *Jeune École* favoured interdiction by cruiser or torpedo boat along the enemy's main trade routes. However, the traditionalists received a tremendous boost in 1890 with the publication of Alfred Thayer Mahan's *The Influence of Sea Power upon History.* Using the Royal Navy as his mean Mahan (an American) argued that a concentration of naval force in battle fleets decided the control of vital sea lanes; that large scale blockades and not cruiser raids were decisive; that naval bases and colonies were more valuable than large land areas, and that possession of these guaranteed nations world status. Mahan aided the development of a 'blue water' navy in the United States, and exercised considerable influence over the composition of the rest of the world's navies. His views accorded well with British naval thinking at the time, ideas that had evolved out of experience during the long wars against Revolutionary and Napoleonic France. British naval doctrine set great store by the decisive victory gained by Nelson over the French at Trafalgar. By the 1880s, Britain had developed her naval strength around homogeneous battle squadrons designed to maintain command of the sea in all weathers by virtue of the power of their guns.

The naval battle of Tsushima in 1905 during the Russo-Japanese War provided further proof, if any were needed, that encounters were going to be won by superior speed, heavier guns, better gunnery control and high explosive shells, all of which the Japanese had possessed. Speed, together with the idea of hitting hard, frequently and at long range, was adopted by the First Sea Lord Sir John Fisher as Britain's theme, providing the design basis for the new Dreadnought class. So revolutionary was the concept of the fast all-big-gun warship that battleships of ever increasing size and strength were given priority by most naval powers over the next fifteen years. Despite the indecisiveness of the only main engagement between opposing fleets during the First World War – at Jutland – the principles of the 'decisive battle' continued to be mouthed and obdurately reiterated during the whole of the inter-war period. The most commonly accepted yardstick for measuring naval strength remained the tonnage and armament of the battleship. The capital ship remained the 'citadel of effective sea power . . . from which all other classes of vessels derive their power'.[9]

The administrative organization of the British and US navies and their position in the defence structure of their respective countries also needs defining. In Britain, the supreme authority rested with the Cabinet, known after September 1939 as the War Cabinet. Advice to the Cabinet on matters of grand strategy came from the Committee of Imperial Defence (CID), which was dissolved after the outbreak of the war in Europe and replaced by such organisations as the Defence Committee.[10] Regular members included the Prime Minister, the Minister for Coordination of Defence and the three civilian service ministers. Much of the work of the CID was based on its sub-committees, the Chiefs of Staff and the Joint Planning Sub-Committee, the latter consisting of the three service chiefs and the three Directors of Plans together with their staffs. As from September 1940 the Joint Planning Sub-Committee was redesignated the Joint Planning Staff.

Within the Royal Navy a distinction was made between the political and naval arms. The First Lord of the Admiralty – a civilian appointee – was technically the head of the navy. He had a seat in and was answerable to Parliament, and was assisted in his endeavours by both a financial and a parliamentary secretary. All naval matters were handled collectively by the Admiralty Board, which acted as a general council of advice for the First Sea Lord who operated at its head. His naval associates, the Second, Third and Fourth Sea Lords in their capacity as Chief of Naval Personnel, Controller (naval construction) and Chief of Supplies and Transport, along with the Deputy and Assistant Chiefs of Naval Staff and a Permanent Secretary, were all Board members. Beneath the Board lay the various Admiralty Departments, plans, trade, intelligence and other divisions led by their service directors, who were professional naval officers. The First Sea Lord acted as the principal advisor to the First Lord on naval matters, and was also principal advisor in an operational sense. Personal responsibility for the actions of the other naval members of the Board therefore lay with him. As Chief of Naval Staff, he also issued instructions and orders to all other Admiralty authorities.[11] The First Sea Lord was assisted, advised and sometimes criticized by the Deputy Chief of Naval Staff (DCNS) – later altered in wartime to Vice Chief of Naval Staff – the Assistant Chiefs of Naval Staff and the various directors.

Within the British Cabinet there was collective responsibility. A firm statement of policy did not stem from the Prime Minister but from the

Cabinet as a collective body. This was not the case in the United States; while the President might seek the opinion of Cabinet or clarification of information, responsibility for decision making rested directly with him. In Britain the same political party controlled both executive and legislature; in the United States the President did not participate directly in the work of Congress, and neither he nor the Cabinet were ever totally masters of the situation. No organisational equivalent to the CID or the Chiefs of Staff Committee existed: Roosevelt created a Liaison Committee in May 1939 with both service and political representation, but it met only seven times between 1939 and the outbreak of war, so infrequently, in fact, that it was felt to be all but useless. The RAF's chief air representative in Washington, Kenneth Slessor, wrote about some of the problems:

> Morgenthau evinced great interest in our Chiefs of Staff and Joint Planning organisation, and asked me to give him a note on the subject . . . One thing that strikes me very forcibly here is the chaotic condition of their organisation – or lack of organisation – for the coordination of defence. They have nothing in any way comparable to our C.I.D. organisation, and the sole authority capable of giving any decision of any importance is the President who – as far as I can see – never gets reasoned, coordinated military advice setting out fully and clearly the various implications, military, political, and economic, of any course of action. Here again a lot of thinking people are well aware of their shortcomings . . .
>
> I am sure the vital thing to get across to these people, who are genuinely out to help us, is that, whereas their declared policy is to do everything short of war, actually on present form they are only doing at most 25% of what they could do . . . I asked Arnold today whether it was not true to say that if the U.S.A. really got down to it they could double their present planned production of 2500 combat planes a month by mid 1942; he said it was perfectly true but that unless they got some one man to control and direct the aircraft industry as a whole they hadn't a hope of reaching even the 2500. It is the same old story – no coordination and centralisation of all real power in one man – F.D.R.[12]

The Secretary of the Navy was the counterpart to the Royal Navy's First Lord of the Admiralty. A civilian appointee, he was responsible to the President and to Congress. Matters of general policy were normally referred by the Secretary to the General Board. The Chief of Naval Operations, the Commandant of the Marine Corps, the President of the Naval War College and the Chief of Intelligence were all ex-officio Board members until 1932 when they were excluded. A total of eight or nine other officers were appointed by the Secretary. The General Board normally provided advice on such areas as naval technical questions and limitations, but it had no executive authority and was limited to a purely advisory role. The function of strategic planning was handled by the Office of the Chief of Naval Operations headed by the CNO and his staff, together with the chiefs of the semi-autonomous bureaus, including the Naval Plans Division. The CNO was responsible for the use of the fleet in war, and he did issue orders in his own name to the bureaus and the field commands, but not to the Secretary of the Navy.

Planning between the US services was coordinated by the Joint Board. This organisation consisted of the Army Chief of Staff, the Deputy Chief of Staff and the Assistant Chief of the War Plans Division, together with the Chief of Naval Operations, the Assistant Chief of Naval Operations and the Director of the Naval Plans Division. Its working arm was the Joint Planning Committee composed of the chiefs of the plans divisions and their staffs. The war planning agencies in each navy were similar. Both had heavy representations of the conservative traditionalists, that is, those that regarded the battleship and the big gun as the main elements of seapower.

During the 1920s and 1930s the key problem for both navies was finance. In Britain the financial year ran from 1 April until 31 March. Naval estimates were divided into categories which were the responsibility of one or more department heads in conjunction with the Secretariat. After scrutiny by the Finance Committee, appropriations would normally be brought before the full Admiralty Board. The First Lord then presented those estimates to the Chancellor of the Exchequer, who in turn passed them on to the Cabinet for approval. The completed programme would be presented by the First Lord in the form of a White Paper to the House of Commons for debate.

In the US the financial year ran from 1 July to 30 June. American naval estimates were prepared by the Navy's Budget Officer, formulated in accordance with the President's own financial programme and what the administration's Bureau of the Budget would allow. Since annual estimates were often prepared some fifteen months in advance, the War Plans Division also had input and a role to play. The proposals were then reviewed by the General Board and the Secretary of the Navy. The appropriations proposals were raked over in turn by no less than four separate committees: the House and Senate Committees on Naval Affairs between them had jurisdiction over all potential legislation, the Naval House and Senate Appropriations Committees concentrated on naval appropriations that were to be voted on by Congress, and building authorisations and other legislation were handled by the Naval Affairs Committees. There were some nine House Sub-Committees, allowing each naval bureau to present its own case at the hearings for cross-examination. The full House Committee would often discuss combined reports and copies would be sent to the Chairman of the Senate Committee for a second round of hearings and discussions. Under the US constitution all bills seeking to raise revenue had to originate in the House so that an Authorisation Bill would be prepared and referred to House and Senate Appropriations Committees for approval. A third and fourth round of hearings would take place, evidence would be heard and a report prepared, usually under the auspices of one or more of the Sub-Committees. Submissions would be made before the full Committee and a naval bureau might be recalled to clear up minor points before the report was passed back to the House and the Senate for approval.

None of these Committees had any power to pass legislation; they could report and recommend but could not legislate. The peculiar system of checks and balances so characteristic of the American government's system was maintained. Neither the House nor the Senate could consider a bill in the appropriate area without it first having passed either the House and Senate Naval Affairs or the Appropriations Committees, and no Senate Committee could accept any legislation unless it had first passed through the hands of the House Committees. After clearing Congress and Senate an Appropriations Bill, for example, would then be presented to the President for approval. He had power of veto over the whole bill but not over individual items. Overseeing the whole operation was the Bureau of the Budget directly responsible to the President, which had the right to revise all estimates submitted. As a bill passed one authority and then another, the language and text might be altered out of all recognition; under such circumstances a Conference Committee – made up of House and Senate Naval Affairs Committee members – would be called, and staff from the Navy Department would have to clear up any conflicting interpretations.

Thus the American bureaucratic system was a great deal more complicated than that of the British. Like the British White Paper, the Secretary published the Navy's Annual Report for the previous fiscal year outlining and detailing all naval activities and the policy that would be pursued over the next year. The Japanese had little need for intelligence information before 1932; until that time the Annual Report was completely open to public access. In practice, then, it was far more difficult for the Navy Department to hide or disguise appropriations from the prying eyes of the Japanese or their own administration, and this was to prove significant as a factor influencing the direction taken by naval relations between the two countries.[13]

Notes

1. H.C. Allen (1954), *Great Britain and the United States: A History of Anglo-American Relations 1783-1952*, London; H.G. Nicholas (1954), *Britain and the United States*, London. See also Corelli Barnett (1972), *The Collapse of British Power*, London, pp. 254–63.
2. Max Beloff (1966), 'The Special Relationship: An Anglo-American Myth', in Martin Gilbert (ed.), *A Century of Conflict, 1850–1950: Essays for A.J.P. Taylor*, London, pp. 148–71; Christopher Thorne (1978), *Allies of a Kind: The United States, Great Britain and the War Against Japan, 1941–45*, London.
3. C.A. MacDonald (1977), *The Roosevelt Administration and British Appeasement 1936–39*, Oxford; Ritchie Ovendale (1975), *'Appeasement' and the English Speaking World: Britain, the United States, the Dominions, and the Policy of 'Appeasement' 1937–39*, Cardiff; Akira Iriye (1967), *Across the Pacific: An Inner History of American-East Asian Relations*, New York; Carl P. Parrini (1969), *Heir to Empire: United States Economic Diplomacy, 1916–23*, Pittsburgh; Frank C. Costigiola (1977), 'Anglo-American Financial Rivalry in the 1920's', *Journal of Economic History*, vol. 37, pp. 911–34; Michael Hogan (1977), *Informal Entente: The Private Structure of Cooperation in Anglo-American Economic Diplomacy, 1918–28*, Columbia, MO; Stephen E. Pelz (1974), *Race to Pearl Harbor: The Failure of the Second London Naval Conference and the Onset of World War II*, Cambridge, MA; Wm Roger Louis (1977), *Imperialism At Bay: The United States and the Decolonisation of the British Empire 1941–45*, Oxford.
4. D. Cameron Watt (1984), *Succeeding John Bull: America in Britain's Place 1900–75*, Cambridge; David Reynolds (1981), *The Creation of the Anglo-American Alliance 1937–41: A Study in Competitive Co-operation*, London.
5. These include Wm Roger Louis (1971), *British Strategy in the Far East 1919–39*, Oxford; Peter Lowe (1988), *Great Britain and the Origin of the Pacific War: A Study of British Policy in East Asia, 1937–41*, Oxford; J.R.M. Butler (1973), *Grand Strategy: September 1939–June 1941*, Annapolis, MD, vol. 2; Mark S. Watson (1950), *Chief of Staff, Prewar Plans and Preparations*, Washington DC; Maurice Matloff and Edwin M. Snell (1953), *Strategic Planning for Coalition Warfare 1941–42*, Washington DC.
6. James R. Leutze (1977), *Bargaining for Supremacy: Anglo-American Naval Collaboration 1937–41*, Chapel Hill, NC; Arthur J. Marder (1981), *Old Friends New Enemies: The Royal Navy and the Imperial Japanese Navy, Strategic Illusions, 1936–41*, Oxford.

7. Works include W.D. McIntyre (1979), *The Rise and Fall of the Singapore Naval Base, 1919–42,* London; P. Haggie (1981), *Brittania at Bay: The Defence of the British Empire Against Japan, 1931–41,* Oxford; Ian Hamill (1981), *The Strategic Illusion, The Singapore Strategy and the Defence of Australia and New Zealand 1919–42,* Singapore; James Neidpath (1981), *The Singapore Naval Base and the Defence of Britain's Eastern Empire 1919–41,* Oxford.

8. Major Harry W. Stark (1928), 'The Selection and Defence of Naval Bases', *Coast Artillery Journal,* p. 150.

9. At Tsushima Admiral Tojo had sixteen 12-inch guns (all on his four modern battleships) together with one hundred and twelve 8-inch and 6-inch guns able to fire in any one broadside. His Russian opponent had twenty-six 12-inch guns (but only sixteen of these were modern) seventeen 10-inch guns and one hundred and twenty-one 8-inch and 6-inch weapons. Admiral Rozhestvensky's Pacific Squadron was practically destroyed in the engagement; his losses included six battleships. The Japanese did not lose a single major capital ship. Influenced by this, the British produced the *Dreadnought,* displacing 17,000 tons, which was the first battleship to be powered by turbines. The greatest revolution, however, was in her armament: ten 12-inch guns and twenty-two 6-inch guns, giving her the firepower of two pre-Dreadnoughts in broadside and the equivalent of three when firing ahead, thanks to the arrangement of five twin turrets (two fore, one aft, and one on each side). See Peter Padfield (1972), *The Battleship Era,* London, pp. 103–4, 174–5, 192–3; Holger H. Herwig (1980), *'Luxury Fleet': The Imperial German Navy 1888–1918,* London, pp. 54–6; Geoffrey Till (ed.) (1984), *Maritime Strategy in the Nuclear Age,* London, pp. 104, 106–9.

10. Indeed the wider representation on the Defence Committee, both civilian and military, meant that the War Cabinet became to a certain extent a rubber stamp for decision making.

11. Stephen Roskill (1968), *Naval Policy Between the Wars: The Period of Anglo-American Antagonism 1919–29,* London, vol. 1, pp. 25–6; Marder, *Old Friends,* pp. 28–9.

12. Letter from Slessor to CAS, 4 December 1940, AIR 8/446.

13. Roskill, *Naval Policy,* pp. 26–7, 204–6; Lt. Commander Carl H. Schmidt (1933), 'The Navy: Its Contact with Congress', *United States Naval Institute Proceedings,* vol. 59, no. 2, pp. 239–45.

Part I

Anglo-American Naval Planning in the Pacific

–1–

The Royal Navy and Far Eastern Naval War Planning

Introduction

A two-power standard had been sustained by Britain from 1889 until the rise of the German Imperial Navy. According to this standard, the Royal Navy was to be stronger than the most likely combination of any two naval powers; Russia and France were the chief naval opponents.[1] The traditional antagonism between Britain and France had revived after the Armistice in 1918. With the elimination of German naval power at the end of the First World War, the attention of the Royal Navy in the Pacific turned to the United States and Japan, who had become natural rivals for sea supremacy.[2] Rather than permitting Britain to continue with her ship building programmes unchallenged, both the Japanese and the United States navies seemed prepared to engage in ruinous naval competition. The Washington Treaty therefore came as welcome relief from the crippling costs of a full scale naval race. In 1922, Britain agreed to a capital ship building holiday for ten years. Through limitations in overall tonnage in certain classes of ships – apart from some replacements – Britain and the USA were limited to twenty and eighteen ships respectively and Japan to ten. New ships could not exceed 35,000 tons: all vessels above 10,000 tons were controlled by the Treaty.

Settlement of the parity issue in capital ships, however, did not naturally lead to arms reduction in other classes. The Treaty left naval powers with a wide measure of freedom in the design and construction of carriers and cruisers, and complete freedom in destroyers, and smaller ships. A tonnage ceiling was established for aircraft carriers – 135,000 tons for Britain and the USA and 81,000 tons for Japan. Carriers were to be limited to 27,000 tons. *Lexington* and *Yorktown* proved to be important exceptions. The Treaty agreed to permit construction of replacement capital ships as from 1931, but the London Conference extended the building holiday until December 31 1936 and it was expected that all three powers would not lay down replacement capital ships until after that date. They agreed, however, to reach Treaty targets of 15:15:9 immediately. Thus Britain, the USA and Japan were effectively reduced to a one-power standard in terms of naval strength for most of the inter-war period.[3]

From Britain's standpoint, the Empire remained the heart both politically and economically of the international post-war order, as important after 1919 as it had been during the nineteenth century. With well over half of imperial territories lying east of Suez, the Far East retained its stature as the 'jewel' in the Imperial crown. Because of the scattered nature of Britain's possessions, seapower was the first line of defence and despite obvious naval weaknesses, protection of trade routes and sea communications remained of paramount importance. Though it was generally agreed that cruiser construction provided the key to local naval defence, it was always felt that such vessels would not be capable of standing against Japan in open battle. Despite the popularity of *guerre de course*, and the lack of a philosophical base such as that provided by Alfred Thayer Mahan in the United States, the purpose of seapower was still seen by the Admiralty as maritime supremacy, depending – even in the Pacific theatre – upon battleship primacy and fleet action.[4] As one naval officer succinctly put it:

> Almost every fleet exercise of the period was planned to end with a battle between the giants; and the admiral who was held by the umpires to have 'won' it gained great esteem. Destroyers and submarines were disposed and employed to attack the other side's big ships; while the functions of carrier borne aircraft was held to be reconnaissance, spotting for the battleships' gunfire, and using their torpedoes on a retreating enemy in order to slow him up and so allow the big ships to finish him off. Perhaps the best example of the continued dominance of the capital ship is to be found in the 'prolonged firing' which the recently modernized battleship Warspite was required to carry out in 1938 in order to test her new equipment. Admiral Sir Dudley Pound, the Commander-in-Chief Mediterranean, took his whole fleet to sea and staged what can only be described as a 'mini Jutland' off Malta. Indeed the study of that fight continued to take a prominent place in the Staff College and Tactical School throughout most of the uneasy peace; while amphibious warfare joined shipping defence as comparatively low priorities.[5]

If, because of the Washington Treaty restrictions, large-scale naval forces could not be permanently stationed in the Far East, it was still vital that a fleet be capable of operating from there in an emergency, and in the event of future major fleet actions an up to date dockyard would be required. On 26 April 1919 the Admiralty's Plans Division produced a paper investigating dockyard development in the Far East which was particularly critical of Hong Kong. It predicted the existing naval base would be blockaded in time of war and naval forces cut off. Since it was expected three months might elapse before the arrival of a fleet, Hong Kong was vulnerable. This served to underline the War Office view that reliance could not be placed on the arrival of naval relief forces. The Standing Defence Sub-Committee of the Cabinet also felt the colony to be indefensible, and recommended the British abandon the base, retaining only sufficient forces to defend the commercial port. A fleet operating in distant waters would require a secure anchorage, one 'well to the south of Hong Kong' yet central to the Australasian and Indian Ocean trade routes. Singapore was the natural and obvious choice.[6]

During the twenty years of its construction, the expenditure lavished on Singapore was on the one hand used to support the proposition that governments were attuned to Britain's imperial defence requirements, and on the other as a justification for the cries of 'extravagance' from the opposition. At various times it was described by successive administrations as a bastion of Imperial defence, formidable, perhaps even impregnable, or alternatively as a piece of war-mongering folly.

There has been a tendency to see a consensus between the services about the objectives of Britain's strategy, and a unity of purpose behind its direction. Constant use of the terms 'Singapore strategy' and 'main fleet to Singapore' have carried with them the implication that British naval interests were directed exclusively towards the relief of the fortress and that the Admiralty was unconcerned if not disinterested in the area north of the Malay Barrier.[7] British naval weaknesses and the early history of the development of the Singapore base have unwittingly lent credence to the view that the use of Hong Kong by the fleet was 'dismissed out of hand' by the Admiralty.[8]

Yet economic and political dominance of both the Indian Ocean and the South China Sea continued to depend on seapower. As far as the Royal Navy was concerned, only the exercise of maritime supremacy in those areas where Britain had possessions, interests and commitments could guarantee the integrity of the Empire, for the loss of any portion of British territory would affect the whole. This idea was but a continuation of the Admiralty's traditional pre-war principles. Commercially, too, British stakes in the Far East were inextricably tied to the investment and trade, or rather the potential, of the China market. Hong Kong's position as the commercial linchpin of Britain's Far Eastern trade was unchallenged; the value of imports was over £61,500,000 in 1922. Some 700,000 vessels – a total of 46.5 million tons – passed through the port per year.[9]

Before the First World War, Britain's main Far Eastern naval base had been Hong Kong. A capital ship fleet was retained there before 1905, and a 'token' three battleships remained until 1911. Despite the concentration of effort against Germany, the Admiralty still planned to reinforce naval forces there with the main fleet.[10] Of course sufficient refuelling, docking and repair stations had then existed to make such a transfer feasible. The increase in draught, the development of external bulges on capital ships for underwater protection and the change from coal to oil rendered most of the Far Eastern and Indian Ocean bases obsolete, but did not obviate the strategy justifying their construction, despite the reluctance to station a fleet there in peacetime. A force known as the China Fleet, consisting of cruisers, gunboats, and submarines – later augmented by a carrier – remained on station post-war, although by the late 1930s the carrier had been withdrawn.[11]

The Admiralty's main contingency planning document for a Far Eastern war was the Far Eastern Naval War Memorandum, first produced in 1920. Originally a series of standing instructions for naval units, by the mid-1920s its horizons had widened to include associated strategic matters such as detailed timetables and tactical information for the fleet. Alterations were made frequently according to circumstance.

Emphasis was laid on the despatch of a fleet to Far Eastern waters, the overall objective being the protection of all Britain's eastern possessions and the decisive defeat of Japan. Three distinct phases of conflict were envisaged. Phase I was the period before relief, when the fleet moved to Singapore and Hong Kong was defended; Phase II the period of consolidation when the fleet moved to relieve Hong Kong; Phase III was the period of advance when dominance of the Sea of Japan would be achieved.[12] It was recognized by naval staff that for this plan to succeed there would need to be naval bases of sufficient size and quality to allow the fleet the freedom to operate north of the Malay Barrier. Without adequate defences in the form of heavily fortified gun positions, mobile artillery and anti-aircraft guns, airpower and an armed garrison large enough to provide security in the period before relief, Singapore and Hong Kong would be vulnerable to attack. Fuel, ammunition, refurbishing facilities and supplies would have to be located at specifically chosen anchorages en route to provide the means to transfer such a fleet to its intended location.

An Admiralty Myth: The Search for an Advanced Fleet Base

As a supplement to the naval arms reduction talks in 1922 a status quo had been declared on bases and fortifications east of 110° longitude, excluding Singapore but including Manila, Guam, and Hong Kong. Any attempt to improve existing facilities or to create additional bases north of Malaya would contravene Article 19 of the Washington agreement, at least until 1936 when the treaty expired.[13] Even investigation of potential bases ran the risk of discovery with all the concomitant disastrous international repercussions for disarmament negotiations that might entail. During the 1920s Admiralty base development plans – even at Singapore – were challenged by Royal Air Force opposition to fixed gun defences (air staff believed that bombers and fighters could prevent any kind of large scale landing on the Malayan coast within 100 miles of Singapore) and hostility on the part of the Labour Party to the whole concept of a Far Eastern fleet base. Twice, in 1926 and again from 1929 to 1932, all work on the base ceased completely; construction that did take place suffered severe financial curtailment at the hands of the Conservatives.[14] The scheme to develop even more bases was certain to be opposed by Cabinet, the remaining Chiefs of Staff and the Committee of Imperial Defence on moral, strategic and financial grounds.

As the Royal Navy's chief planning agency the Plans Division exerted considerable influence upon the Admiralty Board. Between 1920 and 1933, Naval War Memoranda confidently predicted that on completion of Singapore's defences the Japanese would be loath to attack the fortress while the fleet was en route, and unlikely to risk action in Malayan waters. Instead they would remain completely on the defensive, either in home waters or along the line from the Luchu Islands to Formosa. Despite considerable revision of the Naval War Memorandum throughout the inter-war period, the Admiralty's Plans Division never lost sight of the possibility that Phase II (the relief of Hong Kong) could be carried out.[15] As to the location of bases north of the Malay Barrier, as Britain's principal fortified anchorage in the South China Sea, a leading commercial port and the principal objective for Phase II, Hong Kong was the obvious choice:

> Singapore and Hong Kong. . .are from their situation, obviously better suited for use as concentration, supply and repair bases for a fleet operating offensively against Japan; and although neither of these ports is within close striking distance of Japanese naval bases, a fact which would necessitate the seizure and organization of an advanced base nearer the enemy's shores, there can nevertheless be no question that for the successful defence of British interests in the Pacific, including the defence of Australia and New Zealand against Japan, the use of the two ports is essential.[16]

Since any consideration of Phase II would be 'impossible without the successful defence of the Singapore base', completion of facilities there took precedence – even in Admiralty eyes – throughout the inter-war period. Nevertheless it was anticipated that in the offensive phase Singapore's main role would be as the principal base of concentration and leading repair centre, while Hong Kong fulfilled the role of chief advanced base.[17] Despite curtailments in construction, even as late as 1928 the Admiralty confidently predicted that the base would be completed on schedule by 1931, so that finance for additional works might be considered. The build up of Hong Kong's facilities to fleet standard was expected to take fifteen years.[18]

The success of such a strategy, of course, also depended on the size and strength of the fleet, but this was less of a consideration in the 1920s and early 1930s when even a modified one-power standard provided the Royal Navy with a satisfactory measure of superiority over an equally limited Japanese fleet. Only after the Treaty expired in 1937 did naval ratio alterations and an increase in the number of probable enemies contrive to make naval construction and the size of the fleet critical issues, though such matters were being considered and discussed as early as 1934.

Despite the obvious risks, the Admiralty also made several attempts to circumvent or overturn the non-fortification clauses of the Washington Treaty. Lack of financial support, fear of discovery, resistance on the part of both the Committee of Imperial Defence and the Cabinet to major improvements and Singapore's own priority in terms of resources meant that many of these plans were simply wishful thinking on the Admiralty's part, yet the intent behind such activities was clear.

In December 1923, as an aid to rapid concentration of requisite forces, the Admiralty had decided to form a Far Eastern 'Peace Fleet' consisting of three battlecruisers, a carrier and an assortment of auxiliaries. They informed the government that by 1929 this force would be based exclusively at Singapore when the new floating dock would be in position. As far as the Overseas Defence Committee and the Chiefs of Staff were concerned, this fleet's main function remained the protection of convoy routes from India.[19] However, the Plans Division was preparing to augment the China Fleet. In accordance with the strategic view of the Naval War Memoranda, Singapore – with the only capital ship dock east of Suez – would function as the main repair base while the 'Peace Fleet' operated from Hong Kong.[20] In 1925 the Admiralty's Director of Dockyards concluded that its naval yards would handle gun replacement on ships such as HMS *Hood*:

> It is not clear whether, on the despatch of the Battle Cruisers to China in 1928, the authorized reserve of guns and mountings will be sent to Hong Kong, but this would follow in the ordinary course, subject to storage accommodation and cranage being then available.[21]

Provision had already been made in Article 19 for 'such repair and replacement of worn out weapons and equipment as is customary in naval and military establishments in time of peace'.[22] Construction of underground magazines began on Stonecutter's Island in Hong Kong in 1927, yet 'delays' ensured the more vulnerable above-ground warehouses remained in use, providing considerable additional storage space for fleet purposes. The Admiralty planned to convert all seven of Hong Kong's coal sheds and construct four oil storage tanks in their place. As an addition to Hong Kong's firepower, the use of 15-inch gun monitors like HMS *Terror*, whose shallow draught was eminently suited to protection of coastal anchorages, was discussed.[23]

Liberal interpretation of the status quo agreement meant mines and boom defence material could be stored in a port, even though actual construction of minefields and boom defences was forbidden. By 1933 there were some 380 mines in the colony.[24] Though it was unable to convince successive governments to subsidize private dock construction, the Admiralty deliberately encouraged the development of commercial facilities for wartime purposes. Until such time as replenishment tankers arrived, the fleet would have to operate on Hong Kong's existing oil stocks; it was estimated that at least 60,000 tons would be necessary for the first ten days. An unwritten agreement with the Asiatic Petroleum Company yielded some 26,000 tons for emergencies: by 1930 company reserve stocks were assessed at 35,000 tons, while those of Standard Oil stood at 36,000 tons.[25] Understandably, British naval staff refused suggestions that an international tribunal be set up to ensure 'maintenance of the status quo in the Pacific' through an investigation of base facilities.[26]

The anticipated arrival of the 'Peace Fleet' was also used by the Admiralty as a convenient lever to force reluctant administrations to part with finance for items considered essential by naval staff. Early in 1928 Beatty's successor as First Sea Lord, Sir Charles Madden, pointed out to the Chiefs of Staff that a paucity of gun defences at Singapore meant no battlecruisers could be stationed there in peacetime; accordingly in the event of war, the China Fleet must withdraw from Hong Kong. Needless to say, an increase in the size of Hong Kong's garrison and additional gun defences for Singapore received immediate approval. Three months later in April 1928, anticipating that Singapore's fortifications would be completed on schedule, the Admiralty Board altered the main role of the China Fleet in Phase I from 'protection of Singapore' to 'protection of Hong Kong'.[27]

With respect to this 'Peace Fleet', it is necessary to distinguish between peacetime functions and wartime functions. In peacetime it was intended to be a reinforcement for the China Fleet, operating from Hong Kong to maximize the deterrent effect against Japan. If war broke out and Singapore's defences were incomplete, protection of the

Singapore base and the security of the main fleet's route of passage would be the paramount concerns. The China Fleet and battlecruisers would therefore withdraw from Hong Kong to protect the Singapore anchorage. If on the other hand the defences were complete, the Admiralty hoped to achieve a Phase II situation as soon as possible after the outbreak of war. The role of the fleet would then be to harass the enemy from Hong Kong, so delaying their advance long enough for the main fleet to arrive.[28]

However, there remained a considerable difference between what the Admiralty Plans Division and the Board wanted and what the Cabinet and the Committee of Imperial Defence were prepared to accept. In particular, Labour's 1929 election victory put paid to some of the more grandiose Admiralty schemes as the Government continued to pursue its cherished dreams of disarmament. Not until the outbreak of hostilities between Japanese and Chinese troops in Shanghai was there renewed concern about the weakened state of Far Eastern defences. In response to the recommendations from the Chiefs of Staff in their annual review, the Cabinet finally abandoned the Ten Year Rule on 23 March 1932. Treasury preoccupation with balanced budgets, seen as essential to economic recovery from the Depression, together with the National Government's desire to achieve a disarmament agreement at Geneva, prevented any dramatic increases in defence expenditure that year.[29]

In the wake of the 1933 annual review the Committee of Imperial Defence set up a Defence Requirements Committee to formulate a programme for the repair of the worst service deficiencies. However, its brief excluded any consideration of rearmament for war; its aim was 'to bring British forces to the lowest point consistent with national safety' to create a balanced deterrent.[30] Nor did the Navy have first call on resources; government interests dictated that priority must be accorded a European-oriented air policy, fearing the likelihood of strategic air attack. Heavy expenditure could not be catered for in the Cabinet's sanctioned programmes without sacrificing reductions in deficiencies.[31] Finally, there was also considerable disagreement about Hong Kong's ability to withstand attack within government circles and the Committee of Imperial Defence. As the Chiefs of Staff pointed out:

> There is moreover a conflict of opinion over the question of the defence of Hong Kong. . ..There is one school of thought, to which we subscribe, which, while realizing that Hong Kong is a distant outpost of the Empire and that its chances of holding out at the present time may be somewhat feeble, also recognizes that His Majesty's Government could not in practice entertain the idea of surrendering Hong Kong without fighting; nor could

they admit it was indefensible. On the other hand the opinion is advanced that it is useless to consider the defence of Hong Kong because its defence is impossible in practice.[32]

Despite support from the Chief of Staff, the DRC and the Committee of Imperial Defence, the British Cabinet was unmoved by suggestions that Hong Kong's garrison be increased to six battalions. Although agreeing in principle to the removal of treaty restrictions, Neville Chamberlain, then Chancellor of the Exchequer, was still unwilling to commit the government to providing additional finances for fortifications there in 1936. Even as late as 1938 there were still no military aircraft in the colony.[33]

However, the Admiralty continued its commitment. From a naval standpoint and given loopholes in the Treaty had already been found and exploited, there were two ultimate standards of defence possible for Hong Kong under the Washington provisions. If the Japanese continued to abide by the naval limitations agreement, a general build-up of facilities allowable under Treaty provisions might be acceptable. If Japan abrogated those agreements, developments would have to be sufficiently advanced in order that a first-class base could be quickly established once the Treaty expired.[34] Government financial restrictions, the debate about Hong Kong's defences and the drain on naval resources brought on by a multiplicity of needs and deficiencies did limit what the Admiralty Board were able or willing to accomplish: Phase III had been all but dropped by the end of 1935 and greater emphasis was laid instead on economic blockade, yet it was still anticipated that *guerre de course* could follow successful fleet action after a whittling down of the Japanese battle line.[35]

Within these more limited parameters, the Plans Division remained faithful to the vision. Dominion suggestions that the fleet remain in Singapore until Japanese intentions became clearer were simply ignored by naval planning staff. Completion of Singapore's facilities was seen as 'the surest step to facilitate the early relief of Hong Kong from the outbreak of war', a policy in keeping with earlier naval war plans and the 1928 Corrigenda. Hong Kong's overall importance as a potential advanced naval base remained undiminished:

> The use of Hong Kong is necessary if we are to be able to bring our sea power for the protection of our interests in China and for effective pressure on our enemy. Without it we cannot operate with our naval forces in Japanese waters.[36]

> The object is to reverse Japan's position of advantage and to secure Far Eastern territories. The establishment of the British Main Fleet at Singapore and then at Hong Kong can alone achieve this purpose and permit us to

employ our superior naval forces for the successful prosecution of the war. To establish the Main Fleet at Hong Kong it is essential that the Singapore base should be available. As previously stated, however, the garrisons and permanent defences of Hong Kong and Singapore are inadequate (and the security of these bases could only be ensured by naval forces).[37]

As with Singapore, there was little protection from the landward side, but the War Office planned to increase the range of all counter-bombardment guns by improving elevation and resiting them to give better overall cover while providing interlocking fields of fire. The plan was aimed primarily at protecting the anchorage and preventing a seaward invasion, and Admiralty support for the scheme took the form of an agreement to augment those gun defences with naval gunboats.[38] By 1933 the Air Ministry hoped to establish at least four squadrons of aircraft to protect Hong Kong from shore-based air attack; these would arrive from India Command or directly from the United Kingdom. The personal intervention of the First Sea Lord was instrumental in convincing the Cabinet to establish two airfields.[39] Such measures were again in keeping with the 1931 and 1933 War Memoranda:

> The establishment of an air force at Hong Kong is vital to its defence. With this and the garrison up to strength and moderate increases in mobile armament Hong Kong should hold out.[40]

Ultimately the Admiralty Plans Division still hoped to make Hong Kong into a first-class base comparable to Singapore; the First Sea Lord Admiral Chatfield had mooted the idea in the DRC meeting early in January 1934. Later in the year an attempt was made to persuade Cabinet to abrogate Article 19 completely, and in the following year an unsuccessful attempt was also made to redefine the Treaty so as to differentiate between base facilities and fortifications. Anticipating agreement, the Director of Plans resurrected the plan to replace Hong Kong's coal sheds and to construct three storage tanks in as many years, and it was also agreed to improve gun defences beyond Treaty limits by 1940 by transferring a monitor from Singapore.[41] However, this policy was again opposed by Cabinet and the Committee of Imperial Defence. In late 1935 the CID reached the conclusion there was no possibility of preventing Japan from interfering with the harbour or of providing sufficient cover to prevent attack; there would be no abandonment of the colony, but Hong Kong 'could never become a first class naval base'.[42]

However, the Plans Division and through it the Admiralty Board still refused to abandon the hope that the base might be of use to the fleet. By late 1935, with the easing of the international situation as a result of the Anglo-German Naval Agreement, Chatfield became so confident that he predicted:

> It had been argued that in existing circumstances our initial strategy would necessarily be defensive, but taking into consideration the broader view, i.e. the possibility of the strengthening of our forces in the Far East, or the co-operation of allies, we might wish to pass from the defensive. With a secure Hong Kong it would be possible to push forward a closer blockade, and perhaps, e.g. with the aid of the United States of America – a cordon could be established from Hong Kong through the Philippine Islands.[43]

The Silver Jubilee provided an unexpected boon in the form of a £500,000 gift from Sultan Ibrahim of Johore, the first of a series from the Sultans of Malaya. This enabled work on Singapore's defences to be accelerated. Stage I was expected to be complete in 1936–7, which would enable an earlier start to be made on Stage 2. The completion date for Hong Kong's modernization programme was reduced from fifteen years to ten and then, once the Treaty expired early in 1937, from ten years to five, though the extent of those defences had yet to be decided. On 14 February 1938 the King George VI dry dock opened at Singapore, although the full dockyard was not expected to be ready before 1941; though somewhat delayed, Stage I of the defences was now nearing completion, with the first of the 15-inch gun turrets in position later the same year. The Sultans of Malaya also provided £200,000 towards the costs of maintaining two squadrons of aircraft.[44]

As for Hong Kong, during the 1937 Far Eastern Appreciation discussions it was agreed that as a minimum all close defence batteries planned there would be completed by 1940, two 9.2-inch guns would be modernized and all obsolete anti-aircraft guns would be replaced with later models of better design. Two additional battalions, improved barracks facilities, two aerodromes (with suggestions for a third) and a complement of four squadrons were among the developments which received approval. As far as naval facilities were concerned, a mine depot with 2,100 mines plus additional destroyers, six motor torpedo boats and the 15-inch gun monitor HMS *Terror* would all be in position in three years. As the Appreciation pointed out, it was expected:

> The remounting and resiting of coast defences at Hong Kong will bring Starling Inlet under the fire of our guns and coupled with an increasing garrison in 1940, will increase the difficulty of Japanese landing operation: the increased scale of A.A. defences will make Japanese air attacks more costly; and the provision of R.A.F. units at Hong Kong should delay the establishment of Japanese air bases in China, and increase the risks which

any Japanese seaborne expedition will have to face. . ... [The] changes we have enumerated will, as a whole, increase our power of resistance to any form of attack which the Japanese may make upon Hong Kong and will therefore improve the chances that the garrison will still be holding out when our fleet reaches Hong Kong.[45]

Alternate Bases

Until it was finished, or until completion of the modernization programme, Hong Kong would remain vulnerable to attack. Logically – at least until 1942 – other bases north of the Malay Barrier might have to serve as operational centres or refuges for the fleet as adjuncts to or substitutes for the main advanced base. The most cost-effective solution was to exploit and make use of the naval facilities of potential allies. France and the United States were the obvious choices:

> If Hong Kong has fallen before the fleet can arrive in the Far East or falls despite the measures for reinforcement and relief, the first essential for recapture is an adequate overseas base from which necessary operations can be carried out. Although a considerable amount of hydrographic and other local information regarding a possible base is available, selection is complicated by political and other considerations.[46]

The Admiralty was never able to rid itself of reservations about a close naval relationship with France. Whether the French fleet was being used as a convenient mean against which to measure British naval strength or whether the Royal Navy regarded the French with genuine hostility is debatable; certainly the Admiralty had been most anxious to secure arms agreements with the French at the 1930 London Conference. However, even though the Cabinet and the DRC Committee agreed unanimously that war with France should not even be considered a possibility, as late as 1934 the Admiralty still saw France as a potential enemy:

> A proper naval defence is that we should be able to provide in the Far East a naval force of sufficient strength to secure the Empire and our supplies against any Japanese encroachment, and at the same time insure ourselves in Europe against interference by the strongest European naval power – namely France. The Naval Staff would be failing in their duty if they omitted to emphasize. . .the potential threat of the very numerous and strong French light forces and submarines. These forces now exist, and we are not prepared to meet a potential threat to our supplies which enables France at an opportune moment, if she so wills, to bring serious pressure to bear on us in world councils.[47]

Like the US Navy, the Admiralty tended to view the world in Darwinian terms. The first law of the state was self-preservation; international relations were dictated by competition. Control of the sea through maritime commerce and naval supremacy was the means to achieve predominant influence. France had been Britain's traditional opponent, and there was already considerable disquiet within the Admiralty about French territorial annexations in the South China Sea. By mid-1934, France had the formidable total of fifty-four cruisers and had laid down two 26,000 ton Dunkerque class battlecruisers. It was although anticipated that if Italy went ahead with the construction of two 35,000 ton battleships, France would certainly follow suit.[48] It was with the greatest reluctance that the Admiralty agreed to naval conversations about future mutual cooperation in 1938, and it remained distinctly unwilling to exchange technical information or reveal plans fully to the French. The latter remained blissfully unaware of Admiralty intentions regarding Phase II.[49]

There was generally a greater sense of community with the United States than with France. However, hope that the United States might provide help in the event of war in the Far East was tempered by concern over the isolationist mood of American public opinion, and by a fear that Britain might be used as a 'cat's paw' and then deserted.[50] In 1939 a Foreign Office official summed up the dichotomies that plagued British Far Eastern policies in this period:

> If we give way to Japanese demands we shall alienate the Americans, who will regard us as poltroons and not worth saving. If we risk our position in Europe by standing up to Japan with force and get away with it, the Americans will applaud us and do nothing, because it will not be necessary for them to do anything. If we stand up to Japan and get a bad knock, American sentiment may, after an interval, allow the Administration to come to our aid, but in the meantime we may suffer a lot of damage. However, if we do not stand up to Japan we are going to suffer that damage anyway, and alienate the Americans at the same time.[51]

In fact an exchange of letters between the Japanese Foreign Office and the State Department in 1934 suggested that the Japanese would even be prepared to abandon demands for naval parity in return for American recognition of the puppet state of Manchukuo and the dismantling of air bases in the Philippines. Reports that American public opinion was being 'prepared for a renunciation of such interests in China as it cannot actively defend', and developing American support favouring Philippine independence, seemed indicative of a US desire to withdraw from the Far East both politically and militarily.[52] Without some kind of an understanding between the USA and Japan, there were strong fears that internecine quarrels such as the Moro and Sakdalistas revolts, together with what was perceived as inherent internal weaknesses within the future Philippine Republic, would tempt Japan to interfere in the domestic political scene as she had in Manchuria. The establishment of a Formosan fishing community on Davao had quickly led to the spread of Japanese control of agriculture and commerce over the whole province; over 372,000 acres of arable land on Mindanao were controlled by forty-one Japanese corporations, and much more land was owned through 'surrogate' Filipino owners.

The Hare-Hawes-Cutting Bill, which had passed both Houses of the American Congress in 1932, had included many unpalatable provisions for Manual Quezon and his Nacionalista Party which had led the fight for Philippine independence.[53] It was no surprise that the Bill was rejected by the Philippine legislature in March 1933. Quezon immediately set off for the United States to negotiate a new arrangement, but found US authorities too preoccupied with domestic concerns a result of the US federal elections and the problems of economic recovery. Quezon was forced by American indifference to accept an amended Hare-Hawes-Cutting Bill on the understanding that certain provisions would be reassessed later. Under the new Tydings-McDuffie Act, a ten-year transitional commonwealth period provided America with considerable influence in domestic affairs and almost total control over foreign policy. US military and naval bases might be retained after independence, but the US President was also required to negotiate a treaty with other powers to neutralize the islands.[54]

Prompted by the incompatibility between these elements and totally disenchanted with the Act's economic provisions, Quezon made several approaches to the British government about joint guarantees or even Philippine entry into the Commonwealth. The creation of a viable local defence system and the appointment of General Douglas MacArthur as military adviser – on his retirement as US Army Chief of Staff – was designed to offset Philippine security problems, but this could at best provide only a partial solution. Quezon felt he desperately needed the backing and support of a maritime power, even if only as insurance against Japan. Lieutenant Colonel Frank Hodsoll of Warner Barnes and Company, chief representative for Imperial Airways and a former British resident, also exerted considerable influence as the new President's trusted confidant.[55] In 1932 the British vice-consul in Manila suggested Britain occupy Corregidor when American withdrawal from the islands took place. Hodsoll also wrote to Sir Austen Chamberlain (an old friend, now on the government back benches) the following year about the matter, and George Sansom, councillor at the Tokyo Embassy, held private conversations with Hodsoll shortly after Quezon's return from Washington in May 1934. He revealed that Quezon had 'no faith in guarantees of independence' and was prepared 'to go hat in hand to Downing Street'.[56] During the course of Quezon's visit to the United States the following year, enquiries were made through the British Embassy in Washington about a joint guarantee against an attack on the Philippines, and at the end of 1936 Hodsoll called at the Foreign Office to request a formal meeting while Quezon was visiting Britain for the coronation. Quezon intended to sound out the possibility of either incorporation into the British Commonwealth or an alliance with the British Empire; alternatively, he proposed Philippine membership of the League of Nations or an international treaty whereby independence could be guaranteed.[57]

The services favoured a British commitment. The Admiralty's Director of Naval Intelligence (DNI) predicted a total American withdrawal would quickly be followed by economic and then political hegemony of the islands by Japan, a 'dangerous development' which would create 'grave problems' since Japan would be astride the lines of communications between Singapore and Hong Kong north of Palawan, dangerously close to Borneo and Malaya.[58] Nor were the Chiefs of Staff entirely blind to the strategic advantages offered if use could be made of former American bases:

> If we could use Manila as a strategic base in wartime or to a lesser extent if we could use one or other of several natural anchorages in the Philippines for our fleet, our strategic situation at sea would be greatly strengthened. An alternative base on the other side of the China Sea from Hong Kong would greatly strengthen the position of that base, and would simplify the problem of countering a Japanese threat to the territory and communications of Australia and New Zealand via the Japanese Mandated islands.
>
> The Philippines are well situated for guarding against such a threat and at the same time covering Hong Kong.[59]

However, the desirability of making such a commitment was tempered by political concerns. The Foreign Office was intrigued by the suggestion but was uncertain as to its practicality, as it was 'difficult to see what arrangement could be arrived at between the Philippines and the US when the foreign policy of the former will be run by the U.S.'[60] There remained considerable confusion too about the extent of future American military commitments. Reports indicated the United States would demilitarize all bases and withdraw to Hawaii, retain the status quo with existing facilities, or construct a separate 'Gibraltar of the Far East' on Palawan or Mindanao. Even so the idea continued to be part of discussions on Philippine security, until events in the late 1930s rendered the chances of British intervention in the area void.[61] By appointing Paul V. McNutt as Philippine High Commissioner, without the permission of or consultation with the Philippine legislature, President Roosevelt served notice that American political and economic domination of that nation's domestic scene would continue. British authorities began to doubt both Quezon's power to negotiate an arrangement and his capacity to do so. Quezon's poor health was a major consideration (he was slowly dying of tuberculosis)[62] but his constant threat to shorten the Commonwealth period and declare early independence unless the US reassessed the economic provisions of the Tydings-McDuffie Act simply created confusion.[63]

By late March 1936, the Foreign Office had prepared a memorandum for CID outlining the various alternatives concerning Philippine security. An Anglo-American guarantee for the islands was a possibility, but was the USA reliable? The memorandum expressed the innermost fear of the Foreign Office that in the last analysis Britain would in 'left in the lurch'. Philippine membership of the League of Nations was rejected, because while this would commit Britain it would not obligate non-members such as the USA or Japan. Another alternative was to seek a neutralization treaty, but this raised the same problems as an Anglo-American agreement by providing a pretext for US withdrawal. This idea later became associated with Australian suggestions for a regional 'Peace Area', an idea successfully resisted by an Admiralty committed to increasing rather than reducing British Far Eastern base facilities and fortifications.[64]

As far as the Chiefs of Staff and the Admiralty Board were concerned, any change in the status of the Philippines would undoubtedly continue to affect the security of British communications, interests and possessions, and the integrity of the Netherlands East Indies as well. Both were prepared to station naval forces there in peacetime, but they remained reluctant to take on the enormous burden entailed in underwriting defence overall. Instead they preferred to encourage continued American occupation, maintaining the status quo in the hope an Anglo-Japanese conflict would eventually widen sufficiently to bring the United States into any war. Future discussions with the United States might even evolve some leasing arrangement or joint use of bases which could accelerate the timing of such an entry. In the end a definite decision was made to abandon the idea of incorporation into the Empire 'except as a last resort'.[65] But the question of the use of harbours in the Philippines was to be a recurring theme in Admiralty Far Eastern strategy, and would prove of great significance late in 1941.

Fuelling Anchorages

By 1925 detailed timetables, arrival graphs and fuelling berths had been prepared to take the fleet as far as Singapore. As Italy was not regarded as hostile at this stage, no consideration was given to the possible closure of the Suez Canal. The capital ships would refuel at the south end of the Red Sea, pass both sides of Socotra and refuel again at Addu Atoll in the Maldives. One aircraft carrier and a cruiser squadron would refuel at Colombo and the destroyers would refuel at Trincomalee and Nancoury Harbour in the Nicobars, which was the final assembly point. The fleet would then pass between Nicobar Island and Atjeh Head into the Straits of Malacca and on to Singapore.[66]

If the 1920s saw attention being devoted by the Admiralty to the transfer of the fleet to Singapore, the 1930s saw attention being devoted to the problems of its despatch to Hong Kong.[67] An area of unsurveyed shoals, reefs and islands to the west of Palawan – known as the 'Dangerous Ground' – was of particular interest. In 1928 the survey vessel HMS *Herald* began the first of a series of visits, and during March and April 1931 photographic flights by naval flying boats from HMS *Iroquois* covered the Palawan passage. *Iroquois* met with HMS *Herald* and HMS *Bridgewater* at Commodore Reef and Investigator Shoal 'with a view to locating possible fleet fuelling bases and anchorages'. The Admiralty anticipated secure knowledge of this region would enable raids to be carried out on Japanese lines of communications; expeditionary forces proceeding south might be ambushed by British naval vessels who would escape retribution by hiding amongst shoals and reefs to which an insufficiently informed enemy would not have access. General interest in advanced air bases as choke points, and Air Ministry curiosity about using Commodore Reef as an aircraft refuelling base en route to Hong Kong, led to investigation of Half Moon and Royal Captain Shoals in 1932. The report of HMS *Herald* showed Royal Captain as 'doubtful' but others as 'possible'.[68]

All relevant information concerning the area was included in a comprehensive Admiralty survey of the entire Pacific region prepared in 1933. This document is a remarkable example of the advantages accruing from the more traditional uses of seapower. Despite the fact that some locations had so little visible land they were awash at high tide, and others were too exposed or topographically unsuited, all were listed, described and categorized. 'A' class anchorages were seen as suitable for capital ship fleets, 'B' class anchorages favoured vessels up to cruiser standard and 'C' class anchorages were suited to light forces only.[69] The Admiralty recognized that if Hong Kong were heavily under siege, extended operations in the South China Seas might have to be undertaken: other bases would be necessary as adjuncts to the main advanced base or as insurance in case Hong Kong's defences should collapse, while additional bases would, it was believed, facilitate the early relief of Hong Kong itself.

The means to establish such bases had been under investigation since the 1920s. The original intention was to form an independent self-supporting unit which could proceed to any selected position to seize and defend it while a safe refuelling and minor repair base was created. All necessary material would be on shore within forty-eight hours and within a week the base would be secure from destroyer, submarine or air attack. Within a month the base would be operational. Royal Marines based on Cyprus first tested the idea near the Gallipoli Peninsula from 1923 to 1924; later many of the principles were successfully applied to a Mobile Naval Base Defence Organization (MNDBO) at Alexandria during the Abyssinian crisis, though from its inception this unit was always intended for operations in the Far East.[70]

However, suitable sites were limited by the lack of British territory between Singapore and Hong Kong. In 1934, C-in-C China Station suggested Brunei Bay or some other base in North Borneo, reasoning it could guard trade routes south of the line Malaya–Fiji as well as aid the relief of Hong Kong. Even though naval staff agreed to use Brunei Bay and Lambang as fuelling anchorages and Gaya Bay as an advanced fleet base, these were still felt to be too far from the main scene of action.[71] One way to acquire bases was to lay claim to suitable anchorages from among the many islet reefs and atolls north of Singapore. The 1933 'Ports and Anchorages' Survey also considered using bases belonging to potentially friendly powers, and particular attention was devoted to the Indochina coast and the Philippines.[72]

By 1930 the French had annexed Spratley Island and Amboyna Cay, and the following year they laid claim to all islands within the area 7° and 12° North. In July 1933 French title was established to North Danger Reef, Itu Aba and Thi Tu. Despite vehement Admiralty protests, such actions failed to rouse the interest of either the Foreign or the Colonial Office; in fact, the Foreign Office ignored the strategic implications almost entirely. Sir John Simon, then Secretary of State for Foreign Affairs, felt that there was little use in putting forward a claim unless the British case was strong enough to bring before the Permanent Court of International Justice. Legal officers were more concerned with whether discovery carried full right of title or perhaps only an inchoate title which had to be followed by settlement.

All this was rather moot as far as the Admiralty was concerned. Their chief interest lay in contesting the French title to these islet reefs over a large area, not in the legality of the British claim. By the end of 1932 the Admiralty had become so incensed by Foreign Office treatment of the annexation question as an 'academic exercise in jurisprudence' that they threatened to take the whole matter to independent arbitration. In the end no direct challenge to French title was ever made for fear of drawing the attention of the Japanese to this question. Effectively for the next few years the whole area became a no man's land, with the question of annexation being deliberately left nebulous to allow renewal of Admiralty survey work. No agreement was reached but, because they themselves lacked naval support in the Far East, the French in effect looked the other way.[73]

Surveys of the Palawan Passage were included in the Naval War Memoranda from 1933, while charts of the 'Dangerous Ground' and the Paracels were prepared by HMS *Herald* and HMS *Adventure* between 1934 and 1936. Reconnaissance work between 1936 and 1938 revealed that no suitable anchorage existed between Hong Kong and Hainan. Hoihow harbour on the China coast was eventually ruled out by C-in-C China Station, while Nau Chow near the Lei Chow Peninsula was already leased by the French. However, secret sea routes through the South China Sea were nearing completion by 1937, and it was expected by the Plans Division that Kam Ranh Bay might be used as a refuelling base.[74]

The period before relief – defined as the time in which both the Singapore and Hong Kong garrisons must hold their positions – was fixed in March 1937 by the Chiefs of Staff at seventy days and ninety days respectively, not counting time for mobilisation. Under the Naval Plans Division's long-range strategy the fleet was expected to reach Singapore in twenty-eight days from the Suez Canal, or in forty-five days if the route round the Cape of Good Hope was used because the Mediterranean was blocked (since the Ethiopian crisis it had been recognized that the Suez Canal might not be available). A total of ten days was added for preliminary preparations such as fuelling, storing and ammunitioning, and another fifteen days for refuelling, delays and adverse weather. Once the main fleet arrived at Singapore the enemy was expected to withdraw along his lines of communications. British naval forces were prepared to fight a fleet action if their opponent chose to do so under unfavourable circumstances with the British Fleet sheltering under the guns of its fortress. Replenishment and repair of the fleet would then take place, and preparations would be made for the advance to Hong Kong.

Once the fleet steamed out from Singapore the Japanese – still preoccupied with the siege of the advanced base – would be forced to decide between fleet action or the withdrawal of their forces. The 'R' class battleships had a top speed of only nineteen knots compared with the twenty-three knot Japanese battleline, but it mattered little since the onus for action would always lie with the Japanese, and what the British Fleet lacked in speed it more than made up for in defensive firepower. The 'R' class were also felt to be useful as base defence ships. Japanese forces would then be cleared from the South China Sea and cruiser raiding forces would be hunted down throughout the Pacific. It was expected that Japan's main line of communications would extend south from Swatow, north of Hong Kong on the Chinese mainland, so one of the first actions undertaken by the fleet would be to bombard that port and render it inoperable. It was hoped this action would facilitate the relief of Hong Kong if still under siege. If the Japanese Fleet refused action en route to the advanced base, it might still be drawn into a main fleet engagement by the need to protect its own supply centres. During Phase III economic strangulation would be imposed, though it was expected to take two years before Japan surrendered.[75]

By early 1938 the choice of alternate sites had narrowed to three possible locations. In April 1937 British authorities reached agreement on joint Anglo-Chinese development of Hainan, which included among other things a railway construction programme and the creation of harbour facilities for civilian and naval use. If Hong Kong was to be relieved, fuelling would be possible at Kam Ranh Bay or the Paracels. However, to facilitate continued operations in the vicinity of Hong Kong the Plans Division − with the permission of the Chinese − expected to make use of the MNDBO to establish an advanced naval base on the south side of Hainan at Gaalong Bay. Alternatively, in order to avoid coming within range of Formosa or the Pescadores, the 'relief expedition' would pass through the Philippines to land in the Amani or Okinawan groups. To facilitate the operation, advanced naval bases would have to be established on the east coast of the Philippines. Not unnaturally, the other Chiefs of Staff regarded such plans as over-ambitious and the prospects of the US sanctioning this were seen as 'remote'.[76] That such contingencies were considered at all reveals that many in the Royal Navy had little understanding of political or naval realities concerning the Pacific, or the real implications of a Far Eastern war.

With the sinking of the USS *Panay* by Japanese bombers in December 1937, the possibility of a future economic blockade or joint fleet action was discussed with Captain Royal E. Ingersoll of the American Naval War Plans Division in London in January 1938. In event of future joint operations in time of war, it was agreed that all waters of the United States, including the Philippines, would be available for British warships and all British ports could be used by US naval forces.[77] The

1938 Naval War Memorandum therefore expressed a clear preference for the Philippines:

> If the political situation permitted the ideal harbour for an advanced base would be Manila. Failing the use of American harbours Kamranh Bay would be the most suitable French harbour. If no harbours other than British and Chinese were available our choice is restricted at present to Borneo and the Paracel Islands. The harbours in Borneo are about 1000 miles from Hong Kong and it is difficult to see how effective operations could be staged in that area from so great a distance. The possibility of using the Crescent Group, Paracel Islands had been fully investigated, but it has been found not to be suitable as an advanced base owing to the difficulty of providing adequate protection against air attack.[78]

In April 1937 the Air Officer commanding the Far East enquired whether Itu Aba or Thi Tu were suitable as air bases. But a leasing arrangement would not legally exclude reciprocal arrangements with Japan and, recognising any direct challenge or claim would simply arouse the French, the Admiralty opted for the establishment of joint air facilities through a most favoured nation arrangement. Deeply concerned about any Japanese challenge to its territorial annexations, France was also anxious to strengthen its position and so permitted the Royal Navy to survey all nearby islands in 1938 with a view to joint annexation. Flat Island and West York Island were found to be suitable, but Itu Aba was too small and Thi Tu was troubled by its crusty surface and seepage problems.[79]

By April 1938, C-in-C China Station was reporting that even the MNDBO could only provide partial protection for Gaalong Bay and the Paracels. Some five miles of nets and a three mile long anti-submarine boom would be necessary before either base could be considered 'secure', and such expense could simply not be catered for in Admiralty programmes.[80]

On 7 July 1937, Chinese and Japanese troops clashed at the Marco Polo bridge near Peking, and before long the incident escalated into full scale war. By May 1938 Japan began to undermine Admiralty intentions by advancing along the China coast from Amoy. By October Bias Bay, some thirty-five miles from Hong Kong, had been seized. Although the Admiralty still considered it undesirable that reefs and islands should be allowed to fall into the hands of a potential enemy, they were forced to stand by helplessly as Japan occupied Hainan in February 1939 and then the Spratley Islands in March. Use of Manila's facilities still depended on American political and military guarantees of support, and given the Roosevelt administration's aversion to foreign policy commitments, such an arrangement appeared a remote possibility.[81]

Fatal Miscalculations

The strategies described above were from the beginning based on faulty assumptions about both Japanese and British capabilities. It was presumed that in the event of war Japan would adopt a purely defensive posture. The careful programme of territorial expansion in the 1930s had reinforced the idea of the Japanese as strategically cautious, prone to 'careful consideration before any action', and therefore unlikely to adopt policies which might involve any serious risks.[82] It was expected the Japanese Navy would be equally lacking in terms of enterprise, skill and determination when faced with the imminent arrival of the British Fleet at its 'inviolate' Far Eastern base. The idea that Japan might land expeditionary forces on the Malayan coast seems to have received little consideration from naval planning staff, but then as far as the Admiralty was concerned the security of the naval base was the justification for the presence of military forces in Malaya. There was no reason to expect that Japan would view things any differently.

Japanese naval power was generally underrated by the Admiralty. All courtesy visits by Royal Navy ships to Japanese ports had been suspended from 1936, and Japanese security in and around their naval yards and installations had intensified to such an extent that little in the way of first-hand intelligence was available. The Royal Navy had no more than superficial knowledge of its potential Far Eastern adversary, yet it retained the usual unshakable faith in Britain's own naval tradition. As Sir Samuel Hoare, First Lord of the Admiralty, pointed out at the Imperial Conference in 1937, it was expected that the 'superior fighting qualities of the British Fleet' would provide security even when 'slightly inferior' to Japanese naval forces.[83] As Arthur Marder has so eloquently pointed out:

> Ship for ship, gun for gun, and man for man, R.N. officers thought their Navy had the advantage and that their admirals were probably better. The Royal Navy therefore contemplated with a reasonable equanimity and confidence the prospect of having to take on the Japanese Navy at some future time, assuming there would be secure bases from which to operate and that numerical comparisons in capital ships on the spot would not be one sidedly against them.[84]

Such assessments were also based on assumptions about British, German and Japanese naval construction programmes, assumptions which ultimately proved to be incorrect. Most plans, for example, presumed that the system of naval ratios would continue, particularly with respect to capital ships. From the Admiralty's standpoint the emphasis in any naval rearmament programme was going to be battleship construction. These remained the mean by which seapower was measured. By 1935 the prospect of a renewal of the naval race in all classes of ships – thanks to Japan's abrogation of the Washington treaty system, changes in the French and Italian naval construction and the development of German naval power – endangered the two-ship margin of battleship superiority then considered necessary to guarantee Far Eastern security. In 1935, although primarily concerned with deficiencies and not rearmament, the DRC Committee had recommended a five-year construction programme for replacement of obsolete ships as well as modernization of the remaining vessels. The original DRC programme was to have extended over seven years; parity with Germany and Japan would be achieved by 1942.[85] However, the Committee was also instructed to begin examination of defence requirements on the basis that financial considerations could be set aside and the 'earliest possible security' achieved in the shortest possible time. In effect the Admiralty was instructed to work out a programme for a two-power standard.[86] The 'New Standard' was not intended simply to deter in home waters while providing sufficient strength in the Far East, but to achieve readiness for simultaneous war with Germany and Japan by 1946. Unrealistically, the programme assumed Germany would maintain its existing naval ratios and took no account of Italian naval construction. The Admiralty felt that as long as a superiority of two ships was maintained over the German Fleet an inferiority of one ship with respect to Japan would be 'acceptable', and this yielded a standard of some twenty ships compared with the nineteen possessed by their potential opponents.[87]

But both the Treasury and the Cabinet were united in their belief that economic recovery must take precedence over defence preparations. Officials spoke of the decline of economic strength that might accrue from rearmament, its effect on balance of payments, overseas investments and foreign exchange reserves, and of the diplomatic dangers to any general European or Far Eastern settlement. Despite provision for a £400 million Defence Loan in 1937, which was intended to operate over the next five years, the Government opposed in principle deficit budgeting, heavy tax burdens or cuts in social services. Sir Warren Fisher, Permanent Secretary of the Treasury, personally believed that the three services would abuse Britain's limited resources if independent of financial control. This does not mean to imply that the government opposed rearmament; as early as 1933 a 'shadow' munitions industry had been set up, and by 1939 preparations were well advanced for a quick changeover of much of the private sector to wartime production with minimum delay time and disruption, and without any use of coercion. But even under such conditions, further naval expansion beyond the limits of the DRC. Fleet was bound to be opposed by the Treasury. The period from 1935 to 1939 was therefore characterized by a battle between the Admiralty and the Treasury for acceptance of the 'New Standard' if not for increased appropriations.[88]

The possible creation of a two-power standard was kept alive by the success the Admiralty enjoyed in its other programmes. The Royal Navy made excellent use of Britain's traditional belief in seapower and of its position as the senior service. In 1935 it recommended that seven new capital ships be laid down in three years in order to match the anticipated maximum German and Japanese construction up to 1939. An initial acceleration in construction would tail off only in the last three years of the programme. The Government was persuaded to agree and the laying down of three capital ships in the second half of 1937 was brought forward six months to be part of the 1936 programme. All five of the 'King George V' class battleships were laid down in one financial year, in theory virtually completing the first stage of capital ship rearmament at one stroke.[89] By maximizing construction from 1936 to 1938, the Admiralty were able to lay down all the vessels originally spread over the full seven-year DRC programme. The year 1937 saw orders for three battleships, two armoured carriers, seven cruisers, two destroyer flotillas, seven submarines, two escorts and forty other vessels. This enabled the Admiralty to camouflage preparations for a two-power standard under the convenient cloak of the DRC. By 1938, in their view, they were 'well on the way' to achieving a two-power standard by 1944 rather than 1946 as originally intended.[90]

Although an enlargement of the 1938 programme to three capital ships was turned down, the Government agreed in June 1939 to lay down a third ship in 1940. The decision as to whether three capital ships a year became a permanent feature of naval construction policy was deferred by the Prime Minister pending investigation by the Admiralty and the Treasury, but war intervened before reports could be formulated. Nevertheless, approval for additional gun production facilities at Dalmuir eliminated one possible bottleneck. By mid-year, according to the Admiralty's own figures and in the wake of German abrogation of the Anglo-German Naval Agreement of 1935, the anticipated lead developed by the July programme over German and Japanese capital ship construction meant a two-power standard in that class of vessel would be achieved by 1942. Britain would have twenty ships and Germany and Japan nineteen.[91] However, the First Lord remained deeply concerned about the need to continue the modernization programmes, predicting that the Royal Navy would be unable to maintain its superiority past 1945 without an immediate increase in construction:

> It is equally clear that we are running very grave risks if we do not put ourselves in a position to be able to build three sixteen inch gun ships from the programme of 1941 onwards. . . .the fact faces us that if we do not take steps now, we may be faced in 1945 and onwards with a position that is then irretrievable. It is, of course, easy to say that long before then either war would have broken out or that the political situation would have completely changed for the better. Nevertheless we should be gambling with a tremendous stake if we based our policy on this assumption.[92]

It must be emphasized too that the search for advanced fleet bases and the attempt to create the two-power standard were part of a long-term Admiralty policy designed to provide security for the Far East by around 1942–1944. Faced with a simultaneous threat from Germany, Italy, and Japan at an earlier date, even this margin of strength would not be sufficient.

To place such Admiralty programmes within the overall context of British Far Eastern strategy between 1937 and 1939, it is necessary to differentiate between long-term and short-term policies. In fact, Italian naval construction had been all but ignored by the Admiralty in formulating their construction programmes. Naval staff calculated that from the summer of 1937 to the spring of 1938, and from the summer of 1939 to the spring of 1940, Britain would have a fleet superior to the Japanese by one battleship. From the spring of 1938 to the summer of 1939 they would have one ship less.[93] Despite the dramatic changes that took place in the international situation between 1935 and 1937, both the Review of Imperial Defence and the Far Eastern Appreciation (prepared specifically for the 1937 Imperial Conference) reaffirmed the Eastern Fleet strategy. In the event of war with Germany, Italy and Japan, the British Fleet would leave sufficient strength in home waters to neutralize German naval power and proceed to Singapore. The Western Mediterranean was regarded by the Chiefs of Staff as a French responsibility, and the Eastern Mediterranean would have to be abandoned, 'since no anxieties or risks connected with our interest in the Mediterranean can be allowed to interfere with the despatch of a fleet to the Far East'.[94] So the Far East, as far as the Royal Navy was concerned, remained just as much a strategic priority over the short term as it was over the long term. The period before relief – defined as the time during which the Singapore and Hong Kong garrisons must hold their positions – was fixed by the Chiefs of Staff at seventy days and ninety days respectively.

Unfortunately, neither the Review nor the Appreciation were

particularly clear about this intent: both documents contained a plethora of contradictory policies. Such problems re-emerged during the discussions at the 1937 Imperial Conference, and the result was confusion if not discord. Many of the divisions between the Admiralty, the Chiefs of Staff and the Committee of Imperial Defence were visibly demonstrated and aired. During the conversations with the Dominions, attention was focused on what were considered to be the short-term problems in dispatching a fleet; but, in keeping with the Admiralty's long-range planning, in the service talks that followed the Appreciation and which excluded Dominion representation, less attention was devoted to the question of Singapore's defences and rather more to the problems associated with the completion of Phase II, in other words with Hong Kong's ability to withstand attack, and the transfer of the fleet north from Singapore. Indeed, Chatfield was to remark that the defence of Hong Kong was 'the crux of the whole Appreciation'.[95] But it remained difficult for the other Chiefs of Staff to differentiate between such policies. Discussions about long-term and short-term Far Eastern strategies only contributed to the confusion, and the Admiralty Board itself – for obvious reasons – chose not to clarify. In addition, the Appreciation had to impress the Dominions with the need for greater defence efforts; any indication that it might be difficult to implement Far Eastern naval policy might lead to concentration on local defence at the expense of Imperial contributions. A policy deliberately designed to 'leave them guessing' was therefore adopted. The Chiefs of Staff cut certain 'dangerous' phrases from the Appreciation before showing it to the Dominions, particularly the fact that the period before relief might have to be extended.[96] When the Cabinet's new Defence Policy (Plans) Committee met, it was agreed to point out the fleet 'as it is today' could not fight a simultaneous war on two fronts, but the eventual creation of the two-power standard would offset this.[97]

Stopgap measures would be necessary until such time as a margin of superiority could be re-established. Between 1937 and 1939 the Chiefs of Staff consistently stressed to the Government that it was 'most inadvisable' to risk war during this period of maximum weakness.[98] For the same reason the Admiralty resisted Australian and Foreign Office suggestions that a fleet be stationed in the Far East in peacetime.[99] If war broke out before 1942 the Royal Navy would face the worst possible dilemma with bases vulnerable to attack and a fleet insufficient to its tasks. Under such circumstances the Royal Navy would have to fight within the limits of its resources under conditions then prevailing. So any method, means or policy which could relieve that pressure on Admiralty resources was welcomed by naval staff.

During the 1937 Imperial Conference, for example, both the

Admiralty and the Chiefs of Staff attempted to widen the burden of responsibility by devolving responsibility while seeking greater commitment from the Dominions for the Far East. Australia and New Zealand expressed some interest in this possibility, but the empire-wide cooperative approach to Imperial defence foundered on the rock of Canadian and South African self-interest; these countries simply refused to cooperate.[100] Early in 1938 the Australian Prime Minister, Joseph Lyons, sent a message of assurance to Chamberlain promising further financial support for defence preparations, and as a result the Joint Planning Sub-Committee was able to prepare a summary of likely submissions. Prior agreement with New Zealand about stationing a Dominion garrison on Fanning Island led the Sub-Committee to predict Australian reinforcements for Hong Kong, Singapore or Trincomalee in the near future. Ultimately it was felt that Australia would accept regional responsibility for air defence, with an Australian air officer commanding the whole region.[101]

On the naval side it was hoped to persuade Australia to acquire a battleship, an idea first discussed in 1934 and then resurrected during the 1937 Imperial Conference. A precedent had already been set before the First World War when antipodean contributions led to the construction of two battlecruisers.[102] In May 1938 the Australian Minister for Commerce, Sir Earl Page, and Robert Menzies, then Attorney General, arrived in London to formalize the arrangement. In their absence Lyons presented the new rearmament package to the Australian Parliament, but was forced by concerted opposition to drop the idea of additional financial support. By the end of the month Menzies was pointing out to British authorities that the Australian programme – including two new cruisers – would not stretch to cover a capital ship as well;[103] there the matter rested until November when suggestions were made by Lyons about leasing a 'King George V' class battleship. At the Pacific Defence Conference in April 1939 the Australians revealed they intended to lengthen Sydney's main dock at Cockatoo Island to take capital ships; though the Admiralty were willing to discuss this, they preferred to wait for the next Imperial Conference. International conditions had deteriorated and the fear was expressed that Australian constitutional difficulties might preclude use of the ship outside Australian waters at a time when every capital ship might prove vital to defence. War broke out before the matter could be properly discussed.[104]

At the end of 1937 the Admiralty joined the Chiefs of Staff in recommending a policy of limiting liability, emphasizing to the Government 'the importance from the point of view of Imperial defence, of any political or international action that can be taken to reduce the number of potential enemies and to gain the support of potential allies'.[105]This was by no means a new policy. Many leading policy makers had already canvassed the possibility of a normalisation of relations with Japan, and Anthony Eden even held preliminary talks with the Japanese Foreign Minister. Both DRC Reports had underlined the need for an accommodation with Japan, and as early as 1935 Hankey, as Secretary of the CID, had favoured a two-power standard and a rapprochement with Italy.[106]

However, the main problem was one of finding the correct balance between risks and diplomatic-military priorities in a rapidly changing international environment.[107] There were a profusion of choices here: whether to 'appease' potential enemies or seek potential friends; whether to assign priority to one theatre or another; whether 'friendships' were reliable or ineffective. The Cabinet, the Chiefs of Staff, the Prime Minister and of course the Admiralty were often at loggerheads as those favouring greater commitment to the Far East (known as 'Easterners') vied with those with Eurocentric interests ('Westerners') as well as those who saw Italy as the main enemy ('Centrists'), across governmental, diplomatic and service boundaries. Even within departments, dichotomies in interest existed. Agreement with Japan would inevitably involve recognition of Japanese territorial conquests, perhaps even the abandonment of British interests in China, yet any ceding of British territory or interests was anathema to the traditional concept of one indivisible empire. An association with Tokyo would also offend the United States. Many therefore saw the cost of an Anglo-Japanese non-aggression pact as being too high. The Admiralty's own need for some kind of alliance was tempered by distrust both of the French and the Americans. 'Appeasement' towards Italy would strengthen Britain's position in Europe but weaken Britain's relations with France. A policy of accommodation with Germany might secure safety for the Empire, but could the Germans be trusted to keep their word? Here the Admiralty could advise but not control, for such decisions were political and could only be made at a governmental level.[108]

Within those upper echelons after 1937, one voice dominated proceedings. In 1934, when the first DRC Report had come before the Ministerial Committee for Disarmament, Neville Chamberlain, as Chancellor of the Exchequer, had questioned the Navy's Far Eastern priorities. He had fully agreed with the need to complete the Singapore base, but wanted to limit activity there to submarines and light forces, and to permanently postpone the plan to despatch a Far Eastern Fleet. Seizing on the Report's recommendation that relations with Japan must be improved, and in keeping with the view that Germany was the primary 'ultimate enemy', he hoped Britain would concentrate on home defence (especially the air force) which would also aid the Treasury in making substantial savings.[109]

Both as Chancellor of the Exchequer (1932–1937) and as Prime Minister(1937–1940), Chamberlain questioned the need for expenditure on the basis that Britain could ill afford to prepare for war against both Germany and Japan at the same time. He pressed for concentration on home defence, especially in terms of air power. His implication that the Empire might have to be ceded and the Dominions abandoned had failed to gain widespread support. Nevertheless in the 1930s the most conspicuously perceived threat to peace was believed to come not from Japan but from Germany's Luftwaffe. It was the 'air parity' scare in 1935 that galvanized Britain into rearmament, prompted if not in part cultivated by fear of strategic bombing; this led to the RAF's spectacular 'Scheme F' to create a bomber deterrent force. By 1938 attention had switched to the production of pursuit intercepters and civil defence. Naval construction continued to compete against such policies.[110]

On assuming the premiership in May 1937, Chamberlain determined that there must be an end to the 'drift' in foreign policy of the Baldwin years. Foreign relations would be adjusted to circumstances, and those circumstances dictated that Britain could not face three opponents simultaneously. Chamberlain applied all of his considerable talents and skills towards reaching durable settlements of all outstanding grievances with at least two potential opponents, Germany and Italy. Rearmament was seen as the indispensable counterpart to conciliation: a stronger defence would deter war while diplomacy removed its cause. He continued to feel, however, that rearmament must not be allowed to get out of control, that it must be contained within a framework of financial limits. At the same time he hoped that 'appeasement' might obviate the need for a rearmament programme entirely. Rearmament's priority under the Chamberlain premiership remained the creation of a bomber force and a home defensive force adequate to meet any anticipated scale of attack.

The Admiralty had little understanding of such 'political niceties.' They regarded military power not merely as an adjunct to policy, but as a distinct and individual need. Even an agreement with Germany, Italy or Japan would not alter the scale of defence required.[111] In event of an immediate threat, naval staff calculated that stopgap measures would be necessary and British naval policies aimed at retaining freedom of action. For the same reason the Admiralty resisted Australian and Foreign Office suggestions that a fleet be stationed in the Far East in peacetime.[112] Historians have spent considerable amounts of time and energy discussing the reduction in size of the Eastern Fleet in the period 1937–9, and in detailing the vagaries and vicissitudes of promises made to the Dominions, but few if any have differentiated between the Admiralty's short-term and longer term Far Eastern policies, or noticed that there were considerable differences in approach between the Admiralty, the remaining defence bureaucracy and the British political apparatus.[113]

Presuming as it did that in event of conflict Britain would face only two opponents, the search for a two-power standard was probably just as unrealistic as the search for advanced fleet bases. Most Admiralty calculations were derived from proposed construction plans to 1942 – tabled because of the Anglo-German Naval Agreement – and on limited information about Japan. In reality Germany's 'Z Plan' intended to create a battle force of some twenty capital ships; she planned to lay down at least three battleships and two battlecruisers in 1939, while Japan's '1942 Programme' consisted of three Yamato class vessels and two battlecruisers. In 1939 the First Lord of the Admiralty calculated Britain's own construction on the basis that Germany and Japan would be able to lay down only two ships and one ship a year respectively.[114]

Success and Sacrifice – The Myth Reaffirmed

By 1937 there remained considerable division within the administration and the Committee of Imperial Defence about Hong Kong. Some favoured increasing Hong Kong's power of resistance, others felt it unlikely the fleet would ever make use of facilities. Opinion about the scale necessary for future defence ranged from preventing a *coup de main* to impregnability.[115] Though improvements were planned by 1940, under existing circumstances even Chatfield was forced to concede the base would probably be untenable. The Joint Planning Committee's Air Representative Captain A.T. Harris concluded two pages of reservations about Hong Kong – penned as an addenda to the Appreciation – with the request the Government seriously consider declaring an open port and evacuate it in peacetime. These reservations were retained in the unexpurgated report for the Cabinet, but were excluded from the Appreciation given to the Dominions for fear of the repercussions.[116]

Despite the debate, however, the confidence of the Admiralty Plans Division remained undiminished and interest in the area north of the Malay Barrier was unimpaired. Since the Washington Treaty had now lapsed, Chatfield argued in favour of a build-up of Hong Kong's defences without regard to financial limits. When the matter came up before the Chiefs of Staff, the Secretary of the Admiralty, S.H. Phillips, revealed to Major L.C. Hollis, Assistant Secretary of the CID, that plans for an advanced fleet base at Hong Kong were under way. The Naval War Memorandum was altered once more to accord with the 1928 Corrigenda. At the outbreak of war the object for the China Fleet was changed from 'the security of Singapore' to 'the security of all Far Eastern possessions'. Although the scale of defence for Hong Kong was still undecided, priority, however, continued to be accorded to Singapore.[117] Three standards of defence were suggested for Hong Kong: Standard A allowed full protection of the harbour for use by the British Fleet at a cost of £23 million; Standard B permitted the development of a submarine base at a cost of £18 million, while Standard C provided only sufficient forces to deny the enemy the use of the anchorage until the fleet arrived, at a cost of £5 million.

By April 1938 financial limits and industrial problems had curtailed much of Hong Kong's existing modernization programme. The War Office had cut the approved counter-bombardment plans by half. The Committee of Imperial Defence felt that adoption of Standard A or B 'would involve a very large expenditure indeed' in a period of general financial stringency. In any case the War Office expected to be fully preoccupied with existing construction down to 1941.[118] The ability of the base to withstand attack had been undermined by Japanese occupation of the South China coast; the Chief of the Imperial General Staff, Lord Gort, pointed out to CID that the 'Gin Drinkers' Line near the direct border with China could not be held whatever standard of defence was adopted. Though it was still hoped the base could be made secure from air attack through provision of bomb-proof shelters, anti-aircraft guns and fighter aircraft, Hong Kong's topography made it impossible to keep the Kowloon area and the anchorage safe from land attack from the mainland.[119] Distrust as to whether the Admiralty seriously intended to retain naval forces in the area, lack of financial support and a lack of confidence about the ability of the base to resist the probable scale of attack led the CID to adopt Standard C as the standard for defence:

> The recommendations of the Chiefs of Staff . . . are that the defence of the island should be secured and that sufficient defences should be maintained to deny the use of the anchorage to an enemy. There would be no ultimate attempt to protect ships in the anchorage or naval installations on Stonecutter's Island and on the mainland. Defences would be designed for the purpose of fighting a delaying action on the mainland and holding the Gin Drinker's Line for as long as possible before finally withdrawing to the Island itself.[120]

After such disappointment one might have expected the Plans Division to abandon any hope of relieving Hong Kong. But by agreeing that Standard C would be subject to periodic review and to unspecified spending above the £5 million limit, the Committee of Imperial Defence unwittingly kept alive the hopes of the Division's Director that 'it might still be possible to establish an advanced base at some point beyond Singapore'.[121]

One of the main criticisms levelled by the Chiefs of Staff and the Committee of Imperial Defence against the Admiralty's long range development plans for Hong Kong concerned the vulnerability of naval facilities to shore-based artillery. As a result, late in 1937, the focus of naval attention began to swing away from the Kowloon-Stonecutter's Island area and towards Hope and Lamont docks at Aberdeen on the south side of the island, outside the range of Japanese guns. This was by no means a new policy. The Admiralty Board had tried to persuade the Government to subsidize private dock construction and repair facilities in the 1920s, and in 1933 the Plans Division initiated a study about leasing these facilities. It had been expected the Aberdeen area would provide accommodation for Leander class cruisers, destroyers, submarines and minesweepers, but both Hope and Lamont had not been used for nearly twenty years and were in a state of total disrepair. Between 1933 and 1938 the financial costs of improvements were too great.[122]

The new scheme, presented by the Director of Plans to the Admiralty early in 1939, called for the purchase of the Aberdeen docks and adjacent environs from the Whangpoa Dock Company and construction of underground storage tanks, an ammunition depot, a controlled mine and a torpedo depot. Ostensibly the base was designed to provide facilities for local naval defence but, as the Director of Plans revealed to the Board, it would also act as an advanced fleet base. Provision was made for an underground rail track and a jetty for oilers, and a large mooring area some two miles in circumference was set aside in the Aberdeen Channel: facilities beyond those required merely for local defence.[123] By May 1939, C-in-C China Station was planning to augment coast defences by placing improvised naval batteries at Bluff Head and on Aberdeen Island, while naval gunboats were selected to cover the approaches. In late July the Admiralty asked the War Office to provide additional anti-aircraft guns and fortifications for the area. By late 1939 about twenty pillboxes had been constructed around the base and an entire British battalion was charged with its defence. Reacting to a report by the Ports Defence Committee in November favouring re-provisioning of Hong Kong rather than relief, Tom Phillips urged that since

Hong Kong is our most exposed outpost. . .we should do all we can to defend it without too many arguments; if it comes to war we should man the defences and fight as our forefathers did in many similar positions. . .I consider that the C.I.D. report in question takes a thoroughly defeatist view of the possibility of holding Hong Kong against the Japanese – and I believe that an adequate British garrison and adequate defences should make that hidebound nation think very hard. And there will always be the fear of the British Fleet coming out to interrupt their siege – they must always depend on seaborne supplies for their forces.[124]

The Plans Division anticipated the Aberdeen works would take some three years to complete at a cost of £1,387,000, with an additional £2,465,000 for modernisation of the dock facilities. But progress in construction was slow. After all, the improvements had no priority. The Committee of Imperial Defence still suffered under the mis-apprehension that the plan was for local defence, so financial support was not forthcoming. Nevertheless in the second half of 1939 a purchase price was agreed with the Whangpoa Dock Company, and £163,000 was approved for a start to be made on underground magazines.

In November the Admiralty challenged the Committee of Imperial Defence directly about the standard of defence ultimately required for Hong Kong.[125] The First Sea Lord and his Deputy were much in favour of Standard A:

When the question of storing Hong Kong came up I said I was in disagreement with Plan C and it ought to be Plan A, modified as necessary so that Hong Kong could hold out even though our Fleet could not near it. Everything should be part of Plan A.[126]

Personally I have always felt that this decision to adopt Standard C was fundamentally wrong and not in accordance with our position as a great maritime power. Hong Kong is our most exposed outpost and ought to be properly defended with 15" guns and everything else we can put there. No other country would leave an outpost of this nature in an improperly defended state.[127]

The Board approved £405,000 for storage facilities and a mine depot, arguing that all defence proposals should now be part of a scheme to develop Standard A. The view was taken that only those parts of Standard C which would be of value if Standard A were adopted were worth proceeding with, and the Aberdeen programme was seen as the right basis for an 'A' class base. But the Committee of Imperial Defence was unmoved by Admiralty arguments, and on 11 January 1940 its reaffirmation of Standard C created two policies, with the Board trying to implement the Standard A proposals and the CID claiming that the programme was incompatible with existing policy. By mid-1940, urgent Treasury demands for stringent economies and the need to concentrate on the defeat of Germany, forced the Royal Navy to defer the full defence scheme. Those parts of the Aberdeen programme not directly connected with local defence were deferred until after the war.[128] By August 1940 the Director of Plans was admitting:

> In the event of war in the Far East, our policy with regard to Hong Kong would be to treat it as an outpost to be held as long as possible. We should not be able to relieve it, and it could not be used as an advanced fleet base.[129]

Notes

1. 'Post War Naval Policy', Memo by First Lord of the Admiralty, 12 August 1919, ADM 116/3610.
2. 'The Development of Imperial Defence Policy in the Far East', Memo by Secretary CID, CID 172 Mtg, 17 June 1923, CAB 2/3.
3. John Robert Ferris (1989), *The Evolution of British Strategic Policy, 1919–1926,* London, pp. 100–1; Christopher Hall (1987), *Britain, America and Arms Control 1921–1937*, New York, pp. 29–30.
4. Mahan argued that political power depended on the possession of colonies. These in turn required a merchant marine and a blue water navy to protect shipping and territorial possessions. See William L. Livezey (1947), *Mahan on Seapower*, Norman, OK, p. 42; Geoffrey Till (1988), 'Naval Power', in Colin McInnes and G.D. Sheffield (eds), *Warfare in the Twentieth Century*, London, pp. 83, 95. For the British application of this see also James Neidpath (1981), *The Singapore Naval Base and the Defence of Britain's Eastern Empire 1919–1941*, Oxford, pp. 3–12; W.R. Louis (1971), *British Strategy in the Far East 1919–1939*, Oxford, pp. 209–10. For overall background on naval strategy see Geoffrey Till (ed.) (1984), *Maritime Strategy in the Nuclear Age*, London.
5. Ibid., pp. 108–9.
6. 'British Imperial Bases in the Pacific', Memo by Admiralty Plans Division, 26 April 1919, ADM 1/8570/287; 'Defence of Hong Kong', Memo by Secretary of War, 7 January 1920, CID Paper 120C, enclosed in ADM 167/58; Note by Mr. Balfour, Foreign Office, 3 May 1921, ODC, CAB 8/8.

7. See for example Ian Hamill (1981), *The Strategic Illusion: The Singapore Strategy and the Defence of Australia and New Zealand*, Singapore; Arthur J. Marder (1981), *Old Friends, New Enemies: The Royal Navy and the Imperial Japanese Navy; Strategic Illusions 1936–1941*, Oxford, particularly pp. 36–45, 50–61; Paul Haggie (1981), *Brittania at Bay: The Defence of the British Empire against Japan 1931–1941*, Oxford; W. David McIntyre (1979), *The Rise and Fall of the Singapore Naval Base, 1919–1942*, London; and Neidpath, *The Singapore Naval Base*, to name but a few.

8. Haggie, *Brittania*, pp. 11–12; McIntyre, *The Rise and Fall*, pp. 4–5.

9. It should be pointed out, however, that Hong Kong was not as important a centre for Far Eastern trade as a whole. Shanghai and Yokohama captured a greater proportion of the volume of trade. Cabinet Committee on Replacement of Fleet Units other than Capital Ships and Singapore, RS 1st Mtg, 27 February 1924, CAB 27/236; Neidpath, p. 47.

10. 'Singapore: Development as a Naval Base', 7 June 1921, CID Paper 143, CAB 5/4; CID 172 Mtg, 19 June 1923, CAB 2/3.

11. 'Imperial Navy Defence', Naval Staff Paper, 4 August 1919, ADM 1/8571/295.

12. Naval War Memorandum Eastern, 1924, ADM 116/3125; Naval War Memorandum Eastern, 1931, ADM 116/3118.

13. N. H. Gibbs (1976), *Grand Strategy* vol. 1: *Rearmament Policy*, London, p. 22.

14. McIntyre, *The Rise and Fall*, pp. 53–102.

15. Ibid., pp. 112–13. McIntyre has charted no less than eight alterations between 1920 and 1934.

16. 'Singapore Development as a Naval Base', Memo by Naval Staff, 7 June 1921, ADM 116/3125

17. Naval War Memorandum Eastern, Corrigenda No. 1, 17 August 1925, ADM 116/3125.

18. Ibid.

19. Naval War Memorandum Eastern, 1924–1929, ADM 116/3125; 'Singapore, Establishment of a Naval Base: Scales of Naval Military and Air Defences', Memo by ODC, CID Paper 237C, 31 December 1924, CAB 5/5; COS 18 Mtg, 5 May 1925, CAB 53/2.

20. James Neidpath and W.D. McIntyre have argued that the 'Peace Fleet' was intended to operate exclusively from Singapore, a view that obviously requires some qualification. See Neidpath, *The Singapore Naval Base*, pp. 94–8, 103; McIntyre, *The Rise and Fall*, p. 47.

21. Minute by Director of Dockyards, 19 May 1925; also Minute by

Director of Naval Ordnance, 26 March 1925, ADM 116/2401.

22. For details of this codicil see Minute by Director of Supply, 8 March 1928, ADM 116/2401.

23. Minute by D of P, 29 June 1926; Ltr Fourth Sea Lord to Deputy Chief of Naval Staff, 6 December 1926; Ltr ADM to C-in-C China Station, September 1926; Minute by D of S, 8 March 1928; Minute by D of P, 1 March 1929, ADM 116/2401.

24. Tel C-in-C China Station to ADM, 6 January 1936, ADM 116/3121.

25. 'Passage of the Fleet, Singapore, Singapore to Hong Kong', Memo by D of P, 6 January 1926; Minute by the Civil Engineer-in-Chief, 27 March 1930, ADM 116/2401.

26. Minute by PAS, 27 March 1925, ADM 116/2401.

27. 'Singapore: the Scale of Attack', Note by Chief of Naval Staff, 18 January 1928, ADM 116/3126; COS 64 Mtg, 23 January 1928, CAB 53/2; Minute by D of P, 18 April 1928, ADM 116/3126; Naval War Memorandum Eastern, Corrigenda No. 2, 10 August 1927, ADM 116/3125.

28. Naval War Memorandum Eastern, Corrigenda No. 1, 17 August 1925, ADM 116/3125.

29. COS Annual Review, CID Paper 108, 23 February 1932, CAB 4/21; CAB 19 (32), 23 March 1932, CAB 23/70.

30. DRC Final Report, 23 October 1934, CAB 16/109; Ministerial Committee on Disarmament, 50 Mtg, 25 June 1934, CAB 27/507.

31. Malcolm Smith (1977), 'The Royal Air Force, Air Power, and British Foreign Policy 1932–1937', *Journal of Contemporary History*, vol. 12, no. 1, pp. 161, 165; Malcolm Smith (1978), 'Rearmament and Deterrence in Britain in the 1930s', *Journal of Strategic Studies*, vol. 1, no. 3, pp. 313–37, 118–21; G. C. Peden (1979), *British Rearmament and the Treasury 1932–1939*, Edinburgh, pp. 118–21, 128–33, 152–60; Gibbs, *Grand Strategy*, chaps 4, 5 and 14, pp. 175–7, 532.

32. 'Hong Kong – Plans for Defence, Relief or Recapture', COS Paper 344 (JP), 16 July 1934, CAB 53/24.

33. 'Report of the Singapore Conference January 23–27 1934', ADM 116/3121; Ltr Chatfield to Dreyer, 7 August 1934, Chatfield Papers; CID 280 Mtg, 10 June 1936, CAB 2/6; COS 217 Mtg, 11 October 1937, CAB 53/8.

34. Notes on the Naval Staff Memo 'Status Quo in the Pacific' by CIGS, 23 November 1934, WO 106/2361.

35. Notes for Discussion with Admiral Sir Frederick Dreyer by D of P and DNI, 25 January 1936, ADM 116/3338.

36. Tel ADM to C-in-C China Station, 25 April 1933, ADM 116/3475; Naval War Memorandum Eastern, 1931, ADM 116/3118.

37. Tel. ADM to C-in-C China Station, 25 April 1993, ADM 116/3475; Naval War Memorandum Eastern, 1931, ADM 116/3118.

38. Hong Kong's 9.2-inch gun defences would appear to be woefully inadequate and undergunned against the full might of a Japanese 16-inch gun battle line. However it was anticipated that 15-inch guns would eventually be installed, and in the meantime the relatively shallow waters and the presence of intervening islands would mean that the Japanese would be forced to close the distance to almost point blank range to engage. Nor was it anticipated that the Japanese would occupy the landward side and bring the defences within range of shore-based artillery. See Notes on Naval Staff Memo by CIGS, 23 November 1934, WO 106/2361; COS 132 Mtg, 24 July 1934, CAB 5/5; Report of Meeting between C-in-C China Station and GOC Hong Kong, 27 December 1935, ADM 116/3490.

39. CID 258 Mtg, 6 April 1933, CAB 2/5; 'Hong Kong: Selection of a Site for a Second Aerodrome', COS Paper 384, 26 May 1935, CAB 53/24; DRC 5 Mtg, 18 January 1934; DRC 7 Mtg, 9 January 1934, CAB 16/109.

40. Naval War Memorandum Eastern, 1931, ADM 116/3118; Naval War Memorandum Eastern, 1933, ADM 116/3475.

41. 'Status Quo in the Pacific', Memo by Naval Staff, COS Paper 359, 22 November 1934; 'Status Quo in the Pacific', Report by the CID Sub-Committee, COS Paper 360, 27 November 1934, CAB 53/24; CID 273 Mtg, 30 January 1936, CAB 2/6; COS 170 Mtg, 31 March 1936, CAB 5/5; Report of a Meeting between C-in-C China Station and GOC Hong Kong, 9 December 1935, ADM 116/3490; 'Deficiency Programme and the 1936 Estimates', Memo by CNS, 6 August 1935, ADM 116/3437; Note by D of P, 1 April 1936, ADM 116/3338.

42. CID 271 Mtg, 14 October 1935, CAB 2/6; Note by D of P, 1 April 1936, ADM 116/3338. Unfortunately CID Paper 471C remains closed for fifty years.

43. COS 151 Mtg, 4 October 1935, CAB 53/5.

44. McIntyre, p. 137; CID 271 Mtg, 14 October 1935, CAB 2/6; 'Far Eastern Appreciation', COS Paper 579 (JP), 7 May 1937, CAB 53/32.

45. Ibid.

46. 'Plans for the Relief and Recapture of Hong Kong', COS Paper 344 (JP), 16 July 1934, CAB 53/24.

47. 'Requirements for the 1935 Naval Conference', Naval Staff Appreciation, April 1934, ADM 1/8802. This is not, of course, to argue that there were not pro-French admirals within the ranks of the

Royal Navy, Admirals Sir John Kelly and Sir Dudley North for example.

48. Tel. British Naval Attaché Paris to Sir Eric Drummond, 28 June 1934, ADM 116/2998.

49. Extracts from Record of Anglo-French Conversations, April 28–9 1938, DP (P) 27, CAB 16/183A.

50. Minute by Harison, 5 March 1934; Minute by Sir V. Wellesley, 7 March 1934, FO 371/18160; COS 208 Mtg, 26 May 1937, CAB 53/7.

51. Minute by Brenan, 6 July 1939, FO 371/23551.

52. Minute by Randell, 14 June 1934; Minute by Orde, 16 June 1934, FO 371/18098.

53. For details on the Philippine movement towards independence see Theodore Friend (1965), *Between Two Empires: The Ordeal of the Philippines 1929–1946*, New Haven, pp. 98–145.

54. Carol Petillo (1981), *Douglas MacArthur, the Philippine Years,* Bloomington, pp. 167–73; Despatch Harrington to Secretary of State for Foreign Affairs, 20 September 1933, FO 371/1661.

55. Ibid.; Nicholas Tarling (1977), 'Quezon and the British Commonwealth', *Australian Journal of Politics and History*, vol. 23, no. 2, pp. 185–6.

56. Despatch Vice-Consul Founds to Secretary of State for Foreign Affairs, 5 September 1932, FO 371/15877; Tel Sansom to Orde, 11 May 1934, FO 371/17576.

57. Tel Osborne to Craigie, 12 April 1935; Memo by Hodsoll, 21 August 1936, FO 371/19823; Memo by Troutbeck, 11 December 1936, FO 371/19824.

58. Notes for Discussion with Admiral Sir Frederick Dreyer by D of P and DNI, 25 January 1936, ADM 116/3338; 'Requirements for the 1935 Naval Conference', Naval Staff Appreciation, April 1934, ADM 1/8802; Minute by Rovell, 14 June 1934; Minute by Orde, 16 June 1934, FO 371/18098; Despatch Blunt to Secretary of State for Foreign Affairs, 15 May 1935, FO 371/18762; 'Japanese Designs on the Netherlands East Indies', COS Paper 380, 29 May 1935, CAB 53/24.

59. 'Future Status and Security of the Philippine Islands', COS Paper 1331B, 17 June 1937, CAB 53/32.

60. Minute by Gore-Booth, 13 February 1935, FO 371/18763.

61. Minute by Stanhope, 5 March 1934, FO 371/18160; Notes of a Conversation between C-in-C China Station and Admiral F.B. Upham at Manila, 23 March 1934, FO 371/18098; 'General Strategic Situation in the Western Pacific vis-a-vis Japan', Memo by C-in-C China Station, 8 August 1935; Notes for Discussion with

Admiral Sir Frederick Dreyer by D of P and DNI, 25 January 1936, ADM 116/3338.

62. Ltr Fletcher to Findlater Stewart, 16 January 1934, FO 371/17576; Despatch Blunt to Holman, 23 December 1934, FO 371/19823; Despatch Blunt to Secretary of State for Foreign Affairs, 19 May 1934; Despatch Blunt to Eden, 18 March 1936, FO 371/19823; Minute by Allen, 23 March 1937, FO 371/20650.

63. Ibid. For background on this whole question see the following files: Despatch Harrington to Secretary of State for Foreign Affairs, 19 May 1934, FO 371/17576; Minute by Hogg, 28 May 1934, FO 371/17622; Memo Lindsay to Simon, 15 February 1935, FO 371/18762; Despatch Blunt to Secretary of State for Foreign Affairs, 31 May 1935, FO 371/18762; Despatch Blunt to Hoare, 18 December 1935, FO 371/19823; Minute by Troutbeck, 23 January 1936, FO 371/198221; Despatch Foulds to Eden, 31 August 1936, FO 371/19823; Ltr Hodsell to Mallet (Washington), 15 February 1937, FO 371/20650; 'General Strategic Situation in the Western Pacific vis-a-vis Japan', Memo by C-in-C China station, 8 August 1935, ADM 116/3338; D. Clayton James (1970), *The Year of MacArthur* vol. 1 *1880–1941*, London, pp. 510–12.

64. Memorandum by the Foreign Office, 8 April 1937, FO 371/20650; Ltr Hodsoll to Mallet (Washington), 15 December 1937, FO 371/20650.

65. 'The Future Status and Security of the Philippines', COS Paper 592, 7 June 1937, CAB 53/32.

66. Naval War Memorandum Eastern, Corrigenda No. 2, 10 August 1927, ADM 116/3125.

67. This is a feature all but ignored by historians such as Neidpath and Haggie who have generally remained preoccupied with the 'relief of Singapore' scenario.

68. Report by HMS *Iroquois*, 1 May 1931, ADM 116/2842; Minute by D of P, 22 March 1932; Minute by D of P, 28 April 1933; Ltr Secretary of the Air Ministry to ADM, 5 October 1931; Notes of a Conference in Hydrographer's Office, 26 November 1931; Ltr Foreign Office to Secretary of the ADM, 7 January 1932; Report by HMS *Herald*, 20 May 1932, ADM 116/2812.

69. Survey of the Pacific Islands, 'Ports and Achorages', 1933, ADM 116/2812.

70. Report by the MNB , 30 June 1920; Minute by Dickens, 30 August 1920; Minute by AD of P, 20 March 1926, ADM 116/2335; ADM 116/4182, *passim*.

71. Tel. C-in-C China Station to ADM, 14 November 1934; Minute by DNI, 24 February 1936, ADM 116/3338; Report by C-in-C China

Station, 12 July 1935; Ltr Ronald, Foreign Office to Secretary of the Admiralty, 16 January 1937, ADM 116/3605.

72. Survey of the Pacific Islands, 'Ports and Anchorages', 1933, ADM 116/2812.

73. Ltr Colonial Office to Foreign Office, 28 April 1930; Minute by Mallet, 21 July 1930; Ltr ADM to Foreign Office, 27 August 1930, FO 371/14916; Ltr ADM to Foreign Office, 29 December 1930; Ltr Foreign Office to Secretary of the Admiralty, 6 March 1933; Ltr Law Officers Department to Sir John Simon, 29 July 1932; Conference on French Claims in Far Eastern Waters, 29 June 1933; Minute by D of P, 28 April 1933; Minute by Haunch for Head of M, 15 March 1933, ADM 116/2812.

74. Naval War Memorandum Eastern, 1933, ADM 116/3475; Survey of the Pacific Islands, 'Ports and Anchorages', 1933, ADM 116/2812; Minute by DOD, 29 January 1937; Minute by Syfet, 12 August 1937, ADM 116/3936.

75. Naval War Memorandum Eastern, January 1938, ADM 116/4393; 'Forecast of British Naval Strength on Dec. 31 1942 for Transmission to Germany', Memo by the Admiralty, DP (P) 35, 19 October 1938, CAB 16/183A.

76. 'Far Eastern Appreciation', COS Paper 579 (JP), 7 May 1937, CAB 53/32; Professional Notes (1937), *United States Naval Institute Proceedings*, vol. 63, no. 6.

77. 'Possible Staff Conversations with the U.S.A.', Report by Naval Staff, 17 December 1937; 'Memo of Meeting with Captain Royal E. Ingersoll', by Chatfield, 5 January 1938, ADM 116/3922.

78. Naval War Memorandum Eastern, January 1938, Section XI, ADM 116/4393.

79. Tel C-in-C China Station to ADM, 7 April 1937; Minute by S.A. Phillips, 29 July 1937; Tel E. Phipps to Foreign Office, 22 December 1937; Minute by Hydrographer, 14 March 1938; Report by HMS *Herald* to ADM, 25 April 1938, ADM 116/3936

80. Minute by D of P, 16 September 1938; Memo by C-in-C China Station, 6 April 1938, ADM 1/9530; Marder, *Old Friends*, pp. 45–6; Neidpath, *The Singapore Naval Base*, p. 164.

81. 'Report of the Anglo-French Conference held at Singapore 22–27 June 1939', COS Paper 941, 11 July 1939, CAB 53/52; Minute by D of P, 9 March 1939, ADM. 1/9951; Minute by D of P, 6 March 1939, ADM 1/11326.

82. This is revealed in the following documents: Minute by D of P, 16 September 1938, ADM 1/9530; Minute by D of P, 11 April 1939, ADM 116/4087; Minute by Backhouse, 24 March 1939, ADM 1/9909; Interview between Stirling, Australian External Affairs

Officer, First Lord of the Admiralty, and DCNS, 4 April 1939, PREM 1/309; Memo on Seapower by Churchill, 27 March 1939, PREM 1/345. For a view of the Army plans with respect to the defence of Malaya see Louis Allen (1977), *Singapore 1941–1942*, London.

83. 'Efficiency of the Japanese Navy', Memo by Naval Attaché Tokyo, 18 February 1935, ADM 116/3862; COS 304 Mtg, 20 June 1939, CAB 53/11.

84. Marder, *Old Friends*, pp. 352–3.

85. DCM 65 Mtg, 1 July 1935, CAB 16/112.

86. CP 187 (35), 7 October 1935, CAB 24/257; DPR 52, 21 November 1935, CAB 16/139; 'Resumé of the Present Position regarding Defence Requirements', CAB 10 (36), 25 February 1936, CAB 23/133; 'Naval Defence Requirements', Memo by CNS, 9 October 1935, ADM 1/8774; DRC Third Report, 21 November 1935, CAB 29/112.

87. DRC 21 Mtg, 25 May 1936, CAB 16/136; 'A New Standard of Naval Strength', Memo by the First Lord of the Admiralty, DP (P) 3, 29 April 1937, CAB 16/182; COS 209 Mtg, 1 June 1937, CAB 53/7.

88. Gibbs, *Grand Strategy*, Chapter 8; Peden, *British Rearmament*, Chapter 3; For more detail on the whole rearmament question see G.C. Peden (1979), 'Sir Warren Fisher and British Rearmament Against Germany', *English Historical Review*, vol. 94, no. 370, pp. 29–47; D. Cameron Watt (1973), 'Roosevelt and Neville Chamberlain: Two Appeasers', *International Journal*, vol. 28, pp. 185–204; D. Cameron Watt (1965), *Personalities and Policies: Studies in the Formulation of British Foreign Policy in the Twentieth Century*, London, pp. 100–16; R.J. Pritchard (1973–1974), 'The Far East as an Influence on the Chamberlain's Pre-War European Policies,' *Millenium*, vol. 2, pp. 7–23; R.A.C. Parker (1975), 'Economics, Rearmament and Foreign Policy: The United Kingdom Before 1939 – A Preliminary Survey', *Journal of Contemporary History*, vol. 10, pp. 640–7; John Lippincott (1976), *The Strategy of Appeasement: The Formulation of British Defence Policy*, D. Phil., Oxford, pp. 211–375.

89. Construction problems and labour difficulties in the end delayed completion of these vessels. Nevertheless *Duke of York, Prince of Wales,* and *King George V* were all in action by 1941. Work on *Anson* and *Howe*, however, ceased for one year to allow production facilities to be concentrated on armoured merchant cruisers. See John Roberts (1981), 'Penultimate Battleship: The Lion Class 1937–1946', *Warship,* no. 19, pp. 167–83; G.A.H. Gordon (1988),

British Seapower and Procurement between the Wars: A Reappraisal of Rearmament, London, pp. 186–7, 192–3.

90. Gibbs, *Grand Strategy*, pp. 301–19. This process had a long period of gestation. This can be followed by looking at the following: DPR 52, 21 November 1935, CAB 16/139; Note by Coxwell, Admiralty Estimates Branch, 27 November 1936, ADM 116/3631; DPR 88, 23 June 1936, CAB 16/139; DPR 24, 3 July 1936, CAB 16/136; Board Minute 3380, 24 June 1936, ADM 167/94; Ltr Duff Cooper to Inskip, 21 July 1938, ADM 1/9672; 'A New Standard of Naval Strength', Memo by the First Lord of the Admiralty, DP (P) 3, 29 April 1937, CAB 16/182; Note by Bridges, Treasury, 8 May 1937, T 161/780/S42000; Defence Expenditure in Future Years', Memo for DP (P) Committee by Minister for Co-ordination of Defence, 9 February 1938, CAB 16/182; and finally 'Defence Expenditure in Future Years', CP 24 (38), 8 February 1938, CAB 16/181.

91. Gibbs, *Grand Strategy*, pp. 337–8; Roberts, 'Penultimate Battleship', pp. 179, 182; Revised New Programme for 1938, Memo by Chancellor of the Exchequer, 14 February 1938, CAB 16/181; Gordon, *British Seapower*, p. 175; Ltr First Lord of the Admiralty to Prime Minister, 12 March 1938, PREM 1/346; 'The Capital Ship Position', Memo by the First Lord of the Admiralty, 27 June 1939, CAB 16/183A; CAB 39 (39), 26 July 1939, CAB 23/100.

92. CID 364 Mtg, 6 July 1939, CAB 2/9.

93. Marder, *Old Friends*, pp. 41–6; Ltr Runciman to Prime Minister, 19 June 1939, PREM 1/316.

94. Ltr Vansittart to Ismay, 15 February 1937; COS 198 Mtg, 18 February 1937, Appendix 2, CAB 53/7; 'Far Eastern Appreciation', COS Paper 596, 14 June 1937, CAB 53/32.

95. COS 198 Mtg, 1 March 1937, CAB 53/7.

96. Gibbs, *Grand Strategy*, pp. 409–18; DP (P) 2 , 11 May 1937, CAB 16/181; COS 204 Mtg, 6 May 1937, CAB 53/7.

97. DP (P) 2 Mtg, 11 May 1937, CAB 16/181.

98. COS 209 Mtg, 1 June 1937, CAB 53/7.

99. Haggie, *Brittania*, pp. 112–13, 129–32; Marder,*Old Friends*, pp. 41–6.

100. ICM 7 Mtg, 26 May 1937, CAB 32/128; Record of Discussion with Australian Minister of Defence, 17 June 1937, ADM 1/9134; J. Eayrs (1965), *In Defence of Canada,* Toronto, vol. 2, pp. 55–61; see also Corelli Barnett (1972), *The Collapse of British Power*, London.

101. Record of Discussions with Australian Minister for Defence at the Admiralty, 17 June 1937, ADM 1/9134; E (PD) 37 Mtg, 26 May 1937, CAB 32/128; CAB 33 (38), 20 July 1938, CAB 23/94; Minute by Balfour, 12 June 1939, FO 371/22793.

102. For details on the early development of the Australian Navy see Alun Evans (1986), *A Navy for Australia*, Sydney, pp. 82–5, 89–93. See also I.C. McGibbon (1981), *Blue Water Rationale: The Naval Defence of New Zealand 1914–42*, Wellington, p. 261. For information about the request made from 1937–39 see R.G. Neale (ed.) (1975–6), *Documents on Australian Foreign Policy 1937–49*, Canberra, vol. 1, 1937–38, pp. 310, 315–16, 336, 368–70, 507, 511–13, 534–6; vol. 2, 1939, pp. 60–1.

103. Ibid.

104. Tel. First Naval Member Naval Board Melbourne to First Sea Lord, 14 March 1939; Minute by Backhouse, 15 March 1939, ADM 1/9831.

105. CP 296 (37), 12 November 1937, CAB 24/272; 'Comparison of the Strength of Britain with certain other Nations as at January 1938', Memo by CNS, COS 227 Mtg, 19 January 1938, CAB 53/8; Ltr Chatfield to Inskip, 26 January 1938, Chatfield Papers.

106. DRC Final Report, 23 October 1934, CAB 16/109; DRC Third Report, 21 November 1935, CAB 29/112; 'Italy, Some Notes of a Holiday Visit', Memo by Hankey, 27 September 1937, CAB 21/563. See also Lawrence R. Pratt (1975), *East of Malta, West of Suez: Britain's Mediterranean Crisis, 1936–39*, Cambridge, pp. 31–2.

107. Changes such as the German reoccupation of the Rhineland, the Abyssinian crisis, and the outbreak of the Spanish Civil War. There were signs too of a developing relationship between Britain's potential enemies.

108. For details about the dilemmas facing British foreign policy and defence planners see Maurice Cowling (1975), *The Impact of Hitler: British Politics and British Strategy 1933–40*, London, pp. 176–206, 293–312; Bradford A. Lee (1977), *Britain and the Sino-Japanese War 1937–39: A Study in the Dilemmas of British Decline*, Stanford, pp. 205–21; D. Cameron Watt (1975), *Too Serious A Business: European Armed Forces and the Approach to the Second World War*, London, pp. 129–32.

109. DC (M) (32) 120, 20 June 1934, ADM 116/3436.

110. Malcolm Smith (1980), 'Planning and Building the British Bomber Force, 1934–1939', *Business History Review*, vol. 54, no. 1, pp. 37–8.

111. DP (P) 2, 11 May 1937, Cab. 16/181.

112. Haggie, *Brittania* , pp. 112–13, 129–32; Marder, *Old Friends*, pp. 41–6.
113. These will be dealt with in more detail in the next chapter.
114. 'The Capital Ship Position', Memo by the First Lord of the Admiralty, DP (P) 63, 27 June 1939, CAB 16/183A. For an outline of the German and Japanese programmes and the failure of British intelligence to detect them, see Edward P. von der Porten (1969), *The German Navy in World War Two*, London; Pete C. Smith (1977), *The Great Ships Pass,* London, pp. 46–9; Wesley Wark (1985), *The Ultimate Enemy: British Intelligence and Nazi Germany 1933-1939,* Ithaca; Peter Lowe, 'Great Britain's Assessment of Japan Before the Outbreak of the Pacific War', in Ernest R. May (ed.) (1984), *Knowing One's Enemies: Intelligence Assessment Before the Two World Wars*, Princeton, NJ, pp. 456–75. Most of the reports about Japanese naval construction were provided by a single individual, a Chinese worker employed at various Japanese naval yards. His evidence was looked at askance by the DNI and was generally regarded as dubious. My thanks to Ned Willmott for information about this. See ADM 116/5757 for details.
115. COS 207 Mtg, 18 May 1937, CAB 53/7; 'Reports by the Chiefs of Staff on the Far Eastern Appreciation', COS Paper 591, 1 June 1937, CAB 53/32; COS 198 Mtg, 1 March 1937, CAB 53/7; Minute by D of P, 15 January 1938, ADM 116/3863.
116. COS 198 Mtg, 1 March 1937, CAB 53/7; COS 217 Mtg, 11 October 1937, CAB 53/8; 'Far Eastern Appreciation', COS Paper 579 (JP), 7 May 1937, CAB 53/32.
117. Ltr S.H. Phillips to Major Hollis, 27 August 1937, CAB 104/68; Ltr C-in-C China Station to ADM, 10 July 1937; Minute by D of P, 5 October 1937; Tel. ADM to C-in-C China Station, 13 October 1937, ADM 116/3863; 'New Policy Report August 1938', 26 August 1938, WO 106/2367.
118. 'New Policy Report August 1938', 26 September 1938, WO 106/2367; Note on COS Paper 564 by the War Office, 17 February 1937, WO 106/2362; CID 312 Mtg, 7 April 1938, CAB 2/7; CID 328 Mtg, 30 June 1938, CAB 2/7.
119. CID 329 Mtg, 19 July 1938, CAB 2/7.
120. Minute by D of P, 12 August 1938, ADM 116/4356.
121. Minute by Director of Dockyards, 5 August 1938, ADM 116/4356; CID 329 Mtg, 19 July 1938, CAB 2/7; Minute by D of P, 16 August 1938, ADM 1/9530.
122. Minute by D of P, 30 May 1933; Minute by DNC, 20 June 1933, ADM 116/4356; Minute by DOD, 18 June 1935, ADM 116/3663.

123. Minute by D of P, 24 January 1939; Minute by D of P, 27 February 1939, ADM 116/4356.
124. Report on the Defence of Hong Kong, 1 May 1939, WO 106/2371; Defence of Hong Kong 1939, WO 106/2379; Ltr S.H. Phillips to WO, 18 July 1939, ADM 1/9865; 'Hong Kong: Period Before Relief', Memo by the Ports Defence Committee, COS Paper 176, 23 December 1939; COS 3 Mtg, 4 January 1940, CAB 79/3; Minute by DCNS, 8 January 1940, ADM 116/4271.
125. 'Defence of Hong Kong', Memo by Whitaker for Civil Engineer in Chief, 2 January 1940; Minute by Edelsten for D of P, 22 August 1939, ADM 116/4356; Minute by Director of Victuals, 16 June 1939, ADM 1/10199.
126. Minute by First Sea Lord, 4 January 1940, ADM 116/4271.
127. Minute by DCNS 3 January 1940, ADM 116/4271.
128. Minute by D of P, 2 January 1940; Minute by Rosines, 30 October 1940, ADM 116/4356.
129. Minute by D of P, 13 August 1940, ADM 116/4356.

The United States Navy in the Pacific

Out of the USA's early years as a major seapower two basic naval strategies emerged. Long-standing rivalry with Germany was already a strong feature of US naval policy long before the First World War; misunderstandings with Admiral Dewey in the Philippines over blockade regulations had resulted in near confrontation with a German cruiser squadron during the Spanish-American War.[1] US war plans were colour coded, and War Plan 'Black' evolved as a result of the German-Venezuelan crisis of 1902, reflecting America's traditional support for the Monroe Doctrine. The plan envisaged defence against a German battlefleet strike across the Atlantic to seize Caribbean bases, while the American Navy's role was altered to preventing the destruction or blockading of the Panama Canal.

In the post-war world US naval staff were just as concerned as the Royal Navy about any outbreak of war in the Atlantic, despite the destruction of German seapower in 1918, and were equally anxious to retain forces to counter European maritime developments. While Britain saw France as the main Atlantic threat, it was Britain that assumed the mantle of potential hostile in American eyes. As the General Board admitted:

> In the Atlantic our most probable antagonist is Great Britain. In the Pacific our most probable opponent is Japan. In case of war between the United States and Japan within the next few years, Great Britain would probably remain neutral, but in case of war with Britain Japan would undoubtedly join Great Britain in order to avail herself of the opportunity thus presented to seize United States possessions while our military and naval forces are engaged in other vital operations.[2]

By March 1920, approved by the Secretary of the Navy Josephus Daniels, the War Plans Division portfolio included both a strategic war plan for the Pacific and a combined Atlantic and Pacific war plan. By 1926 the Joint Board had established an order of priority: 'Orange' (Japan), 'Red' (Britain), and 'Red-Orange' (an Anglo-Japanese coalition). The 'Red-Orange' strategy against an Anglo-Japanese coalition called for a major effort in the Atlantic while a deterrent force composed of the older battleships, destroyers and submarines tried to confine Japan to the western Pacific.[3] Fleet concentration on the Atlantic side of the Canal would be followed by an amphibious landing on Trinidad and the seizure of British possessions off the east coast of the United States such as Bermuda, Jamaica and the Bahamas. The British Fleet – it was hoped – would be deprived of bases south of Nova Scotia and confined to Newfoundland waters, while the Great Lakes waterway was secured and Vancouver attacked.[4] In the meantime the Army plotted an overland campaign and the seizure of Halifax. From the US Navy's standpoint the potential of an Anglo-American war remained a dominating feature of relations between the two countries in the 1920s. Indeed, the 1927 Geneva Conference foundered because of naval visions of a 'perfidious Albion', and the administration only succeeded in arranging an agreement on cruiser tonnages at the 1930 London Conference by ignoring naval representation entirely.[5]

Planning against Japan was of an entirely different character than against Britain or Germany. Asiatic interests and an insular empire would have to be defended against a competing political and economic system along the rim of the USA's oceanic frontier. 'Orange' therefore 'envisaged an offensive war, primarily naval, directed towards the isolation and harassment of Japan through control of her vital sea communications and through offensive sea and air operations against her naval forces and economic life'.[6]

Two considerations prompted a decision to move rapidly into the western Pacific at the start of such a conflict. The Japanese were expected to make the first move; according to the Joint Board, war would break out either because of Japan's refusal to continue to recognize the 'Open Door' principle, through US interference with Japan's political and economic ambitions in China, or as a result of restrictive anti-Asian immigration policies in the USA. Manila and the Philippines were felt to be so strategically important they would have to attract Japan's attention sooner or later. If the Japanese were quick enough they might also attempt an amphibious assault on the Hawaiian islands, and at the very least they would seek to fortify and establish bases in the Marshalls and the Carolines. Joint Board planners therefore maintained that success depended on the speed of the US reply, and on retaining a base west of Hawaii close to the main scene of action. Once US strategy became known Japan, it was felt, would assume a defensive posture anchored on the Central Pacific island chain and try to whittle down the US Fleet to manageable proportions by attrition.

Like the Admiralty's Naval War Memorandum Eastern War Plan, 'Orange' predicted three distinct phases of conflict. During Phase I the

US Fleet would concentrate its forces in the eastern Pacific, either on the west coast or preferably on Hawaii. During Phase II the fleet would advance to the western Pacific and proceed to the rescue and relief of Manila. In Phase III, the Fleet would move to Japanese waters where close economic blockade and occupation of Japanese territories would eventually force surrender.

Neither the Admiralty nor the US Navy Department seemed to have had any faith in international agreements or organisations. Both preferred to act unilaterally against what they perceived to be an 'aggressive and militaristic' Japan, which aimed at 'hegemony of the Far East'.[7] The Navy Department and the Admiralty thus approached Far Eastern defence from a similar standpoint. Both felt command of the sea was the primary object, while battleships were the main arbiters of power; both had potential enemies on two fronts yet their own fleets were limited in size to a one-power naval standard; and both faced essentially the same problem, of getting the fleet into a position where it would do the most good.

The main logistical requirements were also exactly the same, namely adequate supplies of food and water, ammunition, repair facilities equipped with machine tools, dockyards and fuelling facilities. As early as the Spanish-American War the importance of these had been brought home to the US Navy. At that time the United States had no coaling stations or naval establishments of sufficient size to re-supply its naval forces anywhere in the Pacific, so Admiral Dewey was forced to rely almost entirely on supplies purchased from Hong Kong. Without British coaling facilities, the US campaign in the Philippines would have been impractical.[8] The Navy Department favoured the development of one key base and at least one or perhaps two advanced bases. As to location the US Navy expressed a preference for its own territorial possessions. Construction in peacetime of a Far Eastern fortress with impregnable defences ashore and afloat was the most logical solution, but the US government refused to countenance such a project and traded away any such prospect at the Washington arms negotiations. There was the additional problem that, although the central Pacific route provided the quickest way to the Far East, there were neither large land masses nor operating seaports of any size between Hawaii and the archipelagos of Asia. One solution was to rush the fleet to the Philippines and improvise a base as soon as war began; in fact, the length of any war became dependent on the time it took to establish a western Pacific base and the time it took the fleet to get there. This was the accepted naval strategy through much of the period between 1906 and 1934.[9]

Though the Philippines were not as vital an area of investment for the United States as Hong Kong was for Britain, the area was still important. By 1933, for example, it was estimated some 76 per cent of the industrial enterprises in the islands were US-owned.[10] Standard Oil's stocks reached 105,000 tons by 1941 and company investments totalled $6,673,000.[11] As far as the Philippine economy was concerned, the US market was absolutely essential to prosperity. Secondary industry was totally dependent on the United States. Nearly all of the sugar produced was exported to the United States, and this alone made up 36 per cent of income and contributed 46 per cent of the country's total revenue. Some 600,000 tons of coconut products and 28,000 tons of tobacco were shipped to the west coast every year.[12] Little wonder that in the early 1920s the naval representatives on the Joint Planning Committee and the General Board were in agreement that any contemplated US withdrawal would be detrimental to the interests of the Filipino peoples and 'tantamount to abandonment of American interests in the Far East'.[13] Others even saw it as an 'incitement to war'.[14]

War Plan 'Orange': The Search for an Advanced Fleet Base

Before 1922, attempts by the US Navy Department to establish a Far Eastern fleet base were frustrated by early rulings (1909 and 1916) emphasizing protection of the West Coast, while the Washington Treaty meant no major development was supposed to be undertaken west of Hawaii. In any case, given the logistical difficulties, improvements could not be made in the Far East until a main base was completed on the Hawaiian Islands, so the General Board pushed ahead with the development of facilities there.[15] By 1920 some 44,000 tons of fuel oil was stored at Pearl Harbor, and a one thousand-foot dry dock capable of taking battleships had been put in place. By August 1919, machine shops, hoisting equipment, a one thousand-foot wharf and a hospital had all been completed. Pearl Harbor's minefields were ready and in storage, and the searchlight programme was far advanced. A torpedo storage depot and an ammunition plant had been completed on Kuahua as well.[16]

As to an advanced fleet base, the General Board had hoped to develop both Cavite, on the south side of Manila Bay, and Guam to equal standards, but there was considerable confusion about this. Cavite was not the Navy's first choice. In October 1901 a board under Rear-Admiral Henry C. Taylor, Chief of the Bureau of Navigation, had completed a plan for a heavily fortified self-supporting base at Olongapo at Subic Bay, and between 1901 and 1905 some $1,069,395 was set aside to make a start. During the 1907 war scare the Joint Army and Navy Board recommended concentration of defence measures there and not at Manila Bay.[17] But Army officers stationed in the Philippines felt the surrounding hills made Subic as vulnerable to shore-based artillery attack as Port Arthur. Forced by Army intransigence to choose Cavite, the Navy still continued to maintain dual facilities at Olongapo.

Like the Army, the Joint Board and the Navy Department at first strictly adhered to Article 19.[18] Later the Department – like the Admiralty – sought to bypass Treaty restrictions by placing emphasis on mobile rather than fixed defences. Captain Williams of the Navy Plans Division, for example, tried to differentiate between coast defence, which he defined as covering every aspect of the system, and coast defences, which covered only works and batteries.[19] However, Captain, later Admiral, William Veazie Pratt rejected such interpretations as being 'against the spirit of Article XIX' and the Joint Board underwrote his conclusions.[20] However, the Board did see submarines as a valuable deterrent, while destroyers might 'wreak havoc' on Japan's lines of communications; by 1924 three squadrons of patrol craft and a seaplane tender had been added to the defences.[21] By 1931 the Asiatic Fleet consisted of one cruiser, eighteen destroyers and twenty-four submarines.[22] Destroyer and submarine tenders, together with an oiler and a dry goods ship, were also made integral parts of the Asiatic Fleet. This, it was hoped, would maximize reliability and ensure independence from shore-based support.[23]

The Navy Department also sought to improve facilities at Cavite. In 1924 a 24,000 ton capacity tank was purchased from private sources for naval use; construction of a fuel depot was undertaken the following year, and a total of $373,000 was forthcoming for repairs to the dilapidated Cavite wharf.[24] By 1926 some 14,285 tons of fuel oil was in storage, and in 1928 long range radio facilities were added to the primitive submarine base.[25] Captain M.R. Standford's report on the facilities in Manila Bay pointed out Cavite's unsuitability – due to shallow water – for anything of deep draught like a drydock, so the Department persuaded the administration to allow the area around the base to be dredged to a depth of thirty-five feet, which was carried out between 1928 and 1932. By the late 1920s, thanks to the construction of half a dozen new oil-fired shallow draft gunboats specially designed for Chinese waters, C-in-C Asiatic Fleet was intending to augment the Army's gun defences on islands like Caballo and Corregidor with naval gunboats from the Yangtse Patrol.[26]

The Army too were seeking ways to bypass the Treaty. The Commander of the Philippine Department, Brigadier-General Kilborne, announced in a routine dispatch to the War Department his intention to tunnel a road for the air garrison at Kindley Field on Corregidor's tip, and the Ordnance Bureau was persuaded to part with several thousand tons of condemned TNT for the task. In 1922, by using the entire post maintenance fund for one year and drafting in one thousand convicts from the Bilidad Prison and salvaged mining equipment from an abandoned gold mine at Baguio, Kilborne was able to start work on the Malinta Tunnel. Work was completed in stages over the next ten years. This helped maintain the Navy's interest.[27]

Some 4,000 mines were also placed in storage, but the Army continued to have primary responsibility for all coast defences, including air patrol, minefields, nets, booms and the forts across the entrance to the Bay, and it jealously guarded its domain. Since the Army preferred the M3 controlled system, Manila's minefields operated on a somewhat unstable electrical circuit.[28] The Navy provided two minelayers to augment the stocks, but the United States had not developed a truly efficient floating mine at this stage; indeed the Navy's principal mine could not even be retrieved once it had been laid. When Admiral Hart finally closed off the approaches to the Bay in mid-1941 with floating mines half of them exploded. Even by the end of 1939 there were still no nets or booms in place.[29]

By leasing part of the naval reservation to private enterprise, the Navy Department also encouraged private dock construction. Valdero de Manila, the Earnshaw group and the Honolulu Iron Works were encouraged to construct patent slips to carry out large-scale repairs. However, most of these were far too small for fleet use, being under 1,100 tons in capacity. Private contractual work with the San Nicholas Iron Works enabled the Navy to keep its ships' boilers in prime condition. In event of war the Department also hoped to use Manila's harbour facilities; here there were 1,250 acres protected by a 10,000 foot breakwater wall, with 9,000 feet of berthing space available, and heavy cranes with a lifting capacity of seventy-five tons.[30]

Alternate Bases

As it was recognized Manila's defences might not hold, alternative sites were also considered. The choice depended on the route taken by the US Fleet, and here the matter was more complicated than for the Admiralty, for there were three possible approach routes. In 1927, after flying to Japan, Charles A. Lindbergh completed a report on the Aleutian island aerial route that led to requests from the Department of Commerce for further investigation. Though the Army Air Corps established bases at Dutch Harbour and Kiska, low temperatures and appalling weather conditions meant constant operating difficulties would be faced for naval craft. Considerable numbers of ice flows meant sea conditions would be particularly dangerous, making it unlikely that the route might be used.[31] Nevertheless in 1938, as a defensive measure, the Hepburn Board proposed a line of patrol air bases from Kodiak to Dutch Harbour; by 1941 the programme had centred on the creation of a base at Dutch Harbour and an advanced base at Adak.[32]

If the route chosen was across the central Pacific, then it was initially felt that Guam would have to be held or recaptured. Yet from the defence standpoint, Guam's demise had begun from the moment the Washington Treaty was signed. In 1922 there was a small force of 546 Marines armed with two 6-inch guns and six aircraft guarding the island.[33] By 1932 there were no aircraft, no artillery and only 146 Marines left. In January 1925 the C-in-C Asiatic Fleet, Admiral Washington, had transferred Marines from Cavite to the International Settlement in China and deficiencies had been made up from Guam; in 1927 another 15 officers and 246 men followed, this time directly from the island itself. By 1929 Guam was categorized as 'F' on the priority list. Existing defences would not be reinforced on the outbreak of war, and in event of attack by superior forces the defenders would rely on 'sabotage and demolition'.[34]

By 1931 the Navy Department was reporting to President Hoover that Guam 'no longer has any military value'. Hoover therefore agreed to reduce all activity down to the lowest possible level, that required merely for operation of a civil government.[35] By 1936, with that traditional mistrust of military power so characteristic of American administrations, President Roosevelt was threatening any naval officer who dared to raise again the question of forming a Naval General Staff with immediate transfer there 'for the duration', an indication that Guam had sunk so low on the naval scale it was now equivalent to the British Outer Hebrides.[36] Captain Lademan, commander of the main naval supply vessel to Guam, left a vivid portrait of the relative backwardness of the island as a naval base:

> Submerged coral heads clogged most of Apra harbour surrounding the small mooring area. There were no docks for deep draught ships. Little steam launches (formerly officers liberty boats in the days of coal burning battleships) towed miniature lighters from the ship up a Lilliputian channel to a wharf at the village of Piti where a cluster of tin roofed sheds masqueraded as a Navy Yard. It took twelve days of round the clock back breaking work to unload the ship.[37]

However, elements within the General Board continued to hope that if restraints on financial expenditure could be lifted, base facility improvements up to fleet standard at Pearl Harbor, Cavite and elsewhere might be possible. The Navy Department suffered periodic bouts of overconfidence in this regard. In 1938 the President had been sufficiently impressed by testimony before the House Naval Affairs Committee concerning the paucity of facilities in the Pacific during the Vinson Construction Bill's passage through Congress, to create a board under Rear-Admiral Hepburn to investigate the state of Far Eastern defences. The Hepburn Board proposals, submitted in December of that year, called for a massive $325 million expenditure programme on some twenty-five bases. The Bureau of the Budget immediately cut this back to $94 million for completion of only twelve bases. Under this reduced programme provision was made for facilities in both oceans, but the main emphasis was on the Pacific. Kaneohe Bay, Midway, Wake, Johnston and Palmyra were to be developed as secondary air bases for land-based aircraft or naval seaplanes. One of the most interesting developments was the brief re-emergence of Guam as best choice for advanced fleet base, at an estimated cost of $39 million. To a large extent the Navy Department was playing 'Corinthian Bagatelle with a ball called Guam on a board called Congress'. 'Top score' was repair facilities for all classes of vessels, re-establishment of fortifications and the build-up of a strong protective garrison, all of which had the support of those favouring a swift trans-Pacific offensive. 'Minimum score' comprised only authorisation for some dredging, extra seaplane ramps and accommodation, at a cost of $5 million, which satisfied those desiring hemispheric defence.[38]

But despite Leahy's plea that expenditure would be spread across five years, the President was not prepared to accept the financial outlay, stipulating that no money must be spent before 1940 and reducing the bill to $20 million. Even this limited programme was unacceptable to both the State Department and the Naval Affairs Committee, and so the Guam proposals were dropped from the bill. In its preliminary study on future war plans in April 1939 the Joint Planning Committee noted the Navy's desperate need for an advanced base, but convincing the administration seemed unlikely. Writing about the Guam proposal in 1941 for United States Naval Institute Proceedings, John Masland pointed out:

> The failure of Congress to authorize the Guam appropriation was a clear indication of its unwillingness and of the unwillingness of the public to support the sort of naval policy required to uphold traditional American political policies in the Far East. It was true that large sums were being voted for the expansion of our fleet and shore facilities, some of them in the Eastern and mid-Pacific. But as late as the winter of 1940, this expansion was thought of in terms of the defense of our immediate Continental home.[39]

Early in May 1940, Stark pointed out to the Naval Affairs Committee the desperate need over the long term for re-fortification of Guam and the creation of an 'impregnable' base in the Philippines. Estimates for completion ranged as high as $50 million for Pearl Harbor and $225 million for Cavite and Guam respectively. At this stage, there seemed little hope for such a project.[40]

One alternative, of course, was to seize and occupy Japanese bases in the Mandates. This would require the creation of some kind of Marine amphibious all-arms force specifically designed for the task. However, the training and philosophy of the Marines at this stage was concerned more with occupation of advanced bases than with seizure. In 1922, Lieutenant-Colonel Ellis and his first-hand studies of the problems of defending Guam led General Lejeune to recommend the establishment of a mobile self-sufficient unit ready for action within forty-eight hours, which could conduct land operations against a hostile naval base to seize it from the enemy. By 1927 tactical studies were emphasizing the need to secure bridgeheads and landing points; disembarkation timetables and gunfire support had become the core of the Marine Manual.[41]

However, finance was a distinct problem, and new commitments in Nicaragua and China dispersed the Marine Force. By 1928 there were barely enough resources present to keep Quantico and Mare Island running, and after 1925 there was no further amphibious training for nearly a decade. Even those exercises that did take place were not altogether successful. The first training exercise in amphibious landing at Culebra in the Caribbean in 1923 ended in total confusion. The naval bombardment was regarded as ineffective, transports were badly loaded and landing craft poorly designed. A second exercise at Oahu the following year, demonstrating a brigade-sized landing, simply underlined the problems.[42] Once again, the likelihood of seizure of all of the Mandates appeared unlikely. US military policy continued to emphasize the landing role of the Marines, but even as late as October 1939 only two cargo ships were attached as transports to the US Fleet on a permanent basis:

> In January of 1941. . .the shore party for a brigade size landing consisted of one elderly major and two small piles of ammunition boxes. The ship to shore movement of fuel was a nightmare. We had no force level transportation, no engineers, and no supporting maintenance capability worthy of the name. In short, the combination of the parsimonious years and our own apathy had left us next to helpless where logistics were concerned.[43]

> I am of the opinion that the average naval officer has no conception of amphibious warfare. His idea is to lay offshore, slap a brigade of Marines

on the beach, and impatiently await their return aboard ship. During recent manoeuvres I was surprised to find out that only in rare instances would a naval officer observe land operations.[44]

Guam's demise during the 1920s indicated the central Pacific route would not gain administrative support. Even before 1922 the attention of the Naval War Plans Division had therefore been drawn further south. If the southern route was chosen, however, it was felt that other bases in the Philippines would probably be necessary. Indeed one of the main objectives for the Fleet under the 1924 War Plan was 'the establishment of an advanced fleet base at Manila or at some other location'. By 1929 the range of choice had narrowed to four possible locations. Tawi-Tawi Bay in the Sulu archipelago lacked suitable locations for shore installations. Coron Bay's defence was complicated by no less than four separate entrances, and the base was well within the 'typhoon belt'; Malampaya Sound on Palawan was felt to be vulnerable to land-based air attack from Manila. That left Dumanquilas Bay, about eighty miles northeast of Zamboanga on Mindanao as the most likely candidate. It was closer to Hawaii than any of the other sites, and was protected from weather and sea bombardment by a range of hills. Good positions for storage, housing, airfields, coastal and AA batteries were available, and timber, coal and fresh water were in plentiful supply. The Navy planned to establish a naval repair depot, two air stations, three major storehouses and a large refrigeration plant, barracks and housing for at least a battalion of troops, while storage facilities would be sufficient for three months supply of food, fuel and equipment.[45]

The first revision of War Plan 'Orange' in October 1926 therefore created a specific starting point from which all actions would be measured. Since it was unrelated to warnings from civilian authorities, M day was not the day on which war was declared, but rather the date upon which the mobilization schedules were based. It was expected that the main fleet and fleet train would be concentrated at Hawaii by M+30. Base material would leave the West Coast at the same time. Dumanquilas Bay would be occupied until M+180, when the Manila Bay-Subic area would be recaptured. These would then become the main outlying Western bases. However, the Department expected no money to be forthcoming in peacetime towards the cost of such facilities; the base would have to be established after war had broken out, with the required material and personnel being transported to its intended location once the fleet regained control.[46]

As regards fleet bases in the islands around the Philippines, several possible arrangements were discussed by the Navy Department. The Naval War Plans Division suggested that some of the economic provisions of any independence act be modified to favour the Philippines in return for leasing arrangements on Aparri, Palawan, the Sulu archipelago or Corregidor. Some naval officers even hoped to apply a form of self-determination, for there was already a natural boundary between north and south based on racial, religious and cultural lines; the predominantly Muslim Moro population on Mindanao regarded the Roman Catholic north as their hereditary enemy, and were anxious to preserve an American presence to guard and protect their culture. In 1935 General Parker, then commander of the Philippine Department, suggested permanently leasing a British base in North Borneo; however, while favouring arrangements for joint leasing, the Admiralty were not prepared to support any ceding of British territory.[47]

The idea of an alternate base to Manila proved remarkably long lived. By 1940 President Quezon was making it clear to Admiral Hart, the current CINCAF, that he personally favoured retention of a US naval base in the islands. The General Board now looked to Dumanquilas, Tutu Bay or Tawi-Tawi. Hart expressed his preference for an island chain, which could be more easily protected than a mainland base.[48] On 11 September 1940 the Secretary of the Navy decided a special board under Admiral Greenslade would investigate the whole naval base problem.[49] Greenslade was a revisionist, more interested in the creation of a defensive 'strategic front' extending from the Aleutians to the Philippines and thence to Guam than in establishing an advanced fleet base for offensive purposes; fleet bases would be useful but only to hold the apex at each side of a defensive triangle.[50] Nevertheless, the General Board concluded that Dumanquilas and Polillo were the most suitable main fleet bases in the Philippines; Tawi-Tawi and Davao would be secondary cruiser bases, and Malampaya Sound a temporary operating base. As a long-range strategy this could ultimately provide a deterrent for the islands, but for the time being Cavite and Guam would remain mere secondary outlying bases. However, Army planners continued to object to the very existence of a central Pacific route, preferring instead to dispatch reinforcements to the Philippines round the Cape of Good Hope and through the Indian Ocean, kept open by Britain and France.[51]

Fuelling Anchorages

Along the southern route, at least one air station and a battalion of troops was planned for Malampaya Sound, while no less than twenty naval fuel stations, each with storage for 75,000 tons of fuel, were also seen as being useful. Separate naval air stations and naval repair depots with storehouses, crane ships with 400,000 pound lifting capacity and ten acres of oil storage would also be needed. In order to aid the repair of ships, floating dry docks would also be required. Because of cost it was expected that these would have to be built and transported after war had broken out. Two would be based at Manila by M+530 and M+650 respectively. All the necessary construction work would be completed by specially organized labour battalions, the forerunners of the 'Sea-bees'.[52]

As many coral reefs, islands, and islets as possible would have to be used. Advocates of the southern approach like the C-in-C Asiatic Fleet, Admiral Albert Gleaves, thought in terms of the Galapagos, New Caledonia and American Samoa. Gleaves also recommended construction of bases at Tahiti, the Marquesas and Tuomatu Island, suggesting that France discharge her war debts by transferring her island possessions to US control.[53] In 1921 Secretary of State Hughes had requested a strategic estimate on the southern Pacific islands from the Navy Department. Johnston and Palmyra islands were then seen as being of greatest importance, while Nukuhiva, New Caledonia and the Admiralties were of 'moderate value' as naval bases.[54] In May 1923 the recently completed cruiser *Milwaukee* was sent on a training/working-up cruise into the Pacific. Carrying two seaplanes for photographic reconnaissance she travelled from Hawaii via Taongi, Eniwetok, Mortlock, Truk, Hall and Wolea to the Dutch East Indies. On the return journey, the ship visited spots on the northwest coast of New Guinea, Brisbane, Sydney, Auckland, Noumea, New Caledonia, the Fiji Islands and Samoa. Some ten islands were listed by the Navy's War Plans Division as suitable anchorages in event of an 'Orange' war, and *Milwaukee* visited five of these.[55]

Between 1923 and 1924 the Navy was also involved with the Department of Agriculture in an examination of islands southwest of Hawaii. Scientific expeditions were despatched to Nichoa, Ocean, Johnston, Fanning, Baker, Howland and Washington Islands. In 1926 the Director of the Naval War Plans Division submitted a memorandum on the strategic advantages of Christmas Island as a submarine or seaplane base, and the Department recommended the British claim be challenged. By July it was proposing a wholesale takeover of French Oceania as well, but the State Department wisely rejected both proposals. Nevertheless the 'showing the flag' exercises by both the Great White Fleet in the Southern Pacific in 1908 and the Coontz expedition of 1925 had much in common.[56] Both looked at the southern route option, both showed the speed of United States naval reaction to a crisis, both were a demonstration as to how the support services might triumph over distance, and both demonstrated the ability of ad hoc provisioning and mobile bases to cope with fleet needs.[57] From 1927 to 1933, however, interest in the southern route appeared to wane; survey efforts were instead concentrated on the Caribbean side of the Canal, though some 9700 soundings of the North Pacific were taken by the USS *Ramapo*.[58]

The utility of air power in the Pacific was one major difference in emphasis between the Royal Navy and its US equivalent. The increased emphasis on airpower in the United States services was reflected by an Army round-the-world flight and by naval enlistments of air personnel. While recruitment remained fairly constant at about 85,000 between 1922 and 1932, the number of men assigned air duty in the Navy rose from 4,247 in 1923 to 10,771 in 1930.[59] Indeed, it was hoped air power might reduce the need for fleet action and make up for deficiencies created by the lack of bases and auxiliaries. Naval interests included both defensive patrol and offensive capability, with both land-based and sea-based systems. With the introduction in 1926 of a five-year programme to create a combined service force of 1000 aircraft, the Navy began actively to compete with the Army Air Corps for a share of land-based aircraft and landing grounds.[60] Six naval air stations were established in the continental United States, and Ford Island in Hawaii became the main establishment in the Pacific for land-based naval aircraft. As the Army had responsibility for all coastal defence, it resented the Navy's introduction into service of such aircraft as the Marlin twin-engined bomber.[61]

In the area of sea patrol, the PN-10 seaplane with its extended cruising capability was serving with the Navy by the late 1920s.[62] In October 1933 an aeronautical design breakthrough created an aircraft that fulfilled all the Navy's hopes for an extended range flying boat, the Consolidated PBY Catalina. This monoplane had a radius of action of more than 1,000 miles, and the Navy even began to discuss their use as attack planes. Admiral King believed that the flying boat would be able to haul twenty-four tons of explosive, almost as much as the air wings of the carriers themselves, across vast distances to enemy targets. He even envisaged operating them with torpedoes.[63] The PBYs would also provide cover for the fleet while on passage.

The Navy also investigated the possibility of mobile bases. One possible solution to the air base problem was the placement of sea dromes west of Hawaii. Each drome would have weighed 25,550 tons, and would have been 1200 feet long, 200 feet wide at the ends and 400 feet wide in the middle with a draft of 160 feet, with accommodation for 160 people incorporating weather, radio and fuelling facilities; the Navy hoped to extend these to create naval fuel stations for the Fleet. The first of seven was to have been completed in 1929 and anchored halfway between Bermuda and New York, but in the end the design proved too unstable in rough weather.[64]

Naval air stations also served as the main servicing and maintenance centres for naval air afloat. Here too there were substantial differences in practice from the Royal Navy. In general British naval aviation and carrier doctrine lay in direct contrast to that of the US Navy. From the beginning the US Navy placed greater emphasis on the use of carriers in the Far East:[65]

> To ensure air supremacy, to enable the United States Navy to meet at least on equal terms any possible enemy, and to put the United States in its proper place as a Naval power, fleet aviation must be developed to the fullest extent. Aircraft have become an essential arm of the Fleet. A naval air service must be established, capable of accompanying and operating with the Fleet in all waters of the globe.[66]

> It is the Navy's mission to protect our coasts, our sea borne commerce and far flung possessions. Once war is upon us we must take the offensive and win it. The Navy is the first line of defence and naval aviation as an advanced guard of this first line must deliver the brunt of the attack. Naval aviation cannot take the offensive from shore; it must go to sea on the back of the Fleet.[67]

Consequently, the visits to Pacific Islands mentioned above served multiple purposes. They allowed the United States to 'keep an eye' on Japanese activities in the Mandates. Surveys could be carried out on islands of use, which could either become part of the alternate route to the Philippines or be incorporated into an aerial 'defence screen' with patrols protecting Hawaii from surprise attack. Patrols could also supply additional aerial cover over the fleet itself to supplement naval air power on the aircraft carriers. At the heart of this emphasis lay a more accurate realisation of Japan's surface naval strength. US naval staff had fewer illusions than the British about Japanese capability:

> The Japanese sailors are well trained. The efficiency of the personnel of the Japanese Navy is equal to that of the British or American navies. The morale is excellent. The Japanese Navy is modern, well balanced, and ready for prompt service. The Combined Fleet works on a schedule of employment that is certain, with the equality of its personnel, to produce a highly efficient organization, and one that will operate smoothly and effectively in time of war.[68]

> The Japanese are not inferior to the other foreign navies – including the United States – in ordnance, engineering, and aviation. Thus, in general, the material condition of the Orange Fleet may be said to be very good. . .It is considered that the Orange Navy is a well organized efficient force which

is from a material and tactical standpoint ready for war. . .the zeal and care with which they pursue their duties leads to the conclusion that the Orange Navy is a competent and well drilled force, manned by officers and men that know their business and who are loyal and enduring.[69]

In July 1934 the new cruiser USS *Astoria* was despatched on a training cruise southwest of Hawaii. Stops included Palmyra, Christmas, Howland, Baker and Nukulaelae; the ship proceeded to Australia and then back through the Pacific via Noumea. Nukulaelae in the Ellice group was felt to be suitable as a seaplane base, and Baker and Howland as bases for airfields.[70] By the end of 1934 Wake, Johnston and Kingman Reef had been placed under naval jurisdiction by Executive Order,[71] and by the end of 1935, with naval assistance, Johnston, Palmyra and Kingman Reef had all been surveyed.[72] During test exercises at Hawaii that year some forty seaplanes, using these islands, launched an attack on a 'Battle Fleet' approaching from Midway. That same month PAA's expedition to Wake was accompanied by naval officers, and landing field and seaplane sites were marked out.[73]

Having seen reports of the 1935 expeditions, the C-in-C US Fleet concluded that four seaplane bases, one each at Midway, Pearl Harbor, Palmyra and Tutuila, would create an impenetrable aerial barrier protecting Hawaii, while the Naval War Plans Division felt Wake and Samoa would assist reconnaissance of the Mandates.[74] By March 1936 Howland, Baker and Jervis had been placed under the jurisdiction of the Department of the Interior. The Bureau of Aeronautics reported that aerial coverage for the Fleet's passage 1,000 miles west of Hawaii was to be provided by seaplane tenders moored at islands en route.[75] Christmas Island was seen as being of particular value, and Canton, Fakaofu, Danger Reef, Penrhyn and Suvarov were also likely sites; as well as operating as advanced bases these could be used for defensive patrol. It was the continuing interest in this region that was to bring Chamberlain's administration into political conflict with the US Government in 1937.[76]

The Navy's 1939 report on aviation wartime requirements called instead for the establishment of air patrol bases in the southern Japanese Mandates. This had the advantage of allowing a rapid transit across the Pacific, thereby opening an immediate line of communication to Singapore, but the route was subject to flank attack by the Japanese and it culminated in a dangerous bottleneck around the Mindanao-Morotai-New Guinea area where the numerous islands limited easy passage. Torres Straits was rejected because it was feared that in event of war it might be mined.[77] Navy planners favoured seizing Truk as a buffer against interference while the Fleet proceeded south from Hawaii to Fiji and thence into the Java Sea via the Moluccas, where it would link up with the Asiatic Fleet and join in the defence of the Malay Barrier. Tawi-Tawi and Jolo in the Sulu chain between Mindanao and Borneo were considered likely sites, and Quezon indicated he would be willing to make available southern Philippine bases. By February 1940 the Department finally announced the despatch of six patrol aircraft to Canton. Earlier, in August 1939, a list of islands it felt must be claimed was passed to the State Department.[78]

This preoccupation with the southern route continued under the Rainbow Plans. In Rainbow 2, incursions from the south were seen as useful to shorten the line of communications to the Philippines. Under Rainbow 3, Blue would advance from the vicinity of Rabaul and establish a fleet base either in the Palaus, at Tawi-Tawi or at a port somewhere near Borneo.[79]

Anglo-American Naval Planning Begins to Deviate

Since the Far Eastern war plans of the British and US navies were similar, one might be forgiven for seeing the principles of seapower as some kind of Holy Writ. After all, both navies were motivated by exactly the same principles, operated under similar limitations and were equally misunderstood by their respective administrations. Yet there were differences that, as they evolved and emerged, had the effect of separating the plans and the strategies of both navies.

The idea of a speedy transfer for the Fleet across the Pacific had been the central core of War Plan 'Orange', but as the 1930s wore on that notion became a political football within the US Navy. Increasingly, US naval strategy became trapped in a three way battle between what might be termed the 'hares', the 'tortoises' and the 'armadillos'. All three schools of thinking were committed to absolute victory, but they disagreed about targets, routes and especially the timing of any advance. According to Miller, 'tortoises' held sway in the middle ranks of the US naval planning positions while the 'hares' were entrenched in the upper rankings. The latter argued that America would never be stronger than at the beginning of a war. Time was expected to favour the defence, so their view – to use the words of Nathan Bedford Forrest, one of the great Confederate cavalry commanders – was to get there 'fustest with the mostest.' While the defeat of Japan might be expected to take years, the object was to advance the reconquest of the United States Far Eastern territories as far as possible before Japan became organized. Success would be made easier by the construction of an American Gibraltar, but until it was built the fleet would have to use improvised advanced naval bases. The quick advance dominated US planning from 1906 to 1934, and exerted periodic influence afterwards, but by the late 1930s the 'hares' were coming under constant attack.[80]

The 'tortoises' accepted that war with Japan was almost certain to be a lengthy affair. The Navy's customary mission – control of the Pacific – still required a superior fleet served by advanced fleet bases, but the Philippines and Guam would almost certainly fall to the Japanese, rendering any dash across the Pacific a gamble in the extreme, entailing hasty initial preparation, vulnerable communications and an uncertain destination.[81] To endanger the fleet by sailing into the teeth of the Japanese defences was seen as foolhardy, given the advances in aircraft and submarine design that had ensued during the 1920s. A more conservative approach would preserve and conserve the battleships, enabling the US industrial machine to begin flexing its not inconsiderable muscle. They proposed to move the Fleet slowly across the Pacific, step by step in a measured advance, securing islands en route as advanced naval bases, either through the Mandates or along a southern Pacific route. It was expected that the advance might last as long as two years before reaching the area surrounding the Japanese home islands.[82]

By the late 1930s a third group, the 'armadillos', had emerged with a very different approach. From 1937 to 1939 the international scene changed considerably; the prospect of a global war seemed much closer, with Japan on the verge of forming a partnership with Fascist Italy and Nazi Germany. The prospects of an outright Axis threat to US interests appeared high. Under conditions where the United States faced three potential opponents, the aggressiveness of 'Orange' appeared out of kilter with prevailing conditions. Politically it appeared more acceptable with current US isolationist policy to adopt a defensive stance, supporting the Allies in the Atlantic and maintaining the Pacific as a secondary theatre of operations. Naval officers who were defensive minded were initially opposed by a determined band of naval offensivists labouring to preserve the essence of the 'Orange' plan. For example in 1937–38 Admiral Leahy sought to preserve 'Orange' against direct attack by the Army, but towards the end of his tenure in office even he was forced to accept that the island bases needed to support such ideas would not be forthcoming.[83] It was these dichotomies that were to provide the basis for many of the difficulties that later beset Anglo-American naval relations in the Pacific.

The Admiralty was able to sustain its commitment to a speedy offensive to a greater degree than the US Navy. It is interesting to know why this was so. After all, they were beset by almost exactly the same needs with regard to Far Eastern defence and had devised the same method of meeting the Japanese threat. However, it is clear there was far less internal support for the original tenets of War Plan 'Orange' calling for a 'fast track' offensive than there was for the Far Eastern Naval War Memorandum. There were three reasons for this. First, the US Navy found it far more difficult than the Admiralty to hide its plans and its expenditures; second, it was shackled by a lack of base development that extended from the west coast right across the Pacific, making it unlikely that a quick full scale naval offensive was even feasible. Finally, there was a great deal less confidence about the ability of the United States Far Eastern possessions to hold out for the time required for rescue.

As the senior and more respected of the British armed services, the Royal Navy had certain advantages. British bureaucratic organization and administration provided enough loopholes for the Admiralty to re-direct finance. Though the Royal Navy was not always able to garner support for its projects, it was able to make considerable improvements at Hong Kong and to keep those improvements from prying eyes. In the United States, on the other hand, there was an inherent distrust of military matters and of the armed services in general. Any suggestion that a General Staff be formed along the lines of the Prussian model was regarded practically as a direct threat to democracy. Given the divisions between congressional, presidential, and judicial responsibility, the administration felt duty bound to create a system of checks and balances designed to restrict and regulate armed service authority. This was achieved by creating Senate and Congressional sub-committees to investigate every aspect of service life. Held in a inquisitional spirit of judicial enquiry, these proceedings had right of call on any and all personnel. Perhaps in no other country in the world were the armed services so closely and so publicly scrutinized, which made it extremely difficult if not impossible to disguise what was spent and the way in which it was spent. Naval appropriations, for example, were looked into by no less than four separate committees as well as the Director of the Budget. On the one occasion the Department did try to cut a passage through the Washington Treaty provisions, the 'Teapot Dome' scandal proved so disastrous it simply made the Navy even more cautious and hesitant about making improvements west of Hawaii.[84]

Absence of Bases

Another factor differentiating the Admiralty from the US Navy was the latter's general lack of base development. Even if the US Fleet reached the Far East, there remained serious doubts as to whether it could be maintained there. Even before the question of Philippine independence was raised, priorities under Monroe had begun to vie with the priorities under Mahan; continental defence competed directly with defence of empire.[85] The United States lacked the experience that Royal Navy tradition provided; it was new to the concept of a blue water navy and base possession. There was no equivalent on the west coast of a Scapa Flow, an Alexandria or a Gibraltar. On the American seaboard the facilities necessary to support fleet activities had simply not been available before 1900, and even by 1919 development was only in its early stages. On the east coast, New York and Chesapeake Bay were the two main bases, and supplementary facilities for cruisers, destroyers and patrol craft were developed at Charleston and Guantanamo Bay. Separate facilities were needed at both ends of the Panama Canal. In the Pacific, Puget Sound, San Francisco Bay's Mare Island and Hawaii were to be developed as first-class bases, with San Diego as a supplementary base. In 1919, however, a naval board of inspection reported that there were only six docks capable of dealing with battleships in the Pacific.[86] Facilities at Mare Island and Bremerton were found to be 'totally inadequate' for fleet tasks:

> There was no developed operating base south of Bremerton that could berth the big ships, so they rolled outside the breakwater off San Pedro. The Puget Sound area was becoming the Pacific Fleet's summer drill grounds, but the fogs, currents, and lack of good anchorages made operations difficult and a bit hazardous. The Admiral noted particularly in a routine report to the Secretary, that smoke from forest fires was as dangerous as fog in the late summers and early fall. The southern drill area at sea between San Pedro and San Diego was ideal, but the lack of a shipyard to handle battleships was bothersome.[87]

It was intended to deepen the shallow water around Mare Island and to develop other facilities in the San Francisco Bay area, but in terms of resources, base development on the west coast was subject to fierce competition from both the Atlantic seaboard and the Canal, where Britain was regarded as the most likely opponent. It seemed expedient to mount 16-inch guns for the protection of New York Harbour and Chesapeake Bay. Both Chesapeake and Hell Gate required extensive dredging, and $700,000 was spent on this alone in 1924. Following the Culebra exercises, Admiral H.P. Jones reported a long list of deficiencies at Panama. Faulty grouping of the existing shore artillery exposed the Miraflores lock to sea bombardment, and certain vital parts of the Canal were felt to be susceptible to air attack. Directly as a result of the 1929 exercises, a second list of deficiencies had to be drawn up and changes made.

Sectional interests also had a part to play in diverting resources away from the Pacific. Because Mare Island had limited anchorage space and silting problems, it was regarded as unsuitable as a fleet base by the Navy Department, which preferred Alameda, California. However, pressure from local opinion prevented development. Some 51.25 per cent of naval appropriations came from the seven main coastal states, so these had inordinate influence over expenditure. Some important refitting work could only be done on the east coast, and in wartime this would mean the battleships would have to journey back there from beyond Hawaii.[88] Rear-Admiral Thomas P. Magruder's criticisms were accurate indeed:

> In this respect the Navy has become 'a political football'. Every seaboard state has fought for its own navy yard and, if its harbours were not such as to warrant a navy yard, it must have at least a destroyer and submarine base... The result is that we have today not less than twelve naval yards and naval bases... Only three of these are located on the Pacific Coast and not one is fitted out as a fleet base.[89]

A similar dearth of facilities existed at Hawaii. Here, Army defence plans were not only directed towards protection of the naval facilities, but were also concerned with the creation an impregnable Hawaiian land defence and with the preservation of internal security. Indeed, the internal dangers were felt to be almost as great as the external. By 1930, Japanese made up 37.2 per cent of the population and played an essential role in the life of the islands; they owned 49 per cent of the retail stores and 74 per cent of the arable farmland. Not unnaturally, American planning staff expected sabotage and subversion from the moment hostilities were declared.[90]

Defence preparations on Oahu were never part of any coherent plan; staff studies and requests for funds were based on immediate needs and limited appropriations, so that the defence structure developed in piecemeal fashion. Despite the outlay of $5 million, defence never approached planned levels. Early in 1938 the Hawaiian Department felt $74.5 million would still be necessary to achieve a satisfactory state of defence.[91] The establishment strength in anti-aircraft guns, for example, was listed as 586, but in 1935 there were fewer than 100 on the island and many of these were obsolete. Even by 7 December 1941 there were only 211 anti-aircraft guns present. The war reserve of anti-aircraft ammunition was supposed to be 72,000 rounds, but in September 1934 there were only 40,233 round available. The Army War Plans Division estimated existing reserves would last only eighteen and one-half minutes under attack.

Any anticipated landing, it was hoped, would be halted by the shore installations, but if the enemy succeeded in forming a bridgehead the Defence Plan expected composite mobile combat teams backed by 155mm artillery and 8-inch railway guns to handle the situation. The Federal Aid Road Act of 1924 had entitled Hawaii to share in Federal aid appropriations, with the proviso that preference was given to programmes providing a highway system geared to defence. However, this had been all but ignored by the Territorial Government, with the result that there was no comprehensive system of military highways and even a list of desirable projects was not drawn up until 1934. Nor was there ever sufficient railway gauge available to provide area defence.

The existing mobile searchlights, tractors and the guns themselves were in any case on the verge of obsolescence and in poor mechanical condition. Aircraft and airfield facilities were also in short supply. In 1924 the Army had agreed to vacate Ford Island field leaving all the facilities in naval hands, but the first of the replacement fields at Hickam was not begun until 1935 and the Army was still in partial occupation of Ford in 1939. In 1932, test exercises revealed that the defending air forces would have ceased to exist had operations continued past the fifty hour mark. Oahu's combat planes were found to be 'obsolescent and ineffectual'. Replacements took three years to arrive from the date of application. Even if such an unstable defence system managed to survive the initial assault, it would only be able to hold for forty days before the food ran out.[92]

The Hawaiian islands also suffered more than most from the lack of financial support. From 1922 to 1934 a total of only $9 million was spent by the Navy Department on development projects there. By 1931 there were 531,272 tons of naval fuel in storage at Pearl, though because of volcanic activity and the dangers of earthquakes, much of this had to be contained in above ground tanks which were vulnerable to air attack.[93] Pearl Harbor had always been a poor choice as a main fleet base. Its entrance channel was only 150 yards wide, which meant vessels entering or leaving could do so in safety only in single file. Until an extensive mooring area was cleared round Ford Island, harbour capacity was sufficient for only four battleships. Some nine million cubic yards of earth had to be shifted to make the base usable. Because Ford Island lay at its centre there was a general lack of sea room for manoeuvring inside the harbour, and the presence of both a naval air station and a submarine base meant harbour control was a port authority nightmare. As the base was twenty miles from the nearest entertainment centres, the 14th Naval District command was plagued by social problems, and because money was not available for the transfer of families from the mainland, morale suffered. Little wonder then that the Navy preferred Lahaina Roads as the main fleet anchorage, but this was entirely open to the sea and there were no anchor points for nets or booms. It was not until 1934 that the Fleet was based entirely inside Pearl Harbor for the first time.[94]

Finally, based as it was on past traditions and historical commitment, US naval strategy presumed United States territorial possessions and interests in the Far East would be worth defending; but there was never an absolute political guarantee that this would be so. The United States was wedded more to a commercial doctrine of behaviour based upon moral obligation – the 'Open Door' policy – than to a realistic foreign policy. In 1935 the Far East took but 6 per cent of the foreign investment of the United States, and China took only 1 per cent of that. Given the nation's isolationist temper and its lackadaisical response to Japan's aggressions in China, commanders of the Asiatic Fleet such as Admiral Charles V. McVay, Montgomery M. Taylor and F.B. Upham were not confident that American interests in China would ever be worth defending. This was in direct contrast to the views of the Royal Navy. Though they might disagree with the Government's standpoint, the Admiralty at least knew what that standpoint was and could frame their proposals accordingly. Organizations such as the Chiefs of Staff and the Committee of Imperial Defence provided a forum for discussion. Since there was a clear understanding of the political position, and since Britain had territorial possessions of considerable importance politically, strategically and economically, the Admiralty could reasonably expect Hong Kong to be defended.[95]

American service departments, on the other hand, not only wrangled about the scale of defence but also about whether the US even intended to stay in the Far East. For example, there was considerable confusion about Philippine independence. The 1916 Jones Act pledged freedom from US control 'as soon as stable government can be established'. The Filipinos themselves felt Japan would pose no threat to the islands; they believed peaceful agreement and international arbitration could provide the necessary security, and at this stage they had faith in the pronouncements of Japanese politicians. Consequently at each session the Philippine legislature bombarded Washington with requests for a US withdrawal. The only thing that delayed the immediate granting of independence was the feeling – shared by both the Harding and Coolidge administrations – that the Filipinos were not sufficiently prepared to take on the necessary burdens and responsibilities. By the end of the 1920s, however, certain powerful trade organizations with considerable political influence were committed to severing all ties with the Philippines. Farm interests, the American-Cuban sugar group, the cordage industry and a number of related labour unions were united in their belief that Philippine economic interests provided unfair competition and were cutting domestic products out of the United States market. As a result of the Democrat victories in the polls of 1930 and 1932, there was a growing conviction in Congress that the islands were no longer a political or an economic asset.[96]

By 1931 there were still no air raid shelters on Corregidor and many facilities, including Topside Barracks, had yet to be bomb-proofed. In 1919 a small airfield – Kindley – had been constructed on Corregidor's tip. By 1928 the Army Air Corps had forty-nine observation planes, eleven pursuit aircraft and nine bombers in the Philippines, but there were unfortunately only sufficient crews for nine pursuit craft and five bombers.[97] By 1934 the Army War Plans Division had reduced the authorized number of anti-aircraft guns from thirty-two to twenty-four, simply because there were insufficient personnel to man any more. In any case there was a general shortage of guns not only in the Pacific commands but overall; in 1932 there were only sixty-two 3-inch AA guns in the entire Army and no heavy artillery apart from three 155mm guns. Even by mid-1940 there were no more than 1,800 pieces, substantially fewer than the British were using to guard London. In 1934 the Commander of the Philippine Department pleaded for an increase in the authorized strength of AA ammunition from 48,000 to 64,000 rounds, but this was turned down by the Army's War Plans Division. The garrison was short of establishment strength by 12,551 rounds.

The Views of the Army

The Army also expressed disquiet about existing US Far Eastern strategy, particularly the ability of both the Philippines and Hawaii to hold out in event of attack. As it was bound by the status quo arrangement, the US garrison in the Philippines remained fairly constant in the inter-war period at around 10,000–11,000 troops, of which 6,000 were Philippine Scouts officered by Americans. There were also 5,500 members of the Philippine Constabulary to maintain internal security. Lack of sufficient troops meant defence of the islands would have to be confined to Luzon alone.

The Navy felt that the primary task of the garrison should be to protect the Manila Bay area for the arrival of the Fleet. The Philippine Department, on the other hand, hoped to protect the entire Luzon coastline by creating three native divisions, one each for the northern and southern sectors and one in reserve. Because of poor service conditions and the general unattractiveness of army life to native Filipinos, attempts to attract recruits for a militia proved singularly unsuccessful. In addition there was a natural antipathy on the part of the

War Department about supplying arms to what might prove to be an anti-American anti-democratic movement which outnumbered the white minority.[98]

All these things – the paucity of bases on the West Coast, the lack of facilities at Pearl Harbor and the vulnerability of defences in the Philippines – directly affected war planning. By 1928 the Army staff members of the Joint Planning Committee were already casting doubts on the ability of existing forces to hold Luzon and even the entire Manila Bay area. They suggested that as soon as war was declared the US garrison must withdraw to the Bataan Peninsula. New directives altered the Army's mission: in event of an 'Orange' war its task was to 'hold' indefinitely the entrances to the Bay, but to defend the Bay area itself only 'as long as possible'. This was included in the Joint 'Orange' War Plan for 1928.[99]

The political consequences of Philippine independence and its undoubted effect on US military establishments had first been considered by the Joint Board between March and April 1924, but there was considerable division within the Joint Planning Committee about what to do. The Army planners recommended the withdrawal of the garrison once independence was granted; the Navy planners hoped to retain fortified bases on Luzon and in the southern islands in perpetuity. In its report the Committee pointed out the discrepancy but did not resolve it. Opinion within the Joint Board was troubled by the lack of a definite political programme regarding America's future in the Philippines.[100] By 1930 it was agreed that if limited self-government was granted, the bases should be retained. Under conditions of full independence, however, complete US withdrawal was the best solution. Yet in October 1931 in its second review of the situation, the Board reversed its decision: continued possession of the islands was felt to be 'indispensable' for the United States. Withdrawal was expected to upset the balance of power both in the Far East and within the Philippines themselves; it would deprive the US of a valuable entrepôt into trans-Pacific trade, as well as prevent the Army and Navy from completing their assigned missions in the Far Pacific.[101]

Yet many Army officers recognized the illusory qualities of War Plan 'Orange'. The quantity of supplies and manpower listed were good indications of what was desirable, but no indication at all of what was feasible. By M+18 the Army was expected to concentrate 16,000 troops and another 20,000-man expeditionary force on the Pacific coast. By M+45 there would be 55,000 troops together with 40,000 for the expeditionary force and a 10,000 man Marine force on Hawaii. Yet for the whole of the inter-war period, the entire US Army never exceeded 155,000 men. In a memo handed to the Commanding General of the

Philippine garrison, Major Stanley G. Embick, commander of the harbour defences at Manila and Subic, pointed out that the land defences necessary to secure Luzon from attack were not present, harbour facilities could not support a fleet and the fleet had now declined in relation to Japan, while Japan now controlled the Mandates and commanded the area of any chosen route. It would therefore be 'an act of madness' to proceed with 'Orange'.

To Embick's mind, there were only two possible solutions. If 'Orange' was retained as the main strategic plan, the Navy would have to undergo expansion to an unprecedented level and a new base would have to be constructed at a less vulnerable location, but he personally felt that neither the government nor public opinion would be prepared to support such expenditure. Violation of the Treaty might provoke Japan into a new naval arms race. The only viable alternative was to 'scrap "Orange" completely and 'pull out of the Far East entirely', moving the garrisons in China and on Luzon back to the Alaska-Oahu-Panama triangle. The mainland United States would then become the citadel and the outlying possessions merely outposts. If necessary Embick was even prepared to cede Oahu, so long as the mainland continued to be retained as the heart of the defences. Such an arrangement eliminated the need for any large naval establishments, removed the weak links in the American defence chain and eased the drain on the national budget. In the event of war the United States would gradually build up sufficient power behind its defensive screen and resume the offensive at the appropriate moment. Embick himself predicted that it might be two to three years before Japanese naval forces could be matched in Asian waters.

Though Embick could not win over the Army planners, he did give the planning agencies food for thought; later in the 1930s, his views would become the core of dissenting opinion about Far Eastern strategy.[102] Under the 1928 War Plan 'Orange', the decision to begin the trans-Pacific offensive was taken away from the C-in-C US Fleet and responsibility was given instead to the President; under the 1934 version, the Philippine Department was asked only to hold the Manila Bay area for fifteen days before beginning evacuation.[103]

The Views of the President

Roosevelt too had clear opinions about War Plan 'Orange'. At the second Cabinet meeting of the new administration, the President elaborated a plan of action calling for an American withdrawal from the Philippines. He argued that some 30 per cent of the Fleet would have to be diverted to furnish supplies and maintain communications; for every thousand miles travelled the Fleet would lose 10 per cent of its efficiency.

In 1934, rejection of the Hare-Hawes-Cutting Bill by the Philippine National Assembly led Quezon to try to negotiate a completely new independence act, or at the very least modification to the economic provisions. The President was not amenable to such changes, but he promised to set up an investigatory committee, to negotiate a neutralization treaty and to find a solution to the base question within two years. In many ways the Tydings-McDuffie Act was an amalgam of the many views of the self-interested groups in Congress; its provisions included a ten year transition period to independence, restricted and later total exclusion of Filipino immigration into the United States, upper limits on the export of coconut oil and hemp and a graduated tariff.[104] As far as the President and Senator Tydings were concerned, independence must be followed by US withdrawal:

> When the flag of the United States comes down and there is raised the flag of the new Filipino nation, the responsibility for your national defense passes from the hands of the United States to the new Filipino Government. To expect the United States to bear responsibility for the acts of a nation over which it had no control whatsoever would be as illogical as it would be to ask the Filipino people, once they are independent, to defend the shore of the United States. Sovereignty and responsibility walk hand in hand. Without sovereignty there cannot be responsibility.[105]

On 16 November 1936 the President, the Acting Secretary of State and the US High Commissioner to the Philippines, Francis Sayre, met to discuss future US involvement in the Philippines. Over the previous two years the President had made his own opinions perfectly clear. In April 1935 Swanson, then Secretary of the Navy, had approached Roosevelt with a proposal for alternative base sites on the Sulu archipelago. Roosevelt had immediately criticized the proposal's basic premise, namely that a base even needed to be retained in the islands.[106] In December he made it obvious to Swanson he no longer felt the Philippines to be an economic or a political asset. As he pointed out to Sayre, it would take the United States two to three years before an open attack could be launched on Japan. US strategy should be one of 'moving westward, making our position secure on one Pacific island after another'. In the meantime the United States 'would have to let the Philippines go temporarily'. Neutralization therefore appeared to be the most attractive alternative, and Roosevelt called upon the State Department to furnish him with detailed proposals.

The draft memo prepared by Maxwell Hamilton of the State Department's Far Eastern division provided a 'core agreement' to respect mutual rights and insular possessions. Codicils made it possible to extend the initial arrangement to outlying states such as French IndoChina or the Netherlands East Indies; obligations reaffirmed the Kellogg-Briand Pact and bound the signatories to continue and even extend non-fortification. However, primarily because it was felt Japan could not be trusted to keep such an arrangement, the State Department was unwilling to support renewal of the non-fortification clause, and the General Board strongly supported this stand; but the President dismissed such recommendations as 'defeatist'. He pursued his own policy line through Norman Davis, his personal representative in London. In March 1937 Davis approached Alexander Cadogan of the Foreign Office and the British Prime Minister himself about neutralization. However, internal discussions reveal the Admiralty was opposed to the scheme, and Chamberlain was unwilling to demilitarize Hong Kong without a greater demonstration of faith from Japan.[107]

The idea of a trans-Pacific offensive was equally anathema to the pervading spirit of American pacifism and to the image of the American services as 'non-aggressive', a view adopted both by public opinion and successive administrations. The Navy Department mounted a powerful publicity campaign to convert national consciousness and to lobby Congress about the need for a strong Navy through such organizations as the Navy League and the Army and Navy Register, but was unable to canvass substantial support.[108]

Fatal Miscalculations

By 1929 the General Board had developed a construction programme to raise the US Navy to Treaty standards by 1936, but President Hoover was appalled by the estimated costs. Battleship replacement alone was expected to be $1.1 billion. Needless to say, Senator David I. Walsh's resolution calling for such an amount was defeated in the US Senate. Hoover preferred to emphasize the nation's potential for construction rather than actually building. The administration was willing to create 'a reasonable force' to assure the Navy had 'a fair chance', but it did not support the idea of an 'adequate force providing absolute certainty'. In other words, a Navy capable of maintaining the home defence area could be justified, but not one powerful enough to keep open sea lanes or defend island possessions. For the London Conference in 1930, the General Board was forced to scale down its cruiser requirements from twenty-five to twenty-one. The non-naval delegation then reduced this even further to eighteen, and the United States agreed not to begin construction of its sixteenth cruiser until 1933.[109]

By then the Fleet was estimated to be at 65 per cent of Treaty strength allotted and Admiral Pratt, Chief of Naval Operations, was forced to provide a floating rotating reserve making up nearly one-third of existing US naval forces. Severe manpower difficulties accentuated this problem. In his first report to the Secretary of the Navy, Admiral Adams noted that the Navy required 97,400 men but there were only 84,500 on paper. To bring the Fleet up to Treaty standards, Adams estimated 8,500 line officers and another 137,557 men would be needed. In 1935 the battleships of the Fleet were manned to only 81 per cent and carriers and cruisers to 70 per cent of complement.[110] Although partly due to financial limitations, this deficiency can also be attributed to the general unpopularity of the US Navy as a career in the inter-war period. Poor salaries, bad working conditions and inadequate housing tended to take their toll. In Admiral Arleigh Burke's class of 1922, for example, there were 412 graduates; five years later there were only 269 left and by 1940 there were only 193 of the original class still serving.[111]

As President, Roosevelt was not entirely immune to naval needs. Much of his concern, however, was with defensive self-sufficiency – with the creation of a self-contained US security zone – than with preparations for a trans-Pacific offensive. Admiral Pratt had approached the President with a plan for the creation of a two-power standard by 1948, but Roosevelt was more concerned about balanced budgets; financial support for the Navy was thus doled out in meagre proportions.[112] By comparison with British rearmament that of the United States was slow, even lackadaisical. Not until 1940 did America opt for a large-scale naval construction, though an earlier supplementary programme had been approved in 1938; even this bill was introduced by Senator Carl Vinson on his own initiative.[113]

The blame for this cannot be laid entirely at the President's door. All Vinson's bills had particularly rough passages through Congress. The President's own attempt to secure funds to begin four new battleships in the 1938–9 fiscal year was also defeated by Congress late in 1938, so he could not help but be deeply impressed by the need for caution. Even though appeals to Mussolini and Adolf Hitler in 1939 went unanswered, Roosevelt continued to be committed to the idea of a just international order based on law.[114] In strategic terms too, America was less deeply committed to naval rearmament than Britain; reflected in a certain lack of response even from within the US Navy. Naval programmes were graduated and leisurely; there was little pressure to speed up production. Timetables were attuned more to 1946 than to 1941.[115] In 1936 the Department had initially expected to construct only one battleship for the 1937 fiscal year, and late in 1937 the programme for fiscal year 1938–39 included only two battleships. On his own initiative Vinson added plans for two aircraft carriers to his bill. On 10 November 1937, Leahy had written to the President to inform him the US Navy no longer needed more aircraft carriers because of the efficiency of flying boats 'in both, offense and defense. . .as compared with carrier based planes'. The Navy was indeed fortunate that the carrier Hornet was even laid down in 1939.[116]

With its main choice as advanced fleet base threatened by Philippine independence, its west coast and its remaining Pacific bases in a less than satisfactory state, with few auxiliaries to offset these deficiencies, lacking trained personnel to man an increasingly over-aged fleet already underweight in allowable Treaty tonnage, the US Navy was obviously in a worse state than its British counterpart and was therefore less capable of carrying out its intended war plan. The Navy Department also suffered from much less financial support and political guidance. As with the Royal Navy, the range of political choices were distinctly limited. To bridge that gap meant either to 'cut the cloth to suit existing resources', which could mean abandoning both the 'Open Door' and Mahan's doctrines, or building up of those same forces to required levels, which meant abrogating the Washington Treaty. By implication the Philippines would either have to be abandoned or the right to fortify renegotiated; at a minimum some kind of military or naval base in the islands would have to be retained. For the General Board, the choice was clear. National security had to rely on the Fleet. War Plan 'Orange' not only provided justification for naval construction but guaranteed the US Navy the key role in any future war.

One alternative was to develop a relationship with one or more potential allies, a view favoured by the Naval War College in their own preparations for the 1935 Naval Conference and later supported by Admiral Leahy. The most likely candidate was Britain, but the very idea of intimacy between the two countries was alien to the Navy War Plans Division and the Department itself. The General Board was convinced that the Washington Treaty had critically weakened the US Navy and British manipulation was felt to be primarily responsible: in American eyes, Britain had preserved her own sea power at little cost to herself but at enormous cost to the United States The spirit of active competition could not be eradicated, and Britain remained the chief opponent against which the state of the US Fleet was measured. The doctrine of 'perfidious Albion' did not preclude the possibility of common understanding in London in 1935, but it did preclude the possibility of an alliance or common military or political action in the Far East, as the 1938 Ingersoll Mission clearly demonstrated.[117]

War Plan 'Orange': The Myth Repudiated

As early as 1931, the Navy Department as a whole was admitting that 'Orange' could not be carried out with the naval forces then existing.[118] At the Naval War College at Newport, Rhode Island, the plan had been repeatedly tested by students on paper. Sixteen games carried out between 1919 and 1941 involved the American seizure of a central Pacific base in the Mandates; nine others concentrated on a fleet advance to the Philippines and eleven more on the defence of US territorial possessions. In the 1923 exercise, fifteen capital ships had made a successful passage across the Pacific, but during the 1928 exercise only ten were able to complete the journey.

The 1933 Fleet Problem presupposed Japan had already launched an attack on the Manila base, and 'Blue's initial objective was to recapture its advanced base or an alternative equivalent in the southern islands. As commander of 'Blue' Force, Captain Ernest King was forced to watch, fuming, as his ships battled their way to Dumanquilas Bay at enormous cost. Captain van Auken expected that Manila would hold for only two weeks 'at best', while Harold C. Train's critique pointed out that the US would have difficulty in defending the slow and obsolete fleet train from air and submarine attacks launched from out of the Mandates. Since only seven battleships survived the journey at the end of the exercise, it was still problematic whether the new base could be defended. All would still have to be staked on major fleet action somewhere in Philippine waters. In the 1935 exercise, because of a lack of fuel and a shortage of tankers, the Fleet failed to hold its advanced fleet base, and by 1936 the Naval War College had all but abandoned the idea of a rapid advance across the Pacific.[119]

There was, however, no sudden switching of priorities, no rapid reverse in strategy. The Navy Department and the Naval War Plans Division continued to resist change at every turn. The idea of some kind of swift trans-Pacific offensive continued to be part of naval thinking well into 1940, but the gradual erosion of the 'quick offensive' under War Plan 'Orange' was inexorable. Under prevailing financial restrictions and with the Japanese astride the main line of advance it was recognized – albeit reluctantly by the Navy – that the Plan could not be carried out with existing resources. Many of the necessary pre-war preparatory steps would have to be initiated after war had broken out, when resources were less impeded by financial control and when solutions to the many problems could be found. 'Orange' was less a realistic war plan than a hope, one that extended the period before relief for the Philippines to years rather than months. The main strategic problem was that between 1937 and 1940 American planning agencies were unable to make any firm decisions about US Pacific strategy. By 1935 the Joint Planning Committee had agreed to a more carefully staged advance, one calling for seizure of Japanese bases in the Mandates before proceeding. 'Base-Type 1', with anti-submarine nets and facilities for 150 planes, was expected to take forty-five days to create; 'Base-Type 2' would take considerably longer to develop, as it would comprise five sections with separate handling facilities for each class of ship.[120] As to the Philippines, the Committee finally accepted the Philippine Department's view that evacuation to Bataan must become part of the garrison mission. However, rather than confining naval defence to protection of the Bay entrance, the Asiatic Fleet was given the task of attacking Japanese lines of communications.

It was tacitly assumed that Manila and Cavite would inevitably fall, probably within a short space of time. Those sections of plan 'Orange' dealing with the use of Malampaya Sound and Dumanquilas Bay were cancelled, although a recommendation that Palawan be ceded to the United States – adopted unanimously by the Palawan provincial board – kept alive the idea of an alternate fleet base.[121] Early in 1937 Admiral H.E. Yarnell, C-in-C Asiatic Fleet, investigated several possible sites but expressed considerable doubts that such a base could success-fully resist attack for the time required, even if the Government did provide the necessary finance. As an alternative, Yarnell suggested America might avoid such expenditure by relying entirely on light forces, naval aviation and submarines. By forming a common front with other nations in the Pacific, he felt Japan's dependence on external resources and its economic vulnerability might be exploited by com-mercial strangulation 'without huge armies or dubious fleet encount-ers'.[122] This view seems to have exerted a strong influence on the President.[123]

By 1936 the cumulative effects of one and one-half decades of cut-backs led the Acting Secretary of War and the Secretary of the Navy to call for a complete re-examination of the US military position in the Far East. The gulf between the Army and Navy planners had become so wide they were forced to submit separate reports. Their views were now directly opposed. The views of Embick and Parker had been accepted by the Army and the new Chief of Staff Malin Craig, and the Philippines was now seen as a definite military liability. In the face of the Independence Act it now seemed unlikely any new base would be constructed, or that re-fortification of existing bases would be renewed.[124] As far as the Army planners were concerned:

> From a military point of view, therefore, our military (including naval) position in the Philippines is untenable; to strengthen it adequately during

the continuance of their Commonwealth status is impracticable; and any attempt on our part to do so would probably provoke war with Japan. However, in view of our commitments in these islands, our military and naval strength there would not be decreased during the life of the Commonwealth.[125]

Because of these uncertainties about the situation in the Far East, Navy planners preferred to defer making definite decisions until such time as War Plan 'Orange' needed to be revised. Tentatively, they were anxious to preserve the right to intervene in Philippine affairs after independence, and they hoped that existing military forces might be augmented in the future. Since the Joint Board had no brief to produce a unified study, it merely passed on both reports. Effectively, planning was deadlocked on this issue for the next two years.[126]

In late October 1937 the new head of the Army's War Plans Division, Walter Kreuger, warned that in light of the outbreak of the Sino-Japanese War 'Orange' had become 'dangerously inflexible'. The CNO, Admiral Leahy, agreed that major revision was long overdue. In November, Army planners submitted a plan for protection of the Alaska-Panama-Hawaii triangle. Navy planners on the Joint Planning Committee, however, continued to insist that plans must provide for the eventual defeat of the enemy. That could never be achieved by a purely defensive strategy. With stalemate once again all too likely, the Chief of Staff suggested the new Deputy Chief of Staff, Stanley Embick, and Rear-Admiral James O. Richardson be appointed to negotiate a compromise. Their revised plan retained the Army's defensive stance and the Navy's trans-Pacific offensive. In return for removal of stipulations concerning the need for Presidential approval before proceeding west of Hawaii, statements referring directly to offensives or even a timetable for action were eliminated. During the initial stages of any war American forces would assume 'a position of readiness', while naval forces gathered strength. Once 'the signs were favourable', the Navy would begin to move via the Mandates or the South Pacific route. No reference was made to the length of time before relief, and no provision was made for reinforcement of the Philippines. However, in 1939 the Department did provide $50,000 to begin work on naval extensions to the Malinta Tunnel, though Yarnell's plea for additional naval forces went unanswered, and the Asiatic Fleet's operating plan now called for the creation of a raiding force to attack Japanese lines of communications from as far away as the Indian Ocean so as to draw Japanese warships away from the Philippines.[127] As for the Army as General Krueger pointed out to the Chiefs of Staff:

The idea of a definite period of self-sustained defense is no longer a part of our present concept of the defense of the Philippines in an Orange war, nor is it authorized under any approved Joint Board action now in force. Whatever form the new Joint Army and Navy Basic War Plan 'Orange' may take, it is highly improbable, as matters now stand, that expeditionary forces will be sent to the Philippines in the early stages of an Orange war. . . The Department Commander should accomplish his mission for the maximum time possible with the personnel and reserves then available to him.[128]

The Rainbow Plans

In late 1938, after the Munich crisis, the first tentative but definite steps towards hemispheric defence were taken. On 20 November 1938, the Board directed the Joint Planning Committee to analyse a situation where one or more fascist powers violated the Monroe Doctrine. That same month the Atlantic squadron, consisting of seven heavy cruisers and seven destroyers – which had been formed in early September as a deterrent force – went on exercise for the first time.[129] The 1939 Army programme called for strengthening of the outpost line from Panama to Alaska, and from Hawaii to Puerto Rico. Continental defences would be protected by five trained divisions with special units to reinforce the forward positions. However, by the middle of the year the US Army did not have a single complete regular division, and could put together only four part divisions and five part brigades.[130] It was felt by the Chief of Staff that such weaknesses might be offset by increased reliance on potential allies, and in December 1938 the Lima Declaration emphasized the need for common defence among the Pan American nations. In April 1939 the Joint Planning Committee submitted a report on the possibility of cooperative action from the South America Republics in event of Axis intervention, but their inherent military and political weaknesses made the United States reluctant to make firm commitments and it was decided 'cooperation' would be confined to requests for limited base facilities. The need to guard the southern flank had the effect of stretching the United States already limited resources; in February the Chief of Staff, General Marshall, asked the Army War College to determine the force necessary to protect Venezuela and Brazil.[131]

In its first preliminary report on the subject, the Joint Planning Committee recognized that if facing an Axis attack, US naval forces would not be able to undertake immediate offensive action in the Pacific without at least 40–50 per cent superiority over Japan. It was assumed that Japanese hegemony required the seizure of Hong Kong, Singapore, parts of the Australian coastline and all US bases west of the 180 degree meridian, and unless adequate bases were prepared in advance it was predicted that Japan would seize all these positions. Priority was given to the central position (that is the Americas themselves) the Canal and the Caribbean; defensive forces based on Hawaii would have to screen US interests and guard the lines of communications while offensive action was carried out against German and Italian shipping.[132] To keep the enemy at bay reliance was placed upon aircraft carriers:

> There can be no doubt that the vital interests of the United States would require offensive measures in the Atlantic against Germany and Italy, to preserve the vital security of the Caribbean and the Panama Canal. If this is done it will be necessary to assume a defensive attitude in the Eastern Pacific. . . Giving active use to our superior seapower, however, might take the form of occupation of the Marshall, Caroline, and Marianas Islands. . .or it might take the form of counter-aggression against German or Italian advanced or colonial bases in the Atlantic (if established). The decision as to the direction and extent of offensive operations must, of course, be guided by the aspects of the situation that actually arises.[133]

By June 1939 the planners were being asked to prepare a set of plans, each for a different strategic situation. Rainbow I presumed Germany and Italy were using both the Azores and the Cape Verde Islands, and that Brazil was in open revolt with the revolutionaries receiving direct Axis assistance. It was presumed the US would, without allies, defend the Western Hemisphere, which was defined as extending to Greenland in the east, to American Samoa and Wake to the west and to the bulge of Brazil around the 10 degree meridian to the south. Protection of the western Pacific would be confined to forces available locally while immediate priority was given to the protection of Panama and northern Brazil; in the eastern Pacific the Navy would defend Hawaii, Midway, Wake, Johnston, Samoa and Palmyra. Sea operations would be launched to cut enemy lines of communications while merchant shipping was commandeered and a programme of naval construction instituted; a GHQ of the Army Air Force would be re-established on the East Coast and a strategic reserve of two army corps created. Two advanced bases in Brazil would be developed, one a B-1 type at Maranhao and the other a B-2 base at Bahia. The entire Marine expeditionary force would be transported to Natal, followed by 20,000 Army troops and ninety-three aircraft. Rainbow 4 provided for an even greater commitment of forces to South America and forcible occupation of the Azores and Cape Verde Islands.[134]

However, not everyone on the Joint Planning Committee agreed that Rainbow 1 accurately reflected the US's future position. As the Navy planners had pointed out in April 1939, any Axis alliance would undoubtedly provoke armed opposition from Britain and France as well as the United States. Under a planning directive in June the Joint Planning Committee was asked to consider 'alternate situations that would develop, if the US should support, or be supported by one or more democratic powers'. Reliance might have to be placed on the main European naval powers; if that occurred American commitment to the Atlantic would be confined to its existing naval squadron, which would enable the United States to project its forces into the Pacific. Rainbow 2 presumed a minimum commitment to the Atlantic but a Japanese threat that now extended to British and French possessions as well as those of the United States, which meant the latter had greater responsibility in the Pacific. Rainbow 5 on the other hand, projected US forces into Europe or Africa 'as rapidly as possible', while at the same time maintaining a defensive position in the eastern Pacific.[135]

The Rainbow plans were really a mirror of the disarray that existed within US planning agencies, and were a direct result of the lack of a coherent coordination organisation within the services. Rainbows 1 and 4 encapsulated all the innermost fears of the supporters of hemispheric defence; Rainbow 3 repeated the time worn formulae of a trans-Pacific offensive; Rainbows 2 and 5 placed their faith in a common front which it was hoped would offset the US's own military weaknesses. In many respects they were also a reflection of the period 1939–41, which saw the United States emerging from its policy of isolation from international events.[136]

Work was initially concentrated on Rainbow 1. On 14 August 1939 the plan was approved by the Secretary of War and the Secretary of the Navy, and once the war in Europe had broken out, the Declaration of Panama established a three hundred mile neutrality zone around the Americas. A neutrality patrol was also instituted. The President himself finally signed his approval to Rainbow 1 in October, and the following month an Executive Order established defensive sea areas and aerial reservations round the five main bases in the Pacific, together with American Samoa and Kingman Reef. By the spring of 1940 arrangements had also been concluded with all the governments of the Caribbean providing for defence of their ports, airfields and other vital installations.

Thanks to the Hampton mission in June 1939, US naval authorities were aware that all British Far Eastern ports would be available to US warships. They also knew Britain now intended to send 'a token force' of two to three battleships to Singapore in event of conflict breaking out in the Far East in 1939.[137] Under Rainbow 2, the planners had to calculate just how far Japan would extend her hegemony and power before the United States and 'other Democratic powers' began to react. By April 1940 naval planners had evolved three hypothetical alternatives. If Japan moved south in strength from Formosa, the US Fleet 'might' move to Manila and certain groups would visit Kam Ranh Bay, Hong Kong and Singapore to deter further aggression. If operations had already begun and Japan had seized Kam Ranh Bay and Hong Kong and was about to launch an attack on the Netherlands East Indies, US forces would react by moving to the far Pacific. Japan in turn would begin operations against the Philippines and Guam. Under the third alternative, Japan already controlled the Netherlands East Indies and was in a position to capture Singapore and the Philippines, in which case the scenario would be the basic 'Orange' war situation. Since extensive operations in the far Pacific at an early date appeared out of the question, planning on Rainbow 2 proceeded on the basis Japan had already captured Hong Kong and Kam Ranh Bay, dominated the coast of IndoChina and had initiated operations against the Netherlands East Indies including British Borneo. The main object was to establish US forces in the East Indies area and 'in concert' with others, drive back the Japanese from there.[138]

Each of the plans that followed in the wake of Rainbow 1 was pre-empted by the statement that US forces would continue to prevent 'violation of the Monroe Doctrine by protecting the territory of the Western Hemisphere'. A kind of priority had therefore been established, though the fear that all the old strategic arguments might be re-opened prevented US naval planners from asking the most vital question of all: what would be done if the objectives under Rainbow 1 began to compete or threatened to exclude those under Rainbow 2? What if Monroe began to compete with Mahan? In a way it was perhaps fortunate Rainbow 2 was never passed to the Secretary of War or the Secretary of the Navy for approval. The plan entirely ignored the political dimension, for it was patently obvious that Congress would never sanction outward or clandestine cooperation with any foreign power; the secrecy surrounding the Ingersoll and Hampton missions clearly indicated this.

There were clear limits to the cooperation that any ally might expect from the United States. As Rainbow 2 pointed out, US naval planners felt Hong Kong, the Philippines and Guam would only be returned to their rightful owners after the peace was signed. Japan would be defeated by economic strangulation; major fleet action would be kept to a minimum. There would be no political commitments or alliances, nor would the United States underwrite the defence of British, French or Dutch Far Eastern possessions by assuming command responsibility for the area. As with Rainbow 1, the US was careful to ensure that its own requests for cooperation were confined to little more than access rights to base facilities. US naval commanders were specifically excluded from responsibility for British or French ships or from any kind of combined command structure, just as British and French naval staff were deliberately excluded from exerting control over US warships. The 'democratic powers' were expected to cooperate in the strategic sense by parallel rather than by joint action. They would retain separate commands, and tactical cooperation would be kept to an absolute minimum. As the Hampton mission showed, the US had no war plans detailing the form of any strategic cooperation with Britain.[139]

Like War Plan 'Orange', Rainbow 2 was more futuristic than realistic. In August 1939 the Navy Department carried out an investigation of the state of US naval forces if war should break out immediately. The first of these 'Are We Ready' studies demonstrated that numerous shortages continued to plague the naval administration, which would have operationally crippled US seapower in the Pacific. San Francisco still lacked sufficient storage and handling facilities for the Fleet, while Bremerton remained 'little more than a naval yard'. The Navy Department was desperate to complete the air bases at Pearl Harbor, and the main facility there was still 'inadequate' in terms of dry docks and repair space and with respect to the depth of water in the entrance channel. The secondary Pacific air bases were expected to take from two to five years to complete, and there was the 'greatest need' for a western Pacific advanced base such as Guam. As regards the Fleet itself, personnel had not kept pace with construction. American ships were operating at only 78 per cent of full complement, and another 150,000 men and 1,087 pilots were felt to be necessary. The high-pressure steam boilers of the new destroyer models were suffering teething problems. The US Navy was deficient in cruisers and AA armament. Though it was still hoped that private vessels might be commandeered for naval service, local navy yards had not begun any preparations. There were crippling shortages in seaplane tenders and, both in terms of speed and fittings, most of the existing fleet auxiliaries were totally unsuited to the task required. Even if the political will had been present the United States Navy could have done little to prevent much of Southeast Asia from falling into enemy hands. It was patently obvious too that once Britain and France were under direct threat in the Atlantic, Germany would come to be regarded as the main danger. Resources would have to be duly switched to Europe, to the detriment of Pacific developments. The 'Are We Ready' study also reported that existing facilities could not in any case serve aircraft carriers or fleet requirements in that theatre of operations.[140]

Conclusions

Contrary to long held historical beliefs, the area north of the Malay Barrier was a focal point for Admiralty attention, and because of the preoccupation with a Phase II situation, considerable effort was expended in seeking out possible advanced naval bases there. As far as the Plans Division was concerned, the 'Main Fleet to Singapore' concept was part of a wider scheme directed not merely towards the relief of that base but also Hong Kong.

Yet there was limited strategic initiative in the Admiralty's Far Eastern planning. The Plans Division seems to have exerted undue influence within the Royal Navy. In a vain attempt to secure general acceptance for its unrealistic priorities north of the Malay Barrier, it pursued its long-term ends for nearly twenty years with singular determination against the main stream of strategic thinking within the other services and despite opposition from Britain's political masters. Even in 1939, despite dramatic changes in the international situation, it continued to cling to its outmoded long-range programme. Until this programme could re-establish necessary security, the Admiralty sought over the short term to offset its own vulnerability either by diplomatic means or by shifting responsibility for defence onto others, primarily Australia and New Zealand.[141] Neither proved to be an effective solution, and reliance instead had to be placed on existing inadequate resources and equally inadequate strategies. In future, considerable differentiation will have to be made by historians between Royal Navy planning and that of the other services, between the short-term and the long-term designs of the Admiralty, and the desires of the Plans Division compared with those of the other naval departments.

Preservation of the Empire remained the paramount concern, and indeed the failure to create an advanced fleet base was not due to any lack of Admiralty conviction but to the combined opposition of the Cabinet, the Committee of Imperial Defence and the remaining Chiefs of Staff, and to the limits both of finance and policy. Such planning schemes could never have succeeded in practice, for they were strategically naive and grossly over-optimistic in their assessments. In the end such self-delusion merely contributed to Britain's gross overestimation of her own resources and gross underestimation of Japanese capabilities, and these were to have detrimental ramifications for Anglo-American naval relations in the Pacific.

The US Navy Department expected the necessary seapower to be transferred into a position where it could achieve contact with the enemy and ultimately overpower them, even if that meant traversing vast distances of ocean. As the Washington Treaty had guaranteed naval superiority over Japan until 1936, carrying out such a strategy had depended less on the number of capital ships than on ancillary elements such as fuel, supplies, repair facilities and dockyards. American naval staff therefore sought to solve their strategic problem in the same way as the Admiralty, namely by establishing one main base and at least one Far Eastern advanced base en route to enemy waters. As Britain and the United States shared similar motivations and mutual desires and means, War Plan 'Orange' and the Far Eastern Naval War Memorandum were equivalent. However, by legally preventing the development of suitable facilities of fleet capacity and by establishing a limited fortification zone, the Washington Treaty became the nemesis for the strategic plans of both nations.

Since hierarchically they were constructed along similar lines and seemed motivated by similar doctrinal motivations, it was perhaps only natural that the Admiralty and the Navy Department should have sought ways to by-pass the Treaty restrictions, to 'weather the storm' while achieving what they could in the hope their respective administrations could eventually be converted to their way of thinking. However, the Navy Department was afforded even less support than the Royal Navy. In the United States, rather more emphasis was placed upon domestic political consensus than upon defensive preparations, and moral, strategic and financial considerations played an even greater role in limiting improvements in the US Fleet. From the perspective of the post-war world of the 1920s, such aggressive policies were anathema to the new spirit of American pacifism and to the Congressional conservative coalition.

From the beginning, War Plan 'Orange' was just as faulty in its estimates as the Far Eastern Naval War Memorandum, for the Navy Department overestimated US resources. Unlike the US, Britain's traditional commitments meant base possession was a clearly established policy in the mind of British governments. The United Kingdom possessed the largest merchant marine in the world, and its fleet was supported by a powerful force of naval auxiliaries. Lacking these advantages was bad enough, but the US Navy was also deprived of its most natural choice for an advanced fleet base and received little political direction from its administrative masters about governmental policies and intentions in the Far East. It was perhaps naive of the US Navy ever to have adopted War Plan 'Orange' in the first place, particularly when it was patently obvious that America lacked sufficient bases, auxiliaries, repair facilities and fuel to provide even the minimum necessary support. In some sections of the Department this was clearly recognized, for relations between the bureaus were characterized by considerable disarray over technological improvements, and War Plan

'Orange' eventually crumpled in the face of concerted resistance from the 'tortoises' and 'armadillos' as well as opposition from without. The General Board placed its faith in the Democratic Party in the hope it would reverse the austerity of the Republicans, but for a variety of reasons rearmament was slow and half-hearted. Roosevelt has been seen by historians as a naval supporter, but it is clear the President was as equally to blame as Congress, public opinion and the Navy itself for the lack of development of an efficient construction programme.

One effect of this, at least, was that by the middle of the 1930s an element of rationality had crept into Joint Board planning. The outbreak of the Second World War in the Pacific was to prove the careful step by step advance, requiring an enormous build-up in resources and large-scale base development to support the necessary logistical tail was a better option than a speedy trans-Pacific offensive. By contrast it was the Admiralty's very success in creating at least some defences and dockyards in the Far East, in establishing fuelling stations en route and in dramatically improving naval construction that falsely reinforced the feasibility of its own time-worn formulas. In the end the Royal Navy was more capable of despatching a fleet to the Far East should an emergency arise, but was less capable of maintaining that fleet in position once it arrived. The Navy Department was less capable of sending a fleet over the short-term but at least its plans recognized that war against Japan was bound to be a long drawn out affair; Japanese forces were already established astride the main line of communications to the Far East. From that perspective US Naval Far Eastern planning was probably more realistic than that of the Admiralty. Yet it must be remembered that the strategies eventually adopted by both the Navy Department and the Admiralty did not derive from choice but were thrust upon them by their mutual lack of resources and inherent weaknesses. Even in mid-1940 the Navy Department and the Admiralty continued to support the trans-Pacific strategy, but both were forced to abandon that strategy under the pressure of events.

When in 1941, after long delays, both sides eventually sat across the conference table from each other in an attempt to formulate a mutually satisfactory joint Far Eastern naval war plan, it was this difference in strategy, this essential dichotomy, which was to be at the nub of the problem between them. Though the Admiralty had abandoned the hope that Hong Kong would ever become the key advanced fleet base, they still affirmed their faith in the Phase II strategy of the Naval War Memorandum. Royal Navy planning continued to emphasize preservation of British Far Eastern territorial possessions. The US Navy Department, on the other hand, preferred to play safe, and its planning continued to display willingness to cede most of the Pacific as long as the ultimate defeat of Japan was guaranteed. British Far Eastern strategy was dominated by the need to relieve her bases as soon as possible; because of its lack of resources, American strategy was dominated by the need to re-capture them after they had been allowed to fall. Finding common ground between these divergent views was to prove to be a difficult hurdle to cross.

Notes

1. Richard W. Turk (1978), 'Defending the New Empire, 1900–1914', in Kenneth J. Hagen (ed.), *In Peace and War: Interpretations of American Naval History, 1775–1978,* New York, pp. 186–7.
2. Michael Vlahos (1980), 'The Naval War College and the Origins of War Planning against Japan', *Naval War College Review*, vol. 33, no. 4, pp. 28–9; Report of the General Board on the Limitation of Armaments, Washington, 1921, pp. 4–5.
3. It is interesting to note that the 'Red-Orange' scenario also provided the basis for the 'Europe First' strategy of the Second World War.
4. Memo Naval Planning Committee to Army Planning Committee, 10 October 1919, JB 325, Serial 74, RG 225.
5. William R. Braisted (1977), 'On the American Red-Orange Plans, 1919–1939', cited in Gerald Jordan (ed.), *Naval Warfare in the Twentieth Century 1900–1945: Essays in Honour of Arthur Marder*, London, p. 169.
6. Memo McKean to All Concerned, 29 October 1919, Classified Records of the Secretary of the Navy 1919–1926, PD 198–2, RG 80; Gerald L. Wheeler (1959), 'The U.S. Navy and the War in the Pacific 1919–1941', *World Affairs Quarterly*, vol. 30, no. 2, pp. 202–3.
7. Memo Joint Planning Committee to Joint Board, May 1923, JB 325, Serial 207, RG 225.
8. Indeed, the first version of War Plan 'Orange' expected the American Fleet to steam across the Atlantic, through the Suez Canal, to the Indian Ocean, where it would link up with the Asiatic Fleet in the Seychelles, proceeding via the Sunda and Macassar Straits back to the Philippines. See John H. Maurer (1981), 'Fuel and the Battle Fleet: Coal, Oil and American Naval Strategy', *Naval War College Review*, vol. 34, no. 6, pp. 60–1.
9. Edward M. Miller (1991), *War Plan Orange: The U. S. Strategy to*

Defeat Japan, 1897–1945, Annapolis, pp. 35–6.

10. Harriet Moore (1933), 'The American State in the Philippines', *Foreign Affairs*, vol. 2, no. 3, pp. 517–20.

11. Irvine H. Anderson, Jr (1975), *The Standard-Vacuum Oil Company and United States East Asian Policy 1933–1941*, Princeton, NJ, p. 202.

12. E. Voltaire Garcia II (1968), *U.S. Military Bases and Philippine-American Relations*, Quezon City, p. 4.

13. Senate Committee on Territories and Insular Possessions, Hearings on Philippine Independence, 68th Congress, 1st session, February 1924, pp. 25–6, 98.

14. Captain William Veazie Pratt (1922), 'Some Considerations Affecting Naval Policy', *United States Naval Institute Proceedings*, vol. 48, no. 11, pp. 1845–62.

15. 'Strategic Problems in the Pacific', Memo by the GB, 15 January 1917, PD 196–1, Classified Records of the Secretary of the Navy 1919–26, RG 80.

16. Annual Report of the Secretary of the Navy, 1920, pp. 1–5, 10; Annual Report of the Chief of Army Engineers, vol. 13, no. 863, 1920, pp. 38, 1934.

17. Ibid.

18. Indeed, some twelve 240mm howitzers and fourteen 3-inch guns were en route to Manila, and were offloaded at Hawaii when the Treaty was signed. Memo Pershing to Sec. Nav., 17 May 1922, JB 303, Serial 169–A; 'AA. Defense of Cavite', Memo Colonel B.H. Wells ACOS for COS, 24 May 1922, JB 303, Serial 169A; Memo Overstreet to JB, 29 April 1922, JB 303, Serial 179, RG 225.

19. Ltr Williams to CNO, 29 April 1922, PD 226–103, Classified Records of the Secretary of the Navy 1919–26, RG 80.

20. Memo JB to Sec. Nav., 7 July 1923, JB 305, Serial 208, RG 225.

21. Annual Report of the Chief of Naval Operations, 1924, p. 32.

22. Stephen S. Roberts (1977), 'The Decline of the Overseas Station Fleets: The United States Asiatic Fleet and the Shanghai Crisis of 1932', *American Neptune*, vol. 38, no. 3, pp. 186–7.

23. Annual Report of the Asiatic Fleet 1924–29, Annual Reports of Fleets and Task Forces of the US Navy, Roll 12, M971. Unfortunately half the latter were the infamous 'S' class. Grossly obsolete and practically crippled operationally by their slow diving time, these craft were designed more for coastal work than for fleet patrol. Throughout their service history they were plagued by oil leaks and electrical faults and by 1928 the bulk of them, much to the intense relief of American submariners, had been placed in reserve. See Professional Notes (1930), *United States Naval*

Institute Proceedings, vol. 56, no. 12, p. 1048.

24. Annual Report of the Secretary of the Navy, 1924, p. 56; House Committee on Naval Affairs, Hearings on the 1926 Naval Appropriations, 68 Congress, 2nd session, 17 November 1924, p. 29; 'War Plans from a Naval Point of View', Lecture by Captain W.S. Pye, 1925, AY 1925, WPD Lecture II, United States Military History Research Collection; 'Estimate of the Situation and the Base Development Programme', Memo Eberle to Wilbur, 6 April 1925, Classified Records of the Secretary of the Navy 1919–26, Box 22, RG 80.

25. These had been installed before the Washington Treaty.

26. Army Strategic War Plan 'Orange', 1928, RG 94; Robert William Love Jr, p. 43.

27. Ltr Kilbourne to War Dept, 2 May 1922; 'Military Position of the Philippine Defenses', Memo by JPC Phil. Dept, 7 August 1928, AG 660–2.

28. Ltr CG Phil. Dept to War Dept, 8 June 1928; Ltr War Dept to CG Phil. Dept, 12 June 1928, AG 093.5; E. Dupuy (1956), *The Compact History of the U.S. Army*, New York, p. 213; Army Strategic War Plan 'Orange', 1928, RG 94.

29. Ltr CINCAF to CNO, 4 July 1941, Box 4, Hart Papers; James R. Leutze (1981), *A Different Kind of Victory: A Biography of Admiral Thomas C. Hart*, Annapolis, p. 208.

30. Ltr Bristol to Rear-Admiral H.O. Dunn, 6 May 1928, MLB 214–28 (A), Bristol Papers.

31. 'Annual Report of the Secretary of the Navy', 1932, p. 103; Memo DWPD to CNO, 5 October 1932, GB 416–2.

32. 'Report on the Need for Additional Naval Bases to Defend the Coasts of the United States its Territories and Possessions', December 1939, 76 Congress, 1st session, Document 65.

33. 'Some Effects of the Washington Conference on American Naval Strategy', Lecture by Captain H.F. Schofield, AY 1924, G-2, Lecture 3, 274–A3, United States Military History Research Collection.

34. Bernard D. Cole (1983), *Gunboats and Marines: The United States Navy in China 1925–1928*, Deleware, p. 39.

35. Herbert Hoover (1976), *Public Papers of the President of the United States, Herbert Hoover*, 1931, Washington, Doc 219, pp. 290–1.

36. Ltr FDR to Daniels, 27 October 1937, President's Secretary File (hereafter cited as PSF), Navy Files, Box 19, Roosevelt Papers.

37. J.U. Lademan, Jr (1973), 'U.S.S. Gold Star: Flagship of the Guam Navy', *United States Naval Institute Proceedings*, vol. 99, no. 12, p. 69.

38. Memo Knox to Roosevelt, 8 December 1941, PSF Section II, Navy Department 1940–41, Roosevelt Papers; Minute by Air Attaché, 28 February 1939, FO 115/3419/422; Report on the Need for Additional Naval Bases to Defend the Coasts of the United States its Territories and Possessions, December 1939, 76 Congress, 1st session, Document 65.

39. Dorothy Borg (1964), *The United States and the Far Eastern Crisis 1933–38*, Cambridge, MA, pp. 249–50; John W. Masland (1941), 'Public Opinion and American Pacific Navy Policy', *United States Naval Institute Proceedings*, vol. 47, no. 7, p. 988.

40. Ltr Taussig to Chief Bureau of Navigation, 6 May 1940, Classified Records of the Secretary of the Navy, 1926–42, A 16–NP, RG 80.

41. Kenneth J. Clifford (1983), *Amphibious Warfare Development in Britain and America 1920–1940,* New York, pp. 22–7; Robert Debs Heinl, Jr (1962), *Soldiers of the Sea: The United States Marine Corps 1775–62*, Annapolis, pp. 301–6; Major General John Lejeune (1926), 'The Marine Corps, 1926', United States Naval Institute Proceedings, vol. 52, no. 10, pp. 1961–9. For details on the ideas surrounding amphibious assault consult US Marine Corps (1927), *U.S. Marine Corps Landing Manual, 1927,* Washington.

42. John P. Campbell (1964), 'Marines, Aviators, and the Battleship Mentality 1923–33', *Royal United Services Institute Journal*, vol. 109, no. 1, pp. 46–7; Professional Notes (1923), 'The Fleet Problem – 1923', *United States Naval Institute Proceedings*, vol. 49, no. 6, pp. 1021–9.

43. Lt. Colonel Frank O. Hough (1969), *Pearl Harbor to Guadalcanal: History of United States Marine Corps Operations in World War II*, Washington, p. 21.

44. Heinl, *Soldiers*, p. 308.

45. 'Study of Bases, with Advantages and Disadvantages', Memo by Captain Coxe, OP-12C, Strategic Plans Division, Miscellaneous Subject File Series III, Philippine Islands Naval Base Studies, 1932; Joint Army and Navy Basic War Plan 'Orange', 1928, JB 325, Serial 280, RG 225.

46. Joint Army and Navy Basic War Plan Orange, 6 October 1926, JB 325, Serial 280, RG 225; Louis Morton (1959), 'War Plan "Orange": Evolution of a Strategy', *World Politics*, vol. 11, no. 2, pp. 232–3.

47. Memo Cox to Sec. War, 2 February 1934, WPD 2289-6, RG 165; Memo CNO to JB, 5 February 1934, JB 305, Serial 525; Ltr JPC to JB 28 February 1934, JB 305, Serial 525, RG 225; Notes for Discussion with Admiral Sir Frederick Dreyer by D of P and DNI, 25 January 1936, ADM 116/3338.

48. Ltr Hart to Stark, 12 April 1940, Hart Papers; Memo Chrmn GB to Sec. Nav., 27 August 1940, Classified Records of the Secretary of the Navy, 1926–42, A 16-NP, RG 80.
49. Ltr Sec. Nav. to Greenslade, 11 September 1940, Command File, World War II, Study 404.
50. Greenslade was definitely a defensist. For the definition of 'hares','tortoises' and 'armadillos', see later in this chapter.
51. 'The Greenslade Report', 6 January 1941, Command File, World War II, Study 404; 'Comments on the Greenslade Report', Memo by DWPD, 25 March 1941, Box 45, Series III, Miscellaneous; Memo CNO to DWPD, 3 December 1940, A 16-3/ND 16, Box 92, Series V, Subject Files, Records of the Strategic Plans Division; Army Draft Study No. 17: Rainbow 2, 1939, JB 325, Serial 642–2, RG 225.
52. Joint Army and Navy Basic War Plan 'Orange', 1928, JB 325, Serial 280, RG 225.
53. Ltr Gleaves to Sec. Nav., 6 October 1919, PD 218–1 and 219–1, PD 196–8, Classified Records of the Secretary of the Navy 1919–26, RG 80.
54. Memo Coontz to Secretary of State, 5 April 1921, PD 196–8, Classified Records of the Secretary of the Navy 1919–26, RG 80; 'Papers Relating to the Pacific and Far Eastern Affairs Prepared for the Use of the American Delegation on the Limitation of Armaments 1921–22', Memo prepared by Admiral Gleaves, 1922, pp. 1074–5.
55. Memo DNI to CNO, 31 May 1923, GB 409; Memo Sec.War to Secretary of State, 28 December 1923, File 811.014/96, RG 59.
56. Samuel Carter 111 (1971), *The Incredible Great White Fleet*, New York; Robert E. Coontz (1930), *From the Mississippi to the Sea*, Philadelphia, pp. 463–4.
57. For details see Miller, *War Plan*, p. 79.
58. Ibid.; Ltr JPC to JB, 16 October 1931, JB 305, Serial 499, RG 225.
59. Commander H.H. Frost (1931), 'Naval Aircraft in Coastal Warfare', *United States Naval Institute Proceedings*, vol. 57, no. 1, pp. 9–16.
60. Gordon Swanborough and Peter M.Bowers (1968), *United States Navy Aircraft since 1911*, London, p. 2.
61. Annual Report of the Secretary of the Navy, 1929, p. 36; US Office of Naval Operations (1970), *United States Naval Aviation,* Washington.
62. William J. Armstrong (1978), 'Aircraft Go To Sea: A Brief History of Aviation in the U.S. Navy', *Aerospace History*, vol. 25, no. 2, pp. 79–91; Richard C. Knott (1979), *The American Flying Boat: An Illustrated History*, Annapolis.

63. Miller, *War Plan*, pp. 177–8.
64. Professional Notes (August 1929), *United States Naval Institute Proceedings*, vol. 55, no. 8, p. 728.
65. This area will be discussed in more detail in a later planned work. However, those interested in this question would do well to consult Geoffrey Till (1979), *Air Power and the Royal Navy 1914–1945: A Historical Survey*, London, chapters 3 and 6, and Norman Friedman (1988), *British Carrier Aviation*, London. For detail on American carrier aviation see C.M. Melhorn (1974), *Two Block Fox: The Rise of the Aircraft Carrier 1911–1929*, Annapolis.
66. 'Strategy in the Pacific', Report of the General Board, 8 September 1919, GB File 425.
67. Rear-Admiral W.A. Moffett (1925), 'Some Aviation Fundamentals', United States Naval Institute Proceedings, vol. 51, no. 10, p. 1871.
68. 'Combat Estimate: Japan', Report by NID, 20 July 1939, Box 61, Series IX, Plans, Strategic Studies and Related Correspondence 1939–46, Records of the Strategic Plans Division.
69. Change No. 1 to WPAF-1: 'Orange-2', December 1938, Box 147-B, Series IX, Plan Strategic Studies and Related Correspondence 1939–46, Records of the Strategic Plans Division.
70. 'Report on U.S.S. Astoria', Enclosure to Memo CNO to Sec. Nav., 6 June 1934, E-A 21–5, Secret and Confidential Correspondence of the Secretary of the Navy 1927–39, RG 80.
71. Ltr DWPD to D Central Division, 13 November 1934, EG 12–2, A 21–5, Secret and Confidential Correspondence of the Secretary of the Navy 1927–39, RG 80; Memo Acting Sec. Nav. to Secretary of State, 16 October 1934, File 811.014/311.
72. Memo by Colonial Office, December 1936, AVIA 2/1994.
73. Memo Puleston to FDR, 30 October 1935, A 21–5, Secret and Confidential Correspondence of the Secretary of the Navy 1927–39, RG 80.
74. Extract Washington Post, 29 December 1935, AVIA 2/1994.
75. Memo by Colonial Office, 29 December 1936, AVIA 2/1994.
76. See chapter 3 for details.
77. Memo Rear-Admiral Horne to CNO, 17 May 1940, A 21–2, Secret and Confidential Correspondence of the Secretary of the Navy, RG 80; 'Studies of Strategic Areas: The Singapore–Torres Strait Line' by the Naval War College, WPD Miscellaneous File; 'Studies of Strategic Areas: East Indies Area' by the Naval War College, WPD Miscellaneous File, RG 4; Ltr JB to JPC, 23 June 1939, JB 325, Serial 642.
78. Memo CNO to Sec. War and Sec. Nav., 10 August 1939, JB 325, Serial 642, RG 225; Memo CNO to Admiral Bloch, 29 August

1939, Bloch Papers; Entry 5 March 1939 and 6 April 1939, Leahy Diary; Memo Sec. Nav. to Secretary of State, 21 February 1940, PG/177, State Department File 811.0141, RG 59; Tel. Lindsay to Halifax, 22 August 1939, pt VI, AVIA 2/2017.

79. Rainbow 2, 1939, JB 325; Rainbow 3, 1940, JB 325, Serial 642–2, RG 225. Miller, *War Plan*, p. 247.

80. Ibid., pp. 80, 86.

81. Ibid., p. 116.

82. Ibid., p. 139.

83. Ibid., p. 214; Robert Greenhalgh Albion (1980), *Makers of Naval Policy, 1798–1947*, Annapolis, pp. 383–4.

84. Two directly opposed environmental philosophies had pervaded the Harding administration. One group, exemplified by the Secretary of the Interior Albert Fall, was determined to open the natural resources of the United States to private development. This view was diametrically opposed by Senator Robert la Follette and others, who were dedicated to the preservation of those same resources and to the regulation and restriction of US business involvement in the resource area, which they believed had resulted in the inexcusable squandering of forests and mineral deposits. The lack of sufficient fuel for a trans-Pacific journey was a perennial problem for the Fleet. Even by 1924 there were only 33,285 tons of oil at Pearl, but the Fleet used well over one and one-half million tons a year. In trying to solve this difficulty the Department unfortunately became involved in the Teapot Dome Scandal. Ostensibly the Teapot Dome and Elk Hills fields were part of the Navy's No. 4 Reserve under the exclusive control of the Secretary of the Navy. In April 1921, Fall convinced Secretary Denby that since the Doheny Company deposits on the edge of the fields were draining off naval supplies anyway, jurisdiction should be transferred to Fall and his Department for leasing. In return for Dohenys' access the Navy was bribed by oil certificates which could be cashed for refined oil. As part of the first payment Doheny agreed to provide a massive tank farm with a capacity of 879,283 tons at Pearl and some 422,000 tons of fuel oil. Just as the Admiralty used private enterprise to supplement its own supplies, the US Navy hoped to by-pass the Treaty restrictions and at one stroke, by using Doheny, solve many of its fuel problems. But Fall's information was totally incorrect. Indeed Fall had received $400,000 in bribes to encourage private leasing on the Teapot Dome fields. Once this matter became public – as a result of la Follette's investigation – Denby was forced to resign and Fall committed suicide. Fortunately the first thirty tanks had already been completed, while construction on the second

set was so far advanced it could not be abandoned. See Burl Noggle (1962), *Teapot Dome: Oil and Politics in the 1920s*, Louisiana; James Leonard Bates (1978), *The Origins of Teapot Dome: Progressives, Parties, and Petroleum 1909–1921*, Westport CN.

85. If Mahan established that a nation's greatness depended on colonies and on the defence of possessions by a blue water navy, it was the Monroe doctrine in 1821 that established a sphere of influence over and protection for the Americas. The United States chose to remain out of the affairs of Europe.

86. Memo McKean to all concerned, 29 October 1919, Classified Records of the Secretary of the Navy 1919–26, RG 80; Ltr Coontz to Sec. Nav., 15 July 1920, JB 304, Serial 90, RG 225; Report of the Special Board on Shore Establishments, 27 September 1922, Enclosure to Annual Report of the Secretary of the Navy, 1923, pp. 82–96; Report of the Board for the Development of Naval Yard Plans, 11 June 1923, Enclosure to Annual Report of the Secretary of the Navy, 1923, pp. 97–100.

87. Cited in Gerald E. Wheeler (1974), *Admiral William Veazie Pratt U.S. Navy: A Sailor's Life*, Washington, pp. 155–6.

88. 'Report on the Navy Base Development Programme', Memo Assistant Sec. Nav. to Sec. Nav., 26 June 1923, Enclosure to *United States Naval Institute Proceedings*, vol. 49, no. 9, pp. 1728–31; William Howard Gardiner (1923), 'What the U.S.N. Costs and Who Pays For It', *United States Naval Institute Proceedings*, vol. 59, no. 5, pp 828–42; 'Fleet Problem for 1923', Navy and Military Record, 25 April 1923, pp. 1–2; Professional Notes (1929), *United States Naval Institute Proceedings*, vol. 55, no. 4, p. 342; 'Order of Importance to the Navy of Harbors in the Continental United States', Memo CNO to Sec. Nav., 9 July 1931, JB 303, Serial 495, RG 303; Lt. Commander P.V.H. Weems (1924), 'Shall We Outgrow the Panama Canal', *United States Naval Institute Proceedings*, vol. 50, no. 1, pp. 7–13; Professional Notes (1931), *United States Naval Institute Proceedings*, vol. 57, no. 10, p. 720. See also Captain George B. Fisher (1930), 'Diplomatic Aspects of the Nicaraguan Canal', *United States Naval Institute Proceedings*, vol. 56, no. 5, pp. 381–6; 'The Fight Over the Navy Yards', *Army and Navy Register*, 25 February 1922, pp. 14–16.

89. Lt. R.E. Krause (1925), 'The Trend of Naval Affairs', *United States Naval Institute Proceedings*, vol. 51, no. 4, p. 527.

90. Andrew W. Lind (1946), *Hawaii's Japanese*, New Jersey, p. 11.

91. 'Hawaiian Defence Plan', Report by Hawaiian Department to War Dept, 5 May 1936, WPD 3620–4; 'Report on the Defensive Fea-

tures of the Hawaiian Islands', Memo by Colonel M. Markham to COS, 10 January 1938, WPD 3879–9, RG 165.

92. Ibid.; Professional Notes (1932), *United States Naval Institute Proceedings*, vol. 58, no. 2, p. 289; US Congress, *Pearl Harbor Attack: Hearings of the Joint Committee on the Investigation of the Pearl Harbor Attack*, 76 Congress 1st session, pt 15, p. 1635; Joint Army and Navy Basic War Plan 'Orange', 1934, JB 325, Serial 280, RG 225. See also Walter F. Dillingham (1930), 'Pearl Harbor', *United States Naval Institute Proceedings*, vol. 55, no. 5, pp. 408–10; James E. Wise, Jr (1964), 'Ford Island', *United States Naval Institute Proceedings*, vol. 90, no. 10, p. 23; Clark G. Reynolds (1976), 'Admiral Ernest J. King and the Strategy for Victory in the Pacific', *Naval War College Review*, vol. 28, no. 3, p. 57.

93. P.E. Coletta (ed.) (1980), *American Secretaries of the Navy: 1913–1972*, Maryland, vol. 2, p. 598.

94. Dillingham, 'Pearl Harbor', p. 410; Report of the Parks–Mckean Board to Sec. Nav., 20 October 1919, Classified Records of the Secretary of the Navy, PD 120–1, RG 80; 'Notes on the Strategic Importance of Oahu', Memo by Major Stanley G. Embick, 3 May 1927, WPD 2966, RG 165; Annual Report of the Secretary of the Navy, 1920, p. 12; Rear-Admiral Yates Stirling, Jr (1934), 'Naval Preparedness in the Pacific', *United States Naval Institute Proceedings*, vol. 60, no. 5, p. 608.

95. Roberts, 'The Decline', p. 188. See for example Ltr Admiral M. Taylor to Admiral Leahy, 24 May 1932, Box 269/2, Taylor Papers; 'Inadequacy of Present Military and Naval Forces in the Philippine Area', Memo CINCAF and CG Philippine Department to CNO and COS, 1 March 1934, JB 325, Serial 533, RG 225. See also 'Notes of a Conversations with Admiral F.B. Upham at Manila', Memo by Admiral Dreyer, 23 March 1934, FO 371/18098.

96. Theodore Friend (1963), 'The Philippine Sugar Industry and the Politics of Independence, 1929–35', *Journal of Asian Studies*, vol. 22, no. 2, p. 179; Gerald E. Wheeler (1959), 'Republican Philippine Policy, 1921–33', *Pacific Historical Review*, vol. 27, pp. 277–90.

97. Harry C. Thomson and Lida Mayo (1960), *The Ordnance Department: Procurement and Supply*, Washington, p. 70; Ltr Brig-Gen. George Simonds to COS, 25 June 1928, WPD 3022-8; Ltr Stanley G. Embick to JPC, 7 September 1927, WPD 3022, RG 165.

98. In 1924, for example, there was a mutiny among the Philippine Scouts; Congress, House Committee on Insular Affairs, Hearings on House Record 7233, 72 Congress, 1st session, 1932, p. 436; 'Report on Mutiny in the Philippine Scouts' by Phil. Dept, 19

March 1925, WPD 522–18, RG 165; Carol Petillo (1981), *Douglas McArthur: The Philippine Years*, Bloomington, IN, pp. 132–3.

99. 'Defense Reserve A.A. Ammunition Philippine Department', Memo Brigadier-General C.E. Kilbourne ACOS WPD to COS, 12 September 1934, WPD 3489–5; Annual Report of the CG of the Philippine Department, 27 August 1939, AG 319–12, RG 94; Ltr JPC to JB, 9 January 1928; Joint Army and Navy Basic War Plan 'Orange', 1928, JB 325, Serial 280, RG 225. See also Louis Morton (1949), 'American and Allied Strategy in the Far East', *Military Affairs*, vol. 39, pp. 22–39.

100. Ltr JB to Sec. War, 14 March 1924; Ltr Acting Sec. War to JB, 10 April 1924, JB 305, Serial 227.

101. Ltr JPC to JB, 19 February 1930, JB 305, Serial 472; Ltr JB to Sec. Nav., 23 October 1931, JB 304, Serial 441; 'Military Value of the Philippine Islands to the United States', Memo JPC to JB, 16 October 1931, JB 305, Serial 499, RG 225.

102. Joint Army and Navy Basic War Plan 'Orange', 1928, JB 325, Serial 280, RG 225; Grace P. Haynes (1953), *History of the Joint Chiefs of Staff in the War Against Japan: Pearl Harbor through Trident*, Washington, vol. 1, p. 3; Memo SDE to CG Philippine Department, 19 April 1933, WPD 3251–15; 'Notes on the Strategic Importance of Oahu', Memo by Major Stanley G. Embick, 3 May 1927, WPD 2966, RG 165. For his earlier views on the defence of the Phillippines, see Captain Stanley G. Embick (1916), 'The Prospect for Coast Defences', *Journal of United States Artillery*, vol. 46, pp. 151–66.

103. Joint Army and Navy War Plan 'Orange', 1928, JB 325, Serial 280; Joint Army and Navy War Plan 'Orange' 1934, JB 305, Serial 525, RG 225.

104. James A. Farley (1948), *Jim Farley's Story: The Roosevelt Years*, New York, p. 39; Memo General Parker to TAG, 1 July 1934, AG 093.5 Phil. Islands; 'Manuel Quezon Missions, 1934–37', Report by Bureau of Insular Affairs, 13 February – 23 March 1937, National Resources Branch, RG 350; Theodore Friend (1965), *Between Two Empires: The Ordeal of the Philippines 1929–46*, New Haven, pp. 95–148.

105. Speech by Senator Tydings quoted by Suzanne G. Carpenter (1976), 'Towards the Development of Philippine National Security Capability 1920–40: With Special Reference to the Commonwealth Period 1935–40', unpublished PhD thesis, New York, p. 209.

106. Ltr Chrmn GB to Sec. Nav., 16 April 1935; Ltr Sec. Nav. to Roosevelt, 22 April 1935, GB 1683.

107. Richard A. Harrison (1988), 'A Neutralization Plan for the Pacific: Roosevelt and Anglo-American Cooperation, 1934–1937', *Pacific Historical Review*, vol. 52, no. 1 , pp. 47–72; Memo of Conversation at the White House between Secretary of State and the President, 16 November 1936, State Dept, File 711 B 00111/6, RG 59; Harold C. Ickes (1959), *The Secret Diary of Harold C. Ickes, The Inside Struggle*, New York, vol. 2, pp. 7, 51; Department of State, *Foreign Relations of the United States: Diplomatic Papers* (hereafter cited as FRUS), vol. 3 , 1937, pp. 954, 973, 975; Borg, *The United States,* pp. 244–7.
108. Gerald L. Wheeler (1957), 'The United States Navy and the Japanese "Enemy" 1919–31', *Military Affairs*, vol. 21, pp. 70–1.
109. Love, *The Chiefs*, p. 65; R.G. O'Conner (1962), *Perilious Equilibrium: The United States and the London Naval Conference of 1930*, Lawrence, KN, p. 49; House Committee on Naval Affairs, Hearings on HR 7359, 70 Congress, 1st session, 1928, p. 520; Congressional Record: Special Session, 71 Congress, 14 July 1930, pp. 319–20.
110. Annual Report of the Secretary of the Navy, 1930, pp. 155–8; Annual Report of the Secretary of the Navy, 1934, p. 13; Annual Report of the Secretary of the Navy, 1935, p. 13.
111. David Alan Rosenberg (1975), 'Officer Development in the Interwar Navy: Arleigh Burke – The Making of a Naval Professional, 1919–40', *Pacific Historical Review*, vol. 44, p. 508.
112. Professional Notes (March 1938), *United States Naval Institute Proceedings*, vol. 64, no. 3, p. 443; Annual Report of the Secretary of the Navy, 1938, pp. 1–5.
113. House Record No. 1899, 75 Congress, 3rd session, pp. 1–2; Professional Notes (1936), *United States Naval Institute Proceedings*, vol. 62, no. 10, p. 1492; Ltr Morell to Asst. Sec. Nav., 2 August 1938, Box 3089, RG 19; Love, *The Chiefs*, p. 112; Louis Stockstill (1961), 'Uncle Carl Vinson: Backstage Boss of the Pentagon', *Army, Navy, Air Force Journal,* vol. 98, no. 25, p. 27; John C. Walter Fall (1980), 'Congressman Carl Vinson and F.D.R.: Naval Preparedness and the Coming of World War II', *Georgia Historical Quarterly*, vol. 114, pp. 294–305.
114. Congressional Record, 75 Congress, 3rd session, vol. 83, pt 5, 20 April 1938, p. 5571; Department of State (1943), Peace and War, Washington, Doc. 128, pp. 455–8.
115. Memo CNO to Sec. Nav., 26 August 1936, GB File 420–2.
116. Ltr Leahy to Roosevelt, 10 November 1937, President's Official File, Box 18, Roosevelt Papers, FDR Library.
117. This is dealt with in greater detail in the next chapter. Hector C.

Bywater (1934), *Sea Power in the Pacific*, Boston, pp. 121–5; Ltr Chrmn GB to Sec. Nav., 18 January 1933, GB 1521–AA, RG 225; Merze Tate (1948), *The United States and the Limitations of Armaments*, Cambridge, MA, pp. 156–7.

118. Annual Estimate of the Situation – 1931, undated, File LI-1, Secret and Confidential Correspondence of the Secretary of the Navy, 1927–39, RG 80; Waldo Heinrichs, Jr, 'The Role of the United States Navy', cited in D. Borg and Shumpei Okamoto (eds) (1973), *Pearl Harbor as History: Japanese-American Relations, 1931–41*, New York, p. 170.

119. Michael Vlahos (1981), *The Blue Sword: The Naval War College and the American Mission 1919–41*, Annapolis, pp. 143–5, 168–78; Ernest J. King and Walter Muir Whitehall (1952), *Fleet Admiral King: A Naval Record*, New York, pp. 236, 242; 'Critique of Operational Problem IV–1933: General Comments', Memo by Captain S.C. Rowan, undated, Box 53/2261-AA, RG 4; Captain Ellis M. Zacharias (1946), *Secret Mission: The Story of an Intelligence Officer*, New York, pp. 133–4.

120. Memo JPC to JB, 23 April 1935; Revision of 'Orange', 8 May 1935; Change WPL 16, No. 5, undated 1935 Appendix 7, chap. 3, War Plan 'Orange', JB 325, Serial 546, RG 225.

121. Morton, 'War Plan "Orange"', pp. 242–3; Professional Notes (1936), *United States Naval Institute Proceedings*, vol. 62, no. 10, p. 1494.

122. Ltr CINCAF to CNO, 11 February 1937; Ltr Cmdr 16, Naval District to Sec. Nav., 28 April 1937, 25 August 1937, NB/ND16, Secret and Confidential Correspondence of the Secretary of the Navy 1927–39, RG 80; Memo CINCAF to CNO, 15 October 1937, Enclosure to Ltr Leahy to Roosevelt, 8 November 1937, President's Official File, Box 18, Roosevelt Papers, FDR Library.

123. Ltr Roosevelt to Leahy, 10 November 1937, PSF Navy Files, Box 15, Roosevelt Papers, FDR Library.

124. Joint Letter of Secretary of War and Secretary of Navy to Secretary of State, 26 November 1935.

125. Report of Army Members JPC, 5 March 1936, JB 305, Serial 573, RG 225.

126. Report of Navy Members JPC, 6 February 1936, JB 305, Serial 573; Memo ACOS for COS, 18 October 1937, WPD 2720–10, RG 165; Morton, 'War Plan "Orange"', p. 243; Memo Pye to CNO, 22 April 1936, Strategic Plans Division Miscellaneous Subject File Series III.

127. Memo JB to JPC, 10 November 1937; Ltr Army and Navy Members JPC to JB, 29 and 30 November 1937, JB 325, Serial

617; Joint Army and Navy Basic War Plan 'Orange', 21 February 1938, JB 325, Serial 618. See also Morton, 'War Plan "Orange"', pp. 248–9, and Mark Skinner Watson (1950), *Chiefs of Staff: Prewar Plans and Preparations*, Washington, pp. 90–3.

128. Memo Krueger to COS, 16 February 1938, AG 660.2.

129. JB Minutes, 9 November 1938; Ltr Acting Sec JB to JPC, 20 November 1938, JB 325, Serial 634; Maurice Matloff and Edwin M. Snell (1953), *Strategic Planning for Coalition Warfare*, Washington, p. 5.

130. Committee on Appropriations, House Hearings no. 6692; War Department Appropriations Act FY 1938, 75 Congress, 1st session, 1937, p. 1; Memo ACOSWPD to DCOS, 15 February 1939, WPD 3748–17, RG 319.

131. Forrest C. Pogue (1966), *George C. Marshall: Ordeal and Hope, 1939–1942,* New York, vol. 2, pp. 336–7; Gerald K. Haines (1978), 'The Roosevelt Administration Interprets the Monroe Doctrine', *Australian Journal of Politics and History*, vol. 24, pp. 332–45; 'Report of Delegation of U.S.A. to the Eight International Conference of American States' by Cordell Hull, 10 December 1938, Washington, Appendix 8; JPC Exploratory Studies, 21 April 1939, JB 325, Serial 634, RG 225.

132. Ibid.; JB Minutes, 6 May 1939, JB 325, Serial 634, RG 225; Memo Sec. JB to JPC, 11 May 1939; Memo JPC to JB, 23 June 1939, JB 325, Serial 642.

133. Joint Army and Navy Rainbow Plan 1, undated, JB 325, Serial 642–1, RG 225.

134. Ibid.

135. Memo JPC to JB, 27 July 1939, JB 325, Serial 642–1, RG 225; Matloff and Snell, *Strategic Planning*, p. 10; Tracy B. Kittredge (1950), 'United States – British Naval Cooperation, 1939–42', unpublished manuscript, Microfilm 226, Naval Historical Division, Section 3, pt 8, p. 43; Watson, *Chiefs of Staff*, pp. 97–100.

136. Memo JPC to JB, 23 June 1939, JB 325, RG 225; James R. Leutze (1977), *Bargaining for Supremacy: Anglo-American Naval Collaboration, 1937–41,* NC, pp. 40–1; Stetson Conn and Byron Fairchild (1960), *The Framework of Hemispheric Defence*, Washington, pp. 7–13, 411.

137. This matter is dealt with in the next chapter.

138. Ltr CNO to Sec. Nav., 6 November 1939, JB 325, Serial 404; Memo CNO to Sec. War and Sec. Nav., 10 August 1939, JB 325, Serial 642–1, RG 225; Memo OCS to Sec. War, 21 May 1940, WPD 3860, RG 165; Kittredge, 'United States–British Naval Cooperation', Section 3, vol. I, no. 83; 'Record of Meetings with

Cmdr. Hampton 12/6–14/6/39', Enclosure Ingersoll File, Series VII, Records Relating to Anglo-American-Dutch Cooperation, Records of the Strategic Plans Division; Memo CNO to Under-secretary of State, 14 July 1939, File A 16–3, CNO Secret Correspondence: Warfare/Miscellaneous; Draft Study Navy Section Rainbow No. 2, 5 July 1939, JB 325, Serial 642–2, RG 225.

139. Ltr JB to JPC, 23 June 1939, JB 325, Serial 642; Army Draft Study No. 17: Rainbow 2, 1939, JB 325, Serial 642–2, RG 225.
140. 'Are We Ready Study No. 1', Report Chrmn of the GB to Sec. Nav., 31 August 1939, GB 425, Serial 1868.
141. This issue will be described further in the next chapter.

Part II

The Anglo-American Naval Scene
1937–1941

—3—

A 'Special Relationship': Naval Relations 1937–1939

Terms like 'relationship' imply community of interest, and there has been a tendency by historians to see the wartime alliance between the two countries, Britain and the United States, as a political expression of an underlying social and cultural unity. In his history of the Second World War, one of Churchill's more important themes was America's 'special position' amongst the 'English-Speaking Peoples'.[1]

A major element in the evolution of this relationship was thought to be the pre-war links that developed between the naval staffs of both countries.[2] Yet in fact, both the British and the American navies evolved their comparable Far Eastern strategies in isolation from each other. Their respective war plans were designed to be executed without assistance from allies. This state could hardly be termed a relationship, intimate or otherwise. Considerable differentiation also needs to be made between the kind of collaborative effort achieved in the Atlantic and the general lack of such intent in the Pacific. What, if any, were the links between both navies? How did they regard each other? Was the basis of their contact cooperative, competitive or both?

To try to find answers to these questions, the issue of trans-Pacific air routes and the combined staff talks that took place in 1938 and 1939 are vital, because on these matters Far Eastern affairs were directly involved. The China theatre has been deliberately avoided; it more directly affected the field commands than it did either Washington or London, where the main command centres were located and where most of the key decisions were made.

Background

On the evening of the 16 December 1938, after a White House reception, Ambassador Lindsay, the chief British representative in Washington, met the President and the Secretary of State in Roosevelt's study to discuss the deteriorating situation in the Pacific. Only a few days before Japanese aircraft had attacked and sunk the American gunboat USS *Panay* on the Yangtse. Several British vessels had also been fired on. Responding to Lindsay's request for a mutual united response, the President suggested a coordinated 'peaceful blockade' of the Japanese home islands. In a broaching the question of naval staff conversations between the two countries, Roosevelt recalled that between 1915 and 1917, when he had been Assistant Secretary of the Navy, Commodore Guy Gaunt – then British Naval Attaché – and Captain William Veazie Pratt had come to an arrangement for the systematic exchange of 'secret information', including war plans. According to Roosevelt, he had been instrumental in setting up these early intelligence exchanges. As a result, when the United States entered the war 'Admiral Sims's well known mission was only of minor importance.'[3]

What is interesting is the confusion this reference caused in British naval circles, for the British record showed that while Roosevelt had been most helpful after the US declaration, there was no indication of a clandestine relationship before 1917.[4] Anglo-American cooperation did not seriously begin until President Wilson reached his fateful decision for war. What followed in many ways set the tone for future relations. From the opening of hostilities, the Americans intended that the European Allies should bear the brunt of the fighting. Before he left to establish direct communication with the British Admiralty, Rear-Admiral William S. Sims was warned by the Chief of Naval Operations, Admiral Benson, not 'to let the British pull the wool over your eyes. It is none of our business pulling their chestnuts out of the fire. We would as soon fight the British as the Germans'. American assistance to the Allied powers was therefore distinctly limited; the United States saw itself as an associated but minor partner. Only reluctantly did the Navy Department abandon its battleship programme until war's end to concentrate on merchant shipping construction; despite glowing promises, the United States never met its merchant tonnage commitments. The Navy was assisted in these endeavours by the country's own wartime leader, for President Wilson was bound and determined to avoid entanglements that would lessen his ability to dictate the postwar settlement. The British became increasingly convinced that the US was developing its shipping programmes with an eye to the future rather than to immediate wartime need; US naval staff were equally convinced that the British were not committing sufficient forces to counter the submarine menace.[5]

'Freedom of the seas' had been quickly adopted as one of Wilson's Fourteen Points for discussion at any peace conference – after all, this had been traditional US policy since the War of 1812. The application of this principle was intended to safeguard neutral and belligerent trade in time of war, but it also made it difficult to institute any form of blockade and would hamper any future British battle fleet operations. As the then First Sea Lord, Admiral Wemyss, pointed out:

> The British idea of freedom of the seas is free and unfettered access in time of peace, to all the seas by those who wish to cross them...in time of war this privilege must be fought for by the belligerent navies, causing as little inconvenience as possible to neutrals, but maintaining the right of capture of belligerent merchant ships and of searching neutral merchant ships in order to verify their nationality and prevent their aiding a belligerent.
>
> Acceptance of this proposal would result in making sea-power of little value to a nation dependent upon it for existence whilst providing a military Power with free lines of overseas communication.
>
> The right to decide for ourselves questions which concern such vital interests, could not be surrendered to any League or combination of nations, for by assenting to the proposal we should give up by a stroke of the pen the sea-power we have for centuries maintained and have never misused. On this basis the British Empire had been founded, and on no other can it be upheld.[6]

Though this impasse resulted in a British victory, it was obvious the Admiralty felt the contribution it had made to the war effort would guarantee it a predominant role over the naval side of the peace negotiations. None of this boded well for future cooperation. Indeed, once victory was assured the traditional Anglo-American differences began to re-emerge. As Admiral Sims wrote to Captain Train:

> When you consider the spirit that is now being shown between the Allies and the practically complete distrust between all of the others you can see that it does not offer very much encouragement for the type of 'League of Nations' which must be based on the brotherhood of men. Since the Armistice was signed a new war began: it is going on here as furiously as it is down your way. You do not see much about it in the papers but it is going on just the same. It is the clash of national and economic interests that is going to give the trouble complicated to a certain extent by the people who have always lived up in the clouds. ...They must reach a common conclusion or else settle down to the same state of affairs before the war.[7]

Competition – in the form of a potentially ruinous naval arms race between both sides down to 1922 – was followed by hostility concerning the nature of naval arms control after the Washington Treaty. Given the lack of naval base facilities, American naval delegates to various disarmament conferences during the inter-war period felt US interests could only be protected by vessels with both extended range and firepower. Heavy battleships and heavy cruisers were seen as vital for US security. However, because of the need to preserve British commerce and the need to protect lines of communications as well as its many and varied naval bases across the globe, the Admiralty required light cruisers and light battleships; in other words, ships that could protect convoys from hit-and-run raids. Finance was an equally important consideration; such light vessels were quick and cheap to produce. British naval delegates therefore argued for 'special circumstances' totally different from those of any other country. The Admiralty felt its needs were absolute, and its naval requirements should not have to depend on the size of the fleet of any other nation. The US Navy Department was not prepared to allow Britain more than parity in each class of vessel. Each was determined to maintain the forces considered necessary for the preservation of national security; questions of quantitative versus qualitative limitation with respect to ship characteristics, numbers and total tonnage became the key considerations.[8] In the opinion of the General Board, the misguided views of US politicians had allowed the British to manoeuvre the United States into accepting a 'paper' parity that served British interests at minimum cost. For their part, the Royal Navy thought that the changes that ensued in US construction programmes meant the United States was playing fast and loose with the arms control arrangements.[9]

Such competition was given a certain vindictiveness because, towards the end of the First World War, America had displaced Britain as the principal financial and banking centre. The United Kingdom emerged from the great conflict an impoverished debtor nation, yet determined to regain its lost markets and even increase its influence in new and prosperous regions such as South America. The United States was equally determined to continue making market gains and to expand on many other fronts, and had built up a merchant marine to accomplish these ends. The foreign trade of the United States rose fourfold between 1915 and 1920. This had an immediate effect on the naval affairs of both nations; in the Middle East, Admiral S. Calthorpe, commanding Royal Navy units in Turkish waters, began to express concern that attempts were being made by US business interests 'to secure a hold on Turkey' under the auspices of relief aid from America. In September 1919 the US Navy's General Board spoke of the 'growing jealousy and alarm' exhibited by British naval staff about the growth of the US merchant marine. British attempts to counter US interests in Middle Eastern oil drew vehement protests from the State Department. Admiral Mark Bristol, then senior US naval officer in Constantinople, saw British presence in the region as 'shot with dark and sinister intrigues.' Evidence suggests that there was generally a hostile rather than a cooperative basis to Anglo-American relations.[10]

Aware of its many weaknesses, the British government attempted to shape world financial arrangements in a way that would minimize the problems and maximize British strengths. The British sought to create a London-based financial bloc to regulate the flow of world capital, reduce the massive war debt and inflate world prices in the hope of stimulating foreign trade. However, Britain continued to meet determined competition from the United States, and in fields such as cost accounting, scientific research, labour relations, food and power supplies, natural resources, industrial equipment, modern technology and capital reserves, the latter continued to dominate. When the First World War began, Britain and the United States had similar levels of exports to Japan; by 1927 British figures had been reduced by one-half but the United States had increased its share by 84 per cent:

> It is quite certain that, unless the characteristics of the market are scientifically studied with the satisfaction of the individual consumer as the governing factor in the whole of the manufacturer's organization, British trade cannot hope to hold its own, still less to advance, when sited against the systematic approach. . .which is displayed by some of our foreign competitors.[11]

The Air Routes and the Naval Base Question

In the 1920s, the US Navy Department had expressed considerable interest in the island chains lying across the Pacific between the Philippines and Hawaii. Under War Plan 'Orange', atolls in the Japanese Mandates had been seen as useful for advance fleet bases; some islands were to be used to screen Hawaii and the Canal Zone from direct attack, while others provided a means of reaching the Philippines without passing through Japanese-held territory. In 1934, because of 'the importance of civil aviation and naval operations', Roosevelt instigated a set of naval studies on the feasibility of air bases en route to the Philippines, and the State Department was ordered to prepare to negotiate with London about potential sites. The matter was first raised in private discussions between Vincent Davis and the Prime Minister, Ramsay MacDonald, in London in June of that year, and the visit to Australia by the USS *Astoria* in July served notice to the British about future American intentions.[12]

Such intentions quickly became linked to the fortunes and progress of the Pan American Airline Company. The Navy Department had already found PAA to be particularly useful on the US mainland and close links had been established; PAA had aided the establishment of installations such as hangers, fuel tanks, loading docks and other paraphernalia, which had all been built to serve military as well as civilian purposes. PAA had also offset costs by sharing facilities; this had enabled the Navy Department to effectively camouflage military airfield construction under the guise of establishing civilian air routes. The company already had administrative jurisdiction over Midway, Guam, and Tutuila. In late December 1934, when both PAA and the South Pacific Company were seeking to extend their existing landing rights privileges in the Pacific, PAA was able to negotiate access to the naval facilities at San Diego and Pearl Harbor.

On 29 December 1934 an Executive Order placed Wake, Johnston, and Kingman Reef under US naval jurisdiction.[13] By the middle of 1935 PAA had begun the first of its clipper services to the mid-Pacific, and was welcomed by the Navy into Midway. The airline agreed to construct facilities on Midway, which the Navy was prevented from undertaking under Article 19 of the Washington Treaty. In August the US Post Office authorized air mail contracts for the new route, and needless to say PAA filed the only bid, although the question of terminal rights remained unsettled. PAA was granted a twenty-year franchise to establish Manila airport but because of pressure from Japan, China refused to grant landing rights at Canton. Reluctantly, PAA was forced to approach the Macao and Hong Kong authorities – initially without success. Clearly then, the only viable alternate route to Asia was by way of the South Pacific and Australia, and press reports now began to reach the British Embassy in Washington about the interest of the US Post Office in establishing an air mail service between Australia and America.[14]

The type of aircraft best suited to Pacific conditions dictated the kind of civil and naval air facilities. Here there was some confusion, which was understandable. In the early 1920s aircraft engines had barely been able to develop over 500 horsepower. By 1935, however, liquid-cooled engines had been all but replaced by the more efficient air-cooled radial engines of 2,000 horsepower or more. Given the distances involved and the required safety factors, both PAA and Imperial Airways placed their faith in long-range seaplanes. The US Navy Department supported that view on the basis of the need for long-range reconnaissance. Based on reports of visits to Kingman Reef and Palmyra, the C-in-C US Fleet favoured at least four main naval seaplane bases – Midway, Pearl Harbor, Palmyra, and Tutuila – while the commander of naval aircraft at Hawaii spoke publicly of Christmas Island as 'the best possible seaplane landing area between Hawaii, and American Samoa'. In 1935 the US coastguard vessel *Itasca* made three survey trips to Samoa, visiting Howland, Baker, Jervis, Palmyra and Kingman Reef. Baker and Howland were felt by the Navy to be suitable only for land based aircraft.[15]

Following these developments with the greatest concern, and with the need to draft an appropriate policy now paramount, the Foreign Office called for comments from all interested parties. Much of the fear about PAA stemmed specifically from the company's activities in the Pacific as well as from civil aviation developments in Australia. Because of 'the short sightedness of British manufacturers in regard to overseas markets', American penetration into the Australian economy was felt to have assumed 'grotesque' proportions. In civil aviation, for example, British competition had been thoroughly undercut. Douglas DC-2s had already been chosen for Melbourne to Launceston route; West Australian Airlines had ordered two Lockheed Electras for the Perth to Sydney run and two more were on order for New Guinea; the new Stinson monoplane was performing successfully from Sydney to Brisbane, and Waco machines were flying from Sydney to Bega.[16] As far as the British Ambassador was concerned:

> There seems to be a definite policy aimed at drawing Australia, in particular, and New Zealand into the American orbit, as well as to increase an existing influence in Canada. Today Sydney seems almost like an American city and Antipodean culture is becoming American; dress, customs, language, and doctors, engineers, and technicians appear to follow the somewhat ephemeral American methods and techniques. It appears to me that the United States has in mind some closer form of association, possibly we shall see the outward and visible sign in a Pacific trade treaty. . .I quoted public utterances by Mr. Roosevelt. . .to the effect that something like an American Empire in the Pacific was contemplated.[17]

Because of the subsidies paid to American shipping lines, P&O had already complained that British Far Eastern sea carriage was now directly under threat. Imperial Airways feared the development of a similar situation from competition with Pan American Airways:

> There seems a grave risk of the Americans and Dutch establishing themselves in such a way that will short circuit our own services and possibly result in British territory being serviced by foreign airlines. PAA had approached our agents in Singapore to handle PAA traffic when they extend from Manila. An extension to Hong Kong is imminent. The Dutch want to extend their service from Tarakan to Manila and connect with the trans-Pacific and their own carriage via Batavia to India and Europe. K.N.I.L.M. is extending its service from Medan to French Indo-China.[18]

> I do not think it can be too strongly emphasized that the Americans are doing everything possible to oust British transport interests in the Pacific. There is another letter in the "Times" today about the swamping of British shipping in that area. Cannot we get the Colonial Office and the Navy to do something to protect these islands in the Pacific which may be of the

greatest importance to British air interests in future? I suggest that even if continuous occupation is too difficult to arrange at the present time, a visit by the Navy and the rehoisting of the British flag over these islands might deter the Americans from their designs upon them.[19]

The Admiralty's Plans Division needed no convincing about the need to advance any and all territorial claims in the Pacific, not only to assist the Air Ministry in the creation of a Pacific air route, but also because these islands were felt to be of strategic value as fuelling bases, landing grounds and wireless stations. It was hoped that if communications networks could be established, the Japanese could be detected and prevented from establishing their own fuelling bases in the area. The Admiralty thus whole-heartedly supported Air Ministry requests that claims be put forward to Howland, Baker and Jervis before con-solidation of any US title; but, as with the Spratley Islands, the Foreign Office was unwilling to press the issue. When an international conference on reciprocal landing and flying rights was mooted, the UK delegates were instructed that Britain would be willing to abandon any claim to Howland, Baker and Jervis, in return for landing rights on US territory.[20] Indeed, the Foreign Office was convinced the 1935 Wellington Agreement (signed between PAA's chief representative in the region, the Australian airman Harold Gatty, and the New Zealand Government) would inevitably lead to the establishment of reciprocal arrangements on Hawaii and the US west coast, because the New Zealand Agreement was subject to withdrawal if reciprocity was not granted: 'if any British company desiring to operate over the Pacific is hereafter refused by the United States Government reciprocal rights of landing in US territory, the New Zealand Government may terminate the contract within one year's notice'.[21]

PAA also negotiated access to Pago Pago with stopovers in Apia and Kingman Reef, and won the airmail contract between San Francisco, Hawaii and Manila. By March 1936 it had been shown that Baker, Howland and Jervis were unsuitable for flying boats, and PAA now switched its attention to Canton, Hull and Fanning Islands. Meanwhile in London an Interdepartmental Committee on Air Communications had been formed, and early in 1936 the decision was finally made to press ahead with British claims.[22] The British were interested in both land-based and sea-based sites. A minimum depth of two fathoms and a minimum length of some two miles, with at least two hundred yards of flat ground either side, were defined as the main base requirements. Visits were arranged by HMS *Wellington* to Flint, Caroline, Vostock, Penrhyn, Starbuck, Malden, Fanning, Christmas and Danger Islands; HMS *Achilles* was released from service and placed on loan to the New

Zealand Government, and photographic reconnaissance was arranged for Hull, Nukonono, Fanning, Christmas, Canton and Kingman Reef,[23] and HMS *Leith* stopped at McKean, Enderbury and Canton. Unfavourable conditions were found on Kingman Reef, Fanning and Nukonono, where blasting was required, but Christmas and Hull were felt to have potential. There was also a division of opinion about Canton. HMS *Leith* found the island a fair anchorage for ships and a good anchorage for planes; *Achilles* reported Canton to be 'useless'. Of all the islands only two, Fanning and Christmas Island, were found to be of direct use as naval anchorages.[24]

The captain of HMS *Leith* took steps to annex Canton, Hull and McKean by leaving notice boards and a Union Jack. Because neither Enderbury nor Phoenix were suitable as air or naval bases no markers were left, and it was decided no action would be taken in relation to Flint, Caroline, Vostock, Starbuck and Malden. In order to establish definite title to Christmas Island, an administrative officer was appointed there.[25] Admiralty opinion on the matter was summed up in a Chiefs of Staff paper early in 1937:

> The Pacific Islands are of strategic value in so far as they provide us with fuelling bases for our naval forces, possible landing grounds for our Air Forces, and position for the establishment of wireless stations. Moreover if our system of communications can be sufficiently developed the chances of Japan using any islands in our possession as fuelling bases would be considerably reduced. We conclude that we should endeavour to establish sovereignty over any of the Pacific Islands offering facilities for fuelling bases or landing grounds. It should be our policy to assist, where possible, the development of those facilities which would be of value in war.[26]

Reports on the defence value of the area by the US Navy's Bureau of Aeronautics in 1936 had pinpointed Christmas, Canton, Fakaofu, Danger, Penrhyn and Suvarov as having potential. US construction on Palmyra was even deferred until 'proper claims to Christmas could be made'. In March 1937, ostensibly to observe a solar eclipse and in co-operation with the Navy, the American Geographic Society despatched an expedition to Canton; in fact, as Admiral Leahy pointed out to the State Department, by using coastguard cutters and civilians to camouflage its operations, the US Navy now planned to establish title and occupy the island. The State Department's Legal Adviser had already informed the Navy that any US claim over the Phoenix Island group would almost certainly be viable, and the Americans did not feel obliged to inform the British about the visit.[27] Unfortunately the arrival of USS *Avocat* at Canton coincided with the survey by HMS *Wellington*. According to British authorities, US naval officers refused to recognize British ownership, despite the fact that the Phoenix Island group and Christmas had been redesignated part of the Gilbert and Ellice group by the Colonial Office in January 1937. A concrete plinth with an aluminium flagpole and the Stars and Stripes was left behind.[28] The disappearance of Amelia Earhardt also sparked a series of US naval exercises in the area:

> The principle value of the search from the Navy's viewpoint was the opportunity it offered to operate ships and planes in a large and little known area of great importance. . . other valuable experience was gained in search tactics, in the 'Lexington's' high speed test, in the fast refuelling operation which the carrier accomplished at Lahaina Roads Hawaii, after her run from the mainland.[29]

On 16 July the British note of protest about the occupation duly arrived in Washington. In the belief that discovery did not constitute title, the President at first backed Leahy's proposals for forcible occupation of the island on the basis that it 'was badly needed as a base for naval airplanes'. But Hull warned that such action would undoubtedly be contested by the Royal Navy. Reluctantly the President agreed, though he now widened the framework of any future negotiation to other uninhabited islands.[30] With respect to Canton itself, Roosevelt stipulated that America would only negotiate as long as the island remained uninhabited:

> The South Polar Continent is an illustration in point. Various explorers – American, British, Norwegian, etc. – have planted national flags all over the place and claimed title. New Zealand has formally annexed a large portion of the Antarctic Continent but the point is that no human beings live on it and use it. It is therefore open to the nationals of any nation to go there permanently occupy the land and acquire quick title. In regard to Canton Island, if we negotiate with the British in regard to it and other Islands in the Gilbert, Ellice, and Phoenix groups, we can make it clear that the British have a good many harbours in the mid-Pacific and that we have none, and that we want several islands in as many parts of the mid-Pacific as possible, which will be useful for aviation purposes, including safe anchorage in clear water.[31]

Unfortunately, the British had already taken the decision to occupy the island. On 5 August 1937 the New Zealand Government landed a naval party from HMS *Achilles*; these were later replaced by a temporary administrative officer and in September a Deputy Commissioner for the Phoenix Islands was appointed. Not until 9 August was the US note, stipulating that future negotiations must be based on the continuation of the status quo, received.[32] By mid-September information had begun to reach the State Department about British annexation of Henderson, Ducie and Oeno near Pitcairn – islands ostensibly with large lagoons suitable for seaplanes. On 20 October 1937 His Majesty's Chargé d'Affairs informed the Roosevelt administration that since the British claim to Canton was 'unassailable', it would not be included in any negotiation. However, the US Government insisted a 'standstill' would not be of earthly use unless Canton was included.

This contretemps had now assumed 'grotesque' proportions. Many in the US State Department saw forcible occupation as the only viable alternative. The US Counsellor of State, Walton Moore, left Ambassador Lindsay with no doubts as to the President's displeasure. The President was 'chaffed. . .about the land grabbing propensities of the British'; he was convinced they were 'the prize claimers of the world' and 'liked to do business on a 90 cents to 10 cents basis'. Lindsay himself favoured conciliation, and Foreign Secretary Anthony Eden was inclined to agree, but the British Office of Civil Aviation was furious and the Admiralty was opposed to any compromise.[33] As the Director of Overseas Civil Aviation, C. J. Galpin, and the Royal Navy's Director of Plans, Captain Tom Phillips, argued:

> Taken by itself the American attitude is preposterous. They grabbed three islands with trumpets in the press and news reels (you will recollect the scene in the "March of Time" shown all over America and this country of British statesmen belatedly hunting up precedents, Japanese admirals gravely conferring, and New Zealand businessmen eagerly welcoming the cornucopia of U.S. enterprise). Now these islands turn out to be useless, while we have reoccupied an island of value, and so we are threatened with the displeasure of the American public, exhorted to think on higher planes and lectured for outmoded manners.[34]

> The despatch of the British Ambassador is very one sided and it ignores entirely the United States action in annexing Howland, Baker, and Jervis Islands without one word to us, while putting in the worst possible light our own annexation of Canton Island to which we might say we had as equally good a claim. . . If we give way to the United States on Canton Island, they will no doubt try to make a case out for getting Hull and the other islands in the Phoenix Islands from us and possibly also Christmas Island. In the circumstances, it may be that we accepted somewhat too readily the United States claims to Howland, Baker, and Jervis Islands, but again it is legitimate to observe that the United States are not showing themselves so accommodating with regard to the islands we ourselves claim.
> The acerbity of the US representations, and the bringing of the President's name into the matter, may well indicate, apart from the fact that the United States recognizes the value of Canton Island, that they realize that their claim to it is very doubtful.[35]

As Britain seemed unwilling to abide by the 'standstill' proposal, a US 'expeditionary force' under the supervision of the US Coast Guard landed on Canton where a British radio post was already located. The island was immediately placed under the jurisdiction of the Department of the Interior, and the State Department representative in Hawaii was instructed to colonize the island with native Hawaiian as well as army and navy personnel. PAA had also been pressing the administration for access to Canton; the company had just concluded an agreement inaugurating an aerial passenger service to New Zealand, and one clipper had already crashed near Pago Pago, so the need for additional bases had become critical.[36] On 29 March 1938 the Department of the Interior granted PAA access to Canton. Amid vehement protests from the Admiralty and the Colonial Office, the President's suggestion that a condominium be formed over the island was accepted by the Foreign Office, but within months the situation had begun to deteriorate again.[37] PAA's licence on Canton made no provision for future agreement with foreign concerns unless the State Department approved them first, and permission to build on the island was directly under the control of the US Secretary of the Interior.

The Colonial Office had originally hoped to settle the overpopulation problems of the whole Gilbert and Ellice Island group by resettling natives on Canton. The decision to retain the colonizing scheme owed less to any positive expectation that settlement would ever materialize, and rather more to the fear that without the scheme the islands might be regarded as unimportant, thereby strengthening the US Government's claims. The British feared that they would be left only with those portions of the island which were of no use to anyone. On 6 May 1938, without permission from British authorities, the US Navy began landing a second survey team with quantities of cement and balloon observation gear. Even though the joint trusteeship had obviously become a 'monstrously bad joke', the Foreign Office was still anxious to avoid serious friction. It was the Admiralty that took the strongest anti-American stance, but then they had always disapproved of any joint administration, particularly under circumstances where the Americans retained control of the air facilities. The Admiralty felt it was better to have no facilities at all, and effectively to demilitarize the whole region rather than allow Japan access to any abandoned facilities created as a result of an anticipated US withdrawal from the Far East. In addition, the US draft agreement on the condominium made no mention of the use of Canton as a joint naval facility, nor did it grant access by British military aircraft to the airfield. America's sudden incursion into Canton led the Royal Navy to recommend the cancellation of PAA's contract on the island and the despatch of a warship.[38] As Balfour pointed out:

In the first place it seems a very unequal division of the spoils and a bad bargain to sacrifice our share in administrative control and sovereignty over the airport, which is commercially and strategically important, in exchange for the colonization scheme which in itself is relatively insignificant. . . it is true that the use of the airport would be thus denied to any belligerent except the U.S.A. for warlike purposes against us, but in any war in which the U.S.A. was not involved as our ally, it seems that we would, if this airport is to be regarded as American territory, lose even what claims we would have to its use under a condominium regime.[39]

Interestingly enough, Hull Island was now looking a better prospect as an aerial refuelling base than Canton, where extensive dredging and the blasting of coral outcrops was found to be necessary. Since all efforts to find a compromise solution to the problem of the trans-Pacific air routes had failed, Ambassador Lindsay in Washington suggested that Canton be abandoned.[40] The Foreign Office was now under considerable pressure. The New Zealand Government was eager for a civil aviation link-up between Suva, Nukonono, Hull and Christmas Island; the New Zealand Air Force expected to be operating two squadrons of Wellingtons by 1940, and was anxious to create strategic air routes for land-based aircraft radiating out from Fiji. In April 1938 the Navy Department flatly rejected any suggestion the British be granted landing rights in Hawaii; Roosevelt refused to recognize that the sovereignty issue and reciprocal rights were even connected. Britain's compromise set of proposals for a four-power conference was not even shown to the President for fear of arousing his ire. Since notice had also been received that the Navy Department intended to expand its surveys to include the whole Phoenix Group in 1939, the Admiralty urged that Britain must 'lose no opportunity' in consolidating its own position upon Hull.[41]

Reluctantly, the Foreign Office agreed that Hull would prove useful, but it was seen only as a 'bargaining counter'. Reciprocal rights, it was felt, might be exchanged in return for American agreement to a four-power conference.[42] By November 1938, to avoid the American proposal for a 'general clean-up' of all remaining Pacific islands, naval personnel from HMS *Leander* were left on Hull, Gardner and Christmas. Hull was staked out, and by the following month advance parties of natives had dug wells there. In December survey parties departed for Nukonono and Fanning Islands, while meteorological equipment and an administrative officer were placed on Christmas. These decisions were underwritten by the Committee of Imperial Defence when, early in 1939, they agreed that there was a definite need to establish British sovereignty over potential intelligence, reconnaissance and seaplane bases. Nevertheless the Admiralty were now prepared to cede certain 'unimportant' islands, but only if America altered her attitude.[43]

There was little chance than this would occur. PAA negotiated renewal of its air agreement with New Zealand with the intention of using Noumea, within easy flying distance of Brisbane and Auckland. In December 1938, the Hepburn Board's report to Congress recommended the establishment of naval facilities in the Pacific for tender-based patrol operations. This necessitated a considerable amount of channel dredging to allow entry to lagoons. In February 1939, Ambassador Lindsay reported that American jurisdiction had now been extended to Midway, Wake, Johnston, Sand, Kure, Baker, Howland, Jervis, Canton, Enderbury Island and Kingman Reef. The US State Department also listed a string of islands from the Galapagos to Noumea and then to the New Hebrides where the US had 'definite interests', namely Christmas, Makin, Funafuti, Oeno, Suvarov and Caroline Islands. US authorities now argued they had complete ownership over Canton,[44] and by July US survey parties had landed on Hull. They erected seven flagstaffs and constructed four one hundred-foot towers, and formal claim to the whole Phoenix Group was made by the administration in September along with twenty-three other islands in the Pacific group, most of them British. It was perhaps fortunate that, as a result of the outbreak of a European war, the United States agreed to a 'standstill' until the conflict ended.[45]

There may well have been many fields in Anglo-American relations where a 'special relationship' did exist, but there was little basis for cooperation in Anglo-American naval relations in the Pacific, except perhaps at the field command level along the Yangtse. In those areas where contact was made between the two sides at higher levels, a heritage of mutual suspicion and hostility had been created. For a portion of the inter-war period, the US Navy Department regarded the Admiralty as an opponent; neither side was prepared to cooperate with the other and a spirit of active competition characterized their relations in the Far East.

Despite this atmosphere two pre-war naval conferences did take place. What were these two meetings about, and how, if at all, did they then contribute to the development of a relationship?

The 1938 Ingersoll Meetings

If the Washington Conference had established a naval ratio of 5:5:3, it was the 1922 Nine-Power Treaty that pledged a strong independent and united China as a future elusive goal. The contracting powers agreed to respect the sovereignty, independence and administrative integrity of that nation, to assist in the creation and maintenance of effective and stable government and industry of all nations and to refrain from seeking 'special rights and privileges'. What this amounted to was a pledge to respect Chinese integrity but without any commitment to defend China if the treaty was violated. Here was a difference in approach between the British and the Americans. The Americans saw in China a people struggling for full sovereignty, and rightly or wrongly assumed they were also struggling for democracy. It is true that many struggles were going on inside China, but these were primarily struggles for power, not nationhood. The concept of the 'Open Door' conveyed the impression of free enterprise, but in the long run it enmeshed the United States in an alliance not with a country but with a belief. The United States espoused a doctrine not a policy, and one insufficiently important enough to her to defend. United States garrisons on mainland China would protect American lives but not China's interests, and there was constant pressure from all quarters to withdraw US troops completely. Although by 1933 the Chinese market absorbed only 2.5 per cent of Britain's exports, British interests in China were far larger than those of the United States. For Britain the significance of China was its potential rather than its reality as a market source. British interests in Hong Kong had to be protected.[46]

In July 1937, incidents between Chinese and Japanese troops began to escalate. At first both Britain and the United States were anxious to contain the fighting, but Secretary of State Hull's failure to support Australia's Pacific Peace Pact proposal, Chamberlain's refusal to respond to suggestions that he visit the United States and Eden's distinct lack of success in canvassing the possibility of a 'joint demarche' marred relations; both sides were unable to exercise sufficient joint pressure to prevent the crisis from becoming a full-scale war.[47] Of even greater concern was the development of closer ties between Germany, Italy and Japan. There were three possible solutions:

1. The use of threats, blockade and even sanctions, that is, making of an example of Japan to offset Axis collusion while possibly deterring Germany and Italy from contemplating similar action. But this inevitably meant further escalation of the Sino-Japanese conflict.
2. To isolate Japan by wooing Germany and Italy away from a possible alliance system.
3. To use a combination of the above.

Britain's Foreign Secretary, Anthony Eden, believed that such threats were unlikely to be heeded unless there was a concerted effort from both Washington and London, and he was prepared to go to any lengths to achieve Far Eastern cooperation. Neville Chamberlain, on the other hand, was more anxious to secure a comprehensive European settlement. 'Appeasement' appeared to be more cost-effective than a highly speculative foray in the Far East. As to the prospect of forming alliance systems, Chamberlain had little confidence in the French and shared the Chiefs of Staff suspicions concerning them. Though he was not opposed to Eden's position, and was prepared to work with the United States in the Pacific, he placed no faith in US overtures, was uncertain that any kind of reliance could be placed on American assistance, was fearful that pursuit would squander valuable resources and was doubtful the Roosevelt administration was serious with respect to Anglo-American cooperation.[48]

From early 1937, there was a distinct possibility that Japan would exercise belligerent rights in Chinese waters (such as blockade, search and seizure of ships and goods). The Governor of Hong Kong and the General Officer commanding the base both demanded, if necessary, some right of reply. By August Japanese and Chinese troops were battling through the streets of Shanghai, and Chinese shipping was blockaded from Sanhaikwan on the Manchurian border to Swatow in the south. By September the innumerable atrocities being committed and the bombing of Nanking, together with a certain frustration at the singular lack of success in the search for a diplomatic solution, led Sir Alexander Cadogan of the Foreign Office to suggest economic measures against Japan. A Cabinet Committee was set up to look into the possibility of sending two capital ships to the Far East as reinforcements to prevent any anticipated Japanese interference with British trade.[49] Asked for his views on the subject from his position as Chief of Naval Staff, Lord Chatfield's reaction was immediate and hostile:

> From this angle the division of our limited force of capital ships between Eastern and Western hemispheres, far from acting as a deterrent to the Japanese might even present a temptation to Japan in offering them at least a possibility of defeating the divided British forces in detail. . . Pursuing this argument to its logical conclusion, therefore, it becomes clear that if a reinforcement of capital ships is to be sent to the Far East such a reinforcement must be in sufficient strength to defeat the full strength of the Japanese Navy.[50]

Alarmed by reports that sanctions were being contemplated, the Admiralty warned the Foreign Office that an outbreak of conflict in Asia would tempt Germany and Italy to act also, at a time when Britain was in a period of maximum weakness. If the United States provided definite assurances of support sanctions were possible, but the Admiralty cautioned that such economic measures would probably have little effect, and if Japan retaliated, the US could not be counted on to provide military assistance.[51] Hopes concerning US involvement were renewed, however, by President Roosevelt's speech in Chicago in October, particularly by his pointed reference to a 'quarantine' of aggressor nations. Exactly what the President meant by the term fuelled considerable historical speculation,[52] and certainly threw his own advisers into a turmoil. Roosevelt did not help matters by giving different interpretations to different people. Both Welles and Davis began to talk of new peace initiatives and of a revision of the Treaty of Versailles; Ambassador Phillips in Rome now feared that America was abandoning her neutrality inside China. Perhaps as David Reynolds suggests, the President had no specific plan in mind; he was simply hoping to develop guidelines for future policy.[53]

It can therefore be understood why Roosevelt's words caused even greater confusion amongst foreign governments. Chamberlain saw the President's actions as 'suicidal', for he felt the temptation for the Fascist powers to act in Europe while Britain was preoccupied in the Far East would be 'irresistible':[54]

> Now in the present state of European affairs with the two dictators in a thoroughly nasty temper we simply cannot afford to quarrel with Japan and I very much fear therefore that after a lot of ballyhoo the Americans will somehow fade out and leave us to carry all the blame and the odium. It is not a very pleasant prospect. . .when I asked the U.S.A. to make a joint démarche at the very beginning of the dispute they refused. At that time before the Japs were involved it might have stopped the whole thing. Now they jump in, without saying a word to us beforehand. . ... We are carrying on some quiet talks with the Japs which might or might not have come to something, but of course these are now wrecked. . .[55]

Even within the Foreign Office – with the obvious exception of Eden – there was little support for the speech. It was seen merely as a test of mid-western isolationist opinion, an attitude rather than a programme, and it was feared that it would encourage the anti–Japanese enthusiasts.[56] Earlier in the year Chatfield had expressed the Admiralty's view when he wrote that 'in event of trouble', Britain 'would undoubtedly have to stand alone and unsupported in both hemispheres' with France 'an uncertain ally' and 'no friend we can trust' providing support.[57] Not even the President's speech could change that opinion:

> I am concerned about the Far Eastern situation and where we may find ourselves dragged by the sentimentalists. I am afraid that Roosevelt's speech may do us more harm than good. . .and yet you may be quite sure that if it comes to any trouble in the Far East the Americans will stand aside. We have got quite enough troubles on our hands in Europe to make it most

undesirable to sent the Fleet out to the Far East. Sanctions are just as likely to mean sending the Fleet out to the Mediterranean. I have, however, warned the Foreign Office of the danger and I hope that wise counsels will prevail.[58]

Chatfield provided the Cabinet Sub-Committee on British Shipping in the Far East with similar views about the possibility of naval reinforcement of Eastern waters, views that were reflected in its final report, and Cadogan at the Foreign Office endorsed the idea that a small number of ships would be counter-productive. Even the despatch of eight or nine capital ships was regarded as dangerous; such a force would have to be accompanied by a considerable auxiliary force which would necessitate denuding the Mediterranean and many other stations. With reference to the Mediterranean, by 1937, Italy's relations with Britain had deteriorated greatly. Italy was now a strong supporter of Franco, had reinforced Libya and was fermenting trouble in the Arab world; in August, British and French merchant ships had been attacked off the Spanish coast by Italian submarines, and the Nyons Conference – not attended by Italy – had led to only temporary improvements in Anglo-Italian relations.

By early November, Italy had joined the Anti-Comintern Pact. Even if a fleet was sent, it could only defend British and Dominion posses- sions from Japanese attack; it could not undertake offensive operations off the Chinese coast and was therefore unlikely to influence Japan to moderate her policies. Economic pressure was possible but a blockade would take two to three years to have any effect. Chatfield was 'pre- pared to do whatever was required' but he was not sure the British Cabinet realized the implications. So while the imposition of sanctions was considered, it was concluded that nothing Britain could do would have any effect without the direct support of the United States;[59] and as Roosevelt told Norman Davis, the first step towards peace was to mediate between China and Japan. At the Brussels Conference called to discuss this possibility, British delegates appeared anxious not to be seen as being over-cautious lest that antagonize either Japan or the United States, but they remained distrustful and feared that the Amer- icans might pull them forward prematurely.[60] On 1 December 1937 America rejected British offers regarding mediation anyway, while Roosevelt's attempt to widen discussions into a world wide forum foundered.[61]

Interest in a naval demonstration was renewed on 12 December when the USS *Panay* and three Standard Oil tankers were attacked and sunk by Japanese aircraft. British gunboats were also bombed and shelled by shore batteries. The British Cabinet was eager not to lose the opportunity for American support, but again they emphasized the need to be cautious.[62]

On the other side of the Atlantic, Admiral Leahy had become convinced the time had come to take a stronger line against Japan. At a conference with Roosevelt on 14 December he urged the President to return the battleships to the west coast drydocks to prepare them for sea. Possible cooperation with Britain was suggested, but for the time being Roosevelt decided to follow the advice of the State Department and settled on a formal note of protest. Hull pointed out to the Foreign Office that the President felt inhibited by public opinion, which made him reluctant to order any kind of joint protest or fleet movements.

On 16 December, Ambassador Lindsay met Roosevelt at the White House and the question of staff conversations was immediately broached. The President wanted the arrangements to resemble the Gaunt-Pratt talks between 1915 and 1917. Lindsay attempted to point out the value of mobilization or a joint naval demonstration, but Roosevelt felt reinforcements to the Far East should be confined to cruisers and light forces rather than battleships. The object of such staff conversations would be to arrange for a future naval blockade of Japan. Lines would run from the Aleutians to Hong Kong, with areas of individual responsibility clearly marked. Denying that blockade would mean war, the President desired implementation of the new measures after the next Japanese indiscretion. Roosevelt also agreed that it might be possible to advance the date of American fleet exercises in the Pacific or send a squadron of cruisers to Singapore.[63]

The President did not appeared to have made up his mind. In the 1920s he had written articles in *Asia Magazine* predicting a Far Eastern stalemate; he was probably also influenced by Admiral Yarnell's report on Far Eastern defence. In mid-1937 Yarnell had advised America to take advantage of Japan's economic vulnerability and wage a more cost-effective war of economic strangulation by concentrating on light forces, naval aviation and submarines.[64] The idea of a common front with other nations to press Japan through the threat of economic action was of particular appeal to a President anxious about balanced budgets and concerned about 'making substantial savings through eliminating or deferring all expenditures which are not absolutely necessary'. In the mid 1930s he had supported the idea of constructing a hybrid – part picket boat, part destroyer, part seaplane tender – and he planned to commandeer 500 yachts adaptable for military purposes as blockade vessels during the first thirty days of any war, despite vehement opposition from the Navy Department. General opinion in the Foreign Office judged Roosevelt's plan to be a 'fantastic chimera', but despite its obvious 'silliness', it was still felt the idea might be transformed, and the President 'converted' to something more workable if Britain were to react.[65] If a naval demonstration was ordered, the Admiralty still favoured the despatch of a full fleet as long as there was full US co-operation:

> It has been decided and His Majesty's Government have accepted that if we send a fleet to the Far East at all this fleet must be in fighting strength not substantially inferior to the Japanese, and that we cannot rely on the fleets from the U.S.A. and ourselves each markedly inferior to the Japanese and depending for superiority on their working together. It would presumably be necessary to notify the U.S.A. of this decision and to obtain their agree-ment, if possible, to they themselves sending a fleet at least equal to that of Japan. . . The passage of the Fleets to the East will require careful co-ordination, and it will be necessary to find out whether the U.S.A. really visualize sending a fleet east or whether their idea would be to mobilize and remain ready. Assuming that the U.S.A. Fleet goes East, it is clearly very undesirable that one fleet, even if strong enough, should be placed so that it might have a fleet action with the Japanese before the other fleet reaches the East.[66]

It was considered undesirable for the US Fleet to proceed alone to Manila, and the Admiralty suggested it would be wiser for both fleets to proceed independently to Singapore and from there north to Manila together. Both fleets then would not only cooperate strategically by general agreement – similar to that currently under negotiation with the French – but would also operate together in a tactical sense. All signal books, cyphers and recognition codes would be exchanged and com-mand would be unified. If the shortest route was chosen, that is, if the US Fleet settled for the southern route via Fiji and Torres Straits and the British Fleet proceeded via the Suez Canal, both fleets could reach the base in six weeks. There was no intention to provoke war unless Japan attacked. The Americans would be asked to assume responsibility for the north and west, while the area from India to Singapore and thence to Hong Kong would remain in British hands. Singapore would only be able to supply British needs; the US Fleet would have to be supplied from Honolulu.

The British plan owed much to the Far Eastern Naval War Memoran-dum, and visibly demonstrated the Admiralty's continued preoccupation with advanced naval bases and the Phase II scenario. It showed too that there was little understanding within the Royal Navy of conditions existing in the US Fleet. The United States did not have sufficient auxiliaries, bases dry docks or fuelling facilities to support such a long range enterprise; its ships were in no fit state or condition from the supply and personnel standpoint to reach Manila, even by way of

Singapore. The British wanted action immediately, the President was only prepared to act at some future date; the President favoured a naval blockade, the Admiralty a naval demonstration in force, albeit reluctantly.[67] As Lord Chatfield pointed out:

> The whole situation as regards the Fleet going East is at present very uncertain; naturally I am averse to sending it as far as possible. . . Obviously the fleet that you will have to take out is not very satisfactory, but if it did go out I think we should be certain to have the American fleet as well and that will make a great difference. . .Anyhow you can never be sure what they will do so we cannot rely on them absolutely.[68]

By deliberately delaying their response to the Japanese attack, the Roosevelt administration allowed time for a peaceful solution to emerge. By 26 December, Japan's note of apology (in which assurances were given that there would be no further incidents of a similar kind; Japan even offered to pay an indemnity) had effectively ended the Panay Incident; by 7 January 1938 Lindsay was reporting that the prevailing feeling in America was one of 'relief that it is over'.[69] Eden remained anxious to take a strong line in the Far East, but the Americans were now reluctant to act on what had become a closed issue.

On 31 December the United States Navy's Director of Plans, Captain Royal E. Ingersoll, arrived in London to begin staff talks. His mission was highly secret; in the United States only Roosevelt and the Chief of Naval Operations received his report, while in London circulation of the relevant papers was limited. No reference was made to the conversations either in Cabinet or under the auspices of the Committee of Imperial Defence. Eden's hope that the groundwork for future Anglo-American political agreement might be laid was immediately dashed by the news that Ingersoll was under strict instructions from the President not to commit the United States to joint action of any kind. He had no political authority to negotiate, and consequently everything discussed with Admiralty authorities was purely theoretical. He preferred to discuss technical rather than political matters; more interest was expressed in the how than in the when.[70] As Chatfield wrote:

> I pointed out to Captain Ingersoll our difficulties in having a very important back door to guard, and that might limit the strength of the Fleet which the Government would be willing to send out to Singapore. I also said the composition of the Fleet we might send out on our own might be different to that which we would send out if the American Navy was co-operating. . . I informed him that we had never envisaged the tactical combination of the two Fleets but rather that they would go in support of each other [this was, of course, patently untrue]. Captain Ingersoll agreed that this policy represented the view of the Naval Board. The most they had envisaged was

a somewhat distant blockade or, as he called it, quarantine. They would be able to support the blockade on the Pacific side with their Fleet based at Honolulu and their ships in a distant circle from the Aleutian Islands through the Sandwich Islands and Johnson Island south-westwards. Would we be able similarly to hold the blockade on the south-eastern side? I said that that would be our intention in such circumstances.[71]

However, when asked if the US favoured a naval demonstration before another Far Eastern crisis, Ingersoll dodged the question, arguing that the mere presence of the fleet at Honolulu would probably deter Japan. In any case Ingersoll argued that Japan was too preoccupied in China to be able to launch pre-emptive strikes on British and American possessions. He revealed that such a large scale naval movement would require full mobilization of the whole US Fleet and a Declaration of National Emergency by the President. The Fleet was only 85 per cent manned, and though vessels already located in the Pacific – if returned to the West Coast and stocked with personnel, fuel and stores – could reach Hawaii in ten to fifteen days, they would have to remain there at least a month before they could proceed. The United States would first have to ensure that the West Coast and the Hawaiian Islands were fully secure and the Fleet made self-supporting before any advance could be contemplated. This of course reflected the current standing of War Plan 'Orange'. Ingersoll was obviously making a pointed reference to the lack of an adequate fleet train. He also revealed America was considering withdrawal of her China garrisons, the gunboats, and those parts of the Asiatic Fleet operating in Chinese waters. Subsequently Ingersoll was to admit that Roosevelt wanted to supplement America's light forces with private yachts.

In event of a distant blockade, areas of responsibility were worked out. It was agreed the British would cover the area from Singapore to the southern Philippines and the New Hebrides, while the Americans would look after Fiji, Samoa, Hawaii and the west coast. However, if an emergency took place it was clear that the Royal Navy was the only force capable of quick reaction. If the US Fleet did proceed west of Hawaii, a preference was expressed by Ingersoll for the less dangerous southern route via Samoa, Fiji and Torres Straits. The news that Singapore would only support one fleet did not help. Both sides exhibited a considerable degree of self-interest during the discussions. In 'a casual way', Ingersoll twice pointed out that the US would like to establish seaplane bases on Christmas and Fanning Islands, throwing doubt on the whole cooperative effort. Less than a week and a half later, Captain Tom Phillips was accusing the United States of conspiring to steal Christmas Island, Hull and the Phoenix group. As for the Admiralty, their interest in advanced fleet bases north of the Malay Barrier has already been noted. In their conversations with Ingersoll British naval staff admitted they much preferred Manila to Hong Kong as an operating base,[72] but Ingersoll put paid to any hope that it could be used by battleships:

> The British inquired further about the facilities at Cavite and Olongapo and were informed by us that Cavite could maintain submarines and that Olongapo could repair and dock all classes of ships up to and including heavy cruisers and that while the dock at Olongapo had sufficient capacity to lift a heavy cruiser the controlling factor there was the length of ship.[73]

The Ingersoll conversations ended with broad agreements on strategic cooperation, respective spheres of action, reciprocal use of facilities and common codes, and mutual war plans were revealed. But all this was of little use without some kind of military and political guarantee. Ingersoll was surprised by the specific nature of the information provided by Chatfield. He had begun the talks by remarking that the purpose of the mission was to exchange general naval information; on 13 January 1938 he ended them by concluding that they had met 'to consider ways and means of cooperation between the two navies, should it ever become necessary'. But was the idea of a joint naval demonstration ever a realistic proposition? The Navy Department was opposed to a blockade involving only light forces; the President was opposed to the use of the fleet or a battleship line. The Admiralty was not prepared to move its own forces without US support, yet even under wartime conditions the US Fleet would only agree to advance as far west as Hawaii. Even if a collaborative effort had been organized, each side would have retained its own distinct command structure and its own separate area of responsibility, for neither side really trusted the other.

By 11 January 1938 the President finally made a decision and threw his weight behind the Welles initiative for an international conference. He hoped for agreements on key issues such as reductions in armaments, right of access to raw materials, the laws and customs of war and the principles of international relations. Because of the seriousness of the world situation he also asked Congress for an increase in the naval budget, and this became the basis of the Second Vinson Act of 1938. Lindsay also reported that a US cruiser squadron – earmarked to visit Sydney – would now visit Singapore, and he announced that if the British Government issued a statement concerning their completion of naval preparations, the Americans would agree to make public their intention to drydock their battleships and advance the date of the annual

Pacific fleet manoeuvres by three weeks. This was a distinct disappointment to the Admiralty; as Chatfield pointed out, it placed the onus for action on Britain. If the announcement of the Fleet's departure did not have the desired effect then it would be a fait accompli; the British Fleet would have to be sent and Chatfield had no reason to expect US naval support to be forthcoming.[74] Indeed, Ingersoll went on to blame British naval intelligence for a leak about Japanese naval construction and accused them of attempting to cover their own agents. Willson left the Admiralty in no doubt that the Ingersoll Mission would not lead to a regular system of visits by naval officers from each country.[75]

Given US unreliability in the past, Chamberlain was reluctant to see the United States meddling in European affairs once again. The 'Peace' Plan with its emphasis on fundamental principles appeared too idealistic and, coming as it did in the middle of delicate negotiations for a bilateral conference with Germany, positively dangerous for 'appeasement'. Yet he did not want to alienate the United States and was prepared to accept their assistance 'when we have done a certain amount of spadework'. After asking Roosevelt to postpone action 'for a short while' Chamberlain followed up the initiative by asking Roosevelt to proceed, but was thankful when this failed to elicit a suitable response. That in turn merely underlined his belief that 'that it would be a rash man who based his calculations on help from the United States'. In the Far East, Chamberlain contented himself with a strongly worded telegram about the latest Japanese outrages. No announcement about the transfer of naval forces was ever made, nor did a 'burgeoning relationship' develop in the Pacific.[76]

If anything, Anglo-American naval relations now went through a hiatus. In the strategic sphere, there was little contact between the two sides for almost a year. In November 1938 an American approach led to a joint démarche by Britain, France and the United States over freedom of navigation in the Yangtse. Once again it seemed the Americans were moving towards a more active Far Eastern policy. On 9 January 1939, Captain Willson asked the Admiralty's Director of Naval Intelligence to bring the previous year's conversations up to date so that the President and Admiral Leahy could be kept abreast of the state of British planning.[77] At first it was felt the two initiatives might be connected, but Admiral Sir Roger Backhouse, the new British Chief of Naval Staff, rejected this as a possibility:

> Unless the situation got much worse, I doubt greatly whether any move in the direction indicated by this paper would be made by the U.S.A. and I also doubt whether our own Government would be prepared to suggest it. The American government have proved to be extremely reluctant to make any

sort of engagement which might commit them to warlike action and the most recent speech of their President does not seem to change their attitude.[78]

The First Sea Lord's doubts proved justified. The United States refused to be drawn by Foreign Office inquiries about the desirability of retaliation, and Willson was found to be acting without any official backing. As he was about to be recalled to Washington, he was merely anxious to complete his own records before making his official report. At the insistence of the United States, both the Admiralty and the British Government did their best to preserve the secrecy of the 1938 accords, yet information about the Ingersoll visit was leaked to *Newsweek* from the American side, and the US Director of Naval Intelligence – a noted Anglophobe – was suspected of being the guilty party. As a result the Admiralty exhibited an unwillingness to provide Willson with another copy, but in any case an internal review revealed that there was no need to revise the general agreement. British naval strategy had not altered so there was little point in additional meetings. Naval staff did reveal, however, that the Fleet was unlikely to exceed seven or eight battleships, sufficient to operate defensively on a line east of Singapore but not sufficient to operate offensively north of the Malay Barrier without US assistance. No capital ships could be expected in Eastern waters before 1941. Willson could not agree that the possibility of tactical cooperation – which had been in the Admiralty's mind since 1938 – had become an important consideration. Rather than having received an impression of an improvement in cooperation, the Admiralty's Director of Naval Intelligence was left with the feeling that Willson felt the situation in the Far East had eased so 'the need for co-operation might not now be so important'.[79]

British Defence Conundrums in 1939

Nothing could have been further from the truth. In the intervening months after the Ingersoll meeting, Japan brought into play certain restrictive practices on foreign trade inside China, took over the management of the northern railroads, set up large Japanese development corporations and limited the operation of all foreign banks. Customs duties were brought under control, as well as the operations of the post office, telegraph and electrical supplies, and restrictions were applied to foreign shipping along the Yangtse. Lord Halifax now feared that the Japanese were about to develop an exclusion zone, and he called for a physical display to support British diplomacy and guard against the creation of such a vast closed area. Yet Chamberlain reaffirmed that British policy must not antagonize but re-establish better, or at the very least stable, relations with Japan as a means of preventing her from exploiting the deteriorating situation in Europe, where the government's attention continued to be focused.

By 1939 the gap between commitments and capability was much as it had been in 1937, but the range of solutions had become more limited. The Anglo-Italian Agreement of 1938 was no more successful than the Gentleman's Agreement of the previous year in settling the differences between the two countries. Chamberlain's summit meeting in Rome in January 1939 failed to separate Italy from the Fascist camp. Indeed, reports that a Triple Alliance was about to be signed between Germany, Italy and Japan began to reach the Foreign Office early in the year. Despite the Munich Agreement, German aggrandizement continued unabated. In mid-March the remaining portion of Czechoslovakia was seized, and the following month Germany abrogated the Anglo-German Naval Agreement, while in April Italian forces invaded Albania. According to British sources, Rumania was 'asked' to provide the Reich with a monopoly over her export trade. The purpose of this economic offensive was German access to the Aegean and the Mediterranean; as far as the British were concerned this was but a prelude to a wholesale penetration of Southeastern Europe. This was incorrect, but it had its effect; British guarantees of support in event of an Axis attack were forthcoming for Poland, Greece, and Rumania.[80]

In event of a European war, the Chiefs of Staff assumed that Britain would be allied with France against Germany and Italy. Understandably uppermost in the minds of British strategists was the prospect of simultaneous war in three corners of the Empire, now more likely than in 1937. Yet the United States was still seen merely as a friendly neutral power, willing to modify her neutrality in Britain's favour but unlikely to actively interfere. In the first half of 1939 the Royal Navy was in an invidious position with only ten capital ships available for service. As the new First Sea Lord, Sir Roger Backhouse, pointed out:

> The fact of the matter is with our present anxieties in Europe as well as in the Far East, we cannot be strong everywhere. Things have been allowed to go back too far, and we are now completing only the second year of a five year rearmament programme.
>
> The position will be very different in 1941, and of course is getting better yearly. I cannot say, however, that I look forward to 1939 with great confidence.[81]

The Joint Planning Committee therefore agreed to raise the period before relief to ninety days for Singapore and one hundred and twenty days for Hong Kong. The Chiefs of Staff European Appreciation, submitted to the CID on 20 February 1939, pointed out that with Italy added to the balance the British capital ship position had become 'critical'. Until the development of the two-power standard altered the situation, the strength of any Far Eastern Fleet would be totally dependent on 'European circumstances'.[82] The Admiralty still felt a 'reduction in the number of our potential enemies is as definite an accretion to our strength as is an increase in the number of our battle-ships', but the prospects for European 'appeasement' appeared dim. British political weakness was one reason the Admiralty favoured diplomatic negotiations and opposed the use of economic sanctions against Japan during the Tientsin crisis.[83]

There appeared to be two possible solutions to the British defence dilemma: to increase reliance on potential allies and/or to establish a priority in one theatre or another. In event of war, perhaps even the abandonment of the Pacific or the Mediterranean would have to be contemplated. A Foreign Office official summed up the difficulties faced by British strategists:

> Faced with an overwhelming opposition on these fronts with no hope of victory on all of them unless the United States of America or France comes to our aid, should our strategy be (1) to risk complete defeat in the Far East, but to endeavour to force a favourable decision in Europe by knocking out Italy, or (2) to make our position secure in the Far East, but to abandon the Mediterranean and jeopardize our chances of knocking out Italy?[84]

Reviewing the European Appreciation, the new Minister for Coordination of Defence, Admiral Lord Chatfield, felt French forces in the Mediterranean must deter Italy while a fleet was despatched to the Far East. The First Lord of the Admiralty, Lord Stanhope, sought on the other hand to persuade the United States to transfer its fleet to Hawaii, to divert Japan and allow the British to concentrate in the Mediterranean. During March and April of 1939, a protracted debate took place in Whitehall as the existing Far Eastern strategy came under direct challenge from supporters of a Mediterranean approach. Two types of Mediterranean offensive were feasible: a quick attack against the Italian Fleet had an advantage in that it would release naval forces as fast as possible for service in the Far East, while a combined offensive with all arms would wear Italy down more gradually but in the longterm might provide better security.[85]

For the Admiralty, the idea of a 'knock out blow' against Italy was a more attractive proposition than any combined offensive. It was the more acceptable strategic framework, given Britain's limited capacity and her reluctance to rely on assistance from allies. Indeed the support of the First Lord of the Admiralty, the First Sea Lord and the Deputy Chief of Naval Staff provided a powerful political lobby for the revisionist strategy. However, evidence would suggest the Mediterranean strategy was never so universally supported, certainly not by the Admiralty.[86] It was Chatfield at the Strategic Appreciations Committee, convened to review the European Appreciation and to recommend terms of reference for the Anglo-French staff talks, who remained the revisionist's most intractable opponent, and his views seem to have continued to exert considerable influence.[87]

Yet even under the best possible scenario, the revisionists regarded concentration in the Mediterranean only as a temporary expedient. Both sides still saw a need for advanced fleet bases in the South China Sea. The real basis of the disagreement was over the timing of the arrival of the Eastern Fleet. As far as the Plans Division and some of the technical departments were concerned the Mediterranean was simply a staging area, with the Suez Canal as the necessary but not vital link to the Far East. Captain V.H. Danckwerts, the Director of Plans and head of the Admiralty delegation, made enquiries at the Anglo-French staff talks about possible French reactions to British abandonment of the Mediterranean should this prove necessary. Danckwerts feared that interminable delays might occur, brought about perhaps by the need to await a favourable moment before attacking the Italian Fleet, and that the Royal Navy's inability to extricate its forces once engaged would allow Japan to conquer much of the Far East without opposition. It would then require a campaign of considerable duration and cost to retake the fallen possessions.[88] The revisionists, however, expected war to break out first in the Mediterranean,[89] and felt that Japan could be 'deterred' while Italy was dealt with. Perhaps it was no coincidence that the First Sea Lord brought Admiral Sir Reginald Plunkett-Ernle-Erle-Drax, formerly of the Naval War College at Greenwich, out of retirement early in 1939 to head a new Operational Planning Committee – thereby undercutting the work of the Plans Division, which continued to favour the commitment to the Far East under any and all circumstances.[90] Even in event of a European war the latter felt that:

> Forces are retained on the China Station and in Australian and New Zealand waters, the military and air garrisons at Singapore are reinforced, and our outlying battalions in North China are withdrawn to reinforce Hong Kong. These measures will make it clear to Japan that we have no intention of abandoning our position in the Far East.[91]

No definite decision about a choice between theatres was ever made by the Admiralty, not even in April when the Italian invasion of Albania made it likely that war would break out. Even before the Tientsin crisis, the Royal Navy had begun to move away from the revisionist strategy. Over the short term, the size of any Far Eastern Fleet continued to depend on such 'variable factors' as the number of capital ships available, the strategic situation both in home waters and in the Mediterranean, the extent of Japanese aggression and the reaction of the United States and the Soviet Union. If Italy was neutral or eliminated from the war, it was estimated by the Admiralty that seven ships would go East; in a war with all three opponents with America neutral, four would be sent; if the United States was an ally, only two would be despatched.[92] Clearly then the Admiralty had no intention of abdicating the British position in the Far East 'without fighting'.[93] In any case it was expected Japan would be too preoccupied in China to contemplate any kind of advance southwards, and in the long term the development of a two-power standard would offset British weaknesses. The premature death of the First Sea Lord, Sir Roger Backhouse, removed one of the main proponents of the revisionist approach; his replacement, Admiral Sir Dudley Pound, was known to favour a defensive stance in the Middle East.[94] Out of a total of thirty-six war plans being prepared in early June, the Admiralty were involved with twelve, of which eight concerned the Far East.[95]

Opposition to the 'knock-out blow' was by no means confined to the Admiralty. Arguments similar to those within the SAC also occurred in the Foreign Office, where the Far Eastern Department sided with Chatfield and the Egyptian Coordination Department with Stanhope.[96] The Joint Planning Committee was dubious. They pointed out that initially Britain would have to assume a defensive posture.[97] Italy's weaknesses might be exploited by applying superior naval and economic power at the decisive point, but 'not at the outset', a view also subscribed to by Major L.C. Hollis, the Assistant Secretary of the CID:

The Impression seems to have grown up that in the very early stages of a war we could deliver what has come to be called a 'quick knock-out' on Italy as being the weak and vulnerable partner of the Axis. I will not waste the Committee's time in tracing the arguments and discussions which gave rise to this impression, but attractive though it may be in theory, it was I think founded on a misconception. Offensive action against Italy as contemplated by the Chiefs of staff is one thing: a 'knock-out blow' which would render Italy innocuous in the early stages of war and thereby release our forces for operations in other theatres is quite another. The Chiefs of Staff have always favoured taking offensive action against Italy when and where the opportunity arises, but they have never argued in the circumstances with which we shall be faced we could, in fact, deliver this 'knock-out blow' at the outset.[98]

In any case according to the Chiefs of Staff, both the 'knock-out blow' and any combined offensive were dependent on active French cooperation. During the Anglo-French negotiations there had been general agreement on the need for action in the Mediterranean, though the French preferred to confine their activity to North Africa rather than face Italy anywhere else.[99] In May talks were held at the regional level to work out detailed joint plans; it was revealed that no general offensive could be expected if Spain intervened on the side of the Axis. In fact France had sufficient troops to hold only the Mareth Line, and at least two months would be needed before any kind of offensive action could be contemplated. Even then the attack would be limited to the seizure of Tripolitania.[100] The dichotomies between the assurances at the London staff talks and those priorities assigned by regional commanders were never solved to the satisfaction of British planning agencies. By 24 July 1939 the Chiefs of Staff were concluding that Italian neutrality was 'decidedly more preferable to her active hostility', though how this might be achieved was unclear.[101]

Strategic policy therefore remained very much in a state of flux throughout 1939. No cohesive picture of the real state of British planning was presented by the respective delegations at any of the three main conferences held with the Dominions, the French and the United States in the first half of the year. In each case the position taken depended upon intent – in other words what was hoped would be derived from the meeting, the type of talks and who was doing the talking.

At the Pacific Defence Conference, organized by the Dominions and held in Wellington, New Zealand, from 14–26 April, the New Zealand Government expressed considerable doubt about the fleet's capacity to reach the Far East. The United Kingdom delegation found themselves in a rather difficult position; on the one hand they did not wish to encourage doubt, yet on the other they did not want to prevent Australia and New Zealand from setting their own local defences in order.[102] There was also a fear that the Dominions might look to the United States or limit their support for British policies. The UK delegation therefore stated that while no guarantee could be given that 'the whole of the Fleet destined for the Far East could be despatched immediately', by the same token:

It was made clear at the Conference. . . the intention of the United Kingdom Government was to despatch a portion of the British Fleet to the Far East immediately on the entry of Japan into the war, to act on the defensive to an extent sufficient to give a measure of cover to Australia and New Zealand. It was further noted by the Conference that the entry of Italy into the war against the United Kingdom would still not affect this intention.[103]

As pointed out by the Deputy Chief of Naval Staff, Tom Phillips, 'no up-to-date' expression of British strategy had been provided for the Conference, a conclusion perfectly in keeping with the state of planning. The strength and date of despatch of a Far Eastern Fleet were still under consideration at the time, pending revision of the Naval War Memorandum and completion of a new Far Eastern Appreciation.[104]

Anglo-French staff talks were held from 29 March to 4 April, and from 24 April to 3 May. British delegates were authorized by the CID to discuss the deployment of three British capital ships in the Mediterranean 'to enable the maximum pressure to be brought to bear on Italy, so that in co-operation with the French, the Italian Fleet could be driven from the sea'.[105] Nevertheless the Admiralty's Director of Plans still stressed the importance of Far Eastern interests and the need to counter Japanese aggression by naval action, preferably from a secure base. The British delegation admitted uncertainties about the size and timing of Far Eastern reinforcements, but continued to insist that if a choice between theatres had to be made 'it would be for the Government of the day to decide'.[106] As the French regarded the Mediterranean as a key area of control, they were naturally concerned about such vague expressions; indeed at one point they actually threatened 'to make peace with Germany immediately should British withdrawal from the Mediterranean take place'. British staff planners admitted the problem was one of 'balancing risks', but would only agree 'the weakening of the British Eastern Mediterranean fleet would not lightly be undertaken'.[107]

One positive element that emerged from these meetings was a mutual recognition that in event of a three-front war, active participation of the United States on the Allied side was vital. If the United States chose to remain neutral, it was hoped the US Fleet would be transferred to the western Pacific, since this could delay Japanese entry into the war long enough for Anglo-French forces to secure control of the Mediterranean. At one point the Admiralty hoped to link talks with the French with those held with the Americans into a mutually binding arrangement, but American fear of active commitment precluded this.[108]

The 1939 Hampton Meetings

During the discussions surrounding the European Appreciation, the First Lord of the Admiralty, Lord Stanhope, suggested that if the US agreed to move its fleet to Hawaii Britain might despatch a deterrent force of two capital ships to the Far East. He claimed the Japanese would be reluctant to send a large fleet as far south as Singapore if there was a danger that their naval forces might be cut off by a hostile United States. As far as many of the British naval staff were concerned, however, the presence of the US Fleet at a point some 3,500 miles from Japan was unlikely to exert any kind of military threat.[109] As the Admiralty's Director of Plans, Rear-Admiral V.H. Danckwerts, pointed out to the French delegation during the Anglo-French staff talks in April 1939, only in the event that the US Fleet operated from the Philippines, Singapore, New Guinea or northern Australia would the Japanese be deterred from undertaking action to the south. Nevertheless, at a party on the evening of 22 March, Lord Halifax and Admiral Chatfield explained the British strategic dilemma to the US Ambassador, Joseph Kennedy, and a request that the United States consider the return of the Pacific Fleet first to the Pacific and then to Hawaii was passed to the President through Sumner Welles and the State Department. Chamberlain also instructed Lindsay to ask Roosevelt if the United States would be prepared to resume the staff conversations begun the previous year.[110] As Chamberlain explained:

> His Majesty's Government cannot leave out of account the fact that they are involved in a European conflict, they might not be able at once to reinforce on a large scale their naval forces in the Far East and that might affect United States naval dispositions.[111]

At the time a German invasion of Poland was expected at any moment, and on 7 April Italy invaded Albania. If Britain was about to adopt new measures in Eastern Europe as well as in the Mediterranean, this could only be done at the expense of the Far East. However, Chamberlain's request was made without reference to the Admiralty, and the latter doubted that staff conversations could achieve what was required, namely a political guarantee of support. The Ingersoll-Phillips conversations had resulted in a broad strategic agreement, but never had there been any definite undertaking to implement such plans. Lindsay reported that the President had agreed to Chamberlain's suggestion, but the procedure was to be different from that of the previous year.[112] Despite the desirability of exchanging Far Eastern operating plans, Danckwerts felt the emphasis laid by the Americans special naval attachés meant that Roosevelt ultimately wanted to establish a permanent mission for the examination of joint intelligence information. Danckwerts was deeply concerned about the effect of establishing a 1915-type system of liaison:

In 1915 we were already at war and therefore knew our circumstance with accuracy and could assess the numbers and quality of our enemies. At the present day we may be faced with hostilities against Germany, Italy, and Japan simultaneously, but have not as yet arrived at that situation. While, therefore, the closest co-operation with the United States is to be welcomed, the dangers of any leakage of information are probably greater under our present circumstances than they were in 1915, when any such leakage would commit the U.S.A. more firmly to our cause; now such leakage might have the most far reaching results, and even possibly deprive us of our power to choose our own political course.[113]

Such reservations were shared by Backhouse and the Deputy Chief of Naval Staff, Admiral Andrew Cunningham. The First Sea Lord felt further political guidance was necessary before the Admiralty could commit itself, and there was little use even in holding conversations unless guarantees were forthcoming. Joseph Kennedy went on to announce that the President had agreed to return the US Fleet to the Pacific by the end of April. Kennedy also alleged that since it had been intended that the Fleet remain in the Atlantic for some time to come, the significance of an early return would not be lost on the Japanese. Admiral Leahy had discussed exactly that point with the President.[114] But renewed confidence within the Foreign Office about a stronger American stand in the Far East was tempered by the views of the British Naval Attaché in Washington and his influence over naval staff in London. He argued that since such American fleet manoeuvres had been worked out long in advance, this was all 'errant nonsense':

It is difficult to understand why the U.S. Ambassador made the statement accredited to him. . .the programme for the U.S. Fleet was made and published months ago and they have always been going to sail from New York on May 16. . . There has never been any question of the Fleet remaining in the Atlantic for three years – such a procedure would have been most unusual and entirely contrary to existing U.S. naval policy.[115]

In one sense the Naval Attaché was right. The Fleet normally visited the Caribbean for manoeuvres at about this time, and had been diverted from a return to the Pacific by the opening of the World's Fair in New York. However, the US response was indeed motivated by conditions in Europe, and in particular by French panic. Both the United States and the French expected a coordinated Axis attack on three fronts, with Albania and Greece, Poland and Singapore as the natural targets. On 11 April the French Foreign Minister Daladier warned the US Ambassador in Paris that if the British Fleet sailed for Singapore, France 'would have nothing more to do with resistance in Central and Eastern Europe'. Bullitt urged the President to despatch the US Fleet to the Pacific to deprive Chamberlain of any opportunity to abandon France. Even before a second telegram arrived from Lord Halifax outlining the British request once again, Admiral Leahy had been ordered to prepare the fleet for the journey. UK guarantees to Greece and Rumania removed much of the need for a transfer, but the movement went ahead anyway. Roosevelt believed he was saving the peace front.

British attempts to get the Americans to hold the anticipated naval conversations in London failed to convince Roosevelt. Republican gains in the 1938 Congressional elections had strengthened the coalition of Republicans and Conservative Democrats that had proved so effective in blocking Presidential attempts to support the democracies in Europe. Because of his desire to amend the mandatory arms embargo on belligerents and to place British and French supplies on a cash and carry basis, Roosevelt was cautious. Above all, he had to avoid the kind of furore that had occurred in January 1939, when the press had discovered that the French were about to close a secret arms deal which would have allowed them to be supplied with Douglas DB-7 aircraft, the latest American bomber. The President had no intention of allowing the talks to take place anywhere but in the United States, where he hoped elaborate security arrangements would prevent disclosure to the press. It was thus decided to send a specially selected British naval officer incognito to Washington, where meetings would take place at a secret location with specific representatives of the US Navy Department.

As far as British naval authorities were concerned the principal objective of the talks was to explain how, over the short term, the ability to send a large fleet to the Far East had come to depend on conditions in Europe. Commander T.C. Hampton, a former member of the Admiralty's Plans Division, was chosen to represent the Royal Navy. He was instructed to familiarize himself with the Far Eastern Naval War Memorandum and with the arrangements for protection of Britain's trans-Atlantic trade. The Admiralty was careful to suggest that if proposals for combining strategy were made, the initiative would have to come from the United States. Under such circumstances Hampton was to stress British needs for assistance in the Pacific. Singapore would be made available for use by the US Navy, and it was also suggested that aid from US cruisers in the western Atlantic would be most welcome.[116]

On 12 June 1939, Hampton arrived in Washington. Because of his fears concerning security, Leahy insisted that no written record of the meetings be kept in case he was 'interrogated' by Congress. For that same reason, Rear-Admiral Ghormley, the US Navy's Director of Plans, had not even read the notes of the 1938 accord, and did not do so until the day before the meeting. At first Leahy confined his remarks to circumstances where Britain and France were engaged in Europe, Japan was involved and America neutral. Under such conditions, as a deterrent to Japan, he felt the President would move the US Fleet to Hawaii. However, he qualified this by pointing out that the US could not make definite agreements or discuss anything other than parallel action.

At their second meeting on 14 June, Hampton distributed copies of British naval cyphers, codes and signal books (by the time war broke out in September most of these had become obsolete). When pressed on the subject of a US commitment, Leahy explained that if Britain were facing Germany, Italy and Japan, with the United States associated, the latter would assume responsibility for the Pacific and the British and French would control the Atlantic and the Mediterranean. Pointing out that any opinions offered were purely personal and not part of any settled war plan, he felt that in that case the US Fleet would move to Singapore with the intent of defeating the Japanese Fleet en route – relief of Singapore would take 120 days – but he stressed that its despatch was dependent on the arrival at Singapore of a 'token force' of British battleships. As regards unification of the forces involved into a single command structure – probably American– Leahy stressed that this was a political decision to be made by both governments at the time.[117]

Despite the display of 'warm friendliness', the results of the Hampton Mission were 'in some respects disappointing'. The extreme secrecy surrounding the mission rendered any effective discussion impossible. The Assistant Chief of Naval Staff, Rear-Admiral Tom Phillips, felt that the conversations had proved useful: that the Americans would contemplate using Singapore was considered 'a great advance on the 1938 discussions when they were inclined to use a US harbour without any real facilities'. However, little in the way of a positive result was achieved. It was brought home to the Admiralty that an American guarantee of support was probably unattainable, and British authorities were left with the impression that the US Navy had no plans for active cooperation with the British Fleet in wartime. Leahy was an Anglophile and a strong supporter of a firm line in the Far East, but his influence on US naval policy was limited as he was nearing the end of his term in office as Chief of Naval Operations. The lack of cooperation exhibited was in direct contrast to the situation in the Atlantic; there Roosevelt was able to use the visit of King George VI and Queen Elizabeth in June to put forward the idea of a western Atlantic patrol to keep the waters of the western hemisphere clear of belligerents and to relieve British ships from some of their responsibilities.

An indication as to how the United States might really act in a Pacific crisis occurred during the Tientsin Incident. On 14 June the Japanese blockaded the British Concession, where there had been a long-standing controversy about its use as a refuge for Chinese guerillas. They demanded the new Japanese currency be recognized and that all silver bullion held there as part of the Chinese currency reserves be surrendered. At first Lord Halifax toyed with the idea of imposing economic sanctions and the Foreign Office hoped to convince the US to move its fleet to Hawaii. This idea was rejected by Chamberlain and the Cabinet: the need to preserve the peace without any loss or damage to British possessions was paramount. This policy was underwritten by the Advisory Committee on Trade Questions in Time of War and by a Cabinet Informal Committee, both of which advised against damaging UK-Asian trading interests. Chamberlain felt that since the US could still not be trusted, the matter had to be settled by peaceful means lest Germany take advantage. Britain could not afford to send a large capital ship fleet to the Far East without endangering the European situation.[118]

Thus the British continued to believe that, if war were to break out before 1941, they would have to defend their Far Eastern possessions alone and unaided. Most of the cruisers of the China Fleet would be concentrated in the Bay of Bengal during Phase I to protect the line of communications to Singapore and to prevent Japanese raiding. The Admiralty's Plans Division had originally intended to establish an outer and inner patrol line, extending some five hundred miles to the north of Singapore between IndoChina and Borneo, but the obvious vulnerability of cruisers to air and sea attack led instead to reliance on aerial and submarine patrols, backed by an inner line of destroyers. Yet the Admiralty refused to adopt a purely defensive posture. It intended to upset the Japanese timetable with raiding forces, and its concerns during Phase I were not limited to the preservation of Singapore.[119]

Swatow, north of Hong Kong, continued to be seen as the most likely base for Japanese naval forces operating in the South China Sea. The possibility of blockading or bombarding the port with fire from cruisers on the outbreak of war and during Phase II, after the arrival of the Main Fleet, was investigated in detail between 1938 and 1939. The Admiralty also intended to pass two 8-inch cruisers (or two 6-inch cruisers) through the Balintang Strait north of Luzon from Hong Kong, arriving some four hundred miles off the Japanese coast seven days after the outbreak of war. After a two-day bombardment this force would withdraw via the main trade route from Yokohama to San Francisco, drawing off Japanese forces and maximizing damage as it went, arriving at Queen Charlotte Sound some twenty-two days later.[120]

At the Anglo-French staff conversations in Singapore in June 1939, the French had been persuaded by the British naval representative to look into the possibility of wartime intervention in southern China, and an agreement was signed permitting joint use of Kam Ranh Bay by British and French naval forces. Discussions were, however, limited to a Phase I situation, primarily because the naval representatives and the Admiralty remained distrustful of French security.[121] In August the Deputy Chiefs of Staff Committee discussed promised assistance from Chiang Kai-Shek's Chinese forces; an attack towards Hong Kong was agreed, but Foreign Office fears about the adverse reaction from Japan, inter-departmental difficulties and concern about Chinese reliability put the issue into abeyance.[122] Nevertheless, it was obvious that some naval representatives had played a major role in designing measures to relieve pressure on Hong Kong during Phase I in anticipation that it would still be possible to carry out Phase II, and at a time when the fleet had never been weaker.

During the Tientsin imbroglio the Far East had again become a focal point for naval attention. By bringing forward repairs and mobilizing the Reserve Fleet, the Chiefs of Staff anticipated that if war with Japan broke out immediately, seven capital ships could be sent. This would necessitate denuding the Mediterranean and, of course, the French would have to be consulted first. However, both the Admiralty and the Chiefs of Staff were prepared to contemplate this step. Numerical inferiority with respect to Japan would be offset by keeping the fleet within range of Singapore's air cover. If Hong Kong was attacked the fleet would not initially proceed to its rescue, since its role would be one of 'defensive fleet in being'; yet by the same token, fleet action 'under favourable circumstances' was still considered a possibility. 'If circumstances permitted', or if the Japanese proved to be less aggressive than expected, a 'forward policy' might even be adopted. After all, as the First Sea Lord himself pointed out, since the Japanese had only nine operational capital ships in 1939, a Phase II fleet would require only one more capital ship.[123]

Some authors, in particular those who have written about the pre-war defence relationship between Australia and Great Britain, have accused the Chamberlain Government and the British service chiefs of deliberately deceiving the Dominions by providing guarantees when they knew full well that they lacked the capacity to fulfil their promises.[124] However, there needs to be some distinction made between the views of the Admiralty and those of the CID, as well as the Chamberlain administration. It is true that the Royal Navy conspired, along with many others, to keep the full knowledge about the real state of British Far Eastern defences from the Dominions, but of all the services the Admiralty was the most unequivocal in its support of naval action in the Far East. There was never any naval staff intent to abandon Australia to its fate. Any deceit necessary on the Admiralty's part was presumed to be justified because it was always assumed the present circumstances were a temporary aberration and the creation of a two-power standard would restore the naval balance to a more favourable level.[125] How much influence the Admiralty exerted in maintaining the Far East as a priority, and in ensuring the commitment to despatch a fleet when required remained 'absolute', is difficult to assess, but at times this influence was considerable.

As for the US military and naval authorities, they were not convinced the foreign concessions in China could even be defended, and favoured the return of all US garrisons to the mainland. On 16 June, Secretary of State Cordell Hull was warned by the Navy Department that maintenance of a forward role by the United States would inevitably embroil it in a single-handed war against Japan. An agreement was quickly reached that any invitation from the British to assume the leadership in Far Eastern affairs was to be politely resisted.

From the US standpoint, the 1939 naval conversations proved of some, albeit limited, use. The Joint Planning Committee was finding difficulty operating under a Joint Board frame of reference that presumed the United States would have to resist Japan alone and unaided. On 11 May 1939, the Committee recommended that all future plans would have to take into account the possibility that the United States might have to face three possible enemies. On 23 June, work began on Rainbow 2; this plan presumed the United States would be fighting on the same side as Britain and France against Germany, Italy and Japan. However, these were first and foremost theoretical scenarios where probable courses of action by the United States under different circumstances were outlined. As the General Board pointed out:

> Whether or not we have any possible intention of undertaking war in this situation, nevertheless we may take measures short of war and in doing so clarify the possible or probable war task that would be involved.[126]

There was little hope that the Americans would underwrite foreign interests in China or British Far Eastern possessions. Even if US intervention was possible, the US Navy was hampered by its lack of personnel, inadequate fuel stocks, paucity of auxiliaries and the absence of bases. In August an attempt was made by the Navy Department to assess whether the US Navy could react to a 'serious emergency'. This first 'Are We Ready' Study concluded that the Fleet could not face the Japanese and was 'seriously menaced through an inability to counter similar Japanese types'.[127] There were serious doubts too that Singapore would ever be of any use to the US Fleet; the base was to open in March 1940 but would not be complete before 1941, and in fact the whole southern route to the East was not yet viable.[128] The C-in-C US Fleet made that clear to Washington naval authorities in 1939:

> It does not appear practicable nor profitable, within necessary fuel limitations, to plan problem operations extending into areas so distant from the Hawaiian Islands. Furthermore, the present development of Canton and Palmyra Islands does not permit the basing of surface forces or patrol planes at those places so that the most cogent reason for projecting the operations well to the southward will not exist at the time these exercises are held.[129]

Shortly thereafter, the State Department laid claim to a large number of islands in the South Pacific. It was feared by the Foreign Office that this might be the price to be paid for US wartime cooperation in the Pacific.[130]

Conclusions

During the inter-war period, no real foundation for cooperation was ever established between the British and US navies in the Pacific. Those points of contact that did exist beyond the field command agreements were based on mutual distrust, competition and in some cases near outright hostility, but not on an active spirit of collaboration.

In their pre-war planning, neither side placed much value on the active cooperation of the other. For the most part they had worked out their strategic policies without consultation and in isolation from each other; as a result, they approached any naval conference with a certain degree of self interest. The British hoped to initiate immediate joint action against specific transgressions committed by Japan inside China, but from the beginning the Admiralty believed no faith could be placed in a US commitment, even where US interests were directly involved. These reservations proved to be justified. Encumbered by their government's insistence that no political commitments or guarantees could be made, the US Navy Department reduced discussion to merely an exchange of naval information. The British spoke of the immediate and the short-term, the Americans of the undetermined, long-range, and hypothetical. By the time the Ingersoll conversations took place discussions about a joint naval blockade were already fruitless. In any case the Admiralty had never supported the idea, and hope of further naval action from the Americans depended on decisions from the political and not the military arena.[131]

The British Cabinet, not unnaturally, dismissed any hope of retaliation against Japan over the Tientsin incident. Without US assistance such action would have been ineffective anyway, and Washington was determined 'not to pull British chestnuts out of the fire'. Further meetings about strategy did not take place until nearly a year later, and between January and June 1939 no US naval attaché was even based in London. Any collaborative action that resulted from the Hampton meeting did not go beyond an exchange of the broad features of respective war plans. The general agreement on divisions of responsibility and operating areas was useful but was not necessarily indicative of a cooperative spirit, for and each still intended to act independently, alone and unaided.

Notes

1. Winston S. Churchill (1948–54), *The Second World War,* vols. 1–3, London; Max Beloff, 'The Special Relationship: An Anglo-American Myth', in Martin Gilbert (ed.) (1966), *A Century of Conflict, Essays in Honour of A.J.P.Taylor*, London, pp. 148–71.
2. In his authoritative two volume work on British naval policy, Stephen Roskill characterized the 1930s as a period of renewed cooperation between the Admiralty and the Navy Department. Arthur Marder has referred to the 'intimacy' of the naval connection, and James R. Leutze implies that there was a continuity in naval relations between the two countries down to the Second World War. Indeed Roskill, Leutze and others have singularly failed to distinguish between the two main theatres of operation, namely the Atlantic and the Pacific. See Stephen Roskill (1976), *Naval Policy Between the Wars: The Period of Reluctant Rearmament 1930–39*, London; Arthur J. Marder (1981), *Old Friends, New Enemies: The Royal Navy and the Imperial Japanese Navy Strategic Illusions, 1936–41*, Oxford, pp. 69–74; James R. Leutze (1977), *Bargaining for Supremacy: Anglo-American Naval Collaboration 1937–41*, Chapel Hill, NC, chapters 2 and 3.
3. Tel. Lindsay to FO, 17 December 1937, enclosed in ADM 116/3922; Leutze, pp. 20–1.
4. Minute by DNI, 17 December 1937, ADM 116/3922.
5. David F. Trask (1972), *Captains and Cabinets: Anglo-American Naval Relations, 1917–1918*, Columbia, pp. 63, 124–5, 175.

6. Quoted by Trask,*Captains,* pp. 320–1.

7. Ibid., p. 353.

8. See for example Christopher Hall (1987), *Britain, America, and Arms Control 1921–1937,* New York; T.H. Buckley (1976), *The United States and the Washington Conference 1921–1922,* Knoxville, TN; R.D. Burns (1968), *Disarmament in Perspective,* vol. 3: *Limitation on Seapower,* Los Angeles; R.G. O'Conner (1962), *Perilous Equilibrium: The U.S. and the London Naval Conference of 1930,* Lawrence, KN; Stephen E. Pelz (1974), *Race to Pearl Harbor: The Failure of the Second London Naval Conference and the Onset of World War II,* Cambridge, MA.

9. For but two examples of this view see Ltr Chrmn of the GB to Sec. Nav., 18 January 1933, GB 438–2, Serial 1584; Minute by the First Sea Lord, 15 June 1938, ADM 116/3369.

10. D. Cameron Watt (1984), *Succeeding John Bull: America in Britain's Place 1900–75,* Cambridge, pp. 43–4; Ltr GB to Sec. Nav., 22 September 1919, GB 420–2; E.L. Woodward and R.A. Butler (eds) (1946), *Documents on British Foreign Policy* first series, vol. 4, 1919, London, p. 651.

11. Michael D. Goldberg (1973), 'Anglo-American Economic Competition 1920–30', *Economy and History,* vol. 16, p. 22; F.C. Costigliola (1977), 'Anglo-American Financial Rivalry in the 1920s', *Journal of Economic History,* vol. 37, no. 4, pp. 911–34.

12. Report of the JB, 6 March 1934; Conversations between Davis and MacDonald, 20 June 1934, Davis Papers; Ltr FDR to Secretary of State, 17 April 1935, File 811–79690, PAA/10–5, RG 59.

13. Memo Secretary of State to FDR, 16 April 1935, File 811–79690, PAA/10–5, RG 59.

14. Extract *Washington Post,* 29 December 1935, AVIA 2/1994; Ltr Barnes to Undersecretary of State, 3 October 1935, ADM 116/3569; Ltr Air Ministry to Undersecretary of State, 2 September 1935; Ltr British Consul Honolulu to SSFA, 24 October 1935; Tel. FO to Lindsay, 30 November 1935; Memo by Colonial Office, December 1936, AVIA 2/1994.

15. Ltr Chrmn GB to Sec. Nav., 5 September 1934, GB 404; Memo CNO to Sec. Nav., 16 November 1934, PPF, Navy Department, Roosevelt Papers; Acting Secretary of State to Sec. Nav., 13 December 1934, A21–5, RG 80; Memo C-in-C US Fleet to CNO, 17 December 1935, A21–5, RG 80.

16. Ltr Woods Humphrey to Shelmerdine, Air Ministry, 2 March 1936, AVIA 2/1994.

17. Ltr Barton to Acheson, CO, 18 October 1939, AVIA 2/1994.

18. Ltr Woods Humphrey to Shelmerdine, 26 September 1935, AVIA

2/1951; see also Ernest R. Gilman (1976), 'Economic Aspects of Anglo-American Relations in the Era of Roosevelt and Chamberlain', King's College, University of London, unpublished PhD thesis, chapter 4.

19. Ltr Woods-Humphrey to Shelmerdine, 2 March 1936, AVIA 2/1994.

20. Minute Scott to DNI, 24 August 1935, ADM 116/3569; Extract from Notes of Discussion at the Chrysler Building, 13 December 1935, AVIA 2/1948; Ltr Air Ministry to Undersecretary of State, 2 September 1935, AVIA 2/1994.

21. Tel. Gov.-Gen. New Zealand to DO, 5 December 1935; Tel. FO to Lindsay, 7 December 1935; Tel. DO to Gov.-Gen. New Zealand, 29 July 1936, AVIA 2/1948.

22. Tel. Lindsay to FO, 30 October 1935; Tel. High Commissioner Western Pacific to FO, 23 March 1936; Ltr Seymour to CO, 2 April 1936, ADM 116/3569.

23. Memo ADM to Asst Secretary IACC, 3 April 1936; Ltr Cmdr NZ Squadron to ADM, 3 May 1936; Ltr Burkett to Rear-Admiral Kennedy-Purvis, 26 May 1936, ADM 116/3569.

24. Ltr Herbert to Jarrett, Secretary of the Admiralty, 29 October 1936; Report by Captain Bevirs, 14 September 1936, FO 371/20445; Report HMS *Achilles*, 29 September 1936, AVIA 2/1994; Ltr Hibbert to Jarrett, 29 October 1936, ADM 116/3569.

25. Report by Captain Bevirs, 14 September 1936, FO 371/20445.

26. 'Strategic Importance of the Pacific Islands', COS Paper 581 (JP), 14 May 1937, CAB 53/31.

27. Ltr Cmdr 14 ND to OpNav., 7 April 1936; Cmdr Aircraft Base Force to CINCUS, 23 November 1936; Ltr CINCUS to CNO, 6 November 1936, A 21–5, RG 80; Memo by Legal Advisor to State Department, 5 March 1937, File 811.0141, PG/13, RG 59.

28. Tel. Cmdr NZ Station to ADM, 29 June 1937, ADM 116/3569; Note of Meeting at CO, 11 August 1937, AVIA 2/1994.

29. Extract from the *New York Times*, 5 July 1937, AVIA 2/1994.

30. Ltr British Ambassador to State Dept, 16 July 1937; Ltr Moore to Southgate, 22 July 1937, File 811.79690, PAA/107; Memo for Secretary of State, 26 July 1937, File 811.0141, PG/11.5; Memo Secretary of State to FDR, 29 July 1937, File 811.041, PG/9A; Memo FDR to Admiral Leahy, 30 July 1937, File 811.0141, PG/12.5, RG 59.

31. Ibid.

32. Tel. Lindsay to FO, 9 August 1937; Notes of Meeting at FO, 29 July 1937; Notes of Meeting at CO, 11 August 1937, pt II, AVIA 2/1994.

33. Memo by European Division, 16 August 1937, File 811.79690,

PAA/114; Memo Moore to FDR, 21 October 1937, File 811.041, PG/24B, RG 59; Memo FDR to Moore, 15 October 1937, PPF 359, Roosevelt Papers.

34. Minute by Galpin DOCA, 29 December 1937, pt II, AVIA 2/1994.

35. Minute by Phillips, 12 January 1938, ADM 116/3570.

36. Tel. Lindsay to FO, 1 March 1938; Tel. Lindsay to FO, 5 March 1938, FO 371/21514; Conversation Between Moore and Gruening, 16 February 1938, Territories, 9–0–7; Ltr Gruening to Black, 16 February 1938, Territories, 9–12–7, RG 126.

37. Ltr Secretary of Interior to Juan Trippe, 29 March 1938, Territories, 9–12–7, RG 126; Draft Tel. to Washington by Balfour and Fitzmaurice, May 1938; Minute by Balfour, 6 July 1938, FO 371/21516.

38. Memo by Lindsay, 6 June 1938; Ltr Balfour to Jones, 22 July 1938, pt III, AVIA 2/1994; Ltr ADM to Balfour, 16 July 1938, FO 371/21516.

39. Minute by Balfour, 26 October 1938, FO 371/21516.

40. Ltr Cochrane to Slessor, 8 July 1938; Minute by Balfour, 10 May 1938; Tel. Lindsay to FO, 25 October 1938, FO 371/21516.

41. Tel. DO to NZ Govt, 7 November 1938; Summary of Events and Efforts made to secure acceptance of the U.S. Government to a Four Party Conference on Air Communications in the Far East, 21 November 1938, pt III, AVIA 2/1994.

42. Minute by Balfour, 26 October 1938, FO 371/21516; Summary of Events and Efforts made to secure acceptance of the U.S. Government to a Four Party Conference on Air Communications in the Far East, 21 November 1938, pt III, AVIA 2/1994; Record of Meeting in Mr. Butler's Room, 24 November 1938, FO 371/21517.

43. Tel. NZ Govt to DO, 31 December 1938; Tel. Mallet to FO, 2 January 1939, pt IV, AVIA 2/1994; CID Paper 1327 B, 1 December 1938, cited in FO 371/21517.

44. Tel. Lindsay to FO, 17 February 1939; Tel. High Commissioner NZ to DO, 30 March 1939, pt V, AVIA 2/1994.

45. Draft Tel. FO to Mallet, 20 July 1939; Tel. High Commissioner Western Pacific to SS for Colonies, 19 July 1939; Ltr Acheson to Balfour, 13 September 1939; 'Observations on United States Claims to Twenty Three Pacific Islands Hitherto regarded as British', Report by FO, 16 November 1939, pt VI, AVIA 2/1994.

46. Barbara Tuchman (1971), *Stilwell and the American Experience in China,* New York, pp. 107, 121–2, 127, 172–3; Aron Shai (1976), *Origins of the War in the East,* London, p. 15; Ann Trotter (1975), *Britain and East Asia 1933–37,* London, p. 18.

47. Cordell Hull (1948), *The Memoirs of Cordell Hull,* vol. 1, New

York, pp. 531–3; N. Clifford (1963), 'Britain America and the Far East 1937–40: A Failure in Cooperation', *Journal of British Studies*, vol. 3, pp. 137–54; Ltr Chamberlain to Morgenthau, May 1937; Tel. Lindsay to Eden, 1 June 1937, FO 371/20660; Ltr Chamberlain to Davis, 8 July 1937, PREM 1/261; Tel. Eden to Lindsay, 12 July 1937, FO 371/20950; Ltr Eden to Dodds, 12–14 July 1937, FO 371/20955; Department of State, *Foreign Relations of the United States* (hereafter cited as FRUS), vol. 3, 1937, pp. 36–7, 158–60.

48. See Anthony R. Peters (1987), *Anthony Eden at the Foreign Office, 1931–1938*, New York, for details about the Eden–Chamberlain split. See also Lord Avon (1962), *Facing the Dictators*, New York, p. 531; Keith Middlemas (1972), *The Diplomacy of Illusion: The British Government and Germany 1937–39*, London, p. 55; CAB 32 (37), 28 July 1937; CAB 34 (37), 8 September 1937, CAB 23/89.

49. Tel. CO Hong Kong to WO, 29 July 1937, FO 371/20955; Memo by Cadogan, 23 September 1937, FO 371/29956.

50. 'Reinforcement of British Naval Forces in the Far East', Memo by Chatfield, 23 September 1937, CAB 27/634.

51. Memo ADM to FO, 4 October 1937, FO 371/21014.

52. Some authors like Dorothy Borg have argued that it merely implied moral isolation. Others like John McVickar Haight, Jr have suggested that a proposal for a naval blockade was being mooted. Dorothy Borg (1957), 'Notes on Roosevelt's Quarantine Speech', *Political Science Quarterly*, vol. 72, pp. 405–33; Dorothy Borg (1964), *The United States and the Far Eastern Crisis 1933–38*, Harvard, p. 288; John McVickar Haight, Jr (1970), 'Franklin D. Roosevelt and a Naval Quarantine of Japan', *Pacific Historical Review*, vol. 40, pp. 203–26; FRUS, vol. 1, 1937, pp. 665–6.

53. Memo Clive to FO, 2 November 1937, FO 371/21016; Avon, *Facing the Dictators*, p. 538; L.R. Pratt (1971), 'The Anglo-American Naval Conversations on the Far East of January 1938', *International Affairs*, vol. 47, pp. 745–63; C.A. MacDonald (1974), *The Roosevelt Administration and British Appeasement 1933–6*, Oxford, pp. 112–13; William L. Langer and S. Everett Gleason (1952), *The Challenge to Isolation, 1937–40*, New York, p. 23; David Reynolds (1981), *The Creation of the Anglo-American Alliance 1937–41*, London, pp. 30–1.

54. CAB 35 (37), 6 October 1937, CAB 23/89.

55. Quoted by Malcolm Murfet (1984) *Fool-Proof Relations: The Search for Anglo-American Naval Cooperation During the Chamberlain Years 1937–1940*, Singapore, p. 68.

56. Minute by Holman, 5 October 1937; Minute by Orde, 6 October 1937, FO 371/20667.
57. Ltr Chatfield to Vansittart, 5 January 1937, Chatfield Papers.
58. Ltr Chatfield to Little, 6 October 1937, Chatfield Papers.
59. Report of the British Committee on British Shipping, 17 November 1937, CAB 43 (37), CAB 90A; Minute by Cadogan, 26 November 1937, FO 371/20959; 'The Suggested Despatch of Naval Forces to the Far East', Memo by CNS, 29 November 1937, FO 371/20960.
60. Note on Meeting between Davis and FDR, 19 October 1937, PSF Box 88, Roosevelt Papers; Sir R. Clive to FO, 2 November 1937, FO 371/21016; Tel. Eden to Lindsay, 10 November 1937, FO 371/21017.
61. Tel. Lindsay to FO, 1 December 1937, FO 371/20960.
62. Paul Haggie (1981), *Brittania at Bay: The Defence of the British Empire Against Japan, 1931–41*, Oxford, p. 115; CAB 46 (37), 8 December 1937, CAB 23/90 A.
63. Entry 13 December 1937, entry 14 December 1937, Leahy Diary; Harold L. Ickes (1954), *The Secret Diary of Harold L. Ickes* , vol. 2, New York, p. 274; Tel. Lindsay to FO, 14 December 1937, FO 371/21021; Tel. Lindsay to FO, 16 December 1937, FO 371/20961.
64. See Franklin D. Roosevelt (1923), 'Shall We Trust Japan?', *Asia Magazine*, pp. 475–8. See also Roosevelt (1928), 'Our Foreign Policy: A Democratic View', *Foreign Affairs*, vol. 6, p. 555; Ltr Yarnell to Leahy, 18 January 1937, Box 3, Yarnell Papers; Ltr CINCAF to Lt. Col. Thomason NWC, 22 February 1937, Box 67, Series IX, Plans Strategic Studies and Related Correspondence, Records of the Naval Strategic Plans Division.
65. Memo Roosevelt to Edison, 10 February 1938, Official File, Box 4, Roosevelt Papers; James Herzog (1973), *Closing the Open Door: American–Japanese Diplomatic Negotiations 1936–41*, Annapolis, p. 179; Minute by Cadogan, 19 December 1937, FO 371/20961.
66. 'Possible Staff Conversations with the U.S.A.', Memo by the Admiralty, 17 December 1937, ADM 116/3922.
67. Ibid.
68. Ltr Chatfield to Pound, 30 December 1937, Chatfield Papers.
69. Ickes, p. 277; Malcolm H. Murfet (1980), 'Anglo-American Relations in the Period of the Chamberlain Premiership, May 1937–May 1940: The Relationship Between Naval Strategy and Foreign Policy', unpublished PhD thesis, Oxford, p. 126; Tel. Lindsay to FO, 7 January 1938, FO 371/22106.
70. Tel. FO to Lindsay, 1 January 1938; Tel. FO to Lindsay, 7 January 1938, FO 371/22106; Records of Conversation Between Captain Ingersoll USN and the Naval Staff at the Admiralty, 3 January

1938, ADM 1/9822; Report by Ingersoll, undated, Box 116, Series VII, Records relating to Anglo-American-Dutch Cooperation 1938–44, Records of the Naval Strategic Plans Division.

71. Report of Interview Between Chatfield, Ingersoll, Willson and James, 3 January 1938, ADM 116/3922.

72. Ibid.; Pratt, pp. 760–3; Agreed Record of Conversations, January 1938, ADM 116/3922; Minute by Phillips, 12 January 1938, ADM 116/3570.

73. Report by Ingersoll, undated, Box 116, Series VII, Records relating to Anglo-American-Dutch Cooperation 1938–44, Records of the Strategic Plans Division.

74. Borg, *The United States,* p. 511; Tel. Lindsay to FO, 10 January 1938, FO 371/22106; Ickes, p. 269; Leutze, p. 19; Roskill, *Naval Policy*, vol. 2, p. 364; Memo by Cadogan for Chamberlain, 11 January 1938; Minute by Chatfield, 11 January 1938; Ltr Chatfield to Cadogan, 12 January 1938, FO 371/22106.

75. Ltr Ingersoll to Willson, 21 February 1938, Box 116, Series VII, Records relating to Anglo-American-Dutch Cooperation, Records of the Strategic Plans Division.

76. Keith Feiling (1946), *The Life of Neville Chamberlain*, London, p. 324; Reynolds, *The Creation*, p. 20; Minute by Cadogan, 11 January 1938, FO 371/22106. See too Chatfield's comments; Ltr Chatfield to Inskip, 25 January 1938, Chatfield Papers.

77. DBFP, series 3, vol. 8, pp. 278–9; Memo FO to ADM, 23 August 1938; Ltr Jarrett to Ronald FO, 9 August 1938, ADM 116/4087.

78. Minute by Backhouse, 10 January 1939, ADM 116/3922.

79. 'Notes of a Conversation with the U.S. Naval Attaché' by DNI, 9 January 1939, 13 January 1939; Minute by D of P, 10 January 1939, 17 January 1939; Minute by Stanhope, 17 January 1939, ADM 116/3922.

80. F.C. Jones (1954), *Japan's New Order in Asia* , London, pp. 71–98; CAB 51 (38), 31 October 1938, CAB 23/96.

81. Tel. Backhouse to C-in-C East Indies, 5 December 1938, ADM 1/9767.

82. COS 267 Mtg, 13 January 1939, CAB 53/10; 'Malaya – Period Before Relief', Memo by the JPC, COS Paper 848 (JP), 27 February 1939, CAB 53/37; 'European Appreciation', DP (P) 44, 20 February 1939, CAB 53/45; CID 348 Mtg, 24 February 1939, CAB 2/8.

83. CID 362 Mtg, 26 June 1939, CAB 2/9.

84. 'Arguments For and Against the Despatch of a Fleet to the Far East in Wartime', Memo by P.B.B. Nichols, 15 March 1939, FO 371/23981.

85. SAC 1st Mtg, 1 March 1939, CAB 16/209.
86. Some historians such as Norman Gibbs and Lawrence Pratt, have argued that the Admiralty entirely favoured the 'knock out blow'. See Norman Gibbs (1976), *Grand Strategy* vol. 1: *Rearmament Policy*, London, p. 423; Pratt, pp. 179–80. Lawrence Pratt, for example, argues that a 'revolution in British strategy' occurred, contending that 'within a month of its appearance as a serious proposal, and with remarkable ease, the nebulous concept of a Mediterranean offensive had been circulated among, and accepted by, British political and military leadership'. See Pratt, *East of Malta*, pp. 175–6, 179.
87. See SAC 2nd Mtg, 13 March 1939, CAB 16/209, but note 'The Dispatch of a Fleet to the Far East', Note by the First Sea Lord, 28 February 1939; 'Despatch of a Fleet to the Far East', Memo by DCNS, SAC Paper 16, 5 April 1939, CAB 16/209 and OPC Papers 10 and 11, 15 March 1939, Drax Papers.
88. Minute by Danckwerts, 22 March 1939, ADM 1/9909; Minute by Danckwerts, 22 March 1939, ADM 1/9897; AFC (J) 23, 4 May 1939, CAB 29/160.
89. Minute by Danckwerts, 22 March 1939, ADM 1/9909; 'Despatch of a Fleet to the Far East', Memo by DCNS, SAC Paper 16, 5 April 1939, CAB 16/209.
90. Revised Draft Section XVII, Naval War Memorandum Eastern, 25 May 1939, ADM 116/3863; Roskill, *Naval Policy*, vol. 2, p. 462.
91. Minute by Danckwerts, 22 March 1939, ADM 1/9897.
92. Minute by D of P, 5 May 1939, ADM 116/3863; Neale, vol. 2, pp. 140–3; CID 363 Mtg, 11 July 1939, CAB 2/9.
93. 'The Despatch of a Fleet to the Far East', Memo by DCNS, SAC Paper 16, 5 April 1939, CAB 16/183A.
94. Dispatch Pound to ADM, 8 May 1939, 10 May 1939, ADM 116/3900.
95. 'War Plans Report', Memo by JPC, JP Paper 422, 13 June 1939, CAB 55/16.
96. Minute by Vansittart, 21 March 1939, FO 371/23981.
97. 'Allied Plans Against Italy', Memo by JPC, JP Paper 382, 27 March 1939, CAB 55/15.
98. 'Notes on the "Knock-Out Blow" against Italy', Memo by Hollis, 20 July 1939, CAB 21/1426.
99. 'Allied Plans Against Italy', JP Paper 382, 27 March 1939, CAB 55/15; COS 309 Mtg, 19 July 1939.
100. 'Record of the France-British Conversations between General Nogues and General Ironside 4–6 May 1939', Annex to COS 305 Mtg, 28 June 1939, CAB 53/11.

101. 'The Attitude of Italy in War and the Problem of Anglo-French Support to Poland', DP (P) 65, 24 July 1939, CAB 16/183A.
102. Statement by Chatfield, SAC 2nd Mtg, 13 March 1939, CAB 16/209; Minute by Hadow 18 March 1939, FO 371/23981; 'New Zealand Co-operation in Imperial Defence', COS Paper 832, 1 February 1939, CAB 53/48.
103. 'New Zealand Defence Conference', Report by Sir Arthur Longmore, Addenda to COS 298 Mtg, 1 June 1939, CAB 53/11.
104. COS 298 Mtg, 25 May 1939, CAB 53/11; COS Paper 937 (JP), 3 July 1939, CAB 53/51.
105. AFC (J) 17, 20 April 1939, CAB 29/160
106. AFC (J) 23, 4 May 1939; AFC (J) 54, 8 May 1939, CAB 29/160.
107. Gibbs, *Grand Strategy*, pp. 675–6; W. David McIntyre (1979), *The Rise and Fall of the Singapore Naval Base 1919–1942*, London, p. 150; Tel. Lindsay to Hallifax, 11 April 1939, FO 371/23982.
108. AFC (J) 65, 5 May 1939, CAB 29/160; Minute by Stanhope, 26 April 1939, ADM 116/3922.
109. CAB 12 (39), 18 March 1939, CAB 23/98; SAC 2nd Mtg, 13 March 1939, CAB 16/209; 'Despatch of a Fleet to the Far East', SAC Paper 16, 5 April 1939, CAB 16/183A; DP (P) 44, 22 February 1939, CAB 16/183A; CID 348 Mtg, 24 February 1939, CAB 2/8.
110. AFC (J) 45, 25 April 1939; AFC 11 Mtg, 25 April 1939, CAB 29/160; FRUS, vol. 2, 1939, p. 88; Minute by the PM's Private Secretary, 28 April 1939, FO 371/23560.
111. Tel. FO to Lindsay, 19 March 1939, FO 371/23560.
112. Tel. Lindsay to FO, 14 April 1939, FO 371/23561; Minute S.H. Phillips to FO, 29 March 1939, FO 371/2354; Minute by First Sea Lord, 27 March 1939, ADM 116/3922.
113. Minute by D of P, 22 March 1939, ADM 116/3922.
114. Minute by First Sea Lord, 27 March 1939, ADM 116/3922; SAC Paper 16, 5 April 1939, CAB 16/183A.
115. Minute by Naval Attaché British Embassy Washington, 12 April 1939, FO 115/3417/70.
116. MacDonald, *The Roosevelt Administration*, p. 149; Robert Dallek (1979), *Franklin D. Roosevelt and American Foreign Policy 1932–45*, New York, pp. 174, 183–4; Tel. Lindsay to FO, 2 May 1939; Tel. Lindsay to FO, 8 May 1939, cited in ADM 116/3922; Memo Danckwerts to Hampton, 22 May 1939, FO 371/23561; Minute by Stanhope, 26 April 1939, ADM 116/3922.
117. 'Report of the Meeting held on 12 June 1939', Memo by Commander Hampton; 'Report of the Meeting held on 14 June 1939', Memo by Commander Hampton, ADM 116/3922.

118. Aron Shai (1974), 'Was There A Far Eastern Munich?', *Journal of Contemporary History,* vol. 9, pp. 161–9; CAB 33 (39), 21 June 1939, CAB 23/100; CP (162) 39, 16 June 1939, CAB 24/288; FP (36) 94, 16 June 1939, CAB 27/627.

119. Minute by D of P, 16 August 1938, ADM 1/9530; Minute by D of P, 11 April 1939, ADM 116/4087.

120. Minute by Gelmer for Head of M, 20 March 1939, China Secret Envelope no. 1, 24 April 1939, ADM 116/4635.

121. 'Report of the Anglo-French Conference held at Singapore 22–27 June 1939', COS Paper 941, 11 July 1939, CAB 53/52.

122. DCOS 183 Mtg, 14 August 1939; Minute by Clarke, 1 September 1939; Minute by Benan, 4 September 1939, Annex to DCOS 183 Mtg, 21 June 1939, CAB 27/625.

123. Cabinet Committee on Foreign Policy 54 Mtg, 21 June 1939, CAB 27/625; 'Situation in the Far East', COS Paper 931, 24 June 1939, CAB 53/50; COS 304 Mtg, 20 June 1939, CAB 53/11; Naval War Memorandum Eastern, March 1939, ADM 116/4393.

124. See for example John McCarthy (1976), *Australia and Imperial Defence 1918–1939*, St Lucia, Qld; David Day (1988), *The Great Betrayal: Britain, Australia and the Onset of the Pacific War*, North Ryde, NSW; Ian Hamill (1981), *The Strategic Illusion*, Singapore.

125. This view can be clearly seen in the following documents: Minute by Phillips, 28 June 1939; Minute by D of P, 28 June 1939, ADM 116/3922; FP 36 (94), 16 June 1939, CAB 27/627; 'The Situation in the Far East', COS Paper 928, 18 June 1939, CAB 53/50; Cabinet Committee on Foreign Policy 54 Mtg, 21 June 1939, CAB 27/625; Minute by D of P, 12 June 1939; Minute by First Sea Lord, 13 June 1939; Tel. Lindsay to FO, 15 June 1939, ADM 116/3767. For information about British government policy towards China see Bradford A. Lee (1973), *Britain and the Sino-Japanese War 1937–39*, London, pp. 179–80.

126. W.L. Langer and S.E. Gleason (1952), *The Challenge to Isolation 1937–40*, London, pp. 152–3; Louis Morton (1959), 'Evolution of War Plan "Orange"', *World Politics*, vol. 2, p. 257; Grace Haynes (1963), *History of the Joint Chiefs of Staff*, Washington, p. 5; Maurice Matloff and Edward Snell (1953), *Strategic Planning for Coalition Warfare 1941–42*, Washington, p. 5.

127. 'Are We Ready No. 1', Memo Chrmn GB to JB, 21 August 1939, Microfilm Roll 5, Strategic Planning in the U.S. Navy: Its Evolution and Execution 1891–45, Scholarly Resources, Inc.

128. James H. Herzog (1964), 'The Role of the United States Navy in the Evolution and Execution of American Foreign Policy 1936–

41', unpublished PhD thesis, Brown University, p. 198; Matloff and Snell, *Strategic Planning*, p. 8.

129. Ltr CINUS to CNO, 6 December 1939, Roll 31, Fleet Problem 21–1940, M 964, Record of Fleet Problems.
130. 'Observations on United States Claims to Twenty Three Pacific Islands Hitherto regarded as British', Report by FO, 16 November 1939, pt VI, AVIA 2/1994.
131. It is difficult to see, as Leutze suggests, the development of an ongoing relationship between 1938 and 1939, though he is correct in emphasizing the emergence of a sense of mutual need. See Leutze, *Bargaining*, chapters 2 and 3.

–4–

Britain Cedes the Initiative: The Road to ABC-1

Prior to 1940, neither Britain nor the United States believed a full-scale commitment to each other was either desirable or necessary. The Chamberlain administration resented the United States's 'unwarranted interference' with their plans in Europe and was distrustful of US activities in the Pacific, while Roosevelt's administration was constrained by its fear of war and the indifference of Congress and public opinion. Nevertheless, by mid-1940 cooperation between the two nations had become essential, not from desire but from need, not as a result of freedom of choice but from the pressure of events. The United States hoped the Royal Navy could provide security for itself in the Atlantic, while the protection of the British Commonwealth in the Far East became increasingly dependent upon a heavy American naval presence.

Outbreak of the War in Europe

When war broke out in September 1939, the Admiralty found itself in a better strategic position than had been anticipated by the planners. Both Italy and Japan declared their neutrality, leaving Britain in the advantageous position of facing only one belligerent. The Royal Navy's transition from peace to war went reasonably smoothly. By 3 September most of the vessels of the Home Fleet were on station, while the Mediterranean Fleet was already concentrated at Alexandria.[1]

Despite these advantages, Britain's limited number of secondary vessels meant there were difficulties in providing sufficient trade protection for the Atlantic. The need to form hunter-killer groups worldwide to counter the raider menace, together with the material required for Operation 'Catherine',[2] placed additional strain on the Royal Navy's already overburdened resources.[3] As early as 7 September the Admiralty was seriously contemplating the complete withdrawal of all cruisers and destroyers from both the Indian Ocean and the Mediterranean, and Admiral Drax even anticipated that it would be six months before any kind of offensive at sea could be launched. In November, Churchill cancelled work on the battleships *Lion* and *Temeraire* to make up critical deficiencies in convoy escorts. Despite vehement protests from naval staff, production was concentrated on armoured merchant cruisers in the hope that one million tons of shipping might be completed in one year.[4]

At the Commonwealth Conference in London in November 1939, it was promised that if a choice between theatres was necessary the Far East would continue to take precedence over the Mediterranean. Significantly, however, such a decision would be taken only if the security of Australia and New Zealand was directly threatened. Even before the Conference began it was obvious that the Chamberlain government was looking to the United States 'to take the lead in holding the fort in the Pacific'. On 2 November the British War Cabinet cabled Lord Lothian, the British Ambassador in Washington, about probable American reactions to Japanese raids against the coastlines of the Antipodes. Lothian replied that since the central Pacific was now an American preserve, the US would be at war long before Australia and New Zealand were endangered. While the Foreign Office recognized that the United States would not act as trustees for British Far Eastern possessions, it was expected that the US Navy 'would act as a watchman who, by patrolling his own house, acts as a deterrent to a burglar who might otherwise approach the house next door'.[5]

Even though the Italians had made arrangements to inform the Admiralty about movements of their warships, Royal Navy staff remained suspicious of Italian neutrality. Admiral Pound determined that the Admiralty must not be caught out as she had been during the Ethiopian crisis, and by 30 March 1940 the transfer of sizable forces to the Mediterranean was arranged. By the following month the First Battle Squadron, consisting of *Warspite*, *Malaya*, *Ramillies* and *Royal Sovereign*, together with the carrier *Eagle*, two squadrons of cruisers and two and one-half flotillas of destroyers, were operating out of Alexandria while a second fleet was created at Gibraltar.[6]

Following the occupation of Denmark in April, German air and seaborne forces landed in southern Norway. Britain and France were forced to abandon the attempt to establish Allied forces at Trondheim in Central Norway. On 10 May, as a direct result of the German invasion of the Low Countries and because of the discontent surrounding the Norwegian campaign, the Chamberlain government fell and a National Coalition took office with Churchill as Prime Minister. After four days of fighting the Netherlands Government was compelled to surrender; on 14 May German armoured columns broke through the French defences on the Meuse and swept towards the Channel. On 28 May the Belgian

Army surrendered, and the following day the British began withdrawing the greater part of their expeditionary force from Dunkirk, completing most of this evacuation by 4 June. The next day the Germans began their first attacks on the reformed French defence lines, which gave way after three days. On 10 June, confident that the Allies were defeated, the Italian Government declared war on Britain and France. On 17 June the new head of the French Government, General Pétain, sued for peace.[7]

Far Eastern Strategy Transformed

While the collapse on the Western Front was taking place, Japan was applying increasing pressure on Churchill's new administration. In June the Secretary of State for Foreign Affairs, Lord Halifax, was told by the British Military Attaché in Tokyo that unless Britain closed the Hong Kong frontier and the Burma Road, war with Japan was inevitable.[8] The British now concluded that the need to contain the Italian Fleet, pressures in home waters and in the North Atlantic and the ramifications of the French defeat meant Britain was incapable of sending a fleet to Singapore. The four capital ships, five modern and two old cruisers, one aircraft carrier, twenty-three destroyers and nine submarines that made up the Mediterranean Fleet – even if transferred to the Far East in their entirety – were plainly inadequate to meet the full concentrated strength of the Japanese Navy; at best such naval forces could only act as a deterrent.

In any case, naval staff doubted that the ships would even be able to reach their destination in time; they feared that unless the fleet was based at Singapore prior to the outbreak of war, it would probably be intercepted en route.[9] Many vessels were already involved either on escort duty in the North Atlantic or in the Norwegian campaign. *Malaya*'s steering gear was on the point of collapse, *Ramillies* needed her stern bushes realigned and replacement 15-inch guns for one turret and *Warspite* was long overdue for dry docking. The Mediterranean Fleet had been heavily involved in the bombardment of the Dodecanese and was in dire need of repair. In fact the whole situation in that theatre had become so desperate that complete withdrawal was once again being seriously considered. Only the partial destruction of the French Fleet at Mers-el-Kebir relieved the pressure.[10]

Japanese presence in southern China and Hainan, the development of airfields in Thailand and the vulnerability of French IndoChina to pressure now made an overland attack on Malaya a more distinct possibility and placed Singapore within reach of hostile land-based aircraft. The Chiefs of Staff found it necessary to defend not merely

Singapore Island but all of the Malay Peninsula. Emphasis in Far Eastern defence – in their view – had switched from seapower to airpower, though they admitted 'air forces required to implement that policy, however, cannot be provided for some time to come'. Colombo and Trincomalee were now preferred by the Admiralty to the more vulnerable Eastern bases.[11]

There were two possible strategies for Britain in the Far East. Defence could be decentralized and control passed to Australia until the European situation stabilized. It had already been recommended that Australia furnish two divisions for service in Malaya, and the Chiefs of Staff hoped Singapore's air strength would be augmented by two fighter and two reconnaissance squadrons.[12] The United States might also be persuaded or 'induced' to help safeguard British possessions while some financial assistance to China would tie down Japanese forces and preserve the 'status quo'. Alternatively, the government would have to seek a general settlement with Japan on the widest possible lines. This option was backed by the Chief of the Imperial General Staff and the Joint Planning Sub-Committee, but was opposed by the Foreign Office and the Prime Minister. The basis of their criticism was that any such agreement with Japan would of necessity have to involve the United States – already known to be hostile to such negotiations – and would necessitate enormous concessions on Britain's part.[13] As the Admiralty pointed out:

> Committed as we are in Europe and without the help of France, we must avoid an open clash with Japan. A general settlement, including economic concessions to Japan is desirable. But the prospects are not at present favourable. Failing this settlement, our general policy must be to play for time, cede nothing until we must, and build up our defences as soon as we can.[14]

In the event of a Japanese attack on Singapore, Australia or New Zealand, Lord Ismay still promised the Dominions 'timely resistance' by Britain, though this could not take the form of stationing a fleet at Singapore before the outbreak of hostilities. The Chiefs of Staff felt that there would still be time to concentrate ships 'to the eastward in ample time to prevent disaster', while the Prime Minister regarded Singapore as a powerful fortress, one easily capable of holding out for some considerable time. Because he felt the primary defence of the base rested with the fleet and 'the great potentialities of seapower', he opposed the Chiefs of Staff recommendations that the whole of Malaya be defended. Churchill felt Japan would be unlikely to advance southward while involved in China unless Britain was defeated by Germany;

he generally underrated Japan's military capabilities.[15] In any case, as Churchill announced to the War Cabinet on 8 August 1940, the risk of heavy attack on Egypt meant Britain must continue to concentrate on the defeat of Italy. Even during the early phases of an Anglo-Japanese war, when it was likely Singapore would be attacked, the Mediterranean Fleet would be retained at Alexandria, and only in the event of an actual invasion of Australia and New Zealand would the Mediterranean be abandoned and forces rushed to the assistance of the Dominions.[16]

Churchill, like Chamberlain, had never been a supporter of the idea of despatching a fleet to the Far East, nor had he ever looked with favour on the Singapore naval base. In 1925 when Chancellor of the Exchequer, he had remarked dismissively that Singapore was 'just another link in the chain of Imperial communications'. The base was merely a 'moral guarantee' to Australia and New Zealand, but he did not feel that Japan would attempt to invade 'in our lifetime or that of our children.' At one CID meeting he deprecated even competitive naval building against Japan, demanding the formation of a sub-committee to review and revise not only the role of the base in defence strategy but also the choice of site and the method of defence. On the very day Cabinet approved the construction of a Far Eastern floating dock, Churchill turned a discussion of the Admiralty's cruiser replacement programme into a review of the Singapore strategy in the hope of delaying or reducing expenditure on warship construction.[17]

By 1940, if war broke out, Churchill hoped the Admiralty would be able to spare the *Hood*, two 'R' class, three cruisers and twelve submarines for the Far East, but Pound felt only one battlecruiser (probably *Renown*) and the carrier *Ark Royal*, together with two cruisers and fourteen destroyers from the Mediterranean Fleet and Force H, could be made available, and these could be sent only as far as Trincomalee. The Chiefs of Staff concluded that the Eastern Fleet would probably be better employed on trade protection duties than in dubious fleet encounters. Reluctantly, Churchill agreed: 'I pray that we may never have to make this widespread distribution, but I am in full agreement with the principles on which the Admiralty would propose to meet the strain'.[18]

Recognizing that there were barely enough ships to cover the East Indian sea lanes, Dudley Pound opposed any extension of cooperative defence measures to the Netherlands East Indies. He feared such activity in the Far East might prejudice the effort against Germany, his criticisms being partly based on the Admiralty's traditional opposition to alliance systems (seen already in relation to France and the United States). It was unanimously agreed by the Chiefs of Staff that if Britain could be certain the United States would go to war over the Netherlands East Indies, she would follow suit. However, there was a difference of opinion between the First Sea Lord, the Chief of the Imperial General Staff, and the Chief of the Air Staff about what to do in the absence of US support. The dispute was finally brought before Churchill, who felt Britain could not afford to wait until Australia and New Zealand were isolated and Japan was making preparations for an attack on Singapore; but he remained confident that the United States could not remain indifferent to such a Japanese invasion. As a result, the War Cabinet instructed the Chiefs of Staff to prepare an appreciation on the basis that support would be given to the Dutch, but this remained a contentious issue.[19]

The Prospects for Anglo-American Staff Talks

Early in 1940 the United States was only a marginal British supply source, providing material unobtainable from domestic production or from within the sterling bloc area. Once the German attack opened in the West, however, the Government began pressing the United States to sell 'surplus equipment' such as aircraft and destroyers. To guarantee supplies, Britain was most anxious that the US should enter the war. Britain became as dependent on an American presence in the Atlantic as it was on an American presence in the Pacific.

Given the United Kingdom's strategic position and past experience in previous military negotiations, it seemed natural to the British that the Admiralty should take the lead in exploring and developing the scope of any American commitment to Britain and to the European conflict. To facilitate such cooperation Admiral Sir Sydney Bailey, a former Director of Plans, and Captain Curzon-Howe, British Naval Attaché in Washington, were recalled to head a new Committee which was set up to examine the forms that US naval operational assistance might take. Information about the direction of the United States Far Eastern policy, the degree of US commitment to the Pacific and the extent to which the US might be prepared to take on additional responsibilities in both regions was required. It was felt the best method of exchange would be by way of a staff conference between the respective service representatives, along the lines of the Anglo-French meetings of the previous year. Captain Arthur W. Clarke was appointed Chief of Mission and Liaison Director in Washington in case that city became the venue for such talks.

The report of the Bailey Committee, completed on 15 July, was based on the assumption that the United States would enter the war in Europe as Britain's ally. The report outlined some twelve possible areas of close cooperation, and also incorporated a considerable body of information about the workings of the Admiralty from tactical issues such as gunnery, minelaying and the use of naval airpower to strategic issues such as intelligence and problems in communications. Its arrangements extended from convoying and command matters in the Bay of Biscay to the basing of American capital ships at Singapore. Before the report was submitted to Washington, however, some provisions were excluded from the final report, including some sensitive technical details which would be obviously unpalatable to the US Navy Department. The Committee continued to act as a main centre for information, and in the second half of 1940 no less than 395 enquiries from the United States were answered.[20]

By mid-October the British Joint Planning Committee had drawn up a draft outline for conversation recommendations. Talks in London and Washington would deal with the general implications of US involvement and the extent to which the US would make up British Far Eastern deficiencies. Talks in the Far East would handle any specific problems as well as the details of coordination. The format of the talks duplicated American planning methodology; just like War Plan 'Orange', conversations would move from discussion of general principles at the higher command levels to consideration of particulars at the field command level. An Anglo-American Standardisation of Arms Committee and an Anglo-Dutch-American (ADA) Committee were formed to implement the agreed accord.[21]

America Foreign Policy and the Far East

At various times in 1940 it did seem that Roosevelt's administration would take a stronger line in the Far East, but at other times this possibility seemed as remote as ever. British naval planners were undoubtedly deceived by the vagaries and vicissitudes of United States Far Eastern diplomacy. Late in 1939, Ambassador Craigie in Tokyo and Parliamentary Undersecretary R.A. Butler had both stressed the desirability of an active settlement of the Sino-Japanese conflict. Even the Chiefs of Staff argued that Britain must avoid war with Japan 'at any cost'. Japanese pressure during the first half of 1940 aimed at forcing a British withdrawal from China, and the Admiralty had been eager to comply. However, Lothian reported from Washington that Roosevelt intended to retain US forces there indefinitely. The President expressed the hope that Britain and France would only withdraw because of force majeure and not by agreement with Japan, and the British had reluctantly agreed.[22]

Nevertheless the US State Department was more sensitive to

Japanese presence and dominance in Southeast Asia than it had been in 1938 or 1939. When the US-Japanese trade treaty expired on 26 January 1940, an investigation was begun into the possibility of applying economic pressure on Japan. By February reports concerning this reached the Foreign Office. Early in April the Japanese declared a special economic interest in the Netherlands East Indies. The US Secretary of State, Cordell Hull, immediately declared preservation of the status quo in the region to be the cardinal aim of US policy. Hull's statement had the effect of strengthening Britain's own resolve; Britain secretly declared its involvement in any conflict between Japan and the Netherlands East Indies to be dependent on the United States, if not on the extent of any US commitment.

On 23 September 1940, demands for bases in IndoChina led to the entry of Japanese troops into the northern half of the country. Under the terms of the Tripartite Pact, Japan's 'New Order in Asia' was acknowledged by the Axis in return for the recognition of German and Italian conquests in Europe. The proposals were decidedly anti-American; each participant was pledged to assist the other if attacked by 'a power at present not involved in the European war or in the Chinese-Japanese conflict'. Japanese aggression also forced closure of the Burma Road. The Foreign Office made enquiries about the kind of support the United States could provide if the road was re-opened. Hull agreed on the need for re-opening, feeling the British, Dutch, Australians and Americans should have 'private conversations on technical problems which would be involved in common action for defence in the near future'. Nevertheless, he emphasized such talks must be purely 'technical' and not concerned with 'political policy', because the administration would not enter into political pledges, and he warned that any US commitment to a Far Eastern war would undoubtedly cut down supplies to Britain. Still, the British Chiefs of Staff were impressed. Previously they had decided not to regard violation of the Netherlands East Indies as a *casus belli*, but they now reversed that decision.[23]

There were even indications that the United States might be prepared to take on additional military responsibilities. On 16 April 1940, the US Naval Attaché, Captain Alan G. Kirk, suggested a plan to forestall further Japanese advances by transferring the US Fleet to the Philippines, though he pointed out that Manila's facilities were unsuitable for fleet purposes. Given the thrust of the Hampton discussions from the previous year, the Vice Chief of Naval Staff, Tom Phillips, concluded that the US Navy Department was hinting at possible use of Singapore by US warships. Washington was assured by the War Cabinet that the base would be available. Once again, however, it turned out Kirk was acting entirely on his own initiative and without approval.[24]

In December 1939 the so-called 'moral' embargo already existing on the sale of aircraft to Japan was expanded to include materials, machinery and manufacturing plants. Though such a policy was more psychological than economic, it became part of the State Department's tougher line in the Far East. The embargo was extended in the second half of the year to aviation gasoline, iron and steel scrap and machine tools. The economic and military elements of State Department policy became inextricably linked. The major portion of the US Fleet, less the newly established Atlantic Squadron, left its west coast base at San Diego on 2 April 1940 – in keeping with its normal operating procedure – for fleet exercises off Hawaii. According to the original schedule, worked out in 1939, it was intended the fleet leave Pearl Harbor on 9 May and return to the mainland. But on 7 May Stark informed CINCUS, Admiral Richardson, that all vessels were to be retained there for another two weeks, and by 15 May the decision had been taken to operate the fleet there 'for some time'. As part of a political rather than a military manoeuvre, and almost by default, the wholly unsatisfactory and poorly served Pearl Harbor became the main fleet base for the US Navy.[25] US naval staff were quite aware of the dangers of this:

> The retention of the major concentration of the U.S. Fleet in the Pacific is a restraining influence against Japanese movement towards the Philippines, Guam, or the Dutch East Indies. However, the Fleet will serve this purpose only so long as other manifestations of government policy do not let it appear that the location of the Fleet is only a bluff.[26]

The United States was now trapped by its own strategy. Any reduction in the strength of the fleet at Hawaii would automatically require concomitant increases in economic pressure to compensate. Twice during 1940 Stark tried unsuccessfully to convince the President to return the fleet to the west coast, but Roosevelt was not prepared to let the United States 'lose face' diplomatically. The failure of the State Department to prevent Japan from signing the Tripartite Pact or from occupying Northern IndoChina drew Roosevelt's administration inexorably first towards supplementing, and then towards extending pressure on Japan.

Thus in the end, Britain's confidence in the United States was never really justified. US policy was directed more towards keeping the war away from the Americas and the Panama Canal than towards support for the Allied or British cause. The creation of a Western Hemisphere Neutrality Zone, extending 300 miles around home waters, was nothing more than an adaptation of a quarantine-blockade scheme first announced by Roosevelt in 1937, and an extension to the Monroe Doctrine's traditional framework. Roosevelt was clearly anxious that the Western Front in Europe be maintained, but he sought to aid the Allies without the entanglements that had drawn the United States into the First World War.[27] The President's initial reaction to the opening of the German offensive on 10 May had been to intensify his efforts to aid the democracies in Europe by exploiting a 'loophole' in the Neutrality Act to secure the release of US military equipment for sale to the Allies. On 16 May the President went before Congress to ask for a massive appropriation for American defence, a measure intended to create sufficient forces for a two-front war. The US Army would be built up to 1,600,000 men. The General Board favoured the introduction of universal military training, but US public opinion was not yet ready for such a step. A selective form of service was introduced instead, but it was estimated it would be March 1941 before a single new army corps could be created. Even this 'balanced military force' could not be established without a 50 per cent reduction in ammunition allotment.[28] The President spoke of 50,000 planes a year, but with three to eight month delays in production even under the old 5,500 aircraft plan, the United States had on hand only 49 new bombers and 150 new pursuit aircraft. It would be 1943 before the United States even approached a two-power standard.[29]

US naval planners therefore estimated it would take a year before the United States could launch any kind of large-scale offensive. On 22 May they urged the President to conserve US military resources by concentrating on hemispheric defence. Counter-attacks, they argued, should be limited to Mexico and South America. Rainbow 1 immediately gained Presidential approval, and by 12 July it had been distributed to all commands. On their own initiative, the Joint Planning Committee renewed work on Rainbow 2. Of particular concern was the danger of an early British collapse. So pessimistic were the planners about the European situation that they recommended protective occupation of British, French and Dutch possessions in the Western Hemisphere (such as Canada and Newfoundland) as well as potential island bases in the Pacific such as Christmas, Washington, Fanning and the Phoenix and Gilbert groups. The Navy Department had not forgotten Britain's lack of cooperation over US territorial demands in the Pacific. On 22 June, after nearly 130 million rounds of ammunition – representing nearly one-quarter of Army stocks – had been despatched to Britain, Marshall and Stark sought to establish a ban on the sales of further military supplies. The President avoided making a definite decision, but he did drop plans to sell Britain twelve B-17s, and he agreed that new orders would only be forthcoming if sales did not affect the United States own procurement. Britain would have to prove that it could survive. By 2 July 1940, the Walsh Amendment prohibiting the sale of equipment considered essential for US defence had been passed.[30]

Resolutions favouring a complete embargo on Japan had been shelved by both Houses in February. Late in June the British and Australian governments asked the State Department to cooperate either in appeasing or opposing Japan. Hull had rejected both alternatives, arguing that American policy was designed to avoid conflict with Japan but not to assent to her actions.[31] In mid-October Roosevelt's Liaison Committee met to discuss the implications of the Tripartite Pact. Among other options, the President considered peacetime reinforcement of the Asiatic Fleet and a complete embargo on all US trade with Japan. When Lothian first suggested talks in May 1940, Roosevelt had evaded the question of staff conversations by resurrecting his 1938 patrol line scheme.[32] He now returned to this idea, suggesting the formation of a picket line from Honolulu to the Philippines and from Samoa to Singapore. Alternatively, special naval missions would increase 'tension pressure' on Japan. Cruisers, accompanied by tankers, would circuit the Pacific at will, appearing and reappearing at isolated points in the Far East and in northern waters. Such trans-Pacific cruises by warship detachments, he hoped, would unnerve the Japanese and prevent the outbreak of war.[33]

Visits were tentatively arranged to Australia and Singapore, but opposition from the Navy's field commanders was vehement. They regarded such action as 'too provocative' and protested at the diversion of vital resources and fuel. The Eastern section of the State Department agreed. Hainan was now occupied by Japan and Singapore was well within range of Japanese submarines. Stark and Marshall felt the timing of such manoeuvres was 'inopportune', if not strategically foolish. Under-Secretary of State Sumner Welles pointed out that neither the State Department nor any member of the Navy could ever agree to such dispositions. With the Presidential elections pending, Roosevelt was especially anxious to avoid risks and deferred making a decision, but it was obvious he intended to return to this issue at a later date.[34]

There was similar confusion about Anglo-American staff talks. Having made the decision to run for an unprecedented third term in office, Roosevelt desired to avoid any suggestion of collusion with Britain. He was particularly sensitive to criticism from the press and from public opinion. Suggestions for a military meeting had been put forward by Lord Lothian on 25 May, but the President discounted the notion that America might ever become involved in a Far Eastern war. Only by promising to discuss British dispositions in the event of surrender was Lothian able to find a way round this impasse.

Roosevelt wanted to limit any 'conference' to a simple exchange between representatives from the Navy Department, the Admiralty and the naval attachés in Washington and London. He was less interested in aiding the UK and more interested in strengthening US defences in case of a British collapse. He envisaged purely naval talks to deal with such issues as the surrender of the French Fleet, the expected entry of Spain into the war and the invasion of Britain.[35] As the President told Rear-Admiral Robert L. Ghormley, the Special Naval Representative for the 'mission', the overall objective for future conversations was be to evaluate British chances of survival.[36] For their part, the Admiralty and the Bailey Committee expected the extent of any US commitment to the war in Europe would be discussed. US suggestions for 'technical' meetings were seen as an extension of the scope of the original conversations of 1938. However, fearful of a breach of security, Churchill was loath to reveal Britain's Atlantic naval dispositions and was just as reluctant to proceed with a staff conference. Halifax, the British Foreign Secretary, was only able to persuade him by promising the Far Eastern situation would be dealt with as well. A US team finally arrived in Liverpool on 15 August 1940.[37]

The American Mission to London

The American Mission consisted of Ghormley, Lieutenant-Commander Bernard Austin and Lieutenant Donald J. MacDonald on the naval side, Major General Delos Emmons from the Army Air Corps and Brigadier General Strong from the Army War Plans Division. Surveys of British defences were conducted, an outline of British strategy and production schedules was provided and a copy of the edited Bailey Committee Report was given to Ghormley for transmission to Washington.[38]

There was, however, a lack of firm direction behind the initiative. The President emphasized that the US representatives were merely observers and could make no political commitments.[39] Strong hoped better coordination of requests for lend-lease on the British side might solve some of the US's own supply problems. Ghormley saw it as purely a fact-finding mission and preferred to promote the exchange of technical information. Having accomplished within a short time all that was possible under their instructions, Emmons and Strong returned home to Washington in September. As professional officers, both men were impressed with the determination of the British to continue to wage war, but they pointed to the distinctly unfavourable naval situation, the dispersal of troops which was seen as weakening defensive capability and the 'ad hoc' running of the economy 'on a day to day basis' which stultified production. A distinctly pessimistic picture of a Britain with a 'dubious future' emerged. Nevertheless, both felt that German air power alone would not decide the issue. Britain was expected to survive for another six months.[40]

Ghormley remained behind in London, and some fourteen meetings were held between him and the Anglo-American Standardisation of Arms Committee. The purpose of these talks was to discuss any criticisms of the Bailey Committee Report by US naval authorities. Initially disappointed that the visit was not a full staff mission, both the Admiralty and the Joint Planning Committee continued to hope that the Americans could be induced or manoeuvred into a conference, and Ghormley himself was the key to this. British authorities saw these meetings as a means to an end; US authorities saw them as an end in themselves. While one side was trying to limit the talks, the other side was struggling hard to expand them.[41]

Ghormley sought to remain 'fireproof' against British overtures. He was prepared to discuss Far Eastern defence questions, but only on his own initiative. He constantly stressed that the opinions expressed must not be seen as official Navy Department policy and that he could make no political commitments. He plainly felt that one man at the end of a long and poorly maintained line of communications was inadequate for the task. Ghormley had good reason to be cautious; in 1917 Admiral Sims was in a similar position and was converted to the British point of view. His Anglophile approach alienated him from the Navy Department and led to a dramatic investigation of his motives and a premature end to his naval career. No one needed to remind Ghormley that he had not been briefed about staff talks.[42] From his actions the British authorities concluded that Roosevelt was waiting for the US elections before committing the United States to a full conference if not the war. Once again they were misreading the signals.[43]

American War Planning and the Far East

Potential aggressors now lay on two fronts. The United States itself was in the process of creating a two-power standard, but this was designed only to provide security in the long term. If war broke out before 1944 the US Navy would face a considerable dilemma, with bases vulnerable to attack and a fleet insufficient to its tasks, and so would have to fight over the short term within its limited resources. Stop gap measures would therefore be necessary until such time as a margin of superiority could be re-established. Any method, means or policy which could relieve the burden was welcomed by US naval staff. The main problem was one of finding the correct balance between risks and diplomatic/ military priorities. There was a profusion of choice: whether to appease potential enemies or seek potential friends, whether to assign priority to one theatre or another, whether friends were likely to reliable or non-cooperative. In other words, the United States faced the same strategic dilemma that had proved so troublesome to Britain from 1937 to 1939.

However, American planners were in even greater disarray. The constantly changing international scene in 1940, the relations between neutrals and belligerents, the need to monitor priorities in production, the alteration in the relative strengths of opposing coalitions – due to fluctuations in the military situation – overwhelmed US military staffs. It proved difficult to formulate a strategic approach in the absence of any firm political directives. Opposition to an offensive strategy from within their own ranks continued to grow. On 1 May 1940 a meeting was held in the office of the Chief of Naval Operations to discuss the war plans situation. Some naval officers continued to favour offensive action in the Marshalls and the Carolines, but success there was felt to be dependent on early aerial and submarine reconnaissance. Yarnell's scheme for a war of economic blockade was discussed, but while Stark remained 'open minded' about this, he was reluctant to project operations too far west of Hawaii, and because of acute fuel shortages refused to sanction planning past the sixty-day mark.

The Rainbow Plans were part of an evolutionary process. Rainbow 4 directly related to Rainbow 1; Rainbow 3 was but a modified version of Rainbow 2, and Rainbow 5 in turn owed a great deal to the principles already established by earlier planning under War Plans 'Red' and 'Black'. Out of the muddle that was Rainbow 2, certain fundamentals about the war and the way in which it would be fought emerged and became part and parcel of US defence strategy down to the outbreak of war in the Pacific. The concept of a Far Eastern war had undergone quite a transformation since the days of War Plan 'Orange'; the idea of a limited war fought with limited means was now one of the key elements of US naval planning. This had been forced upon the Navy Department by its lack of resources, the limitations in its facilities and the needs of the Atlantic, but in other ways it was a reflection of the obvious distaste for offensive warfare felt by Congress and the American public. By mid-1940 the ultimate defeat of Japan was no longer the primary objective; rather, the United States sought merely to preserve the status quo in economic and territorial terms:

> The terms of the coalition implied in the Directive are that the United States will undertake to sustain the interests of the Democracies in the Pacific. The members of the coalition should understand that this does not mean the

economic and military crushing of Japan, or the exchange of the domination of the Far East by Japan for the domination of the Far East by the United States. The United States has no interest in becoming the dominating Far Eastern power, and enjoys an economic position in relation to Japan that it does not care to destroy completely.[44]

US interests in the Far East were also seen as being of much less value to the United States than the interests and possessions of Britain, France and the Netherlands East Indies were to the 'Allied powers'.[45] Rainbow 2 insisted that those nations directly involved must make 'a material contribution to the concerted effort of defence of the Far Eastern theatre', and at a minimum Britain was expected to send at least three battleships to Singapore. Even at this early stage, the main differences between British and US Far Eastern strategies were being drawn; these principles were directly opposed by Admiralty plans.

In the first half of 1940 Rainbow 2 was the current Far Eastern war plan, but it was a strategy hamstrung by the fierce debate surrounding the nature of any Far Eastern war. As it envisaged the advance of the US Fleet to the East Indies via the trans-Pacific route, the plan supported the improvement of facilities at Cavite and Guam up to fleet level. Yet the plan also recognized that once the Fleet reached its destination logistics would be impossible to maintain without Japan interdicting the lines of communication. Emphasis was laid upon the need to deter a Japanese offensive to the south by a speedy American advance, yet when the strategy was tested by the Naval War College it was discovered that the war would continue for almost two years before any advance could be contemplated. Even then, as in the original 'Orange' Plan of 1907, reinforcements would have to proceed across the South Atlantic and through the Indian Ocean using 'Allied' bases en route.[46]

Rainbow 2 provided for the projection of the US Fleet directly to the East Indies area. Rainbow 3 retained the major portion of the US Fleet in the western Pacific, but did not preclude the detachment of some US naval forces to Manila or Singapore. Under existing circumstances, with much of Europe under occupation and with the threat of a British collapse, much of the offensive thinking of earlier US war plans was curtailed.[47] In October, Stark enunciated the principle that became the linchpin of US strategy, that the Pacific was a secondary theatre and of less importance than the Atlantic:

Within the near future the United States may be confronted with the demand for a major effort in the Far East, an effort for which we are not now prepared and will not be prepared for several years to come. If in the near future we should be confronted with the necessity of armed opposition to Japan, that effort probably will be limited to the employment of minor naval, surface, and air forces operating from Singapore and the Dutch East Indies bases plus the interruption of Japanese shipping to the Eastern Pacific.[48]

It was feared the commitment of powerful surface forces to the Pacific region would hamper the transfer of major forces to the Atlantic, where the east coast would almost certainly have to be protected. Thus 'for the foreseeable future', economic warfare replaced battle-fleet action. An advanced group, consisting of four heavy cruisers, one aircraft carrier, nine destroyers and forty-one aircraft would be despatched via Palmyra, Canton, Suva, Noumea and Port Moresby; its primary offensive mission would be to raid Japan's lines of communications, while its primary defensive mission would be to reduce Japan's offensive capacity by contributing to the defence of Malaya by protecting sea communications in the Makassar and Florea Seas. It was not expected that these vessels would be used to directly oppose enemy forces. Except in the early stages of an enemy advance they would be employed south of the Malay Barrier on commerce protection duties, and would assist in the destruction and capture of enemy merchant ships and raiders. Because of limits on radius of action, the employment of 'soft' cruisers was preferred to 'hard' capital ships. As for the main fleet, it would remain at Hawaii to guard the Alaska-Panama-Hawaii triangle and to aid in the seizure of a fleet base at Truk.[49]

Army planners opposed any 'risky' operations west of Hawaii. They predicted that Japan could land 20,000 troops on the US west coast, and as Marshall earlier explained to Stark, Rainbow 3 was predicated on the understanding that Britain and France were not in 'immediate danger'; but by November this was no longer the case. The US Chief of Staff felt America must look to her own defences; operations should, he felt, be limited to the despatch of reinforcements to Alaska and Panama. Because Army authorities refused to cooperate, the Navy plans for Rainbows 2 and 3 were carried forward on the presumption that no Army ground or air forces would be involved; ground and air support would be limited exclusively to the US Marine Corps and the Naval Air Arm. Plainly this would be inadequate. In any case Stark had already expressed serious concern about relying on the Royal Navy in the Atlantic: 'Is such an assumption warranted? I doubt the vision of this set up – Doubt if we can afford (no matter what the British promise) to reduce our forces in the Atlantic to so great an extent'. Concentration on Rainbows 2 and 3, he felt, would absorb much of the military, naval and economic resources of the United States, and all aid to Britain would cease.[50]

It was also felt by the Department that some improvement in US defensive positions in the Far East, in peacetime and over the short term, might act as a deterrent. There was intense debate between the planners about the kind of reinforcements required. In 1939, joint Army and Navy manoeuvres at Culebra on the Canal Zone seemed to demonstrate that amphibious assaults on coastal frontiers might be prevented by rigorous air and submarine interdiction if not through effective anti-aircraft cover.[51] The practicability of increasing military aviation in the Philippines was discussed by the Joint Board in February 1940 but had no effect on overall policy.[52]

Hart had pleaded with Stark for a division of heavy cruisers. He felt that the Asiatic Fleet would be overwhelmed if under conditions then existing, it attempted to flee westwards. Under the Rainbow 3 planning schedule, the Department did make some provision for peacetime reinforcement of Manila by surface ships. By mid-year the unmodernized *Augusta* was replaced by one of her sister ships, the *Houston*, and additional destroyers were provided, but such were the needs of the Atlantic that by December 1940 the plan was no longer viable.[53] The head of the Naval War Plans Division, Captain Richmond Kelly Turner, hoped to incorporate a second aircraft carrier into the 'advanced force' plans to help ferry land-based aircraft to the Philippines, but only at some future date. Nevertheless, patrol plane reinforcement was provided for the islands in August.[54] Rainbow 3 was also the first American war plan to consider using submarines in an offensive mode; some $600,000 was made available in 1941 for work to begin on improvements to Cavite's underwater facilities, and by December Hart had received seven new 'advanced patrol' type submarines with an extended cruising range:[55]

> It appears evident that a) the international conditions in the Western Pacific are decidedly unbalanced and therefore unstable; b) that the continued presence of the U.S. Fleet in strength in the Pacific tends to stabilize this situation; c) that material strengthening of U.S. forces in the Philippines would further stabilize the situation; d) that the recent additions to the Asiatic Fleet of a division of submarines and a squadron of patrol planes plus a patrol plane tender, have placed upon the capacity of the Cavite Navy Yard a load approaching its maximum and that, therefore, further additions will have to be restricted unless Cavite is somewhat enlarged.[56]

Such plans, of course, depended on the Army sending reinforcements to the islands, for only regular troops, it was felt, could provide complete protection for the naval anchorage. When approached on the subject, Marshall agreed that a 20,000 man garrison would be ideal, but as he pointed out, the Army was 'so dispersed, so small, so lacking in material and with so few units available outside the essentials in Hawaii and the Canal, that the outlook for stationing any considerable detachment elsewhere looks hopeless just now'.[57] In the latter half of 1940 the Commanding General of the Philippine Department pressed for more pursuit aviation and anti-aircraft guns, and even requested an increase in the Philippine Scouts to 12,000 men.[58] Adhering to policy decisions made the previous year, however, the Army War Plans Division refused to discuss the issue unless national policy itself was altered to permit such a self-sustaining defence programme:

> The C.N.O. must be informed that it is impracticable to increase the existing strength of Army aviation in the Philippines unless or until the national policy requires the peacetime reinforcement of the Philippine garrison so as to afford a reasonable chance for self-sustained defence.[59]

All the major elements that were to be part of the fundamental shift in US Far Eastern strategy in 1941 were therefore already present in 1940:

1. a growing confidence in the capability of air and submarine warfare in an offensive rather than a defensive role;
2. self-sustained defence of the Philippines being seen as a viable deterrent factor against Japan.

Such plans were, of course, considerably less offensively oriented than the old War Plan 'Orange', but were a step beyond mere defence of the Alaska-Hawaii-Panama triangle. They had one major advantage in that they were both more realistic and more cost-effective than a trans-Pacific offensive. Just like the Admiralty, US naval staff were forced to differentiate between what was desirable over the long term and what was possible in the short term. For the time being the triangle's defence remained the paramount concern.

The Plan Dog Memorandum

In October, General Strong and the US Secretary of State agreed that the absence of clear direction from higher authorities was assuming 'monumental' proportions and producing utter confusion within the planning agencies. This prompted Admiral Stark to formulate a major policy review which he hoped would lead to a sweeping re-evaluation of US naval policy. Having sought advice from the Plans Division, Stark completed the initial draft of the review in only one day, working out of his own home – an indication perhaps either of the rudimentary nature of US naval planning or its secrecy. He referred to the document as a 'general estimate' which he intended to submit to the President.[60] But this was no mere estimate: it was an impassioned plea for direction:

> 'Where should we fight the war, and for what objective?' With the answer to that question to guide me, I can make a more logical plan, can more appropriately distribute the naval forces, can better coordinate the future material preparation of the Navy, and can more usefully advise as to whether or not proposed diplomatic measures can adequately be supported by available naval strength. That is to say, until the question concerning our final military objective is authoritatively answered, I can not determine the scale and nature of the effort which the Navy may be called upon to exert in the Far East, the Pacific, and the Atlantic.[61]

Stark was pessimistic about Britain's ability to maintain the Atlantic blockade without assistance. He was convinced economic warfare and strategic bombing would not be sufficient to force Germany's surrender. Britain would have to undertake a strong land offensive, but the necessary materials and manpower could only come from the United States. As to the Far East, Stark was doubtful that political equilibrium could be maintained there, and he was distrustful of the Dutch, pointing out that they would always seek what was 'in their own selfish best interests'.

The CNO postulated four potential strategies for America:

> 1. hemispheric defence, where America energies would be directed towards the protection of United States interests and security, and provision made against attack from both oceans
> 2. a full scale offensive against Japan in one theatre and a defensive stance in the other, if the British could be trusted to hold the Atlantic indefinitely
> 3. the despatch of the strongest possible assistance to both the British in the Atlantic and Allied powers in the Pacific
> 4. a strong offensive in the Atlantic and a defensive in the Pacific. This meant, however, that the United States 'would be unable to exert strong pressure against Japan'.

For the time being Stark preferred America to continue its concentration on hemispheric defence, which had prevailed since Presidential approval had been given to Rainbow 1 in July.[62] He favoured the fourth alternative as the best medium-term strategy; in the tradition of Rainbow 2 and 3, war in the Far East would have 'a more limited objective than complete Japanese defeat'. Initially Allied naval forces would aim to reduce rather than eliminate Japan's offensive capability; allied strategy would concentrate on holding the Malay Barrier and on raiding Japan's lines of communications, though Stark was not confident that the Malay Barrier could be adequately defended without US help. Indeed, the pressing needs of the Atlantic already meant curtailment of the 'advanced force' idea. The Asiatic Fleet would now withdraw from Manila east and south. Stark also hoped to divert vital Japanese strength away from the Malay Barrier by attacking the Marshalls and the Carolines. By 30 November 1940 the military contentions contained in 'Plan Dog' had been accepted by the President and the State Department.[63]

In the meantime hemispheric defence would help to preserve US territorial possessions and interests, and assistance to Britain would, with luck, keep Germany at bay in the Atlantic. Even if the US Navy had wanted to adopt a more aggressive stance, it was incapable of carrying out such a programme without raising the financial restrictions. The United States was not yet in a position to overtly antagonize or obstruct Japan in the Far East, but by the same token neither China nor Southeast Asia could be abandoned, so there was a line past which the US was not prepared to accept further Japanese southward expansion.[64] In foreign policy terms this left the United States with only one viable line of approach: Japan would have to be deterred from committing acts of aggression by both economic and military measures. If necessary, the United States could survive without Britain. US naval staff calculated it would be at least a year before Germany would be able to deploy a surrendered British Fleet against the United States.[65] Britain, on the other hand, could not survive without the US; it needed assistance in the Pacific and in the Atlantic far more than did the United States. Britain was no longer the equal of the United States at the negotiating table. At first, the Admiralty failed to recognize that this change had taken place; naval staff still believed that they could dominate the military planning process, that Britain could still influence the United States and decide how and where the war would be fought. But, however hard they tried to avoid the issue, the British were increasingly forced to take account of the imbalanced bargaining position in the Pacific, and to pander to American strategy and desires there. Though it had been long in gestation, Britain had now truly entered the phase of decline from its position as the number one world power. Unfortunately, the Americans were also well aware that the advantages lay with them.

The US Navy tried to bring home to the British the thrust of their strategy. In October, under Stark's direction, Captain Kelly Turner had shown Clarke one of the US estimates. Clarke had characterized the US view as 'gloomy'. That was an understatement. Unless massive amounts of US aid were provided, the estimate predicted Axis domination of the Mediterranean preceding German invasion of the British home islands and wholesale collapse. As the United States could not simultaneously conduct offensive operations against Japan and provide lend-lease, the paper advised the US to maintain a strictly defensive posture. As a result, the loss of the Philippines, Borneo, the Netherlands East Indies and even Singapore itself was seen as inevitable. American planners recommended 'that every political expediency should be adopted to preclude a conflict with Japan until the war had been won in the West'.[66]

Misreading the Signals

Much reference was made in Admiralty documents to the early discussions of the 1917–1918 period, when Britain had appeared to be the major partner in the Anglo-American association. As national boundaries and national interests no longer mattered, the United States was felt to be in the same position strategically as Britain. It was thus assumed the US would be prepared to take on responsibility for the whole Pacific region, and the Bailey Committee even assigned to the US the defence of Australia and New Zealand. Neither the Admiralty nor the service planners even considered the political ramifications;[67] they approached the problem of Far Eastern defence purely from a traditional military standpoint. The ultimate objective of the war was the defeat of Japan. To achieve that end the conflict would be divided into two phases. During the first phase preservation of a primary fleet base in the region was the paramount concern and the chosen implement of security the battlefleet; the rescue and relief of all 'Allied' possessions was reserved for the second phase:[68]

> We regard Singapore as the key position to be held at all costs, and as the best base from which strategical control of the Pacific can be exercised. We therefore hope that the U.S. Government will agree to base a fleet on Singapore and of sufficient strength, not at first to take the offensive, but to contain Japanese forces. If this does not prove acceptable to the U.S.A. we might, under certain circumstances, have to send a powerful squadron ourselves to Singapore to the detriment of our offensive in Europe.[69]

The Admiralty remained convinced that the United States would acknowledge and defer to Britain's considerable wartime experience.[70] The Joint Planning staff looked mainly to the 1939 Far Eastern Naval War Memorandum as the basis for future discussion, but the Vice Chief of Naval Staff, Tom Phillips, pointed out that this plan was 'too pessimistic' to be of value, and so the 1937 Far Eastern Appreciation and its attendant Naval War Plan became the new basis. The term 'American

Fleet' was substituted for 'Eastern Fleet'.[71] An exact duplicate of the Memorandum was produced with the exception that US naval forces were expected to operate from Manila rather than Hong Kong:

> We consider Manila (provided local defences are adequate) more suitable than Singapore or Honolulu as the main fleet operational base, with Singapore and its greater resources in the rear and Hong Kong available as an advanced operational base if required and usable.[72]

But for now, with at least five armed raiders and the pocket battleship *Admiral Scheer* at large, the First Lord of the Admiralty, A.V. Alexander, pointed out to Halifax that despite the victory over the Italian Fleet at Taranto, even the despatch of a battlecruiser and a carrier to the Indian Ocean could not be contemplated. The additional sea miles travelled on convoy duty in the North Atlantic meant many of the 'R' class were in desperate need of overhaul. British naval weakness ensured the only real deterrent to Japanese aggression was with the United States. This was simply a form of self-delusion brought on by Britain's own desperation and its complete misunderstanding of both United States diplomatic and military principles and policies.[73]

In reaching these conclusions the service planners were, to some extent, deluded by requests from Admiral Ghormley for information about the real state and condition of Singapore's defences and facilities. There remained considerable confusion too about US defence policy and in particular about Far Eastern strategy. The Foreign Office was anxious to know whether a US squadron could be despatched to Singapore in peacetime. Churchill also suggested that such a visit might be timed to coincide with strategy discussions the British were to have in the Far East. These were to be held with the Dominions and possibly the Dutch at Singapore. It was hoped an American presence might have great value as a deterrent against further Japanese transgressions.[74]

A breakdown in cooperation between the service planning staffs and the Foreign Office contributed to this misinterpretation. Both the State Department and the Foreign Office were being by-passed by the military planners. The visit by an American mission to London in August had opened a completely new channel of communication to the United States, one that led directly from the Admiralty to the Navy Department. The nature of the mission and the Anglophobic tendencies within the US Embassy in London, as well as the President's desire for secrecy, dictated this. Besides, from the US standpoint political commitments were to be avoided at all costs.[75] British military authorities were similarly reluctant to use normal diplomatic channels. Security was a paramount concern; much of the technical information the latter had to impart was vital to British defence, and the Kent affair had already in-creased British nervousness about US reliability.[76]

A strengthening of the military arm at the expense of the diplomatic was in some ways inevitable, and grew out of the war itself. British military staffs had grown increasingly confident in their ability to formulate as well as execute policy.[77] This process had been aided by the creation of such bodies as the Defence Committee under the direct leadership of the Prime Minister. Thus Britain's normally delicate diplomatic touch was noticeably absent from these negotiations, which were hampered by a somewhat amateur approach.

This was unfortunate, as the diplomatic arm had a much better grasp of the limitations on US policy than did the military staffs. Throughout 1940, Esler Dening of the American Department had warned that the United States would not go to war unless attacked herself.[78] Foreign Office officials felt it unlikely the Americans would inform British planning staff about the details of US strategy while the US was still a neutral. They argued that the Admiralty's approach lacked tact, that naval representatives tended to convey – perhaps too directly and openly – their intention to have America 'carry the baby' in the Pacific. They warned also against adopting a hectoring tone which 'would result in an immediate snub and a revulsion of feeling throughout America'. They preferred a policy of cautiously 'educating' the Americans round to the British way of thinking. They even suggested that from a US perspective economic warfare was preferable to main fleet action. All this was excellent advice, which was for the most part ignored. Indeed, the Foreign Office was not privy to the negotiations between Ghormley and the Admiralty; the Head of the American Department, Sir John Balfour, only discovered the existence of the ADA Committee late in November 1940, and even then he could get no explanation as to its responsibilities or functions.[79] As J.V. Perowne pointed out:

It is often very difficult for us to know, in these cases where we are little more than a Post Office and have not been kept fully au courant with the earlier history of any particular question to whom to distribute copies of secret telegrams.[80]

By mid November – despite the fact that Roosevelt had now been re-elected as President – the Foreign Office began to notice a distinct 'cooling off' in American interest in staff conferences. Within Amer-ican circles, Secretary of the Navy Frank Knox continued to favour discussions, but Stanley Hornbeck was beginning to entertain serious doubts. Hull was worried about the political risks in sending a full dele-gation and Stark was now definitely opposed to the whole idea.[81]

However, Britain's need for assistance in the Far East was so urgent and the inexperience of the planners in reading the signs so manifest that these considerations passed them by. The arrival from Clarke of digests of Rainbow 3 and 'Plan Dog' – within weeks of each other – further confused the issue. One plan seemed to give practical consideration to the problems faced by naval forces en route to the Far East. Clarke and Captain Burrell of the Royal Australian Navy had already met US Naval Plans Division officers to discuss the use of Torres Strait and New Ireland by US ships. Under 'Plan Dog,' however, the loss of Southeast Asia was seen as inevitable and the US Navy proposed to confine their activities to the defence of Hawaii.[82] The problem for the British was, which plan was current US strategic thinking?

When the British Ambassador Lord Lothian returned home to England on leave in mid-November, the Chiefs of Staff Committee asked whether the United States could provide some kind of definition of Far Eastern policy. They expressed their disappointment that Ghormley had not been empowered to discuss the strategic and tactical employment of US forces in the event of war. Pound also asked if US authorities would sanction the basing of the US Fleet on Singapore in peacetime. Lothian promised to bring these matters directly to the attention of the President.[83]

The British view of US dispositions expected there to be no need to base battleships on Hawaii, because it was felt that Japan would conduct only 'tip and run' raids against the west coast. Yet if US support was forthcoming, Ghormley pointed out that nine battleships at Singapore would be insufficient even as a deterrent in peacetime; the whole US Fleet would be required. This of course would completely denude the west coast of protection and render reinforcements to the Atlantic an unlikely proposition.[84] Ghormley was equally unconvinced that Manila would ever be useful as an advanced fleet base. Since it intended to abide by its promise to withdraw from the Philippines, Congress had declined to sanction improvements to Cavite; Manila harbour had few mines, no nets or booms and only one dry dock with a maximum capacity of 10,000 tons. According to Ghormley the base would be totally unsuited as a main fleet anchorage, and this represented the official naval view at this time:[85]

> Except for Corregidor the Philippine Islands could be held against a determined Japanese attack for a period of only a few weeks. Corregidor would probably hold out for a longer period, but its retention would serve no purpose more useful than that of containing the small land force that would

be employed for its siege. The additional measures that would be required would be so extensive and time consuming that they would involve an unwise diversion of effort.[86]

For the Prime Minister, however, the choice between Singapore and Hawaii hardly mattered as the Japanese Navy was not expected to venture far from its home bases so long as the US Fleet was present somewhere in the Pacific. Churchill felt it would be possible to contain Japan by long-range patrols. The desire to get the Americans committed overshadowed doubts about US planning, and 'Plan D' was therefore 'strategically sound in principle and perfectly adapted to British interests'.[87]

To British naval planners, however, it appeared that US preparations were still in their formative stages. Hawaii was genuinely felt to be too far away from the main scene of any action and, after all, Singapore was the traditional raison d'être for British seapower in the Far East. They therefore urged that Stark not be allowed to exclude the British point of view before definite strategic decisions were made by US planning agencies. They failed to recognize that the United States transition to an Atlantic oriented strategy was both progressive and irreversible:

> It now appears that the American Naval Staff are urging that policy of what action their fleet is to take should be settled before any conversations with us take place. The conversations would then merely discuss details. It seems most important that Lord Lothian should prevent the Americans making a decision on the policy of their fleet now, otherwise when the conversations do start we shall be presented with a fait accompli. The Admiralty share this view and are asking the Foreign Office to put this to him as a matter of urgency.[88]

Lothian arrived back in Washington on 25 November 1940. In case of war with Japan and because of the deteriorating Far Eastern situation, he urged contingency plans be made. The use of Singapore was to be one of the issues discussed. As Lothian pointed out to Hull, existing arrangements in London were not sufficient for the task. Hull immediately took the matter up with Roosevelt, and on 29 November Lothian was at last able to report that the President had finally agreed to staff conversations in Washington. Roosevelt continued to stress, however, that no publicity must be allowed; the whole operation would be camouflaged by attaching the officers concerned to the British Purchasing Commission.[89]

Ghormley's report of the November conversations – a direct reflection of the British view concerning US dispositions – finally reached the United States at about the same time. Unfortunately the arrival coincided with a second 'cooling off' period in interest on the part of US planning authorities. The Joint Board had just decided that assistance would not be provided to the Netherlands East Indies or to Britain in the Far East until Germany was defeated in the Atlantic. Turner now felt any agreement with Britain should be 'very general',[90] and he threatened Clarke that if the British lost Egypt, Rainbow 3 would be 'out the window'.[91] Meanwhile in London on 4 December, Ghormley submitted a questionnaire to British authorities based on the assumption that the US would restrict its activities in the Pacific to the area east of 160 degrees longitude. It seemed 'totally unrealistic' to the Naval War Plans Division to expect the US Navy to jeopardize its own national interests and the defence of its territorial possessions in order to preserve and protect British possessions and the British Empire.[92]

Even if the motivation had been present, without adequate fuelling bases en route, a sufficient fleet train including repair ships and tankers and logistic support from an adequate main supply base, the US Fleet was physically incapable at this stage of sailing the vast distances necessary to reach the Far East. Even if such a capability had been there, the limitations on Singapore's own facilities precluded its use as a fleet anchorage, a fact the British had sought to hide from American eyes. Indeed Bailey even re-drafted the Admiralty's report on the base in a more favourable light,[93] but US naval staff were perfectly *au fait* with the state of Singapore's facilities.[94] Officers from the Asiatic Fleet had carried out their own detailed investigation already, and their conclusions were indeed a presentiment of what happened early in 1942. Because the facilities were concentrated in a very small area, the base was vulnerable both to air attack and long-range artillery fire from the landward side. Spare parts and shortages in base personnel, it was felt, could only be made up by the United States and there were deficiencies in nets, booms, mines and anti-aircraft ammunition with an average of only 400 rounds per gun. The US Navy Department therefore had a better understanding of the limitations of the base than Britain's own Prime Minister.[95]

On receipt of the Special Naval Representative's report and its enclosures, Stark contacted Ghormley and Clarke, impressing on them that the British report was 'totally unacceptable' as a basis for staff conversations; indeed he warned that if the British conferees were restricted to details about the form of US cooperation, 'no useful purpose would be served by staff conversations at this time'. Nor was he prepared to begin talks on any other basis than Rainbow 3. The British delegation would have to defer to US strategy on all things and not try to force their views upon them.[96] Pound admitted British naval staff had not taken US political factors sufficiently into account, but neither Stark's criticisms nor the advice of the Prime Minister – namely that the United States must 'be in charge in the Pacific' – substantially altered Admiralty policy. The British continued to feel that Singapore was still the best location for any eastern fleet. Admiralty planners admitted the presence of the US Fleet at Hawaii could threaten Japan, but only if carrier air attacks were launched against the Japanese home islands. Since US carriers were 'known to be deficient in their radius of action', they were even prepared to send a British carrier group to assist the US.[97] At any future conference, their intention was to 'educate' American planners just as they had tried to 'educate' Ghormley and re-establish dominion over the planning process.[98]

The sudden agreement by the President to full staff conversations took British planning authorities by surprise. Papers needed to be drawn up and technical and statistical data gathered, and a unified strategic approach by the services had to be created. Delays now followed as British planners underestimated the extent of the preparations required; past US intransigence meant that they were unprepared to begin with. As the Prime Minister was anxious to impress the Americans with British strength, the latest and most modern battleship, 'King George V', was detailed to transport the delegation, but a further gap of three weeks ensued before the ship could be withdrawn from sea duty. A detailed agreement calling for extensive technical exchanges had been approved on 25 October, but the Admiralty had only established a temporary mission in the United States by the end of the year, and no formal invitation to the US was received regarding reciprocal arrangements in London until 20 January 1941. The failure of the Americans to fulfil their promise to deliver combat-ready vessels as part of the base-destroyer deal also resulted in some hesitation in Britain about proceeding with lend-lease. A Lend-Lease Commission had to be appointed to untangle many problems, particularly about the use of British ports by US warships. The Admiralty and the Foreign Office had both stressed the need 'to strike while the iron was hot', now their worst fears were realized.[99]

For these delays meant American fears about 'perfidious Albion' were aroused. There had already been several 'cooling off' periods in relations during the build-up to the meeting. The attitude of the US Navy Department towards the Admiralty was already conditioned by an underlying spirit of competition, where professional jealousy and Mahanite theory provided convenient philosophical justifications. Anglophobic tendencies already simmered just below the surface, although it should be pointed out that the American attitude was no different to the Admiralty's own reaction towards the Netherlands East Indies and the French. Unreliability in the communications network and

the need to preserve secrecy meant Ghormley and Lee were only permitted to see British papers while en route to Washington. As American
Military Attaché in London, Colonel Raymond E. Lee expected the
British delegation to hang onto their proposals 'like leeches if I know
the British character at all'. The United States, he felt, must not be
persuaded to adopt a fait accompli, 'to accept proposals the British have
been cooking up for six weeks without examination'.[100] Across the
Atlantic in Washington, Clarke had already noted the start of a third
'cooling off' period in American commitment:

> I would like to emphasize that the Navy Department has not so far proved
> to be a particularly forthcoming institution. The sudden spate of openness
> which resulted in a view of the Appreciation and the War Plan, and the talks
> which took place round about that time, were certainly caused by direction
> from higher up. Generally they are always willing to listen to anything that
> anyone wants to say to them, but that is about as far as it goes. . . Every
> American believes that we are determined to use him as a tool to achieve
> our own ends, and the Navy Department is determined not to be bounced
> and made to subordinate their ideas to ours. The fact that, underneath, they
> may know that our arguments have much to commend them is beside the
> point.[101]

Heavy Weather at ABC-1

The American-British Staff Conference (ABC) began on the 29 January
and lasted until 29 March 1941. Rear-Admiral Bellairs and the former
Naval Director of Plans, V.H. Danckwerts, were joined by Captain
Arthur W. Clarke, Major-General E.L. Morris, and Air Vice-Marshal
J.C. Slessor. The meetings were dominated by a naval presence; three
out of the five members of the UK delegation were Admiralty staff. The
Americans were headed by Major-General Stanley Embick, and the
party included Rear-Admirals Ghormley and Kelly Turner, who was to
stamp his personality upon the proceedings. Overall the US delegation
was determined to discourage the British from enterprises that might
be considered unacceptable to US policies. Both hoped to see the
'channeling' of the conversation into mutually acceptable areas of cooperation.[102]

From the beginning, the US planning authorities stressed that
agreements reached on military matters would be 'tentative' and subject
to approval by both governments. No political commitments could possibly be made, and the President, the State Department, the Chief of
Staff and the Chief of Naval Operations were all excluded from the
proceedings.[103] During the conference it was emphasized that if Japan

moved into southern IndoChina or Thailand, or seized British possessions in the Far East, it would not be regarded as casus belli. This was confirmed by the President through Lord Halifax, now British Ambassador in Washington following Lothian's untimely death. Because it was feared such action would 'precipitate a Japanese move into the Netherlands East Indies,' the US Navy opposed any extension of an embargo on gasoline or oil.[104] Later in the conference the US delegation also warned that it would be 'a serious mistake for the United Kingdom in making their strategical dispositions. . .to count upon prompt military support by the United States'.[105]

Rather than seeing the war against the Axis as a united joint effort as the British did, the US sought to compartmentalize the conflict. Since 'post war interests were never far removed from British minds', it seemed only right that the United States should likewise guard its own national interests. The primary strategic objective was the defeat of Germany, and the United States also intended to provide some naval support to the Mediterranean. Yet even if Japan attacked first, the main effort would still be made in the Atlantic, and of course it was hoped Japan could be prevented by diplomatic means from entering the war or attacking the Dutch. If conflict did break out then where numerically weaker forces operated in another's area of responsibility, they would retain their own command structure and method of operation. However, US forces intended to operate mainly within their own spheres of responsibility under their own commanders. Strategic control was to be exercised by 'cooperation', but was really subject to the willingness of the respective commander to obey directions, and this in turn was also subject to national interest.

The Far Eastern and Pacific theatres of operation were to be strictly divided into separate spheres of responsibility. The United States would protect its own and British interests east of 180 degrees longitude, and was prepared to support Dominion naval operations south of the equator to the Fiji Islands and as far west as 155 degrees longitude, which included New Zealand but not Australia. In keeping with the Rainbow 3 scenario, the Pacific Fleet would sever Japan's lines of communications and deny use of the Marshall and Caroline Islands by raiding westward. Support would be provided for the defence of the Malay Barrier by diverting Japanese forces from a southern advance. The United States refused to assume command responsibility for the Far East; instead the Asiatic Fleet would aid the defence of the Philippines until the islands were no longer tenable and would then retire southward to a more suitable base, possibly Singapore or Soerabaya. Joint naval, military and air forces – under overall British direction – would then attempt to neutralize the operations of the remaining Japanese forces in the South China Sea by holding them north of the Malay Barrier. The Asiatic Fleet would cooperate strategically but not tactically in this movement at the discretion of CINCAF. However, the Fleet would not begin such 'cooperation' until after the fate of the Philippines had been all but settled, and such dispositions would only be implemented if the United States declared war.[106]

The discussions then turned to the relationship between the Atlantic and Pacific theatres. Since the British line of communication to the Far East was more secure than that of the United States, the US Navy proposed to augment British forces both in the Atlantic and in the Mediterranean, so that Britain would be able to release sufficient ships and despatch them to protect her own Far Eastern possessions. As with Rainbow 2, the United States insisted Britain make a material contribution to the defence of the Malay Barrier. A study was presented by Kelly Turner as chief US naval representative, which presumed Britain was expected to survive another six months; thus the United States would be involved in the war in the Atlantic by 1 April 1941. The US would take over responsibility in that theatre west of 30 degrees longitude and as far south as Rio de Janeiro. The US Fleet would also be divided into two separate and distinct bodies, an Atlantic and a Pacific fleet. It was estimated US naval forces would begin operations sometime between M+14 and M+21, though Turner was not precise about the arrival timetable or the kind of forces to be despatched. There were too many variable factors.[107]

Convinced that US policy might still be revised, the British delegation put forward a three-part counter-proposal. Because of the presence of Japanese airpower in IndoChina and Thailand, Turner argued that since it was now within range of Japanese aircraft, Singapore could not be used by US naval forces. For their part the British rated the Japanese Air Corps about the same as the Italian, and Bellairs reiterated that it was possible to base the Mediterranean Fleet at Alexandria, and to operate the Home Fleet at Scapa no more than 300 miles and 450 miles respectively from enemy land-based air forces.[108] Singapore was therefore still seen as the *sine qua non* of British Far Eastern strategy, and as Bellairs explained, not simply on military grounds alone but for a variety of other reasons:

> The maintenance of a fleet base at Singapore is a cardinal point in British strategy. The conception is based not only on purely strategic but political, economic, and sentimental considerations, which even if not vital on a strictly academic view, are of such fundamental importance to the Empire

that they must be taken into account. We are a maritime power, various Dominions and Colonies held together by communications and trade routes across oceans. The home population is dependent on imported food and overseas trade. The security and prosperity of India is our trust and responsibility. Defence of all their interests is vital to our war effort and depends on the capacity to hold Singapore and in the last resort to base a battle fleet there.[109]

If US planners would not accept the presence of a US Fleet at Singapore, it was hoped they might agree to despatch one or two capital ships there. If the US were irrevocably opposed to this idea, then it was expected they might still be prepared to undertake larger offensive operations in the Pacific. British planners suggested carrier raids against the Japanese home islands, or reinforcement of the Asiatic Fleet by at least one carrier and a division of heavy cruisers. Both options would draw off vital Japanese resources from a southern offensive.[110]

Churchill was furious, not only with the Singapore appreciation but also with the whole approach of the British delegation, which had violated his carefully drafted instructions about avoiding controversy and now threatened to hinder US entry into the war. To his mind 'the first thing is to get the United States into the war. We can then settle how to fight it afterwards'.[111] The British delegation was making 'heavy weather' at the negotiating table. As expected, the Americans refused to accept any of the compromise solutions, nor would they agree to any appreciable division of the Pacific Fleet.[112] No part of the US Pacific Fleet would be sent to Singapore, and there would be no strengthening of surface ships for the Asiatic Fleet. US planners felt Japan would take the threat of US intervention seriously only so long as the Fleet remained united; diversions would be a 'strategic error of incalculable magnitude'. The US Army Committee felt the choice was between commitment of the bulk of US naval forces to the rescue of a doomed command to the detriment of the Atlantic, or abandonment of naval forces in the Philippines to their fate, which would leave the US Pacific Fleet in a weakened state. It was felt that only persistent attacks against the Japanese home islands would really be effective. US planners therefore rejected the British carrier raid concept; they felt their ships were far too vulnerable to interception, and in any case, shortages in the Naval Air Arm reduced the capability of the US Navy to conduct long-range bombing.[113] It was little wonder that the British delegation came away from the conference with 'a distinctly bitter taste in the mouth':

This difference of opinion in major policy is to us so fundamental that we think it will be essential to bring it out in the Final Report. We can make it

clear that the plans we are putting forward are the best that can be formulated in the light of the basic national position of the United States, but we
think it would not be right to create the impression in our Final Report that
we were agreed that plans we were putting forward were the best from the
purely military point of view.[114]

Conclusions

Given the choice, the British and US naval staffs would undoubtedly
have preferred to solve their strategic problems in isolation from each
other without consultation and in the traditional manner. However, in
1940 the deterioration in the international situation and the formation
of the Tripartite Pact meant the range of strategic options, if not policy
alternatives, had become more limited. Without Britain the United
States, over the short term, could not guarantee its own security. In both
the Atlantic and in the Pacific, Britain's own survival and that of her
Imperial possessions became dependent upon US assistance. Cooperation between the two countries resulted from mutual need rather than
from desire or choice.

It took nearly eight months before both sides could actually sit
around the negotiating table. As with pre-war naval discussions, mistrust and suspicion, misunderstandings and misapprehensions continued
to dominate the proceedings. During the latter half of 1940 Britain
did much of the talking and the United States much of the listening.
Relations were more complex but just as non-committal. In both
potential theatres of operation, the United States was aware that the
British Fleet was the US front line, yet US planners remained uncertain
about British chances of survival and were fearful that assistance would
entangle the US in another war. Keeping out of a conflict in the Pacific
was a paramount concern. If a conflict arose, the United States was
going to plan and fight any war on its own terms, by establishing the
parameters both of cost and effect to America, by restricting the Pacific
Fleet to a defensive role and by the use of economic warfare.

US naval planners differentiated between assistance directly to
Britain and assistance to the British Empire. The tendency towards strategic cooperation was counter-balanced by caution and mistrust; aid and
assistance was tempered by the fear generated by an uneducated public
opinion and an isolationist Congress. The debate over the Lend-Lease
Bill ensured that covert deception was the keynote underlying US
policy at the ABC Conference. During the Washington staff talks both
sides did a great deal of talking but there was little real communication.
Britain sought to 'educate' the United States, to persuade it to listen to
the voice of experience and to stamp its dominion over proceedings, but

the cardinal mistake was to misinterpret the willingness of the US to commit itself to the defence of the Far East. However, British planning staff were inexperienced in the diplomatic arena and US policy was so haphazard and ineffectively administered that predicting any pre-determined goal for US policy was difficult. Even US defence agencies had problems in working out their own strategic direction. In the end the Admiralty's single-minded pursuit of the United States was counter-productive; it merely hardened America's opposition to Britain's ideas. Indeed, when Lord Halifax tried to make Hull aware of the strategic deadlock that threatened the conference, the US delegation recessed all meetings until specific guarantees were provided prohibiting any pos-sibility that political control might be exerted over the staff conference.

A blueprint for Far Eastern strategy was agreed to, but only in terms of general principles and on a purely hypothetical basis, for there were no political guarantees. At best it was a convoluted war plan. One member of the Foreign Office described it as 'absolutely crazy'.[115] One thing was certain; for the time being in future matters relating to the defence of the Far East, Britain had ceded its independence in strategic matters to the United States. The Admiralty had made every conceivable attempt to bring the US Navy Department into the fold, to set the agenda and to establish dominion over how the war would be fought and where, and had failed. British Far Eastern strategy now depended less on demands for military action from the Dominions and more on sanctification from the United States. As Rear-Admiral Danckwerts himself pointed out:

> In signing and agreeing to A.B.C.-1 we have to some extent tied our own hands and unless we wish to undo all the good we have so far achieved we must bear their susceptibilities in mind when making arrangements which really concern us and not them.[116]

Notes

1. E.L. Woodward and Rohan Butler (eds) (1955), *Documents on British Foreign Policy 1919–39*, Series 3, vol. 9, London, p. 526.
2. This was First Lord of the Admiralty Winston Churchill's pet project for an offensive into the Baltic.
3. Memo by the First Lord of the Admiralty, DMV (39) 3, 17 November 1939, CAB 99/1; Ltr Eden to Chamberlain, 3 November

1939, FO 371/23572; Note on Conclusions reached in the First Lord's Room, 12 November 1939, ADM 205/2.

4. Minute by Drax, 18 November 1939, ADM 205/4; 'New Construction Programme', Memo by First Lord of the Admiralty, 28 September 1939, ADM 167/105; WP (40) 53, 17 November 1939, CAB 66/5.

5. Ltr Lothian to Chatfield, 25 February 1940, Chatfield Papers; Minute by Mallet, 30 April 1940, FO 371/24716.

6. Memoirs of Admiral Sir Algenon Willis, pp. 6, 26–7; Ltr Cunningham to Pound, 29 May 1940, vol. 9, Cunningham Papers.

7. Basil Collier (1967), *A Short History of the Second World War*, London, pp. 86–145.

8. War Cabinet Mtg 172 (40), 19 June 1940, CAB 65/7; Tel. Craigie to Halifax, 24 June 1940, FO 371/24666.

9. 'Implications of the Capture of the Netherlands East Indies', Report by JIC, 20 May 1940, JP 184 (40) and COS Paper 369 (40), CAB 80/11; Aide Memoire for His Majesty's Ambassador in Washington, 13 June 1940, COS Paper 455 (40), CAB 80/13; 'Assistance to the Dutch in the Event of Japanese Aggression in the Netherlands East Indies', COS Paper 596 (40), 1 August 1940, CAB 80/15.

10. COS 183 Mtg, 17 June 1940; Draft Report by the First Sea Lord and D of P, COS 185 Mtg, 18 June 1940, CAB 79/5. For details on British naval strategy during this period see Stephen Roskill (1977), *Churchill and the Admirals*, London, pp. 150–65, and Arthur J. Marder (1974), *From the Dardanelles to Oran: Studies of the Royal Navy in War and Peace 1915–40*, London, chapter 5, pp. 179–288.

11. 'The Situation in the Far East in the Event of Japanese Intervention Against Us', COS Paper 592 (40), 31 July 1940, CAB 66/10.

12. 'Immediate Measures Required for the Defence of the Far East', COS Paper 528 (40), 25 June 1940; Draft Tel. to the Government of Australia, COS Paper 501 (40), 20 June 1940, CAB 80/14.

13. Aide Memoire by the Joint Planning Sub-Committee, COS 506 (40), 29 June 1940, CAB 80/14; 'Security of Singapore', Memo by CIGS, June 1940, WO 32/9366; Comment on the Draft Report of the Joint Planning Sub-Committee by the Foreign Office, 10 July 1940, FO 371/24722.

14. 'Far Eastern Memorandum', ADA 7 (40), 18 October 1940, ADM 199/1232.

15. Minute by Denning, 10 July 1940, FO 371/24725; Ltr Ismay to Bruce, 4 July 1940, CAB 21/893; COS 317 Mtg, 19 September 1940, CAB 79/6; Minute Prime Minister to First Lord of the Admiralty and the First Sea Lord, 2 August 1940, ADM 199/1930.

16. WM 222 (40), 8 August 1940, CAB 65/14; COS Paper 614 (40), 8

August 1940, CAB 80/16; Tel. Prime Minister to Prime Ministers of Australia and New Zealand, 11 August 1940, CAB 65/14.

17. W. David McIntyre (1979), *The Rise and Fall of the Singapore Naval Base*, London, pp. 45–9; CID 193 Mtg, 5 January 1925, CAB 2/4; NP (25) 2 Mtg, 2 March 1925, CAB 27/273.

18. Minute Prime Minister to Pound, 1 August 1940; 'Redistribution of the Fleet in the Event of War with Japan', Memo by CNS, August 1940; Minute Prime Minister to First Lord of the Admiralty and the First Sea Lord, 2 August 1940, ADM 199/1930; COS Paper 592 (40), 31 July 1940, CAB 66/10.

19. War Cabinet Conclusions, 214 (40), 29 July 1940, CAB 65/14; Paper 568 (4), 27 July 1940, CAB 80/13; COS 236 Mtg, 27 July 1940, CAB 79/5; Tel. COS to High Commissioner in New Zealand, 11 August 1940, FO 371/24709.

20. James Leutze (1977), *Bargaining for Supremacy: Anglo-American Naval Collaboration, 1937–1941*, Chapel Hill, NC, p. 134; Bailey Committee Report, 15 July 1940, ADM 199/1159.

21. Leutze, *Bargaining*, p. 144.

22. Minute by R.A. Butler, 22 September 1939, FO 371/23556; War Cabinet Conclusions, WM 63 (40), 28 November 1939, CAB 65/2; Tel. Lothian to Halifax, 18 September 1939, FO 371/23551.

23. Cordell Hull (1958), *Memoirs of Cordell Hull*, vol. 1, London, pp. 908–9; Tel. FO to Lothian, 29 September 1940, FO 371/24709; Tel. Lothian to FO, 1 October 1940, FO 371/24736; COS Paper 772 (4), 25 September 1940, CAB 80/19.

24. Ltr Kirk to Anderson, 20 April 1940, Box 2, Series 1, Kirk Papers; 'American Policy in the Far East', Memo by Hubbard, 30 April 1940, FO 371/24798; J.R.M. Butler (1957), *Grand Strategy*, London, vol. 2, p. 326; Notes of a Conversation between the American Naval Attaché and the Vice Chief of Naval Staff, 16 April 1940, FO 371/24716; War Cabinet Mtg 95 (40), 17 April 1940; War Cabinet Mtg 96 (40), 18 April 1940, CAB 65/6.

25. Michael Barnhart, 'Hornbeck was Right: The Realist Approach to American Policy towards Japan', in Harry Conroy and Harry Wray (ed.) (1990), *Pearl Harbor Reexamined: Prologue to the Pacific War*, Hawaii, pp. 67–8; Memo DWPD to CNO, 17 June 1940, A 16–3, Warfare Miscellaneous, Box 90, Series IX, Plans and Strategic Studies, Records of the Strategic Plans Division.

26. Memo Stark to FDR, 14 August 1940, CINCPAC Correspondence, Kimmel Papers.

27. Hosoya Chihiro, 'Miscalculations on Deterrent Policy: US-Japanese Relations 1938–1941', in Conroy and Wray, *Pearl Harbor Reexamined*, pp. 56–61; Thomas A. Bailey and Paul B. Ryan

(1979), *Hitler vs. Roosevelt: The Undeclared Naval War*, London, p. 38; *Public Opinion Quarterly for 1939*, vol. 4, pp. 105–11.

28. Patrick Heardon (1987), *Roosevelt confronts Hitler: America's Entry into World War II*, Delkalb, IL, pp. 124–5; Memo Sherman to DWPD, 30 April 1940; 'National Strategic Decisions', Memo by JPC, 22 May 1940; 'World Situation', Memo by General Board, 28 May 1940, A 16–3 Miscellaneous, Box 90, Series V, Records of the Strategic Plans Division.

29. 'Estimate of the Position in Relation to the World Situation', Memo by the Army War Plans Division, 15 September 1940, WPD 4321–9.

30. David Reynolds (1981), *The Creation of the Anglo-American Alliance 1937–1941: A Study in Competitive Co-operation*, London, p. 112; Mark S. Watson (1950), *Chief of Staff: Prewar Plans and Preparations*, Washington, pp. 110–13.

31. 'American Policy in the Far East', Memo by Hubbard, 30 April 1940, FO 371/24708; US Department of State (1940), *Foreign Relations of the United States* (cited hereafter as FRUS), vol. 4, pp. 333–6.

32. 'The International Situation and the Reinforcement of the Asiatic Fleet', Memo by WPD, 16 October 1940; 'Measures of Operations to be Undertaken by the U.S. Fleet', Memo by Murphy, 16 October 1940, in Congress (1946), *Pearl Harbor Attack: Hearings of the Joint Committee on the Investigation of the Pearl Harbor Attack* (PHA), 79 Congress, 1st session, Washington, pt 14, pp. 1006–10. See also Tel. FO to Lothian, 25 May 1940; Tel. Lothian to FO, 26 May 1940, FO 371/24716.

33. Ltr Stark to Richardson, 24 September 1940; Ltr Stark to Richardson, 1 October 1940; Ltr Stark to Richardson, 23 December 1940, in PHA, pt 14, pp. 962–3.

34. Ltr CINCUS to CINCAF, 16 October 1940, A 16–3/ND 14, Box 92, Series V, Subject Files, Records of the Strategic Plans Division; Memo CINCUS to CINCAF, 16 October 1940, War Plans Folder, Asiatic Fleet Miscellaneous, Records of the Asiatic Fleet and Asiatic Defence Campaign; Ltr O'Laughlin to Hart, 8 October 1940, Hart Papers: Testimony by Leahy, in PHA, pt 1, p. 353.

35. Tel. FO to Lothian, 25 May 1940; Tel. Lothian to FO, 26 May 1940, FO 371/24716; Tel. Lothian to FO, 17 June 1940; Tel. Lothian to FO, 24 June 1940, FO 371/24240; Tracy B. Kittredge (1946), 'United States–British Naval Cooperation 1939–42' unpublished manuscript, Section III, pt A, chapter 10, pp. 212–13, section III, pt C, Appendix A, pp. 278–9.

36. Leutze, *Bargaining*, pp. 141–2, and chapter 10 for details.

37. Minute by DNI, 2 July 1940, ADM 199/1159; Minute Churchill to Halifax, 24 June 1940; Minute Halifax to Churchill, 28 June 1940, FO 371/24240. For details see Leutze, *Bargaining*, pp. 132–3 and James R. Leutze (ed.) (1971), *The London Journal of Raymond E. Lee* , Boston, p. 29.
38. Leutze, *Bargaining*, pp. 143, 156.
39. Ltr Ghormley to Stark, 18 September 1940, Box 79, Ghormley Correspondence, Com. Nav. Eu. Files, series II; Minutes of Mtg with Admiralty, 17 September 1940, 'Conversation in London', Microfilm Roll 5, Strategic Planning in the US Navy: Its Evolution and Execution 1845–91, Scholarly Resources Inc.
40. Leutze, *Bargaining*, pp. 158–9; Report by Emmons and Strong to President, 24 September 1940, WPD 4368.
41. 'British–U.S. Technical Conversations,' Draft Report by JPC, JP 401 (40), 26 August 1940, copy in ADM 199/1159; Minutes of ADA Committee, Mtg 10 (40), 17 October 1940, ADM 199/1232.
42. For more information about this see Elting R. Morison (1942), *Admiral Sims and the Modern American Navy*, Boston, chapters 19 to 21. Ghormley's position is fairly clear from the following: Ltr Ghormley to Stark, 23 August 1940, 13 September 1940, 18 September 1940, 20 September 1940, 17 October 1940, 16 November 1940, Box 79, Ghormley Correspondence, Com. Nav. Eu., Series II. See also ALUSNA and SPENAVO, Secret File, Com. Nav. Eu. Files for copies.
43. Tel. Bailey to Clarke, 26 November 1940, CAB 122/4.
44. Rainbow 2, undated, 1940, JB 325, Serial 642–2, RG 225.
45. Digest of Conference in the Office of CNO, 1 May 1940, Box 67, Series III, Miscellaneous, Records of the Strategic Plan Division; Brief of Stilman's Memo by WPD, 19 July 1940, WPD 4250–5.
46. Rainbow 2; 'W.P.L. 43', April 1940, Strategic and Operational Planning Documents; 'Statement of the Problem', Memo by Staff of the Naval War College, Newport, March 1940, Box 26, Series II–A, Naval War College: Instructional Material.
47. 'Estimate of the Position of the United States in Relation to the World Situation', Memo by WPD, 15 September 1940, WPD 4321–9; Rainbow Plan 3, October 1940, Microfilm Roll 5, Strategic Planning in the U.S. Navy: Its Evolution and Execution 1891–1945, Scholarly Resources Inc.
48. Ltr CINCUS to CINCAF, 16 October 1940, Box 90, Series V, Subject Files, Records of the Strategic Plans Division.
49. Rainbow Plan 3; 'W.P.L.–44', October 1940, Strategic and Operational Planning Documents; 'W.P.L.–44', Memo CINCUS to

CINCAF, 26 December 1940, Box 147–J, Series IX, Plans, Strategic Studies, Records of the Strategic Plans Division.

50. Memo Cooke to CNO, 10 October 1940, War Plans Folder, Miscellaneous, Records Relating to the Asiatic Fleet and Asiatic Defense Campaign; Memo McCrea to CINCAF, 14 January 1941, Hart Papers; Ltr Stark to Ghormley, 16 October 1940, Box 79, Ghormley Correspondence, Com. Nav. Eu., Series II.

51. Annual Estimate of the Situation, 15 April 1939, Box 44, Series III, Miscellaneous, Records of the Strategic Plans Division.

52. 'Practicability of Increasing Army Aviation Strength in the Philippines', 2 March 1940, WPD 4192–3.

53. Ltr Hart to Stark, 30 October 1939, Ltr Hart to Stark, 9 March 1940; Ltr Stark to Hart, 23 March 1940, Box 4; Hart Diary, entry 15 November 1940 and 20 December 1940, Hart Papers.

54. 'Measures of Operations to be Undertaken by the U.S. Fleet', Memo by Murphy, 16 October 1940, PHA, pt 14, p. 1007.

55. Rainbow 3; Memo CINCUS to CINCAF, 26 December 1940, Box 147 J, WPL Letters 1939–45, Series IX, Plans and Strategic Studies.

56. 'Estimate of the Situation for 1942', Memo by Naval Plans Division, undated 1941, Box 45, Series III, Miscellaneous, Records of the Strategic Plans Division.

57. Ltr Stark to Hart, 9 February 1940, Hart Papers; 'War Department Policy: Reference to the Defence of the Philippines', Memo by WPD, 10 October 1940, WPD 3251–45.

58. 'Policy Relative to the Philippines', Memo by WPD, undated, 1939, WPD 4192–2.

59. Memo WPD to COS, 2 March 1940, WPD 4192–3.

60. Ltr O'Laughlin to Hart, 8 October 1940, Hart Papers; Ltr Stark to Richardson, 12 November 1940.

61. Ltr Stark to CINCAF, 12 November 1940, PHA, pt 14, pp. 971–2.

62. Ibid. For information about hemispheric defence see James H. Herzog (1973), *Closing the Open Door: American–Japanese Diplomatic Negotiations, 1936–41*, Annapolis, pp. 241–55; and George C. Dyer (1972), *The Amphibians Come to Conquer: The Story of Admiral Richmond Kelly Turner*, Washington, pp. 159–60.

63. Memo Stark to Marshall, 22 November 1940; Memo Anderson to Marshall, undated, WPD 4175–15.

64. Memo DWPD to CNO, 22 May 1940, Box 67, Series III Miscellaneous, Records of the Strategic Plans Division.

65. 'Estimate of the Position of the United States in Relation to the World Situation', Memo by WPD, 15 September 1940, WPD 4321–9; see also Tel. Butler to FO, 31 October 1940, FO 371/25253.

66. 'Historical Sidelights' by Captain Arthur W. Clarke, unpublished manuscript, p. 12; Tel. Butler to FO, 31 October 1940, FO 371/ 24243. See also Leutze, *Bargaining*, pp. 187–8.
67. Draft Report British-Dutch-American Conversation by JPC, JP 520 (S) (40), 6 October 1940, CAB 84/20; Instructions for the United Kingdom Delegation, ADA 6 (40), 17 October 1940.
68. ADA Committee Mtg, 21 October 1940, ADM 199/1232.
69. Minute by D of P, 12 November 1940, ADM 199/691.
70. COS 357 Mtg, 23 October 1940, CAB 79/7.
71. 'Allied Strategy in the Far East', Draft Memo by the UK Delegation, COS Paper 893 (40), 2 November 1940; 'Far Eastern Appreciation', Annex to COS Paper 893 (40), 2 November 1940, CAB 84/22.
72. COS Paper 523, 7 October 1940, CAB 84/20.
73. Ltr First Lord of the Admiralty to Secretary of State for Foreign Affairs, 2 November 1940, CAB 79/8; Minute by Harwood, 11 February 1941, ADM 116/4877.
74. Tel. FO to Lothian, 5 September 1940, FO 371/24719; Minute by the Far Eastern Department, 26 September 1940; Tel. Lothian to FO, 7 October 1940, FO 371/24709; Tel. FO to Lothian, 3 October 1940, FO 371/24736.
75. Mtg Joint Army and Navy Committee, 19 February 1941, Serial 011512–13, US–UK Conversation Minutes.
76. In May 1940 Tyler Kent, a cypher clerk at the American Embassy, was arrested by Scotland Yard and charged with breaches of the Official Secrets Act. Kent admitted that he had been collecting security material because of his Republican sympathies, and that he had intended to use it to expose Roosevelt at the election. Subsequently he was dismissed from his post, thereby invalidating his diplomatic immunity, and he spent the rest of the war in jail. See PHA, pt 2, p. 5523.
77. Ltr DMO and P to CIGS, 24 November 1940, CAB 80/24; Minute by Whitehead, 25 July 1940, FO 371/24708.
78. Minute by Dening, 4 November 1940, FO 371/24243.
79. Minute by Dening, 5 November 1940, FO 371/24710; Minute by Balfour, 2 December 1940, ADM 199/1232.
80. Ltr J.V. Perowne to Col. E.I.C. Jacob, WO, 6 December 1940, FO 371/24243.
81. Tel. OPNAV to SPENAVO, 10 October 1940, ALUSNA and SPENAVO Messages, Com. Nav. Eu. Files; Francis L. Loewenheim, Harold D. Langley and Manfred Jonas (eds) (1975), *Roosevelt and Churchill: Their Secret Wartime Correspondence*, London, pp. 115–16.

82. Tel. Butler to FO, 31 October 1940, FO 371/25253; Tel. Butler to FO, 20 November 1940; Minute by Balfour, 26 November 1940, FO 371/24243.

83. Notes of a meeting with Lothian, COS Paper 383 (40), 8 November 1940, CAB 79/7.

84. Note of a conversation between the First Sea Lord and Rear-Admiral Ghormley, 19 November 1940, ADM 199/691.

85. Hart Diary, entry 15 September 1941.

86. Notes in reply to a British questionnaire by the Navy Department, 10 October 1940, Box 123, Miscellaneous, pt VII, Records Relating to the Anglo-American-Dutch Conversations, Records of the Strategic Plans Division.

87. Memo Churchill to First Sea Lord, 22 November 1940, CAB 84/20.

88. Memo DMO and P to CIGS, 24 November 1940, CAB 80/24.

89. Tel. Lothian to FO, 25 November 1940; Tel. Lothian to FO, 29 November 1940, FO 371/24243; Hull, vol. 1, p. 914.

90. 'Study of the Immediate Problems Concerning Involvement in War', Draft Proposal JPC, 21 December 1940, WPD 4561–10.

91. Note of meeting between Turner, Clarke, Murphy and McCrea, 6 December 1940; Memo McCrea to CINCAF, 14 January 1941, Hart Papers. See also Tel. Lothian to FO, 7 December 1940, ADM 199/1232.

92. Cable Stark to Ghormley, 2 December 1940, London Correspondence, ALUSNA and SPENAVO Messages, Com. Nav. Eu. Files; Ltr Ghormley to Bailey, 9 December 1940, ADM 199/1232.

93. Leutze, *Bargaining*, p. 174.

94. Tel. OPNAV to SPENAVO, 10 October 1940, London Correspondence, ALUSNA and SPENAVO Messages, Com. Nav. Eu. Files.

95. Memo CINCAF to CNO, 18 January 1941, Box 147 J, WPL Letters 1939–45, Series IX, Plans and Strategic Studies; Report of Lt. Commander Mason, 30 November 1940, Box 71, Series III, Miscellaneous. See also Report of Conversations between the Chief of Staff with the Netherlands East Indies Naval Authorities at Batavia, 10 January to 14 January 1941, by Captain Purnell, 18 January 1941, Box 117, Series VII, ABDA-ANZAC Correspondence, Records of the Strategic Plans Division. Compare this, for example, with W.D. McIntyre, pp. 171–2; Martin Gilbert (ed.) (1983), *Their Finest Hour: Winston S. Churchill 1939–1941*, London, vol. 6, pp. 1046–7; Martin Gilbert (1986), *Road to Victory: Winston S. Churchill 1941–1945*, London, vol. 2, p. 7.

96. Ltr Ghormley to Bailey, 9 December 1940; Extract of Minutes DO Committee, 51 Mtg, 17 December 1940; Tel. Halifax to FO, 10 February 1941, FO 371/27886.

97. Minutes of meeting held in D of P's room, 10 December 1940, ADM 199/1232; Ltr Bailey to Clarke, 26 November 1940, CAB 122/4.
98. Minute by Sterndale-Bennett, 11 February 1941, FO 371/27713.
99. Julius Furer (1959), *Administration of the Navy Department in World War II*, Washington, p. 797; Leutze, *Bargaining*, p. 213.
100. Extract of Minute DO Committee, 51 Mtg, 17 December 1940, ADM 199/1232; Leutze, *The London Journal*, pp. 22, 198.
101. Note by Captain Arthur W. Clarke, 21 January 1941, CAB 122/5.
102. Standard accounts can be found in Watson, pp. 367–82; Kittredge, Section IV, pt A, chapter 14, pp. 336–57; Arthur Marder (1981), *Old Friends, New Enemies: The Royal Navy and the Imperial Japanese Navy, Strategic Illusions 1936–41*, Oxford, pp. 188–202; J.R.M. Butler, *Grand Strategy*, pp. 423–7; Maurice Matloff and Edwin M. Snell (1953), *Strategic Planning for Coalition Warfare 1941–42*, Washington, pp. 32–43.
103. Memo FDR to Sec. Nav., 26 January 1941, PSF 80: Navy, FDR Papers.
104. Tel. Halifax to FO, 10 February 1941, FO 371/27713; Tel. DO to Australian PM, 14 March 1941, CAB 80/27; 'Statement by the C.N.O. and C.O.S.', 27 January 1941, Minutes of the US-UK Conversations, Serial 011512–3, Microfilm Roll 5, Strategic Planning in the US Navy: Its Evolution and Execution 1891–1945, Scholarly Resources Inc.
105. BUS (J) 41, Mtg 1, 29 January 1941; 'Statement by the U.S. Staff Committee: The United States Military Position in the Far East', BUS (J) 41, Paper 16, 19 February 1941, CAB 99/5; see also US Serials 09212–7 and 09212–14, WPD 4402–1.
106. BUS (J) 41, Mtg 2, 3 February 1941, Mtg 3, 5 February 1941, CAB 99/5; see US Serials 09212–5, 09212–6, WPD 4402–1; Tel. Bellairs to COS, 1 February 1941, FO 371/26147.
107. Ibid.; Mtg between the Army and Navy Sections, 4 February 1941, US Serial 09212–6; BUS (J) 41, Mtg 3, 5 February 1941, CAB 99/5; Minute by D of P, 13 March 1941, ADM 116/4877; BUS (J) 41, Mtg 11, 26 February 1941, CAB 99/5.
108. 'The Far East Appreciation by the United Kingdom Delegation', BUS (J) 41, Paper 13, 16 February 1941, CAB 99/5.
109. Memo Bellairs to COS, 11 February 1941, ADM 116/4877; See also File BUS (J) 41, Paper 4113, WPD 4402.
110. BUS (J) 41, Paper 5, 29 January 1941, US Serial 09212–4, WPD 4402. See the relevant meetings BUS (J) 41, Mtg 3, 5 February 1941, Mtg 4, 10 February 1941, Mtg 11, 26 February 1941, CAB 99/5. For a summary of the Admiralty position see Tel. Bellairs to

COS, 11 February 1941, CAB 105/36 and Tel. Bellairs to COS, 15 February 1941, 17 February 1941, ADM 116/4877.

111. Minute Churchill to First Lord and First Sea Lord, 17 February 1941, ADM 116/4877.

112. Minutes of meeting of the Joint Army and Navy Sections, 13 February 1941, Microfilm Roll 5, Strategic Planning in the U.S. Navy: Its Evolution and Execution 1891–45, Scholarly Resources Inc.

113. 'Dispatch of United States Forces to Singapore', Memo by Army Committee, 12 February 1941, WPD 4402; Diary of Rear-Admiral Roger Bellairs, entry for 26 February 1941.

114. BUS (J) 41, Mtg 11, 26 February 1941, CAB 99/5.

115. Minute by Bentinck, 16 February 1941, FO 371/27914.

116. Memo Danckwerts to Phillips, 23 June 1941, CAB 122/4.

Cooperation without Collaboration

The creation and operation of any eastern fleet was contingent upon the United States in three ways. The British plan could succeed only if the United States was already at war and an ally of Britain. If the US intervened in the Atlantic – thereby becoming a partner of Britain – and Japan attacked the British Commonwealth, then the United States would declare war on Japan. Similarly, if the Japanese attacked both British and American possessions in the Far East, then the Tripartite Pact which tied Germany, Italy and Japan into a military alliance ensured that a US declaration of war against Germany and Italy would surely follow, since the remaining Axis powers would be bound to be ranged against her. What was less clear was what the United States would do if it was still neutral and Japan attacked only British territories or the Netherlands East Indies.[1] Under wartime conditions, concentration of a British fleet depended on how fast the Americans despatched their reinforcements from the Pacific to both the Atlantic and the Mediterranean. If they reacted too slowly, then the Singapore base would probably fall before the fleet even reached its destination.

Phoenix from the Ashes 1: Resurrection of a Myth

In the wake of the ABC-1 conference, British naval strategy underwent some fundamental changes. The period between the outbreak of war and the relief of Singapore was divided into two phases. During Phase I, protection of British sea communications in the Indian Ocean and clearing a route of passage would be the paramount concerns. Initially the bulk of British naval forces on China and East Indies stations would be assigned to convoy duty. One battlecruiser, one aircraft carrier, one cruiser and five destroyers from Force H would be based at Trincomalee. American naval forces would release some of the 'R' class from Atlantic convoy duty. Once the combined fleet was concentrated Phase II – the relief of Singapore – would be implemented. In the beginning the 'R' class were to proceed to Gilbraltar and relieve Force H, which in turn would be despatched to Eastern waters, but this removed the possibility of any quick transfer of forces so the plan was abandoned.[2] Instead it was decided to re-route both the 'R' class and Force H directly to Singapore.[3] However, as the First Sea Lord pointed out, the arrival timetable as well as the choice of ships for the Eastern Fleet was now at the discretion of the Americans.[4]

Thus, faced with the intransigence of the Prime Minister on the one hand and the intransigence of the Americans on the other, the Admiralty and British staff planners were forced – albeit reluctantly – to resurrect the traditional Far Eastern fleet strategy which a month earlier had been, in their own words, 'dead and buried'. *Nelson* and *Rodney* would be withdrawn from the Home Fleet, together with three of the 'R' class from the North Atlantic and *Renown* from Force H, making a total of six capital ships. These would be joined by the carrier *Ark Royal*, ten cruisers and thirty-two destroyers. Prior to concentration of the Eastern Fleet and on the outbreak of war, one battlecruiser and the carrier *Eagle*, together with a cruiser and five destroyers, would transfer to the Indian Ocean. Once the fleet sailed for Singapore, *Eagle* and *Ark Royal* would be retained in the Indian Ocean as the basis of two hunter-killer groups. Under this modified plan, no naval air cover was to be provided, and once in the Far East, British naval forces would be entirely on the defensive. Pre-war plans favouring cruiser raids were revised. However, since it was US policy to relinquish control of the Philippines, no substantial reinforcement of Manila or raids north of the Malay Barrier were planned. It was felt by US naval authorities that Corregidor would fall long before British naval forces could reach the fortress.[5]

Such were the deficiencies in secondary vessels that the Admiralty had to shift and juggle considerable numbers of ships to even form a fleet. Many stations would have to be denuded. The Admiralty had fifty cruisers in service, but thirteen of these were 'C' and 'D' class unsuited to heavy sea duty, leaving no more than thirty-seven capable of operating in blue water. Ten were with the Home Fleet, seven were in the Mediterranean, eight were with the Dominions (and these would be based in their respective home waters) and two were in the Caribbean. This left ten modern and thirteen old cruisers for both trade protection duties and the Eastern Fleet. The only way to make up cruiser numbers was to secure the loan of four US vessels.[6]

It would also be necessary to denude home waters, Gibraltar and Freetown of modern destroyers for Far Eastern duties. The Admiralty hoped the United States would provide nine destroyers for Plymouth, five for Iceland and eighteen for Gibraltar.[7] British naval staff were distinctly nervous about such dispositions, but given the stance of the US they had little choice in the matter:

The Fleet proposed for the Far East appears inadequate in the light of pre-war appreciation, but it is considered that it should suffice for a defensive role. . . Japanese efficiency and morale may well be low; we cannot be strong everywhere and risks must be taken. It is better to take them in the Far East where we have until recently been contemplating having no fleet at all, than to take them in the vital area at home.[8]

However, even given that the Fleet ever reached its destination unless deficiencies in cruisers and destroyers were made up from Dominion and US sources, it could still be crippled operationally. Six capital ships alone were obviously not sufficient to face the full might of the Imperial Japanese Navy. The success of Eastern Fleet operations depended as well on offensive action by the US Pacific Fleet. As Tom Phillips so succinctly put it, it would be useless to have 'a vast fleet at Hawaii making faces at Japan'. For the strategy to work, the US Navy would have to fulfil its promise to draw Japanese naval forces away from the Malay Barrier.[9]

A blueprint for the defence of the whole of Malaya rather than simply the Singapore base had been approved in principle by the Cabinet on 8 August 1940.[10] Over the short term, however, satisfactory force levels could never be met. By December 1941 the target of nine army brigades would probably be reached, but paper strength could not disguise the lack of equipment and shortage of experienced troops. Front-line air strength was only 158 aircraft, less than double what it had been in 1940 and under half the minimum requirement of 336. Most of these machines were outdated Brewster Buffalo fighters and Glen Martin bombers.[11] Little wonder British naval planners had pressed for reinforcement of the Asiatic Fleet at the Washington Conference in January; this force and US air power were felt to be the keys to any successful early defence of the base. However, Admiral Hart had to be dissuaded from retaining his forces at Manila and persuaded to allow the bulk of the Asiatic Fleet to be transferred to Singapore, preferably before the war but at the very least as soon as possible after its outbreak.[12] Even Sir Robert Brooke-Popham's appointment as C-in-C Far East was a carefully contrived attempt to gain control of all airpower in the area, for as the highest ranking officer in the region, it was assumed he would be the natural choice as AOC over the respective multinational air force the British hoped would be created in the area.

A Stab in the Dark: The Search for a Joint Operating Plan

Agreement at international level requires a certain flexibility, which in turn implies a willingness to compromise: often difficult to achieve when mutually opposed national interests are at stake. ABC-1 had established the general strategic principles and the areas of responsibility involved in a collaborative effort against Japan, but operational timing by the 'associated powers' would be crucial. Such problems of detail could only really be solved by a joint operating plan at the field command level. Early in October 1940, the United States had appeared willing to proceed immediately to full staff conversations in the Pacific. The Prime Minister wanted to hold such discussions in tandem with meetings in Washington and London. British naval staff hoped an 'inter-allied' meeting in the Far East with American, Dominion, British and Dutch representatives would be a valuable deterrent against Japan. Discussions would range from talks about the defence of the Philippines and the Netherlands East Indies to consideration of the strategic problems of the whole Pacific theatre.[13] But while this idea was fine in theory, in practice a plethora of mutual misunderstandings and inexplicable delays, coupled with a poor communications system and sheer bureaucratic bungling, complicated proceedings and made success difficult to achieve. No less than five Far Eastern conferences were held between October 1940 and May 1941, yet unanimous agreement between the participants was no nearer at the end of this period than it had been at the beginning.

The first meeting between the British, Americans and Dutch, held from 22–31 October 1940 at Singapore, failed as an international conference. The Dutch feared taking any step that might provoke a Japanese attack on the Netherlands East Indies. Instead they hoped to escape the problem by strictly maintaining the status quo. The Governor-General of Batavia was also worried about security; Singapore was seen as being rife with spies and there was much concern lest military secrets fall into the wrong hands. The Dutch therefore refused to send any representatives.[14] As for the Americans, the President now backed away from the idea of full staff conversations. Since the preferred American methodological approach was to proceed from the general to the particular, there seemed little point – from the US point of view – in discussing tactical details without having first established the general strategic principles. These were not worked out until March 1941. The motivation for an international Far Eastern conference simply did not exist.

The US Navy Department did send a representative, but Commander A.C. Thomas was not even attached to the Asiatic Fleet; he held the lowly post of Assistant Naval Attaché at the American Embassy in Bangkok. Under strict instructions not to undertake any political commitments, his brief was simply to observe and report. He arrived on 28 October, some two-thirds of the way through the conference. As a result, Brooke-Popham was forced to tear up two pages of questions prepared by his staff specifically for the Americans.[15] What had been intended as an international conference ended as merely a tête-a-tête with the Dominions; and here too the results were distinctly disappointing. The British Far Eastern Appreciation had to be heavily censored by the Chiefs of Staff Committee to strike from it references that might be 'misconstrued by Dominion authorities', particularly those sections suggesting that British commitment to the Far East would be less than whole-hearted. Only a précis was sent as a brief, so the British delegation was required to refrain from discussing force level requirements in detail.[16] Australia was distinctly unhappy about the vagueness of such discussions.[17]

As there was no US Consulate or Embassy in Singapore itself, Thomas was forced to telegraph his initial report through the British Embassy in Washington, though after the meeting he passed on his opinions directly to Admiral Hart in Manila. The use of British channels of communication precluded any direct American commentary or criticisms. From the minutes, Hart concluded that the Dutch would hold the balance of available forces in the Far East anyway, and it would be better to hold future talks with them rather than with the British.[18] Nor did reaction in Washington auger well for Far Eastern cooperation. Stark spoke of the 'wishful thinking' of British planning agencies, of their 'slack ways. . .and their non-realistic views of international political conditions and our own political system'.[19]

A lack of definite political and military guarantees and misapprehensions about the extent and location of naval dispositions continued to be stumbling blocks. The Netherlands East Indies was willing to cooperate, but only in the event of a definite assurance of military support. The British representatives were not willing to make such pledges unless they knew what the US position would be. Neither at the Anglo-Dutch meeting at Singapore from 26–29 November (with the Americans again present as observers), nor during the American-Dutch Conference in Batavia from 10-14 January 1941, were such categorical promises forthcoming.

Anglo-Dutch relations continued to be complicated by a division of opinion within the British Chiefs of Staff Committee. As long as the US scrupulously maintained its neutral position and Britain's own resources remained so limited, the Admiralty felt it would be unwise to extend defence measures beyond the territorial limits of the Far Eastern possessions.[20] The Dutch did agree to be responsible for local naval defence up to the Rhio archipelago and Northern Sumatra. Submarines and aircraft would keep Japan at bay while a Dutch 'fleet in being' deployed to any threatened sector. However, the British would provide no naval forces for the defence of the Netherlands East Indies; even the three 'D' class cruisers from China Station were assigned to protect Penang. The Dutch reciprocated: no provision was made for assistance to Malaya in their plans.[21] The leading Dutch Navy representative, Captain Van Staveren, wanted to know what the Americans would do if Japan attacked by way of the Sulu Sea. Would the US protect Dutch shipping en route to the west coast of the United States? The American reply gave additional cause for concern:

> To the first I replied that we would guarantee the neutrality of the Philippines and to the extent of attacking with all forces available, would notify them as well as other nations of serious breaches of neutrality, and we would probably maintain a benevolent neutrality towards the Dutch and British. To the second I replied that I thought a War Zone would be prescribed and that conditions would be the same as now exist in European waters.[22]

The possibility of mutual Australian-British-Dutch cooperation (without US participation) was discussed at the ADA Conference at Singapore from 22–25 February 1941. The meeting took place at a time when the Japanese Navy, with appropriate displays of might in the Gulf of Siam and the South China Sea, insisted on brokering border disputes between French IndoChina and Thailand. There was considerable fear expressed that Japan would force the French and the Thais to lease their bases, thereby opening the way to Burma, Singapore and the Indian Ocean. A war scare ensued. Amid rumours of a Japanese 'lightning strike', Australian troops were dispatched to Malaya and the Dutch recalled their shipping.[23] The meeting took steps to establish a limit on Japanese expansion by creating a 'chalk line'. It recommended that military action be taken without reference to London if Japan directly attacked the territory of the associated powers, invaded that part of Thailand west of 100 degrees east longitude or south of 10 degrees north latitude, directed naval forces towards the east coast of Malaya or the Kra Isthmus, crossed 6 degrees north longitude between Malaya and the Philippines, or landed on Portuguese Timor, New Caledonia or the Loyalty Islands. Spheres of operational control for naval forces and airpower were also established. The Netherlands East Indies finally agreed to release three bomber and one fighter squadrons for service in Malaya and the British promised to place four bomber squadrons under Dutch control, while Australia agreed to reinforce Ambon and Koepang. Significantly, it was felt Japan would be unable to invade more than one target at a time.[24]

This conference had originally been intended to discuss matters of only general concern. In fact, the New Zealand government was not told in time of specific alterations to the brief of the meeting which converted it into detailed discussions. New Zealand decided not to attend, instead allowing Australia to represent their interests. Understandably, New Zealand refused to accept the 'chalk line' concept as it was an agreement reached without consultation. Without reciprocal American assurances, Australia felt that invasion of the Philippines could not be regarded as a *casus belli*, while the Chiefs of Staff Committee in London refused to accept that any automatic response to Japan could be initiated without London's political sanction.[25] The British had expected the Navy Department to despatch only 'observers', but as the ABC-1 Conference was now underway, US planners assumed any meeting would discuss definite plans for cooperation with US forces. Captain W.R. Purnell, Hart's Chief of Staff, pointed out to British naval authorities in Singapore that the Asiatic Fleet was ready to serve under British leadership in a unified command structure.[26] An early report from London about the lack of British progress there had only just reached UK field commands; it was patently obvious to Singapore staff that Hart was not aware of the general strategic principles being established in Washington. Reluctantly, British planners in Singapore concluded it would be a waste of time to begin independent talks at this stage, and an opportunity to extract definite commitments from the Asiatic Fleet was missed, much to the Admiralty's later regret.[27]

The meeting was also characterized by a violent disagreement between Rear-Admiral Sir Geoffrey Layton, C-in-C China Station, and the chief Australian naval representative, Rear-Admiral R.E. Crace, over trade protection plans.[28] As they intended to concentrate all naval forces in the Tasman Sea area, the Australian Government insisted that all Dominion cruisers be returned to their respective home stations. However, the Admiralty took the view that Far Eastern waters must be considered as a whole, and felt such dispositions would defeat the overall defence objective, which was the protection of Malaya. Attempts to convince the Australians to adopt less local dispositions proved singularly unsuccessful.[29]

All the various participants finally met for what was hoped would be the deciding round of discussions at Singapore from 21–27 April 1941. Though no political commitment was implied, the overall objective was to prepare a plan on the basis of the ABC-1 Agreement, but like so many of the other meetings the organization of this conference left a great deal to be desired. The need to reach a speedy agreement overrode any requirements for careful preparation.[30] Only two copies of the ABC-1 report were available for British staff, and these were in the hands of the Australian and New Zealand delegations.[31] Brooke-Popham had received only a summary of results from Washington, so he was put in the invidious position of having to borrow his own copy.[32] Since the Asiatic Fleet had not been appraised of the situation either, Purnell was forced to borrow his report from the US Army.[33] The Australian delegation sent no naval representatives, so it proved difficult to discuss Dominion naval matters with any degree of competence.[34]

The ADB conference felt that the US Pacific Fleet would have to be maintained at a level equal to that of the Japanese Imperial Navy. Initially, the Asiatic Fleet would be based on Manila and would operate against the flank of any Japanese advance. Once Hart's forces moved south from Manila, Purnell promised they would withdraw on Singapore; it was also agreed that all auxiliaries and tenders would be sent there before the outbreak of war. During Phase I, Britain's defence strategy was to hold, in cooperation with the Dutch, a crescent running from Lashio in Burma to Tonga in the Pacific with Singapore as the focal point. In the Fleet's absence, reliance was placed on airpower for mobile defence with the land forces in a static role. Naval plans envisaged guarding the passages through the East Indian archipelago in conjunction with the air forces, but the majority of British naval forces were to be employed in the Indian Ocean on sea protection duties.[35] The Admiralty agreed that the timetable for Phase I might also be moved forward, the transfer of a battlecruiser and an aircraft carrier to Trincomalee would now take place in peacetime rather than in wartime. Thus during Phase II, the British Eastern Fleet was expected to arrive at Singapore ready to seize the initiative at an earlier date.[36]

To clear up outstanding matters left over from the ADA meeting in February, talks were held between British and Dutch representatives on 27 April 1941 in Singapore (Plenaps) with the Americans present once more as observers. Under Plenaps, the Dutch area of responsibility was now extended, stretching from the line of the Equator from 92 degrees east to 113 degrees east, then northeast to the frontier of Sarawak along the frontier line to British Borneo and the Sulu Sea. In the west the line proceeded to 13 degrees south, 120 degrees east, excluding Seamau, Timor and Molu, to Cape Valsche and 141 degrees east, and then directly north. The Dutch also promised to provide a cruiser at Singapore. The 'chalk line' formula was obdurately reiterated, while the lack of an adequate briefing enabled conference discussions to stray all too freely into areas of political rather than military concern.[37] Indeed, as the C-in-C China Station reported, in terms of detailed operating procedures these meetings were of little real value:

> In April 1941 the first ADB Conference assembled at Singapore, and its proceedings served to confirm the opinion I had already formed as to the

distinct but limited value of these Conferences. The exchange of personal contacts between Commanders and Staffs, and verbal discussions of difficulties are always felt to be of immense value and are indeed the only really way of achieving a real common understanding of definite problems. It is when the Conference gets down to the task of reducing its conclusions to writing that the proceedings begin to develop into discussions of doubtful utility.[38]

To a large extent the conversations at Singapore and Washington were conducted in isolation from each other. Far Eastern commanders were more conscious of the need to survive an initial Japanese onslaught, so it was understandable that the view from the Far East should be at odds with the views from London and Washington. Brooke-Popham and Layton made no bones over the fact that they opposed many of the dispositions outlined by ABC-1, which they felt was too pessimistic. They stressed the need for the United States to take a more forward role in Far Eastern defence by preventing Japan from even reaching the Malay Barrier, and emphasized the desirability of reinforcing the Asiatic Fleet and the advantages of an advanced fleet base at Hong Kong.[39] While it is true the seeds of a new US Far Eastern strategy were already present, the Joint Planning Committee in London was not convinced that offensive action from Manila was likely to have much effect:

> It is also very much open to doubt whether, with the forces at present based there, the Japanese would regard the threat from Manila as sufficiently serious to deter them from activities further to the southward. The Japanese line of communication from Formosa via Kamranh Bay would pass at least 500 miles clear of Manila. Unless it is made very much stronger, Manila is not likely to be of much value as a base for surface forces and submarines and aircraft alone are unlikely to be able to sever the Japanese lines of communication.[40]

There were also political objections; increased interest in the area north of the Malay Barrier directly challenged existing US policy. The Chiefs of Staff Committee was at pains to point out that ADB had ignored the need for a 'soft approach':

> We agree that Luzon is a key position the retention of which would be of great value. It is clear, however, from the report of the recent Staff Discussions at Washington that it is not the present intention of the U.S.A. to reinforce the Far East, and failing considerable reinforcement, there is little prospect of holding Luzon against Japanese attack. In these circumstances it is doubtful if Manila would constitute a serious deterrent to Japan's southern advances. We would welcome any strengthening of the Philippines which could be effected otherwise than at the expense of the

U.S. effort in the Atlantic theatre, but we prefer not to press the U.S. Chiefs of Staff any further on this point beyond informing them of our views at this stage.[41]

Misreading the Signals

As has been seen, distrust was very much a part of the relationship between Britain and the United States in the Pacific. En route to the Washington Conference, the British delegation had refused to allow the Americans access to British planning papers until Ghormley and Lee were actually on board ship.[42] Admiral Hart had arranged for the exchange of naval observers between Singapore and Manila, but the Admiralty insisted US naval staff in the Far East not be given access to 'classified information'.[43] Resistance to the release of intelligence was still a deeply embedded feature of Admiralty policy. Codes, cyphers, intelligence reports, aircraft and submarine signals, as well as outlines of future plans, were denied to the US staff until late in 1941. During the ABC-1 meetings Bellairs tried to discover the US Pacific Fleet's operating plans, but was told by Turner that this was entirely the prerogative of the C-in-C Pacific Fleet. Significantly, no one in Washington professed to have 'any clear idea' about what such plans might be.[44]

Rear-Admiral Danckwerts therefore decided to visit Admiral Kimmel at Pearl Harbor. The results of this meeting, held from 9–11 April, were both disturbing and disappointing. Danckwerts gained a better insight into the peculiarities of US field commands than into US planning. At the time, US Far Eastern planning was in a transitory stage between Rainbow 3 and Rainbow 5; forewarned by Admiral Stark, CINCPAC and CINCAF were told not to divulge specific information. To use his own colloquialism, Danckwerts was given the 'run-around'. His report underwrote Admiral Hart's own conclusions concerning the Pacific Fleet's obsessive preoccupation with battlefleet action and fleet tactics. As he saw it, Kimmel utterly opposed splitting the fleet into detachments. In operational terms there was some discussion about carrier raids into Japanese waters, but Kimmel argued that as far as he was concerned this was not a practical proposition. The Americans gave the impression that the 'mere existence' of the Pacific Fleet at Hawaii would restrain Japan and there were few 'definite war orders'. British policy was going to have to be based 'on the hope' that preparations would be made in future for offensive operations into the Marshalls and the Carolines. Unfortunately, at this stage Admiral Kimmel had no knowledge of 'enemy dispositions' or the location of the Japanese defences.

The American attitude obviously worried Danckwerts, but only hints of this reached Admiralty ears. In his report he noted, for example, 'a latent dissatisfaction, an unhappiness about the role and the strategy' of the US Pacific Fleet. Significantly, in operational terms, CINCPAC was seen as repeating his views almost 'by rote'. Kimmel also 'inferred' that he would have considerable difficulty in overcoming Japanese shore resistance and pointed out that the means at his disposal were 'indifferent'. Had Danckwerts written a stronger report it might have resulted in a fundamental reassessment of strategy by the Admiralty, but unfortunately Danckwerts was confused by the fact that Kimmel himself had not yet received a copy of the ABC-1 Agreement upon which to base an operating plan.[45]

Rainbow Plan 5 and the US Pacific Fleet

Even before the ABC Conference the US Army and Navy delegations in Washington had been unable to agree on a common Far Eastern strategy. During these sessions they disagreed with each other constantly, often meeting separately. The American delegates brought their differences to the negotiating table, much to the embarrassment of the British who had to act as referee. One of the key items of US interservice disagreement concerned offensive operations; the US Army wanted to limit the scope of all operations to the capture of advanced positions in the Marshalls, while Navy representatives wanted to provide for action 'in the Mandates' as a whole. A compromise solution with the wording 'Marshalls and possibly the Carolines' was accepted on the understanding that operations in the Carolines were of a contingent nature, and 'if undertaken at all' would be delayed until six months after US entry into the war. Somehow this was lost in translation to the British. Under the aegis of ABC-1 the Americans agreed to divert Japanese strength away from the Malay Barrier, but the US Pacific Fleet was only asked to 'prepare to capture and establish control over the Caroline and Marshall Island area'. Nothing was said about executing that task.[46]

The US Fleet had been serving in the capacity of deterrent force since April 1940. Once Pearl Harbor became the main fleet operating base, that faction within the Navy Department, the defensive 'armadillos', who dissented from main stream US naval strategy re-emerged. The Commander in Chief of the US Fleet, Admiral Richardson, and his successor, Admiral Kimmel, became vociferous critics both of administration policy and of the forward role played by the Navy at Hawaii. Both men were deeply worried by the lack of political direction from above. Both were concerned lest the President's more aggressive use of economic pressure jeopardize the precarious international situation. Richardson felt that Stark, a Presidential appointee to the job of Chief of Naval Operations, was not adequately representing the naval viewpoint. He saw his own role as a naval 'devil's advocate'. He became convinced the President must be made aware of the real strategic situation. Unfortunately, by suggesting that 'senior officers of the Navy, do not have trust and confidence in the civilian leadership', Richardson interfered directly and indelicately into the area of civil-military relations, if not Presidential responsibility. Unable to tolerate an officer whose attitude was so much at odds with his own, he was marked down by Roosevelt for replacement. Richardson was dismissed before his term of office expired.[47]

As Commander Battle Force, Kimmel had served under Richardson's leadership and to a great extent he was his protégé. From their naval experience, both men had already concluded that US war plans were based on unrealistic presuppositions which could not possibly be carried out. Both opposed any movement of the Fleet beyond Hawaii. This applied as much under the Rainbow Plans as it did under War Plan 'Orange':

> It is extremely doubtful that sufficient Japanese strength will be diverted from the Asiatic theater by the mere denial of Wake and the Marshall and Gilbert Islands. Nor do raids on Japanese sea communications offer much promise. Critical Japanese communications lines and important forces will most probably be confined to areas too far from Hawaii for sustained pressure.[48]

This was not a new policy. The evolution of such doubts through the 1920s and 1930s has already been seen; deficiencies, equipment problems, the lack of an adequate number of auxiliaries and the paucity of base facilities explain why. As far as Richardson was concerned, the deciding factor had been the poor performance of the Fleet during Problem 21 in April 1940. During the second half of the exercise Hawaii, the Aleutians, Tutuila, Wake and Canton were presumed to be under 'Maroon' or US control, with well defended outlying bases at Pearl Harbor and Balboa. 'Purple' possessed an advanced position at Guam. The scenario opened with a 'Purple' Expeditionary Force leaving Manila with a similar force already based on Guam. After ten days steaming both opposing fleets came into contact off Hilo. In a night engagement the battlelines blundered into each other and by early morning all order had been lost. Ships from both sides were 'milling about in circles all over the ocean', and to make a bad situation worse, a detachment of submarines proceeding back to base was caught on the surface in the mêlée. It was a 'miracle' that no ship suffered damage, and the entire exercise had to be cancelled. The US Navy's obvious lack of experience in night fighting proved to be a detrimental factor in the early days of the Pacific war in actions such as the Battle for Savo Island.[49]

The US Fleet was indeed deficient in almost every field of endeavour. In terms of personnel, numbers increased from 110,000 in July 1939 to only 152,808 by November 1940, and the US Navy was still 18,426 men short of establishment strength. Complements on US ships fluctuated between 85 per cent and 92 per cent, and the matter was complicated by a quick turn-over in service and continual need for training back in the United States. Some 17,000 additional petty officers were required if war broke out. The US Navy did not manage to get enough men for operating requirements until late 1942.[50]

Action against the Marshalls and the Carolines depended on adequate aerial reconnaissance. Kimmel had only three squadrons of patrol aircraft, and their effectiveness was jeopardized by a lack of leak-proof tanks, armour protection, oxygen equipment and spare parts.[51] In August 1941 the Commandant 14th Naval District pointed out that aerial patrol activities by the Navy would have to be limited to anti-submarine work.[52] Because of the anticipated pressure on his repair facilities, CINCPAC was loath to risk his aircraft by instituting regular patrols around Hawaii.[53] In addition there were a total of only fifty-two carrier-based planes available, of which only twenty-two were fighters. Of a total of four fighter squadrons, nearly one-third were obsolete. In the words of Kimmel himself, the Fleet was 'severely handicapped with regard to naval airpower.' In any case the number of airfields around Pearl Harbor was so limited that no dispersal plan could be instituted even if numbers had been available. Air space was so crowded and the traffic so heavy that barrage balloons could not even be fitted over the base.[54]

Surface operations were also hampered by the limited availability of light forces, anti-submarine equipment, destroyers and cruisers. Kimmel had on hand only four transports, one general goods ship and two provision ships, estimated at 30 per cent of what would be required for a full expeditionary force to the Marshalls.[55] As with Rainbows 2 and 3, the Army refused to support Rainbow 5, so amphibious assaults were to be handled by the two-division Fleet Marine Force. However, as part of an outer network of defences, Midway was to be completed in 1943, Johnston by January 1942 and Wake by December 1942, and to assist in the protection of these outlying bases the Navy was forced to split one Marine division into defence battalions. That division itself had yet to be built up to establishment strength, while the second

Marine division lacked small arms, ammunition, jeeps, trucks, lighters and sufficient boats for operational requirements. As Stark informed Kimmel, there was little hope that such deficiencies could be made up from naval sources. Because the Navy Department constantly feared that their assault forces would be absorbed by the Army, they refused to sanction increases in the Fleet Marine Force beyond two divisions. As the Army War Plans section pointed out, this 'not only seriously impairs the readiness of the fleet to carry out wartime operations. . . but opens the Navy Department to proper criticism for its neglect in this regard'.[56]

One of the insurmountable problems faced by the US Navy was the limitations on Pearl Harbor as a base as well as the general lack of facilities across the whole west coast. At San Francisco, the Oakland Supply Depot was yet to be finished and Treasure Island in the Bay area had only just been acquired. Four new aircraft carrier berths were planned for San Diego and a new drydock for San Pedro, but these were not yet operating. Two naval air stations were finished, one at Puget Sound and a second at Sitka, but the third at Kaneohe in Hawaii was still only partly completed. Even in 1941, facilities at Pearl Harbor were still considered to be only 70 per cent sufficient. If no dry docking occurred, the build-up of underwater growth would mean US battleships would be able to cruise at a maximum of only 15 knots. A new dry dock was to arrive at the base late in 1941, and eventually it was hoped repair facilities could handle a maximum of 30 per cent of fleet needs, but Pearl Harbor continued to lack cold storage facilities and local products were not produced in sufficient quantity even to supply the fleet. In event of war, Admiral Richardson expected most of the US battleships to return to the West Coast for drydocking and refurbishing. To ease the burden, both Richardson and Kimmel attempted to introduce rotating repair schemes in peacetime. Stark – albeit reluctantly – agreed to this idea late in 1941, and by the middle of 1942 nearly one-third of the Pacific Fleet would almost certainly have been out of action, either under repair or en route to or from yards. Stark stressed that this had to be kept secret at all costs, particularly as the Pacific Fleet had already been denuded by increased requirements from the Atlantic Theatre.[57]

Fuel was also a matter of critical concern. Some $6,500,000 had been appropriated to begin work on underground storage tanks on Oahu, and an additional $350,000 was set aside for bomb-proofing existing facilities, but this was only 12 per cent complete at the end of 1940. From July to December that year 841,000 barrels of fuel oil were delivered, but consumption by the fleet over the whole year was 3,972,000 barrels. Between May and June of 1941, 300,000 barrels reached Oahu, but in March alone consumption rose to 703,036 barrels.

Some 3,495,478 barrels were considered reserve stocks but these were under Executive Order and subject for release only in an emergency, and then only by the express permission of the President. By July 1941, usable stocks had fallen to a meagre 2165 barrels.[58] Despite vehement protests from naval staff about splitting the fleet, Richardson was forced to divide naval forces into two task forces to ease the strain. Each was to be employed at sea and in port on alternate weeks. Later, the loss of extended upkeep and the increase in fuel expenditure forced Kimmel to adopt a three-part task force assignment, with an average of eight days at sea to thirteen in port.[59] Even if additional fuel had been available, Kimmel lacked the means to get it; there were only fourteen tankers attached to the command, and seven of these were obsolete. Some battleships still lacked the ability to refuel at sea.[60] It was little wonder that Kimmel expressed great disquiet to Stark about the assigned Fleet role:

> The role of light forces and particularly carriers in the Pacific, is far more important than casual evaluation of relative strength would suggest. Under Rainbow 5 the Pacific Fleet (perhaps justifiably, in view of the Atlantic situation) is so reduced in light forces and carrier strength that its capabilities for offensive operations of a decisive nature are severely crippled. Quick results may only be hoped for – common sense dictates that it is largely hope, based primarily upon the idea that Japan will make a fundamental mistake. . . In the Pacific, with enemy vital interests so far away and no bases of our own within striking distance the logistic problem is acute. We have not, at present, sufficient ammunition, provisions, cargo ships, or tankers to support active operations in the Western Pacific – where the real battleground will be. We are having trouble, even now, supporting the construction and defense of our own outlying bases.[61]

Because of the limitations on mobile repair facilities, it was felt temporary retirement from the whole area might prove necessary. Advanced fleet bases with full maintenance facilities, repair shops, wharves and dry docks were expected to take between two to five years to complete. Kimmel's orders required an operating plan based on the ABC-1 Agreement and Rainbow 5, but it was patently obvious he was simply going through the motions. As late as October 1941, Stark wrote complaining that no plans for advanced fleet bases in the Carolines had been submitted by CINCPAC. Kimmel's end product, Operating Plan 0-1, adapted existing Task Force designations but was far removed from the original ABC concept. Task Force Three, consisting of eight cruisers, one aircraft carrier and sixteen destroyers, would initially conduct a patrol and sweep operation, supported by land-based aerial reconnaissance. Depending on Japanese reaction, Task Force Two with three battleships, one aircraft carrier, four cruisers and eight destroyers would conduct a reconnaissance in force into the Marshalls area itself. The six battleships, one aircraft carrier, five light cruisers and sixteen destroyers of Task Force One would be held back until 'opposition has been overcome and a position obtained from which solid strength can be brought to bear'. They would then be used to 'cover' the operations of Task Force Two. If successful, Task Forces Two and Three would be combined, and then, and only then, would a raid against Eniwetok take place. All these actions were still conditional on sufficient carriers, auxiliaries, patrol aircraft, and anti-submarine protection. An amphibious landing in the Marshalls was planned but would only take place during Phase II.[62] Considering the reductions in the Pacific Fleet's battleship strength affected by mid-year, even Stark himself was reluctantly forced to admit that limited resources meant limited offensive capability:[63]

> We have seat blood in the endeavour to divide adequately our forces for a two ocean war; but you cannot take inadequate forces and divide them into two or three parts and get adequate forces anywhere. It has been for this reason that almost as soon as I got here I started working on increasing the Navy. It was on the basis of inadequate forces that A.B.C.-1 and Rainbow 5 were predicated, and which were accepted by all concerned as about the best compromise we could get out of the situation actually confronting us.[64]

> While offensives by the Pacific Fleet in the Central Pacific may not draw important Japanese forces in that direction, they ought to have an important effect in pinning the Japanese Navy to northern waters or to bases in the Western Pacific.[65]

A surprise aerial attack on Pearl Harbor had been considered a likely option for some considerable time. Some reports were astonishingly accurate in their predictions, speaking of attacks being launched two hours before dawn, on Sunday or a holiday, from Japanese aircraft carriers 350 miles or so from the Hawaiian coast.[66] The Army report on Fleet Problem 21 had pinpointed the fact that the Navy possessed no adequate aircraft detection equipment. Radar sets had been fitted both to the aircraft carriers and the 'Indianapolis' class cruisers, but these were short-range and only operated in a straight line. It was therefore expected that enemy aircraft would 'be in attack range before being detected'. As the depth in the harbour was so shallow it was not felt necessary to fit anti-torpedo baffles, and the fleet was expected to be secure from this kind of attack.[67] In any case protection of the port facilities was an Army responsibility, and there were fifty-six 3-inch mobile and twenty-six fixed 3-inch guns on Oahu for that purpose. However, because of the lengthy training time required, the Army could provide sufficient personnel to man only seventeen guns. Nevertheless the planners remained confident that if no serious damage was done to the base within the first six hours, existing defences would deter attack. The key to successful defence during those first few hours lay with the Navy, the only other alternative source of anti-aircraft cover within the base area. As long as the capital ships remained in harbour the Army saw no reason to increase harbour anti-aircraft defences.[68]

According to mainstream US naval strategy, base facilities were supposed to exist for the preservation and protection of the fleet; now the fleet was to be used for the preservation and protection of the base facilities. The Pacific Fleet's battleships were inextricably tied to the harbour area. It has often been supposed that if Admiral Kimmel had received adequate warning his ships might have fled Pearl Harbor and escaped intact, but in event of a surprise attack the Base Defence Plan presumed the battleships would remain at anchor. Each ship was assigned a specific field of fire which was to have been coordinated by the Commander of 14th Naval District from shore. Offensive action by the Fleet would have been curtailed by the need to beat off aerial attacks.[69] Even if the facilities and equipment had been available for offensive action, Kimmel would have had little chance to put them to use:

> The existing deficiencies in the defenses of Oahu and in the local defence forces of 14th Naval District impose a heavy burden on the Fleet for purely defensive purposes. Ideally, a Fleet Base should afford a refuge and rest for personnel as well as an opportunity for maintenance and upkeep of material installations. When Fleet planes, Fleet guns and Fleet personnel are required to be constantly ready for defense of its own Base, the wear and tear on both men and material can not but result in impaired readiness for active operations at sea.[70]

Developments in the Atlantic and in the Mediterranean in 1941 also restricted the possibility of offensive action by the Pacific Fleet. Having evicted the British from the Balkan Peninsula the Germans seemed to be poised for a two-pronged drive into the heart of the Middle East, and Wavell's counter-offensive in North Africa was floundering by mid-June. The regular night bombing against British cities intensified, while shipping losses in the Atlantic increased dramatically from a winter average of 365,000 tons a month to 530,000 and 668,000 tons respectively for March and April. U-Boat operations now extended to the eastern coast of Greenland, and surface raider activity had forced the Admiralty to disperse the Home Fleet. By late April the British Government was anticipating an early German seizure of Gibraltar, as well as French, Spanish and Portuguese possessions in the South Atlantic, and preparations were being made for pre-emptive US occupation of the Canaries, Cape Verde Islands and the Azores.[71]

These events reinforced Anglo-American predisposition towards early US action in the Atlantic. The crux of the matter concerned convoy escorts. Two American hemisphere defence plans had been drawn up by US authorities by April 1940. The first, Hemisphere Plan 1, provided for full US naval escort for all merchant shipping as far as the twenty-sixth meridian of longitude. If Axis vessels and aircraft entered the waters of the western hemisphere then they would be attacked. In addition, three task forces comprising battleships, aircraft carriers and cruisers would sweep to the edge of the war zone and back. US warships would be ordered to prevent interference with US flagged vessels. Within twenty-five miles of the US coastline and in the close waters round the Gulf of St Lawrence, the Caribbean and Bermuda, patrols would warn away Axis craft, and attack them if they failed to heed the warning.[72] The second plan, Hemisphere Plan 2, was similar to the first, but US action was limited to patrol activity and to the convoying of only its own ships. All enemy movements, however, would be reported to British authorities. By late April Hemisphere Plan 2 was in force, the patrol area and the US security zone was extended to include Greenland, and on 7 July US ground forces replaced the British garrison on Iceland. However, Roosevelt was not prepared to allow full convoy escorting nor would he implement 'shoot on sight' orders. To aid the patrol activity of the Atlantic Fleet, one aircraft carrier and four destroyers passed through the Panama Canal on 6 May, and three battleships, four cruisers and fourteen destroyers followed them a week or so later.[73] Unfortunately, all these reinforcements had to be taken from the Pacific, and weakening the Fleet there could only weaken the deterrent effect.[74] The loss of *Yorktown* alone deprived Kimmel of nearly one-third of his carrier strength, the absent cruisers and destroyers deprived his forces of desperately needed mobility, and while the lack of three oilers chained the Pacific Fleet ever more tightly to Pearl Harbor.[75]

So concerned with the Atlantic situation did US naval staff become that the British authorities were approached with the suggestion that US battleship strength in the Pacific be reduced to three capital ships. Churchill agreed that a marked advance by the United States Navy into the Atlantic might have a greater deterrent effect than maintenance of a large fleet at Hawaii, but for safety's sake and as insurance, the British urged the remaining command not be reduced below six battleships. British naval authorities, however, remained blissfully unaware of the true condition of the US Fleet at Hawaii.

Hostile Reactions to ADB

With the proviso that the 'chalk line' idea was abandoned and Hong Kong excluded from consideration as an advanced fleet base, the British Chiefs of Staff recommended approval of the ADB Report. By 5 September 1941, British authorities had formally accepted ABC-1, Plenaps and the ADA Agreement. However, there continued to be problems with the Roosevelt administration. Although the US Chiefs of Staff sanctioned ABC-1, the President reserved political approval and made it subject to US entry into the war. Nor was agreement for ADB forthcoming. Admiral Danckwerts reported that the Americans 'have taken it very badly and with their usual suspicious outlook have almost accused me of having pulled the wool over their eyes and of concealing these arrangements during the process of the Joint Staff conversations'.[76] Professor Arthur Marder has argued that British authorities received official notification concerning US objections to ADB as early as 3 July,[77] but in fact this report was purely provisional and unofficial. It took twenty-two days for official confirmation of the US position to arrive from Washington, much to the chagrin of British planning staffs.[78]

These problems developed because of the way in which both sides viewed the ABC-1 Agreement. In order to take into account alterations in the international situation, British planners felt arrangements must be flexible. The ABC-1 Report was seen as an outline, a starting point from which a more detailed joint operating plan would evolve. The Americans, on the other hand, regarded the agreement as their 'Bible': any alteration to the provisions was viewed with suspicion as a surreptitious attempt by Britain to exploit the situation for its own ends.[79] This was not altogether untrue. In May, the British authorities had decided to redraw their area of responsibility in the Far East by creating a new Eastern Theatre. The East Indian, Australian, New Zealand and other British naval stations in the region were to be placed under the command of C-in-C Eastern Fleet, a blatant attempt to bypass Australian and New Zealand preoccupations with local defence and gain control of Dominion naval forces, just as the appointment of Sir Robert Brooke-Popham had been an attempt to dominate airpower.[80] However, this deviation from the substance of ABC-1 aroused the ire of Admiral Turner. In what Danckwerts himself describes as 'an acid discussion', the US Navy's Director of Plans, with obvious relish, proceeded to peel away the British proposals layer by layer:

Admiralty Command Arrangements	Turner's Comments
Para. 1: The Naval Commander in the Far East will be called C-in-C Eastern Fleet.	This is contrary to ABC-1.
Para. 2: On the outbreak of war with Japan C-in-C China assumes the duties of C-in-C Eastern Fleet and continues to do so until the arrival of the main fleet at Singapore or when decided by their Lordships.	The latter part is contrary to ABC-1: the decision should be taken in conjunction with the 'associated' powers and not by their Lordships.
Para. 3: On arrival of the main fleet, or when as directed by their Lordships, C-in-C main fleet, who will have been appointed to command the fleet on passage, will become C-in-C. Eastern Fleet, will remain in command of the main fleet and fly his flag afloat. The title of the fleet will be Eastern Fleet.	This is all contrary to ABC-1.
Para. 4: Duties of C-in-C. Eastern Fleet are: 1) Collaboration with C-in-C Far East and Allied Commanders regarding the general strategy of war in the Far East; 2) exercise of unified stategic direction of all naval forces in the Eastern Theatre and those under C-in-C Asiatic Fleet; 3) distribution of naval forces throughout the Eastern Theatre and generally plan for their employment, C-in-C of each station retained operational command of forces within their stations; 4) exercise of the above powers to be limited by right of any principals to withdraw or withhold forces provided prior information is given to C-in-C Eastern Fleet.	(a) 'Allied' should include 'and Associated'; (b) the Eastern Theater as now defined is contrary to ABC-1; (c) this does not safeguard the position of US Asiatic Fleet and US naval staff do not agree that it is at the disposition of the C-in-C Eastern Fleet; (d) this is unnecessary.

Para.5: On C-in-C main fleet assuming the title of C-in-C Eastern Fleet, C-in-C China will continue to carry out his present duties with the exception of those taken over by C-in-C Eastern Fleet.

Why? This is a complicated and peculiar assumption.

Para. 6: Australia Commonwealth Navy Board, New Zealand Navy Board and C-in-C East Indies will exercise operational control over naval forces other than the main fleet, operating on their station.

No comment.

Para. 7: C-in-C China will deputise for C-in-C Eastern Fleet during the latter's absence.

Is this workable?

Para. 8: C-in-C Eastern Fleet will be provided with a Chief of Staff and a Chief Staff Officer, the former dealing with duties given in para. 4, and the latter with the Fleet. During the absence of the C-in-C Eastern Fleet, his Chief of Staff will be attached to the staff of C-in-C China.

Ditto.

Para. 9: The above arrangements apply to a situation where Japan and the US are belligerent. If one only of these powers enters the war, the situation will be reviewed.

No comment.

General. How can C-in-C US Pacific and Asiatic Fleets collaborate in war preparations, etc. with a commander who is superseded at some unnamed time by some unnamed officer? Such an idea is contrary to ABC-1.[81]

To make matters worse the paper was shown to the Chief of Naval Operations, who proceeded to write an official memorandum rejecting British command arrangements. Incensed by what he considered to be unwarranted interference in British areas of strategic responsibility, Danckwerts wrote a scathing reply:

> I suggest that if, in the future you receive a paper from us whose purpose you do not clearly understand, it would assist the process of co-operation if you were to send for me and ask me to explain it before the Chief of Naval Operations writes an official letter rejecting a paper which is only sent to him for his information.[82]

By the end of the last week in July an official list of US objections to ADB was received by British authorities. Those provisions supporting subversive activities inside Japan and assistance to Chinese guerrillas proved too politically volatile to be accepted by the US Chiefs of Staff. From the military standpoint, the main tactical point at issue was whether British naval authorities would adopt an offensive rather than a defensive posture, or in other words, British concentration versus British dispersal. As the US was now thinking in offensive terms, concentration in the area of as much naval and air strength as could be made available was the goal. For the Admiralty, however, protection of sea communications was still the paramount concern. Because of overall British naval weakness and the fear of submarines, and despite the relative importance of Singapore and the Malay Barrier, only three out of a total of forty-eight British ships were assigned to operate in the vicinity of Singapore. No British vessels were to be committed to the naval defence of the Barrier itself against Japanese forces advancing southward, or to operations designed to deny Japan access to passages into the Indian Ocean.[83] Officers within the War Plans Division were distinctly unhappy:

> Stated another way, all the British plan to do. . .is convoy duty south of Singapore and into the Indian Ocean, and leave the naval fighting to the U.S. and the Dutch, pending the arrival of British Far Eastern reinforcements. Possibly this is all the naval effort the British can make initially, in recognition of which they have strengthened their land forces at Singapore and in Malaya. But in my opinion, I believe the British can do more if they do not scatter their naval strength all through the Indian Ocean and Australian and New Zealand station. A reasonable force could be assembled by them to assist in the holding of the Malay Barrier.[84]

US planners also remained unhappy about the designation C-in-C Eastern Fleet. Under the ABC Agreement it was intended that the Asiatic Fleet should operate from Singapore under British strategic direction while CINCAF remained in Manila with most of the fleet submarines, but the creation of an Eastern Theatre made it likely that US naval forces would be employed in waters of no strategic significance to the United States.[85] More importantly, the US Chiefs of Staff decided to make use of the Asiatic Fleet as a lever to force the British 'to take a predominant part in the defence of the Malay Barrier'. In late July US naval authorities threatened to 'withdraw' their agreement permitting the US Asiatic Fleet to operate under British strategic direction. Unless a new British plan of operation for Phase I was formulated, it was unlikely Singapore could survive a Japanese attack, particularly without US support. The onus for change was placed firmly in British hands.[86]

Purnell promised the British the Asiatic Fleet would withdraw on Singapore, but he had also promised the Netherlands East Indies that US naval forces would link up with the Dutch in the eastern half of the Java Sea. Known by the pseudonym 'Joseph's Tunic', Hart's operational plan favoured using submarines to cloak a wholesale withdrawal. Surabaya was mentioned, but Hart himself remained in a considerable quandary about the direction of retreat. While this had not been discussed with the UK authorities, it had been approved in Washington.[87] By mid–September, Washington's threat to withdraw support had actually been carried out. Hart was given complete independence from any allied obligations:

> I'm no longer tied in and to our prospective allies by any instructions, and am absolutely the boss of all my own forces again. I had intended to disregard that instruction – and had already been told informally that I was to do what I thought was right when the time came. But it is better to have the record straight.[88]

Summit in the Atlantic

Unaware that the Asiatic Fleet had been assigned complete freedom of action, British naval authorities were under pressure to reconvene another Far Eastern conference to discuss the US position. Support for a new meeting came from the British Admiralty Delegation in Washington, which had now grown to a full mission, and from Dutch naval representatives in Singapore.[89] Yet the Joint Planning Staff in London were reluctant to abandon ADB, particularly as the long awaited meeting between Roosevelt, Churchill and their respective staffs at Argentia was pending and they were not prepared to compromise on protection for Indian Ocean lines of communication. Though admitting the Malay Barrier was insecure, they felt British offensive action was more dependent on the activities of the Pacific Fleet 'about which we have not been fully informed'.[90]

Churchill and Roosevelt met at sea in Placentia Bay Newfoundland from the 9–12 August 1941. These meetings fell somewhere in between a 'heart to heart talk' and a staff conference. The sessions involved not only the two leaders but also the highest naval and military authorities of both nations, including the Chiefs of Staff, as well as Foreign Office and State Department representatives. However, attention was focused more on the propaganda value of a meeting between heads of state and on the grandeur of the Atlantic Charter than on the international situation now that Germany had invaded Russia and Japan had occupied southern IndoChina. An assurance of US entry into the war and promises of direct military support were what the British planners required. Vacuous phrases about conditions in a post-war world were not seen as an effective substitute by the military. The meetings also proved to be a bitter anti-climax for the British at the strategic level.[91] As General 'Hap' Arnold, Head of the US Army Air Corps, pointed out:

> The British representatives did not realize the almost impossible load being placed upon us by Army, Navy, Air Force, all asking for what each other wanted – 100% – with no funnel or central sieve to coordinate the various demands. They did not appreciate that on top of this load we had to take care of the needs of China, Russia, British Colonies, and the Dutch East Indies. Then we also had to make such military dispositions as to insure that Japan would think before acting in the Far East.
>
> The British as usual asked for everything they wanted regardless of whether we have or ever will have an Air Force. They never blinked an eye when they asked for 100% of our production. They would have taken all the Army, Navy, British, Chinese and Dutch planes and engines. . . Fortunately we were able to get away without promising or giving away everything we had. As a matter of fact, we might have lost everything we owned, including our pants, but we didn't.[92]

This desire to dominate US aircraft production schedules can be easily understood. By September the Chief of the Air Staff in Britain was warning his colleagues that there was no possibility that the Far Eastern target of 336 aircraft could be met in 1941. The Secretary of State for Air pointed out that supplies to Russia were equivalent to twenty squadrons of bombers and fifteen of fighters. Any increase in the scale of Malayan ground defence was bound to be offset by the dire lack of air cover.[93]

There was an absence of sufficient pre-planning at the Atlantic meeting as well. Roosevelt kept his own counsel about the purpose of the talks. It had been hoped better cooperation would result if officials and officers from both sides became better acquainted, but on the US side there was no exchange of views between representatives as to the agenda, the composition or the size of the US delegation.[94] Nor was the atmosphere of the meeting particularly conducive to decision making, as Colonel Hollis revealed:

> Apart from the opening meeting on the first day to say 'how do you do' we have had only two full joint meetings with a number of individual discussions. Sunday 11 August was a 'dies non' with Church parade on Prince of Wales followed by luncheon and dinner parties. The US Chiefs of Staff were housed in two ships, U.S.S. Augusta and U.S.S. Tuscaloosa, and it was difficult to draw up formal programmes as luncheons and dinners were arranged at short notice, and U.S. feeding times were different. Roosevelt's visit on Saturday 10 August took a large slice of available time. The U.S. Chiefs of Staff do not work as a 'team', and so it was not possible to nail them down to a 'combined service' opinion on any particular major point.[95]

Phoenix from the Ashes 2: Despatching the Eastern Fleet

Two primary catalysts have been seen as being responsible for the decision to send a capital ship force to the Far East. First, the occupation of southern IndoChina by Japan on 23 July led to the conclusion that the Japanese were contemplating further aggression. This brought about a fundamental reconsideration of the capital ship position by the Admiralty. Second, the pressure brought to bear by Australia on British political authorities led to increased emphasis being placed on Far Eastern defence measures.[96] The personal telegram sent by the Australian Prime Minister R.G. Menzies to Churchill on 11 August has been specifically mentioned by historians. This read in part:

> We have as you know, always regarded Singapore and Malaya as our vital outposts. . . We have also assumed that in the event of war with Japan, naval reinforcements as discussed in London with a nucleus of five capital ships would be sent to the Far East. We now say and emphasize that an early despatch of capital ships east of Suez would itself be a most powerful deterrent and first step.[97]

However, it must be remembered that early in 1941 Churchill had argued Japan would be loath to declare her hostility unless the United Kingdom was decisively beaten.[98] The Prime Minister had consistently pointed out that Japan was bogged down in China and as the Japanese must always look to a flank attack from the United States, they would not declare war on Britain. Later in the year he also placed great faith in the possibility of a Russo-Japanese war. As a result, the Far East maintained a low level of priority in his eyes in defence terms, and it was only with the greatest difficulty that the Chiefs of Staff were able to persuade him to send any reinforcements.[99]

When on 16 July Churchill made enquiries about the kind of improvement required for Eastern waters, he stipulated that these must not be allowed to interfere with plans concerning the Middle East. On 12 August the Joint Planning Committee did investigate the question of naval reinforcement, but all these preparations were merely expedients over the short term designed to deter Japan from an aggressive southerly course. At the Atlantic Conference, Roosevelt had initially been anxious to secure a thirty-day moratorium on action by all sides,[100] but the Joint Planning Staff concluded that within the thirty-day period, only one vessel out of all the capital ships already earmarked as part of the Eastern Fleet could be made available. The idea of a 'quick transfer' was therefore abandoned. By 22 August the War Office was informing Brooke-Popham not to expect any reinforcements, and by the end of the month Churchill admitted that with the Japanese 'disposed to parley the situation had eased considerably'. It seems difficult then to subscribe the change in attitude that took place in late August to Japanese occupation of southern IndoChina.[101] As the Prime Minister pointed out in correspondence with Dominion authorities, the rationale behind the decision to despatch a Far Eastern Fleet lay in other directions:

> Nevertheless the growth of our battleships strength, the ravages made in the German Navy, which is now reduced, apart from the Tirpitz and the U boats to very modest proportions, and the measure we have of the Italian Navy, will make it possible in the near future for us to place heavy ships in the Indian Ocean. The Admiralty are carefully considering what is the best dispositions to make. But I should like to let you know that as they became available we contemplate placing a force of capital ships, including first class units, in the triangle Aden-Singapore-Simonstown before the end of the year.[102]

As to Australia's influence on events, the arguments put forward by Menzies had been almost immediately countered by the views of New Zealand:

> Until the United States have agreed to take over the more active role in the Atlantic, and have transferred sufficient capital ships to balance the withdrawal of British naval units, it would in their opinion be dangerous to remove five capital ships from the actual theatre of war.[103]

Not surprisingly, the British Secretary of State for Foreign Affairs characterized the Australian position as 'unduly alarmist'.[104] Menzies' suggestion for a Far Eastern Conference in London was regarded with suspicion by Churchill. Throughout 1941 the Australian Prime Minister had spent more time away from his homeland than in it, much of that time in England. David Day suggests support was increasing for an

Empire-wide Cabinet with full Dominion representation led by Beaver-brook and others from the anti-Churchill faction, and that Menzies was waiting in the wings ready to assume the mantle dropped by the incumbent. There were suspicions too that Menzies was eager to use any excuse to avoid the internal political wrangles that constantly threatened to topple his delicate and unstable majority back in Australia. Anything Menzies said was either ignored or looked at slightly ask-ance.[105] As the UK High Commissioner in Canberra warned:

> Ministers. . .desire to part with him on various grounds including bitter personal enmities, ambitions of would be successors, Menzies' alleged lack of capacity for decision and action, and his lack of popular appeal. There is moreover probably a general feeling among Ministers that the Prime Minister's position continually attacked in the press, will not cease to deteriorate, that the Government as a whole is very near to falling, partic-ularly in view of the Budget, and that the best chance for survival involves leaving Menzies out of the way and some figure with a greater popular appeal in charge such as Fadden who, during his previous spell as Acting Prime Minister worked well with the Labour Party. Some genuine anxiety about the Far East obviously afforded cover for this manoeuvre.[106]

The idea of despatching an Eastern Fleet was not new. In March the Admiralty had proposed a fleet transfer in peacetime 'if the situation permits',[107] and by mid-year the Chiefs of Staff were undertaking confidence measures. They were no longer looking merely to airpower as the cure-all for Far Eastern deficiencies; by late July Malaya Com-mand was to be strengthened by two infantry brigades, including one from India, and an anti-aircraft regiment, bringing the total up to thirty-two battalions: more than had been recommended at the 1940 Singapore Conference. The Japanese invasion of southern IndoChina in itself had little effect on the scale of this reinforcement, for the decision was taken even before the Japanese occupied the area.[108] As a result there were four main naval planning scenarios dominating Admiralty minds late in 1941: a Phase I option (a battlecruiser and an aircraft carrier to Indian Ocean waters), reinforcement of the Cape by capital ships, the creation of a full Eastern Fleet and the formation of a joint operating plan with the Americans.

The genesis of the Eastern Fleet thus had little to do with Empire relations and more to do with arrangements that evolved from the ABC Conference. Gradual adoption by the US of convoy escorting and the expansion of the US sphere of responsibility in the North Atlantic proved instrumental and was undoubtedly the more important factor. Under the agreement, US naval reinforcement of the Atlantic should only have taken place after a US declaration of war, but increased US concern with the deteriorating international situation meant reinforcements were reaching there in peacetime, far earlier than had been anticipated. This had a 'concertina effect' on the Admiralty's own plans, bringing forward wartime dispositions and blurring the division between Phases I and II. It enabled the Admiralty to contemplate the despatch of capital ships to the Far East before the end of the year, as the naval arrangements for the Plenaps Conference revealed.[109] By June it was almost certain that a battlecruiser and a carrier would be on station at Trincomalee before December, and it was 'possible' that four of the 'R' class would be based on the Cape by the same date. Such dispositions 'would counteract the raider menace and assist passage of the Eastern Fleet when required.'[110]

The availability of ships depended on the speed of British repair programmes. Here the United States was of inestimable benefit. Acting on an urgent appeal from Britain and pressed by Averill Harriman and the Secretary of the Navy Frank Knox, Roosevelt agreed to let British naval and merchant ships be repaired in United States yards, thereby supplementing the already overburdened resources of the United Kingdom. This action also doomed any hope that US warships would use Singapore. US naval staff concluded that if Singapore could not handle British capital ship repairs, it was unlikely to be able to handle the requirements of the United States.[111] By 1 July 1941 *Illustrious* and *Resolution* had both completed repair and refits, *Rodney* and *Malaya* were still in US yards, and *Royal Sovereign* was returning to the UK having completed fitting out.[112]

By the middle of June, however, both the British and US programmes had run into delays. Asked by US authorities about the wisdom of transferring another three battleships to the Atlantic, Admiralty staff pleaded for deferment until August, when it was anticipated *North Carolina* and *Washington* would be in service. Transfer of the 'R' class was therefore put back until October.[113] By mid-July, the Navy Department disappointingly pointed out that US battleships originally earmarked to relieve Force H at Gibraltar would now be used as escorts on the North Atlantic run. There would be no capital ship reinforcement for the Mediterranean as had been expected.[114] As Admiral Kelly Turner pointed out:

> It is my considered opinion dated 3 received 26 July that the best interests of Great Britain and of the United States would be served by continuing to base only British ships and units on Gibraltar (until it is no longer tenable as a base) and not to further complicate the difficulties of the situation by basing units there which require different services, supplies and support, and speak a different 'language' as to administration and operations.[115]

To despatch a full Eastern Fleet, as opposed to merely a few capital ships to Indian Ocean waters, required the release of sufficient cruisers and destroyers. It was necessary for the United States to undertake the relief of British forces in the North Atlantic by implementing full convoy escort duties across the region under Hemisphere Plan 4.[116] Agreement on this was reached at the Atlantic meeting, but the US adopted a modified Plan 4, agreeing only to assume responsibility for escorting North Atlantic convoys within the US defensive zone west beyond 26 degrees longitude west. This plan would take effect from September.[117] Clearly the President 'was skating on pretty thin ice' in his relations with Congress, for a bill introducing selected service had just been passed by the narrowest of margins. What was more encouraging was a Presidential promise to wage war without a declaration. According to Churchill, Stark was ordered to attack any U-boat on sight in the hope some 'incident' would occur which could justify opening hostilities. Such promises were offset, however, by the news that US naval forces would not be based on British ports nor would the US Navy relieve British ships in home waters.[118] Attempts by Britain to gain control over all multinational aviation in the Far East had been equally unsuccessful. As the Chiefs of Staff ruefully admitted:

> The refusal of United States naval authorities to consider placing naval aviation under the operational control of another service on the one hand, and the reluctance on the part of the United States Army authorities to place the army Air Corps under the operational control of the Royal Air Force on the other, made it impossible to reach agreement on the question of unified command of air forces.[119]

The introduction of the modified US Hemisphere Defence Plan 4 in early September led to an acceleration in the Admiralty's Far Eastern defence preparations. Rather than drawing upon ships from the Mediterranean Fleet, the Royal Navy now expected *Repulse* and *Hermes* to fulfil Phase I.[120] By September *Hermes* was already operating in the Indian Ocean, but *Repulse* – delayed in home waters – did not reach Durban until 3 November. It was anticipated that *Renown*, with her greater endurance and longer cruising radius would probably replace her in January 1942.[121] The first part of an Eastern Fleet – namely, a peacetime concentration of battleships on the Cape – remained subject to availability and British repair programmes. By August a total of eight out of fifteen capital ships were still non-operational, and seven had still not been modernized by the end of November. Even the more recently constructed battleships were plagued by teething problems. Because of the breakout into the North

Atlantic by the *Bismarck, Prince of Wales* and *King George V* had not completed their 'working up', and *Duke of York* was hampered by construction defects. It was hoped that the situation would be dramatically improved by the end of the year, for all the non-operational ships would return to service between September 1941 and January 1942. Effectively, this meant the Admiralty could not begin to contemplate the despatch of a capital ship force until October 1941, and the arrival of these ships in Eastern waters would be at staggered intervals rather than en masse.

Royal Sovereign, Ramillies, and *Resolution* would not be ready until mid-November 1941, December 1941 and January 1942 respectively. That left *Revenge,* which was expected to complete her refit around mid-September. As a result of experiences in Crete, it was also decided to increase anti-aircraft cover on all'the 'R' class.[122] Only *Revenge* was not able to benefit from this before she was on duty in the Indian Ocean.[123] In August naval staff favoured the transfer of *Rodney* and *Nelson* to the Eastern Fleet, but only as a last resort, though by 28 August Pound spoke of despatching them to Trincomalee in the New Year, where they would later be joined by the aircraft carrier *Ark Royal* or *Indomitable* providing badly needed aerial support for the battleships. It was expected that the presence of a battlecruiser and an aircraft carrier in the Indian Ocean would act to deter Japanese 8-inch cruisers, whereas the 'R' class were to be used primarily as convoy escorts in case of attack by Japanese battleships and cruisers on the Empire's trade routes.[124] British naval intelligence had failed to note that economic warfare was anathema to an Imperial Japanese Fleet dominated by Mahan's 'Blue Water' main fleet philosophy.

From the perspectives of September 1941, there were still too many variable factors impeding any decision to transfer a full Eastern Fleet, with all the paraphernalia that entailed. For example, though the programme for Hemisphere Plan 4 was due to start on 1 September, it did not actually begin until 16 September. On 4 September the USS *Greer* was attacked south of Reykjavik by a German U-boat. By 11 September the United States extended its zone of control to include almost three-quarters of the Atlantic, while Roosevelt implemented a 'shoot on sight' order. No declaration of war followed, but the need for an Anglo-American agreement for the relief of British forces in the Atlantic was now desperate.[125]

The strain on British secondary and auxiliary vessels was even greater than before. At the beginning of 1939 Britain had 103 destroyers, of which 100 were operational. By September 1941 this figure had been reduced to 88 of which only 49 were serviceable.[126] Australia and New Zealand still refused to sanction any transfer of their own forces from protection duties in the Tasman Sea area unless the United States agreed to take over strategic responsibility for regional defence,[127] but US naval planners would not be drawn on the question of a commitment south of the Equator:

> The United States have no intention of making any permanent 'allocations' of U.S. naval forces to this area. The U.S. Pacific Fleet will support British naval forces in the Tasmanian Sea as opportunity offers, or as might prove profitable. Such support, however, could not be continuous nor would it be extended in case of sporadic raiding by a single Axis ship. The U.S. Pacific Fleet will at times be adjoining as seems best with regard to the totality of Pacific alignment of the situation, as it affects the interests of stipulated powers.[128]

Initially it appeared that ADB might be made acceptable to both sides and become the foundation for a joint operating plan. At Argentia the Admiralty did have some cause for confidence. Rather than going through the 'rigmarole' of a new Far Eastern Conference, Turner agreed to allow the British to re-draft the document. British planning authorities felt access to the US Asiatic Fleet was still possible; they did not realize that this option was about to be taken from them.[129]

By 21 September 1941 the re-draft was ready for distribution. The Royal Navy sought to go over all the previous month's decisions. Despite a contretemps with the Prime Minister about the need for a Far Eastern deterrent force, Admiralty strategy had not altered. One 'R' class, one battlecruiser, and an aircraft carrier would be on station in the Indian Ocean before the end of the year, and the remaining 'R' class would arrive on East Indies station by late December. *Repulse* would be relieved by *Renown* in January 1942, and two more capital ships would be sent in the new year. Bringing the Eastern Fleet up to full strength continued to depend on cruiser and destroyer availability. To offset American criticisms about the lack of offensive action the Admiralty stated it was prepared to operate a fast strike force of two 8-inch cruisers and an aircraft carrier from Singapore, and possibly a second strike force from Darwin. Yet because of the perceived Japanese raider threat, the Admiralty was loath to transfer capital ships further east. Shortages in destroyers, it was felt, governed their use away from areas where they might be subject to submarine attack, such as along the Malay Barrier;[130] indeed, as a result of the Prime Minister's personal intervention, movements of battleships without destroyer escort had already been curtailed. Churchill pointed out that 'nothing can be more like "asking for it" than to have a battleship waddling along with a six and a half knot convoy without any effective anti-submarine escort'.[131] As previously agreed with the Americans, all political matters within

ADB were removed and placed in an appendix.[132]

To coordinate British actions with those of the US Pacific Fleet, Danckwerts asked Admiral Turner to allow British authorities to see the Navy Operating Plan – Navy Plan 0-1 – for Rainbow Plan 5.[133] Within the week, however, British hopes that ADB might still be salvaged were irretrievably dashed. On 12 October the American Chiefs of Staff stated an effective combined operating plan was now impossible. The chief criticism was the weakness of the British forces allocated to the defence of the Malay Barrier.[134] US planners argued British strategy was not offensive enough. For his part, Admiral Turner remained adamant that the Pacific Fleet's war plan would not be shown to British naval authorities:

> I think you need have no fears that the Pacific Fleet will remain inactive on the outbreak of war in the Pacific. You can reassure the Australians on that point. I regret, however, that in the interests of secrecy I shall be unable to show the U.S. Pacific Fleet Operating Plan – Rainbow No. 5 (Navy Plan 0-1). Naturally, we would expect to exchange appropriate information of this nature were we both at war in the Pacific, but the Chief of Naval Operations believes, at present, that knowledge of the details of the Operating Plans should be held by a very small number of persons – a view which the British Chiefs of Staff apparently share, as we are never informed concerning the details of projected British operations.[135]

To secure American cooperation in the Far East then it was obvious the Admiralty and the planning staffs would have to undertake a fundamental reassessment of their own Far Eastern strategy, one that had to be based on a more forward projection by British naval forces – including capital ships – into Far Eastern waters. To judge accurately where that reassessment might lead strategically, American predilections would have to be taken into account, and such predilections aimed at a more offensive approach.

Air Power: The United States Reassesses its Pacific Strategy

The idea of undertaking a stronger military stance in the Far East had not been developing overnight. Even in 1940 it had been possible to detect undercurrents of change, based on the notion of creating an adequate deterrent force in the Philippines in peacetime. Airplanes and submarines had been seen even then as the only logical alternative to ground and surface naval reinforcement, but the paucity of resources at that time had rendered such propositions dubious, and the ABC-1 Conference and the Atlantic reinforcement schedule underlined those conclusions. However, in February 1941, Turner was forced to admit that if Japan committed further aggression America would have to chose between increasing economic pressure and reinforcement of the Philippines by additional aircraft and submarines.[136]

There continued to be debate about the extent and type of improvement that needed to be made. As far as the Army Air Corps was concerned 'the most successful defense against an air attack is to prevent it being launched. . . A well led and determined attack in force, once launched, cannot be stopped by the defense'. A 'theater of operations combat airplane' was believed to be required, and heavy bomber reinforcement was favoured.[137] However, defence of naval facilities, Corregidor and Bataan were desired by Admiral Hart and the head of the Philippine Department, General Grunert; they preferred concentration on pursuit aviation and anti-aircraft guns.[138] The War Department stood somewhere between the two positions, favouring a 'balanced' military reinforcement, but would not agree to increase or improve the defences without political sanction unless this was part of a programme creating viable self-defence.[139] In 1939 a 20,000 man garrison and 241 aircraft were estimated to be the minimum require-ment, but following through on this would require virtually a revolution both in national defence policy and in political outlook.[140]

Yet in October 1940, just such a revolution occurred. Since 1938 President Quezon had become increasingly disillusioned with the Philippine National Defense Plan and with his chief military adviser, Douglas MacArthur. In June of that year, without official approval, Quezon had visited Japan in an attempt to obtain a formal pledge of non-aggression, but had been disappointed by the lack of response.[141] The initial revenue granted for Philippine defence measures had begun to evaporate, and by June 1940 Quezon was admitting the programme could not be achieved by 1946 and perhaps never. In an attempt to secure additional finance, the Philippine President approached the US Government and thereby placed the onus for future action on American shoulders. On 7 August and again on 14 October 1940 Quezon sent two messages requesting direct Federal assistance for the military training programme and the release of sugar excise tax funds (kept under American tutelage by the US Treasury Department). Responding to the challenge, the State Department prepared two Executive Orders; one calling into US service Philippine military forces, and the second permitting the US President to invoke emergency clauses in the Philippine Constitution to allow the US Government to exert civil jurisdiction directly and, if necessary, to declare martial law. Although these documents remained unsigned for the time being, they were on file and ready to be invoked. Little wonder that the War Department felt 'funds which have been lacking now can be made available', but they might well have added that at last a political guarantee of support for the Philippines had been provided.[142]

The key to any reinforcement lay in improvement in all the military facilities in the islands. Planned use of the Cavite Yard as a submarine base was all very fine in theory except that the so-called 'base' consisted of a barracks, a torpedo store and little else.[143] One could speak about the desirability of bombers and pursuit aircraft, but there were no completed refuelling points between Hawaii and Manila. In April 1940 it had been suggested a squadron of B-17s be ferried to Pearl Harbor, but at that stage the limitations in engine power and fuel consumption meant these aircraft had to be stripped of all excess weight even to reach Hawaii. The idea had been abandoned as 'too dangerous'.[144] Even if modern aircraft had reached the Philippines, they would not be able to operate there: Clark and Nichols were the only tarmac airfields, both had limited fuel and hangar facilities and neither was long enough to handle B-17s.[145]

By February 1941, however, the War Department was looking into the question of providing longer ranged B-26s for Hawaii and permission had also been given to increase the Philippine Scouts; additional coast artillery support for Luzon was being discussed, agreements were reached for the provision of anti-aircraft batteries and field artillery and perhaps most importantly of all, $1,250,000 was allotted for construction of air bases. Some $150,000 of this was for a new airfield on Bataan and $500,000 was set aside for Nichols and Clark to lengthen the runways so as to be able to handle heavy bombers.[146]

By May, in order to affect a full programme of aircraft dispersal, another $3,500,000 had been allotted for the construction of twenty-one airfields, and a new Far Eastern Air Command was set up that same month. The Army Air Corps agreed to US aircraft production plans for fifty-four groups.[147] That same month a General Staff Estimate spoke for the first time of the need to create strike forces for offensive action outside the western hemisphere. By June studies were well under way for the adoption of an eighty-four group programme,[148] while in May Roosevelt wrote to the Secretary of War stressing that bomber production must reach 500 a month:

> I am fully aware that increasing the number of our heavy bombers will mean a great strain on our production effort. It will mean a large expansion of plant facilities and the utilization of existing factories now engaged in making munitions. But command of the air by the democracies must and can be achieved.[149]

Construction of a submarine base at Cavite was begun in January 1941, and by the end of the year some twenty-three fleet submarines were operating there as part of the Asiatic Fleet. By December 1941 there were more submarines at Cavite than there were at Pearl Harbor.[150] It has always been assumed by historians that the revision in US Far Eastern strategy occurred after 26 July when the 'freezing order' on oil – specifically directed against Japan – came into effect; but in effect Roosevelt's actions merely accelerated a process already begun six months earlier. Both the Army Air Corps and the Navy Department had already made it perfectly clear what their strategic approach was intended to achieve:

The existing air garrison and organization in the Philippine Department is considered inadequate for the air defense of that locality. It is believed that the minimum air garrison for an effective air defense should comprise not less than one long range bombardment wing of three or more groups, together with such additional ground and air components as may be required to constitute a balanced force. Current plans for the improvement of existing facilities should be prepared with the above in mind. If it is the intention of the War Department to so augment the Philippine garrison so as to provide an effective defense, this office recommends the creation of a Philippine Air Force command containing a striking force echelon and an air defense echelon.[151]

The Chief of Naval Operations believes that the major strategic objectives of our potential enemies are not now to be found in the Western Hemisphere. For the time being, their major efforts will be in the Eastern Atlantic, the Western Pacific, and the China Sea. If we enter the present war and hope to achieve important results we must with every feasible means inflict and continue to inflict loss upon the enemy. As many of our combatant forces as possible must seek out enemy forces i.e. our fightingforces must go where the fighting is. The Chief of Naval Operations has therefore decided to use as many submarines as possible in far distant waters of the Western Pacific.[152]

It was hoped by US authorities that war in the Far East might still be avoided, but the strength of the Pacific Fleet had been reduced by transfers to the Atlantic Theatre and the weakening of its deterrent effect was now recognized. To offset this lack of strength, what seemed to be required were concomitant increases in economic pressure. Aware of the mounting threat to IndoChina, Roosevelt decided to use Japan's reliance on foreign imports of oil as a diplomatic weapon. In 1940, 60 per cent of Japan's supplies had come from the United States and another 30 per cent from the Netherlands East Indies and the Caribbean. Though the President was not prepared to advocate a complete embargo, it was decided to freeze Japanese assets in the United States and to apply a licensing system to the export of oil. On 26 July Roosevelt issued two Executive Orders, one calling for closure of the Panama Canal to Japanese shipping and the second for the entry of the Philippine Army into the service of the United States. Undeniably the new plan went well beyond previous limited proposals.[153] Following Japanese occupation of southern IndoChina, a new Far Eastern command was set up with MacArthur as commander.[154] That same day the Chief of the Air Staff was ordered to look into reinforcement of the Philippines with heavy bombers in the 'shortest possible time'. Nor was the suggested American reinforcement limited to air power alone; the overall programme was designed to create self-sustained defence in the Philippines.[155] By the end of the month the Navy had agreed to transfer twenty-eight PBYs and eleven submarines to Manila, while the Army was looking for an increase in manpower to a 50,000 man garrison. For the first three months some $10,000 was set aside by the President from emergency funds, but it was expected that most of the financial costs would be paid for eventually by the Philippine Government through the use of sugar excise funds.[156] An appropriate Bill was already before Congress when the Japanese struck in December. The problem of financing defence had never been far from the President's mind throughout the 1930s, which is perhaps why he supported increased air reinforcement. Airpower, after all, was believed to be a most cost-effective defence system.

One other factor explaining the sudden interest in Philippine defence lies in an entirely different direction. Having recently gained official representation on the Joint Board, the Army Air Corps was most anxious to carve out a role for itself. One of the key motivations behind the decision to transfer B-17s to Manila was not the strategic value of such aircraft, or even the need to create a viable deterrent, but the desire of the Army Air Corps to revenge itself upon the Navy for the privations suffered at their hands during the inter-war years. Nothing less than complete destruction of the traditional American defence posture was considered satisfactory. Under the new scenario the Air Corps would no longer merely support naval operations; instead, naval operations would support the Army Air Corps. The augmentation of air strength in the Philippines was therefore seen by Air Corps officers as being 'primarily for the purpose of enabling the army to participate in the strategic offensive':

> It is believed that the time has come to recognize that control of the seas is no longer a function the discharge of which is solely a naval responsibility. The lessons of Norway, the action of the British Fleet (as such) in the

evacuation of Dunkerque, the impotence of the British Mediterranean Fleet at Crete, have proved that naval forces cannot operate within the radius of strong land based aviation. Therefore, the security of the above areas against a seaborne threat is in the final analysis, a mission in which the Army through its Air Forces will have a paramount interest. This responsibility, and the prerogatives which accompany such responsibility, should not be turned over to the Navy on the pretext that air forces can operate over the sea or against sea craft only as a subordinate agency of the Navy. The Navy is well aware of the influence of air power in the control of the seas. It will make every effort to gain control of land based aviation and other aviation to boost its waning power. Each and every concession made to the Navy in subordinating Army air forces to Navy control will strengthen its endeavour to secure control of land based aviation and to eventually take over air force operations and with it coast defense.[157]

This conflict of interest was part of a twenty-year dispute between the services regarding divisions of responsibility over aerial matters. The Navy had taken the view that if aircraft flew over the ocean such aircraft must come under naval control. The Army's view was that the question of responsibility could only be decided by the location of the airfield itself. Naval planes using naval airfields would obviously be under naval control; Army planes using army airfields would come under Army control. Because the Navy had maintained land-based bombers and pursuit aircraft, there had been much duplication of facilities in and around stations like Pearl Harbor. In 1931 General MacArthur, then Chief of Staff, and Admiral Pratt had reached a compromise whereby the Army's mission was to be limited to coastal defence, while naval air power would be based on the fleet,[158] but by 1934 each was accusing the other of breaking the agreement.[159] In May 1938 three long-range bombers were despatched on a navigational exercise, intercepting the Italian liner *Rex* some 600 miles out into the Atlantic. Naval complaints about this manoeuvre forced the War Department to issue orders prohibiting Army aircraft from flying more than 100 miles from the coastline.

By 1941 this dispute had extended to the Far Eastern commands. As the Pearl Harbor Attack Hearings pointed out, one of the major factors behind Japan's success was the lack of agreement concerning responsibility for long-range aerial patrol.[160] There was a singular absence of communication on this subject between Kimmel and the Army commander, General Short. Admiral Hart was also involved in a bitter wrangle with MacArthur over the same matter less than a week before the Japanese attack.[161]

At what point did British authorities learn of this strategic change of direction? On 20 August 1941, General George Marshall had informed the British Mission in Washington that US policy was to build up sufficient strength in the Philippines 'to be able to constitute a menace to any Japanese movement'.[162] All through September the British followed US negotiations with Dominion authorities for the establishment of a southern air route across the Pacific via Rabaul, Port Moresby and Darwin. Yet there had been even earlier hints that a major revision in US Far Eastern strategy was under way. The ADB Report stressed the importance of the presence of air and submarine forces on Luzon, the need for additional reinforcements and the desirability of creating an aerial strike force. Visiting the Philippine islands late in May, Group Captain Dorvall of the RAF had reported increased airfield construction and predicted Manila's state of defence would improve dramatically over the next four months.[163] By September it had become obvious that the Americans were trying to create a new advanced defence line running from Hong Kong through the Philippines to the Pelews, with Luzon as the key element.[164] The garrison in the islands had already been increased to 17,000 and it was planned to send another 15,000 men. A complete anti-aircraft regiment, a battalion of tanks and fifty anti-tank carriers were already en route. Nine B-17s had been sent from Hawaii and plans were to increase heavy bombardment forces to at least two air groups, while fifty P-40 pursuit aircraft had already been shipped.[165] The decision by the British Chiefs of Staff to send two additional battalions to Hong Kong appears to have been motivated less by General Maltby's confidence than by dramatic increases in US defence measures. It was now being expected by British authorities that Hong Kong could not only be defended but held.[166]

Phoenix from the Ashes 3: The 'New' Eastern Fleet Strategy

The moment was more than opportune for the Admiralty to review the state of their own planning. The Americans had threatened to cancel British arrangements concerning the Asiatic Fleet, and they were plainly on the point of rejecting the ADB-2 draft. If a joint operating plan was ever to evolve, the Royal Navy would have to be prepared to defend the Malay Barrier with substantially greater forces and probably with capital ships. Without adequate protection for the naval anchorage, Singapore would be useless as an operating base. It had already been pointed out by the Chiefs of Staff that the necessary British air and ground reinforcements would not reach Malayan waters for some considerable time. Manila, on the other hand, was being rapidly built up with ground, air and submarine forces. If the Americans intended forming an advanced defence line, surface naval reinforcement would be vital for success, yet the US Navy Department had stated unequivocally that they would not send capital ships to the Philippines. In keeping with the traditions of pre-war planning, it may have seemed to the Admiralty's Naval Plans Division that Phase II could be brought to a more logical conclusion with substantially less effort if use was made of Cavite, for Manila was within easy sailing distance of Hong Kong.

Even though they had not seen Rainbow Plan 5 or Navy Plan 0-1, the Admiralty were familiar with the principles behind War Plan 'Orange' and Rainbow 2, and they had received a précis of Rainbow 3 from Captain Clarke.[167] They were well aware that US naval war planning was concerned with a staged advance across the Pacific back to the Philippines. If the British Eastern Fleet moved 1,300 miles closer to Hawaii an anticipated link-up with US forces would become a more distinct possibility, and a British presence would force the US Pacific Fleet to act more aggressively. By initiating a British military commitment to defend United States territorial possessions, the Admiralty may well have hoped to secure a reciprocal arrangement. The long-awaited political guarantee of American support would be made, and at one stroke one of the main problems that had previously plagued Anglo-American naval relations would be solved. Nor was the Admiralty alone in its support for a 'new' approach; the need to attack Japan's lines of communications was also stressed by the Joint Planning Staff as the best means to regain the initiative in the Far East at the earliest possible stage. The latter felt the 'greatest importance' should be attached to denying the enemy a 'foothold' along the line of the Netherlands East Indies.[168]

All these ideas passed through Admiralty minds in the last week of September, culminating in a meeting on 30 September 1941 in the office of the Vice Chief of Naval Staff, Tom Phillips. The purpose of the meeting was to discuss an aide-memoire about the future need for a joint operating plan with the Americans. After some debate, it was decided British naval forces could be sent to Manila; to bypass any American command objections, British ships would be assigned specific tasks under ABC-1 arrangements. Manila was regarded as 'invaluable' in the role of advanced fleet base, so it was only natural that the Royal Navy should now seek to retain it, particularly as Phase I was to take place in peacetime. This decision was reached nearly two weeks before Churchill's dramatic confrontation with Pound and the Admiralty about Far Eastern naval reinforcement:

> We should therefore regard Manila as a perfectly feasible fleet base from the point of view of air attack, provided reasonable A.A. defence and fighter aircraft were made available. V.C.N.S. directed that D. of L.D. (Director of

Local Defence) was to be instructed to prepare a plan for anchoring the fleet at Manila and defending it there. Its position on the flank of the Japanese communications to the China Sea makes it undoubtedly the best base from the strategical point of view.[169]

Such a policy was no mere short term solution to overcome problems with the Americans; rather it was the logical culmination of the Admiralty's preoccupation with Phase II and a duplication of pre-war principles where the emphasis was on the relief of British Far Eastern possessions, particularly Hong Kong. In seeking to use Manila, Admiralty strategy had come full circle. It is perhaps remarkable that almost a year to the day since the idea of despatching a British Eastern Fleet had been abandoned and plans were focused instead on Manila as a substitute for Hong Kong with US naval forces acting as a surrogate for the British, the Admiralty was discussing whether to inform the C-in-C Far East about their intention to base the Eastern Fleet on Manila, well to the north of the Malay Barrier. During the first week in October, naval staff, led by the Director of Plans, drafted a revised aide-memoire incorporating the new strategy.

Capital ships earmarked for the Eastern Fleet were still to be moved to the Indian Ocean, but would be based on Singapore. The transfer would be completed in peacetime by early 1942. Since only cruisers and destroyers would be required to affect a fleet concentration after war had broken out, Phase II would be of short duration. While Singapore was the main repair base, Manila would become the main advanced base, subject to availability of aircraft and anti-aircraft guns. If the United States continued to be neutral then Singapore would remain the sole fleet base.[170] By 15 October this draft plan had been approved by the First Lord of the Admiralty, A.V. Alexander, as the basis for negotiation with the Americans. True to their word, the Admiralty informed C-in-C Mediterranean on 10 October that *Rodney* and four 'R' class battleships would be sent to the Indian Ocean 'and probably further East as soon as possible'.[171] As the Prime Minister was known to be opposed to the transfer of ships, he does not appear to have been either consulted or informed about this. Perhaps the Admiralty hoped that with the mass of paperwork passing across Churchill's desk there was a good chance the message might be missed. To their chagrin, however, they were caught trying to sneak the measure past him. Churchill reacted almost immediately, commenting: 'This major Fleet movement has not yet been approved by me or the Defence Committee. No action must be taken pending decision'.[172]

Churchill versus the Admiralty

The scene was set for a major confrontation between the Prime Minister and the Admiralty over Far Eastern strategy.[173] What must be remembered is that this was not the first time the subject of a Far Eastern deterrent force had come up. If anything, this had been a perennial problem for the Admiralty, particularly since the Shanghai crisis in 1937. At that time a special Cabinet Committee, formed to look into the whole question of Far Eastern reinforcement, had recommended that two battleships be despatched to Far Eastern waters.[174] In June the following year the Far Eastern Department of the Foreign Office came up with a similar suggestion;[175] in November 1938 Sir Josiah Crosby, British Ambassador in Bangkok, suggested a squadron of battleships and cruisers visit Singapore;[176] in January 1939 a memo was written by Fitzmaurice of the Foreign Office on the same subject; and in October 1940 the suggestion was put forward during a Strategic Affairs Committee meeting that the despatch of a capital ship to Singapore 'would act like a magnet to U.S. forces'.[177]

Throughout these debates the Admiralty had always maintained the same position. In peace or in war they felt only a fleet could provide absolute security in Far Eastern waters. This was because they thought in terms of the worst possible scenario; they were motivated not by political considerations but by military concerns. In case of the outbreak of war, those concerns dictated that a fighting fleet be sent, and this was just as true in 1941 as it was in 1937. The fleet to be transferred in round numbers was less than under pre-war planning schedules, but the Admiralty did not realize the limitations that had been placed on offensive action by the US Pacific Fleet, nor did they know that the Asiatic Fleet was no longer bound by ADB. If the US Pacific Fleet acted according to agreements, the Admiralty believed those numbers would be sufficient. In March 1941 the Director of Plans had suggested retaining the 'R' class permanently on convoy escort duties while withholding *Nelson* and *Rodney* from Eastern waters.[178] Pound had opposed such dispositions, arguing that the best chance lay in sending out 'full forces', that is, a full fleet.[179]

As early as 28 April 1941, Layton had been informed by the Admiralty thata separate C-in-C would command the Fleet on passage and would assume general control over Far Eastern naval forces. On 11 May he was told that Tom Phillips would be selected for the position, and on 3 October he was informed that Phillips had now definitely been appointed C-in-C Eastern Fleet and that his own command was about to be abolished. On 21 October the Admiralty signalled that Phillips would leave shortly for the Far East.[180] Such communications provide demonstrable proof of the Admiralty's long-term intention to station a fleet in Eastern waters.

As the First Sea Lord pointed out to Churchill on 28 August in an earlier confrontation, his task was to create a homogeneous force in terms of speed and firepower. The strongest battle group that Pound could recommend as a deterrent force was the battleships *Nelson* and *Rodney*, the battlecruiser *Renown*, and the aircraft carriers *Hermes* and *Ark Royal*, all of which could have been based on Singapore by April 1942. In an emergency the carrier *Indomitable* might also have been added. However, Pound was quick to point out that if war broke out this force would have to withdraw to Trincomalee, and plainly that was unsatisfactory.[181] The Admiralty were quite aware of the tactical limitations of the 'R' class. These ships had been designed for North Sea conditions; they were patently unsuited for tropical conditions, and were hampered by poor endurance, limited fuel capacity and range, insufficient water storage facilities and poor ventilation. However, US arrangements in the Atlantic meant there were no other ships than the 'R' class available in the required time, and since it was still expected the onus for action would lie with the Japanese, speed was a less vital concern than firepower. The 15-inch guns of the 'R' class were expected to exact a severe toll on the 14-inch gun 'Kongo' class in the Japanese battleline. *Nelson* and *Rodney* were included because their 16-inch guns were seen as equally invaluable over the longer ranges.[182] As to the function of the 'R' class, even in Eastern waters they were regarded as being perfectly suited to the role required of them in accordance with established pre-war principles:

> Our older battleships whatever might be their value as ships of the battle line, which is certainly not negligible, would be of unquestionable use in subsidiary roles, such as escorts for important convoys against powerful raiders or as base ships at any advanced or undefended base we might use in war.[183]

On 30 September the Secretary of State for Foreign Affairs had submitted a memorandum to the War Cabinet suggesting that the moment was ripe for a 'display of firmness' in the Far East to 'deter Japan from war'.[184] A day later C-in-C Far East and C-in-C China Station stressed 'the propaganda value of even one or two battleships at Singapore', and on 17 October the new Australian Prime Minister, John Curtin, urged the despatch of capital ships 'as soon as possible. . .in view of their deterrent effect and possible decisive influence'.[185] Bolstered by this support, Churchill's principle object was to prevent the outbreak of war. With the enormous pressures on British resources and heavy commitments already in the Mediterranean, he was seeking the most economic utilization of deterrent forces. The dispatch of a 'formidable, fast, high class squadron' to Eastern waters was seen as the best way 'to cope with a superior force'. There it would 'show itself in the triangle Aden-Singapore-Simonstown', where 'it would exert a paralysing effect upon Japanese naval action' just as the German battleship *Tirpitz* was tying down Admiralty ships in the Atlantic. For Churchill, Imperial, political and economic considerations were the dominant preoccupations.[186]

Churchill therefore opposed the idea of creating – even in the Indian Ocean – any kind of fleet, 'costly in maintenance and manpower', which would consist of what he saw as 'slow, obsolescent or unmodernized ships', which 'can neither fight a fleet action with the main Japanese force nor act as a deterrent upon his modern fast heavy ships'. Regarding the use of the 'R' class as convoy escorts, Churchill recognized their value as a counter to enemy cruisers, but he was less than sanguine about the breach of deterrent principles implied by such dispositions and was deeply concerned about the threat from Japanese fast battleship detachments. The presence of the 'R' class in Eastern waters was felt to be dependent on refitting schedules and 'one or two fast heavy units'; otherwise the 'R' class would be merely 'floating coffins'.[187]

In order to understand what transpired at the defence meetings of 16 October and 20 October 1941, it is necessary to look at events somewhat in reverse. Only then can what had really transpired be clearly understood. In the wake of these meetings, there were still unsolved issues of contention concerning numbers, roles and destinations. On 21 October an Admiralty signal to all naval stations confirmed that *Prince of Wales* would soon be en route to Singapore, but the day before it had been agreed with Churchill to despatch the ship only as far as Capetown 'where the situation would be reviewed'.[188] Indeed, on 1 November Churchill's minute to Pound queried: 'If it is decided that P. of W. should go to Singapore. . .', and the next day Pound had replied: 'It is my intention to review the situation generally just before P. of Wales reaches the Cape'.[189] But on 24 October, the Admiralty's Director of Plans admitted that the Prime Minister's naval dispositions upset only plans with regard to *Nelson* and *Rodney* but would not affect plans regarding the 'R' class – a significant point.[190] Between 20 October and 5 November, Churchill sent telegrams to Dominion authorities (Australia, New Zealand, Canada and South Africa), the USSR and to President Roosevelt, informing them about the new dispositions. Each of these documents contained certain common features: they all referred to the creation of a deterrent squadron of one or two capital ships based on Singapore but operating in the Aden-Singapore-Simonstown triangle, and to the movement of the 'R' class to Eastern waters 'as ready'.[191] As the first draft of his telegram to Australian authorities indicated, the Prime Minister still expected the 'R' class to fulfil a convoy escort role.[192] Admiral Pound had already succeeded in neatly sidestepping that issue. As he told the Prime Minister:

> I think it would be a pity to be more definite than is necessary as regards the use of any of these ships, as it might hamper Phillip's dispositions later. Also, the Australians are always so keen on having battleship escort for their troops it would be undesirable to be too definite about the use to which the 'R' class are to be put.[193]

The U boat attack on the destroyer USS *Greer* on 4 September had provided the opportunity for the President to announce a clear-cut system of escort and protection. By 13 September, US naval patrols were protecting all merchant ships within the western hemisphere defence zone, and on 17 September US warships began escorting the first British convoy. The inclusion of Iceland within the American zone under Hemisphere Plan 5 now extended American defensive waters as far west as 10 degrees longitude; it now included virtually three-quarters of the Atlantic. By 25 September the British had withdrawn completely from the area.[194] One month later to the day *Prince of Wales*, with Tom Phillips on board, left the Clyde bound for Eastern waters, and at the same time C-in-C China Station informed Admiral Hart that Phillips was en route and that the 'remainder of his fleet. . .will be following him very shortly'.[195] By 4 November the Admiralty had told US naval authorities that ADB-1 and 2 no longer met existing circumstances; they pointed out that the introduction of Hemisphere Plan 5 by the United States on 22 September now meant they were 'able to start forming a capital ship force in Far Eastern waters before the outbreak of war', thereby further reducing the difference between Phases I and II. *Repulse* and *Revenge* were already in the Indian Ocean and *Prince of Wales* was on passage. *Royal Sovereign* and *Ramillies* would leave during November, and *Resolution* in December.[196] However, the very next day Churchill sent the following telegram to the Canadian High Commissioner:

> In view of the threatening situation in the Far East, and the need for doing all we can to make Japan understand what she might be faced with if she persists in going to war, we have decided to place a force of capital ships before the end of the year in the triangle Aden-Singapore-Simonstown.
> Our original idea had been to send the battleships Rodney and Nelson and

the four R class (Royal Sovereign, Revenge, Resolution, and Ramillies) based mainly on Singapore. This scheme, however, became impossible in its entirely owing to the recent injury to the Nelson.

What we have now decided is to send forthwith our newest battleship Prince of Wales to join the battlecruiser Repulse, which is already in the Indian Ocean. The Prince of Wales will be at Capetown quite soon. In addition the four R battleships are being moved as they become ready to Eastern waters and later the Repulse will be relieved by Renown which has greater radius.[197]

Yet 'in the new conditions', as the Admiralty pointed out to Stark, they were now considering disposing a capital ship force on the Philippines north of the Malay Barrier with the object of attacking Japan's lines of communications. Before very long, and in peacetime, an Eastern Fleet might even be based at Manila. The Admiralty were even prepared to supply and install underwater defences there, and suggested that since the need for a joint operating plan had become urgent, a conference should be held at Singapore when the C-in-C Eastern Fleet arrived.[198] Of course this strategy was no new development recently arrived at, but the by-product of several weeks preparation and was based on traditional long-term pre-war principles. Admiral Harwood summed up the 'new approach' when he wrote on 29 October:

I quite agree that our Eastern Fleet when it is established at Singapore should look upon Manila as its advance base and probably operate from there. The question has been discussed during the last few weeks, particularly with C. in C. Eastern Fleet. We have been into the various anchorages that might be suitable. . . Very briefly, since we put up ADB-1 and ADB-2 we have completely changed our outlook and come much nearer to the American viewpoint, i.e. to operate our ships north of the Malay Barrier.[199]

In the wake of the Defence Committee meetings, the Prime Minister's interpretation of British Far Eastern naval strategy was clearly radically different from that of the Admiralty. Churchill believed *Prince of Wales* was bound for Capetown. It was in fact being sent to Singapore. He believed a small deterrent squadron would be concentrated on Singapore, providing fire support for the 'R' class ships, which would be operating as convoy escorts protecting the Indian Ocean trade routes. Subject to US approval, these ships were now bound for Manila as part of an Eastern Fleet, operating north of the Malay Barrier against Japan's lines of communications. At no time during October did Churchill give any indication he was aware of the Admiralty's negotiations with the Americans or of the new strategic approach being offered.

This enables a reassessment to be made of the dramatic Defence Committee confrontation between Churchill and Pound over the despatch of naval reinforcements to the Far East. The meeting, on 17 October, was attended by Churchill (in the chair), Attlee, Beaverbrook, Eden, Cadogan, Ismay, the Service Ministers and the Chiefs of Staff. Churchill had opened the discussions by arguing that the gradual build up of a fleet comprising old, slow, obsolete ships would not solve anything. It 'seemed to him wrong to send a squadron of Capital Ships that were neither strong enough to engage the weight of the Japanese Navy, nor yet fast enough to avoid action except in circumstances of their own choosing'. Using the *Tirpitz* analogy, the Prime Minister favoured at least one fast modern capital ship in Far Eastern waters which he hoped would have the same effect on the Japanese. *Repulse* was already in the Indian Ocean and should proceed to Singapore, where she would be joined by *Prince of Wales*.

The First Lord of the Admiralty, A.V. Alexander, countered the deterrent force proposal by stressing the need to have modern capital ships ready for action both in the Mediterranean and in home waters. He told the Defence Committee that 'any Eastern dispositions would be governed more by the need to protect our own trade routes than to raid Japanese shipping'. Attlee criticised this proposal for being too defensive minded. He pointed out that the Admiralty's arguments 'assumed that we would be prepared to remain on the defensive in Malayan waters even if Japan attacked Russia. We should find such action hard to justify in the circumstances'. The Vice Chief of Naval Staff might have sprung to the Admiralty's defence but instead, wisely, he chose to make no reply; to have done so would have been to reveal the Admiralty's secret preparations. A. V. Alexander too was being less than honest with the Defence Committee. Two days earlier he had proposed to retain in the Indian Ocean only the 'minimum forces necessary for the security of our sea communications' so as 'to adopt more offensive courses of action in the early stages of the war', and had agreed to employ British forces northward of the Sumatra-Darwin line with 'as powerful a British force from Manila as the destroyer strength would permit', yet he too made no comment. Tom Phillips did deal with Churchill's criticisms of the 'R' class. He argued strenuously that Japan's older battleships were inferior to them; indeed that the addition of *Rodney*, *Renown*, and *Nelson* (when repaired), the Fleet 'operating under cover of shore based aircraft, would be a match for any forces the Japanese were likely to send against them'. Churchill wound up the proceedings by inviting the First Lord to consider the deterrent force idea. It was agreed that a decision would not be made without first consulting the First Sea Lord on his return from an inspection tour of the Home Fleet.[200]

On 20 October, the Defence Committee met again to consider the issue. It was this meeting that was characterized by the hostile confrontation between Churchill and Pound. The Prime Minister pointed to the improved naval position in home waters and to the more active role of the US Fleet in the Atlantic, which meant the War Cabinet would be prepared to accept the shipping losses that might occur if *Tirpitz* broke out. He then alluded to the great deterrent effect of a fast modern ship in the Far East. Pound felt that all three 'King George V' class ships would be needed to hunt down the German battleship, which meant retaining *Prince of Wales* in home waters. The First Sea Lord also did not believe that one fast battleship in the Far East would succeed as a deterrent, since Japan could put 'four big ships' into any convoy carrying an expeditionary force south.

Pound suggested that only the presence of six battleships at Singapore (now no longer the Cape or the Indian Ocean) would uncover Japan's defences to US naval forces. Significantly, no mention was made of Manila or of operations north of the Malay Barrier, though Pound did deliver one half-truth when he correctly pointed out the Admiralty had never in any of its war plans 'envisaged moving our battle fleet northward of Hong Kong'. The Prime Minister stated he understood the 'R' class battleships would be used in the Indian Ocean as convoy escorts; Pound deftly replied that this was so 'until it became necessary to concentrate in the Far East. The aim had always been to constitute a battle fleet with this as the nucleus', but he gave no indication as to where or when such a concentration would take place, or whether it was to based on Singapore or elsewhere. Churchill went on to argue that the main danger in Eastern waters was not from an attack in force, but from attacks on trade routes by Japanese battlecruisers. The former would be sufficiently powerful to sink an 'R' class and its escorting convoy. He felt the only thing that would induce caution would be the presence in Eastern waters of a fast striking force, a decision now underwritten by the Defence Committee itself.[201]

In the light of the evidence already presented, the Defence Committee meetings need to be reinterpreted. It seems obvious that the Admiralty entered into these discussions with certain necessary and clearly defined ends in mind. Keeping the new strategy from the prying eyes of the Prime Minister was a key consideration. Pound, Phillips and A.V. Alexander knew that Churchill was bound to oppose the creation of any Eastern Fleet, or even the basing of a reasonable capital ship force on Singapore, never mind Manila. They knew also that he would oppose use of the 'R' class in any battleline. It is interesting to note that no attempt was made to relieve the Prime Minister of his misapprehensions concerning the role of such vessels, misapprehensions based on obsolete Admiralty plans given to him two months earlier. By whatever means the Prime Minister had to be persuaded to sanction the transfer of the 'R' class to 'Eastern Waters' under the control of C-in-C Eastern Fleet. The Admiralty did not lie outright to the Defence Committee: they simply kept their cards close to their chest and did not tell the whole story. One can only admire the deftness with which Churchill was diverted from the main issue.

As Eden correctly diagnosed, the presence of a modern deterrent squadron in Far Eastern waters was 'only a secondary consideration'. It did make better sense tactically to concentrate ships of similar speed if one was forming a battleline, and so it was probably safer to retain the 'King George V' class in home waters, but these were matters of only conditional concern. Fast capital ships in Eastern waters might be valuable if raiding operations north of the Malay Barrier were planned, but the presence of only one or two capital ships, alone and unaided, were unlikely to convince the Americans of British intentions to defend their Far Eastern possessions. In company with other capital ships, however, these might exert a strong influence on US policy.

Once the transfer was sanctioned, the Admiralty moved with considerable speed. There was no hesitation, no last minute attempt to block the despatch of the *Prince of Wales*. By 21 October all naval stations had been told Singapore was the intended destination, and the following day the Americans were informed.[202] Was this issue critical enough to have warranted Pound's accusations of 'unsound dispositions' and threats of resignation? After all, *Prince of Wales* was only going to be transferred as far as Capetown, and it was intended to review the situation anyway when *Nelson* – torpedoed on 27 September – had been repaired. Unless there was some other ulterior motive for his attitude, Pound's reaction appears to be 'making mountains out of molehills'.

The Royal Navy had always held a fascination for the Prime Minister and his contact with the service was extremely close. He had after all served as First Lord of the Admiralty at the beginning of both world wars. Since 1939, Pound had been dealing with him on a day to day basis. He therefore knew Churchill verywell; he knew his ideas and his thinking processes. The deterrent force question took up an inordinate amount of time at the Defence Committee meetings. Was this merely fortuitous circumstance or was Pound's opposition an inspired piece of tactical maneuvering, a psychological ploy designed to divert discussion away from examination of the role of the 'R' class? By opposing the despatch of Churchill's favourite ship *Prince of Wales*,

Pound must have known that the Prime Minister could not fail to take up the issue. The more the First Sea Lord protested, the more determined Churchill would become.

At what point then did the British prime minister become aware of what had transpired? The critical date would seem to be 5 November 1941, one day after the Admiralty had informed the Americans of the new dispositions. Churchill was now faced with a fait accompli: if he acted against Admiralty strategy, negotiations with United States naval authorities might be fatally compromised and other more serious ramifications might follow in its wake. The risk that this might affect the Anglo-American diplomatic and economic relationship was too great. American reaction to the proposal would first have to be gauged. Churchill approved the Admiralty telegram, though significantly he made no other comment except for a signature; on the same day he was persuaded by Pound to agree to retain *Prince of Wales* in Eastern waters only until *Nelson* was repaired and *Rodney's* guns replaced. By 12 November the First Sea Lord was informing the War Cabinet that if the United States remained neutral and Britain was attacked in Eastern waters before Christmas, a Far Eastern battle fleet would be based on Singapore, operating along and north of the Malay Barrier line by January 1942: a policy first outlined by the Assistant Chief of Naval Staff, Sir Henry Harwood, on 29 September 1941 and which had been sanctioned by the Admiralty in the first week in October.[203]

Contrary to the views of almost every major historian who has dealt with this subject, Pound did not give way to Churchill; rather it was the Prime Minister who surrendered to the Admiralty, and the Prime Minister's surrender was total and complete. As Pound pointed out in a telegram to Stark dated 17 November 1941:

> It was very satisfactory that we should have had the same feelings about the A.D.B. papers now that we are able to send ships to Eastern waters. I have no intention of raising it officially but as I think you know I have never been convinced that the present dispositions are correct. If we had a strong Anglo-American Fleet at Singapore with advanced forces in the Philippines I do not believe there would be any question of the Japanese making a move to the Southward.[204]

A Question of Support: Roosevelt's Political Guarantee

All the careful British preparation for a joint operating plan would still be an utter waste of time until or unless political and military guarantees of support were provided by the United States. Even by November 1941 there seemed little likelihood that the undeclared war in the Atlantic would evolve quickly into full-scale conflict with Germany. Despite Churchill's public statements of 24 August and 10 November that in event of the outbreak of war between the United States and Japan 'a British declaration would follow within the hour', in the absence of a reciprocal arrangement both the Chiefs of Staff and the Prime Minister studiously sought to avoid action that might directly provoke Japan. Of necessity, any Pacific war would have to be a US-Japanese conflict, and the fear that an Anglo-Japanese war might break out without the United States being involved in any way, was of deep concern to both the services and the Prime Minister down to the end of 1941.[205] John G. Winant, American ambassador in London, summed up Churchill's dilemma when he wrote:

> He asked me if I thought there was going to be war with Japan. I answered 'yes'. With unusual vehemence he turned to me and said: 'If they declare war on you we shall declare war on them within the hour'. 'I understand that Prime Minister. You have stated that publicly'. 'If they declare war on us will you declare war on them?' 'I can't answer that Prime Minister. Only the Congress has the right to declare war under the United States Constitution'. He did not say anything for a minute but I knew what was in his mind. He must have realized that if Japan attacked Siam or British territory it would force Great Britain into an Asiatic war and leave us out of the war. He knew in that moment that his country might be 'hanging on one turn of pitch and toss'.[206]

Roosevelt's promise of support for the ADB cause, delivered to Halifax on 1 December 1941, has been a matter of considerable historical debate.[207] That same day, Halifax also held an 'off the record' interview with Sumner Welles. Welles stipulated that the United States could never tolerate Japanese hegemony in an area so economically vital to the US war effort and to US trade, but that the American domestic scene dictated that this point 'remain in the background'. Undoubtedly it was this statement that turned Roosevelt's vague 'aside' (as Halifax put it 'that in event of an attack on ourselves or the Dutch we should obviously all be together') into a political pledge.[208] Two days later, Halifax returned to ask whether Roosevelt's use of the term 'support' meant 'armed support'. Roosevelt replied that it did.[209]

Controversy has surrounded use of this term.[210] What interpretations fail to take into account is that by the time of the meeting Roosevelt had already defined the scope of any American military assistance. The discussion on 1 December had been prompted by an urgent telegram from Sir Robert Brooke-Popham to the War Office on 27 November 1941. Based on intelligence reports received on 26 November, it seemed likely Japanese convoys were bound for Thailand. 'Matador' –

a pre-emptive strike on the Kra Isthmus joining Malaya to Thailand – was predicated on a definite pledge of US support. Sanction for the operation was urgently required.[211] On 1 December the President approved British plans to occupy the Kra Isthmus if Japan attacked Thailand or built additional bases in IndoChina as jumping off points for further aggression. While still hoping for a diplomatic solution, he spoke of military support from the US 'by an air group in the Philippines and long distance naval blockade, which of course means shooting'.[212]

Formal requests had been already sent to Britain, the Netherlands East Indies, Australia and New Zealand on 30 September, requesting cooperation for the development of air bases at Singapore, Darwin, Rabaul, Port Moresby and Rockhampton. The Army Air Corps had already agreed that when the number of B-17s reaching the islands increased to the level of four bombardment groups, two of these were to be used outside the Philippines.[213] Although Roosevelt told Halifax on 3 December that the form of any support would be decided by the Joint Chiefs of Staff, he had bypassed his own military services and was proceeding with his own course of action.[214] Later, Turner pointed out that the matter was discussed at the General Staff level, but that no definite decisions were reached; yet on 1 December, Roosevelt had directed that three small vessels be dispatched as pickets towards the IndoChina coast. One was to be stationed between Hainan and Hue, another between Kam Ranh Bay and Cape St Jacques and the third off Pointe de Camau. These ideas – naval blockades, picket lines and the like – were a culmination of the President's preoccupation with limited wars fought with limited means and can be traced back to 1937; they were an inevitable outcome of the President's obsession with the reduction of costs in any full-scale war against Japan.[215]

Admiral Phillips and the Manila Conference

One of the main problems preventing the formation of any Eastern Fleet remained the lack of destroyers. Even by stripping Force H completely, returning all Dominion naval forces to their home stations for reassignment and detaching four escorts from the Mediterranean Fleet, only sixteen destroyers could be raised, and after adding all the units on China and East Indies stations together, the Royal Navy still found itself eight destroyers short of the minimum required for fleet purposes.[216] By 25 October, however, news arrived that if the United States entered the war she might be prepared to supplement British destroyer deficiencies, though no definite assurance of support had yet been received.[217] On 7 November the Chief of Naval Operations did agree to the use of two destroyer divisions from the Asiatic Fleet, but only under wartime conditions. Nevertheless, this offered a potential solution for Admiralty difficulties. The CNO at last appeared willing to sanction use of Luzon 'as an advanced base for naval and air forces'.[218] Galvanized into action, Pound wired Phillips on 9 November informing him that he must not lose any time in reaching Singapore. His stay in Capetown was to be limited, allowing little more than a short visit to General Smuts. So anxious was Pound to respond to Stark's gesture, C-in-C Eastern Fleet was ordered to proceed by the quickest route and at maximum speed, detaching his destroyer screen when clear of the Cape – a somewhat dangerous move – which immediately drew an angry response from the Prime Minister. He minuted: 'I do not quite see what this haste is to arrive at Singapore for a pow wow'.[219]

Pound therefore readjusted the arrival schedule from 1 December to 6 December to allow destroyers to provide escort.[220] On 13 November the Admiralty received the official American reply to its recent 'new approach' proposals. US naval authorities agreed to the Royal Navy's dispositions and consented to a Far Eastern conference to be held to sort out the question of a joint operating plan; however, they preferred that an initial meeting first take place between C-in-C Eastern Fleet and Admiral Hart in Manila. In keeping with the United States own recently implemented defence programme, the Philippines were now being seen as a powerful deterrent if not a positive threat to Japanese advances.[221] As Admiral Stark and General Marshall pointed out to the President:

> The Philippines are now being reinforced. The present combined naval, air and ground forces will make attacks on the islands a hazardous undertaking. By about the middle of December 1941, United States air and submarine strength will have become positive threat to any Japanese operation south of Formosa. The United States Army Air Force in the Philippines will have reached its projected strength by February or March 1942. The potency of this threat will have then increased to a point where it might well be the deciding factor in deterring Japanese operations in the areas south and west in the Philippines. By this time, additional British naval reinforcements to Singapore will have arrived. The general defensive strength of the entire southern area against Japanese operations will then have reached impressive proportions.[222]

While the Army War Plans Division was confident that the Philippines could be defended against Japanese attack, the Navy Department was never quite so certain. They felt Manila lacked sufficient anti-aircraft guns, aerodromes and gasoline reserves.[223] Stark warned against over-estimation of Army strength, which he felt 'will by no means positively insure the Philippines or your bases against determined attack'.[224]

As Ingersoll reported to the Joint Board in early November, what was required were more submarines, more US troops, more training for the Filipino Army and more British strength at Manila.[225] Stark believed that the maintenance of heavy forces at Cavite 'may not be practicable' but that this 'would not rule out the occasional use of Manila Bay as an advanced base by the British Fleet'.[226] This uncertainty and hesitation was transmitted to British authorities by Stark:

> The question of permanently basing the British Far Eastern Fleet in the Philippines in case of hostilities cannot be decided definitely at this time. Arrangements for the defense of naval bases in the Philippine Islands are as yet far from adequate. Repair facilities are sufficient only for the United States Asiatic Fleet. Stocks of fuel and other naval materials are not great. . . It is therefore, questionable whether there is justification, at least initially, for selecting Manila as a main base for the British Far Eastern Fleet. On the other hand, Manila and other harbours in the Philippine Islands would be made available and could be made reasonably suitable for use as advanced operating bases.[227]

After further refuelling stops at Mauritius and at Addu Atoll in the Maldives – which had only just been completed in time – *Prince of Wales* reached Colombo on the evening of the 28 November. *Repulse* and two destroyers (detached from the Mediterranean Fleet) rendez-voused with her there.[228] On 13 November, suggestions that ABC-1 be modified to take into account the new US reinforcement schedules were put forward by the Americans. Under the original ABC-1 report, the term 'defend' had been deliberately selected to convey the idea that the Associated Powers could not maintain selected territories indefinitely, whereas the word 'hold' carried with it the expectation territory would be permanently retained. Under the new provisions air, land and sea forces of the Associated Powers were asked to 'defend' Hong Kong, the Philippines and the Netherlands East Indies, but were required to 'hold' Luzon, Malaya, Singapore and Java against Japanese attack. US naval forces now agreed to 'prevent the extension of enemy military power' in the Australian-New Zealand area:

> The reasons for the changes. . . have to do with the defense of bases, such as Rabaul, which may be needed by the U.S. Pacific Fleet in operations against forces in the Japanese Mandates, with protection of shipping through Torres Strait and approaches, and with the use of air forces both for the support of naval operations of the Associated Powers and for a general offensive air effort.[229]

By 29 November, the US authorities had informed all their Far Eastern military commands of the alterations and were pressing the British to complete their end of the arrangement. Anxious to assist and eager to begin formulating the long awaited joint operating plan, Pound ordered Phillips to proceed independently to Singapore by air. The departure and passage of *Prince of Wales* and accompanying ships from Colombo was also accelerated. Force G arrived in Singapore on 2 December, and the following day Phillips hoisted his flag as C-in-C Eastern Fleet.[230]

At issue was whether the British Government would give C-in-C Far East, in overall command, authority to mount Operation 'Matador'. The Chiefs of Staff continued to take the view that no action should be taken without a firm US guarantee of support.[231] On 5 December Phillips arrived in Manila by air from Singapore.[232] The following day's conference was divided between morning sessions with MacArthur, with Admiral Hart in attendance, and an afternoon session with CINCAF alone. Historians have presumed that no records of the discussions exist, but in fact Admiral Hart retained a copy of the morning's minutes.

Not surprisingly, the conference was less concerned with a joint operating plan than with the security of Manila Bay as a base for future naval operations. For Phillips the key question was whether the US defences were capable of protecting a fleet sheltering in the harbour. From the cross-examination that followed, it emerged that anti-aircraft defences were concentrated in and around Corregidor and Clark Field. Though Manila Bay itself was practically defenceless, MacArthur hoped to have barrage balloons in place by February and additional anti-aircraft equipment was en route. Pound had already promised the US authorities some British stocks as well. In the meantime, Hart pointed out that the most secure anchorage topographically, hydrographically and from the point of view of anti-aircraft defence was Mariveles Bay close to Corregidor. Both sides expected a bombing attack to penetrate the defences, but they hoped the Japanese would be mauled so severely a second attack could never be launched. Neither side expected the bombers to be accompanied by fighters as the range was felt to be too great. Interestingly, in view of what transpired on 10 December, Phillips saw the main danger to the fleet coming from dive bombers, not high level bombing or torpedo aircraft. He stressed the need for pursuit aviation, particularly long-range fighters capable of operating over the sea, and urged formulation of a fully coordinated plan to meet aerial attack.

Phillips then immediately plunged into a report concerning his own dispositions and the Eastern Fleet's intended concentration. He decided to base British preparations on US reinforcement calculations. Initially, British naval forces would be based on Singapore for 'defensive purposes' until the whole Fleet concentrated. By 1 April 1942 facilities at Manila Bay would be sufficient to operate the Eastern Fleet, but Phillips warned he would continue to lack carrier support; *Indomitable* had run aground in the West Indies and he had been unable to secure the services of *Ark Royal*. Yet if American pursuit aviation fulfilled its role the absence of a carrier would make no difference.[233]

During the afternoon session, Hart and Phillips went on to discuss specific dispositions and the drafting of an agreed report. Within the next four weeks Phillips expected *Revenge* and *Royal Sovereign* to join *Repulse* and *Prince of Wales* at Singapore. These forces, together with the cruisers *Mauritius* and *Achilles* from New Zealand, *Tromp* and *de Ruyter* from the Netherlands East Indies and possibly *Australia* and *Hobart* from Australian Station, plus ten British and six Dutch destroyers, would operate from Singapore as a strike unit. A cruiser task force consisting of *Australia* or *Canberra*, *Perth*, *Leander*, *Cornwall* and three armoured merchant cruisers would cooperate with *Houston*, *Marblehead* and four US destroyers along the line East Borneo-Surabaya-Darwin. However, Phillips neglected to inform Hart he had yet to secure Australian or Dutch cooperation. Given Britain's naval weakness offensive action in the Marshalls was still vital to success, so Phillips also enquired about a timetable for the movement of the US Pacific Fleet to Truk.[234]

On 3 December, Pound had directed C-in-C Eastern Fleet to try to secure immediate use of two divisions of destroyers from the Asiatic Fleet.[235] Having read copies of the hostile response to earlier overtures, Phillips, on his own initiative, scaled down his requirements to four destroyers. He had every reason to be confident that Hart would comply. The United States had already agreed to make up deficiencies 'if war broke out and the United States were involved', and Phillips had just been informed of the President's political pledge of support.[236] Despite confirmation about the US promise from his liaison officer in Singapore, Hart had no official word from Washington of this matter even as late as 7 December, and he was suspicious that this was some kind of British plot designed to wrest control of his own naval forces away from him. Hart pointed out to Phillips that the British could make better use the destroyers assigned to the local defence of Hong Kong at Singapore, and a telegraphic enquiry was dispatched immediately to Washington asking for confirmation that a political commitment had been made. He assured Phillips that the US offer would be kept but only if the US was actively in the war.[237]

It was perhaps fortunate that the conference abruptly terminated late in the afternoon of 6 December. Hudson aircraft of the Royal Australian Air Force, flying from Kota Bharu, sighted three separate Japanese convoys off the southern coast of IndoChina steering towards the Gulf of Siam. Phillips at once recalled *Repulse,* at that stage en route to Australia for a goodwill visit, and prepared to depart for Singapore. At the very last moment Hart relented and provided C-in-C Eastern Fleet with the necessary destroyers he required. According to the Hart narrative, Phillips had already decided that if hostilities followed he intended to take his ships to sea and attack the enemy. The events surrounding the actual outbreak of war and the subsequent fate of Force Z will be taken up in future research.[238]

Conclusions

What had been achieved strategically and tactically by the 'allied' or 'associated' powers by the end of 1941? A joint operating plan with all the participants (that cherished Admiralty goal) was only slightly nearer than it had been at the beginning of the year. A preliminary plan had been signed, with the Americans allowing a British Far Eastern Fleet to begin operating from Manila in cooperation with the US Asiatic Fleet by March 1942. On 8 December, formal approval of the new dispositions was received by Admiralty authorities from the CNO Admiral Stark. He promised that sufficient equipment would be provided to make Manila into an advanced operating naval base. A vague promise had been extracted from Admiral Turner stipulating that Kimmel's command would indeed conduct 'offensive operations' into the Marshalls to draw off the Japanese, though US authorities would provide no details; British perceptions as to what such operations entailed were a world away from reality. The Admiralty never knew just how far US offensive operations had been curtailed by Kimmel and the Navy Department. There remained serious doubts about the Dutch contribution, and more particularly about that of the Australians. Could they ever have been persuaded to cede responsibility for the control of their own naval forces to the British? In any event, with the Japanese poised to strike against Pearl Harbor, Thailand, Malaya and the Philippines, there was little chance that these dispositions would be completed in time. It was a case of too little too late.

Who then should bear responsibility for the Force Z disaster? It would seem that though Phillips was Vice Chief of Naval Staff and should bear at least some of the blame for the decision to despatch naval forces to the Far East, the strategy adopted owed less to individual action and rather more to a collective decision reached by the Admiralty itself in the summer of 1941. That decision was based upon naive and unrealistic expectations and a gross underestimation of enemy capabilities, conditions that had characterized the Admiralty's approach to

Far Eastern naval defence throughout the inter-war period. In that sense Admiral Phillips was just as much a victim of Admiralty policy as its instigator.

Notes

1. BUS Mtg 4, 7 February 1941, CAB 99/5.
2. Tel. ADM to C-in-C China Station, 25 February 1941, ADM 116/4877.
3. Tel. ADM to C-in-C China Station, 4 April 1941, ADM 116/4877; Minute Everett to D of P, 4 April 1941, ADM 1/11855.
4. Minute Pound to Churchill, 13 February 1941, ADM 116/4877.
5. Tel. COS to Bellairs, 19 February 1941, 24 February 1941, 27 February 1941, CAB 105/37.
6. Memo First Sea Lord to PM, 13 February 1941, ADM 205/10.
7. 'Situation if the United States Enters the War and Japan Remains Neutral', Memo by the Plans Division, 6 March 1941; Tel. ADM to All Stations, 13 May 1941, ADM 116/4877.
8. Minute by D of P, undated February 1941, ADM 116/4877.
9. COS Paper 578 (41), 18 September 1941, AIR 9/144. For more information on British strategic thinking about Malaya see S. Woodburn Kirby (1957), *The War Against Japan: The Loss of Singapore,* London, vol. 1, pp. 162–3, 506–11.
10. COS Paper 614 (40), 8 August 1940, CAB 80/16; COS Paper 676 (40), 28 August 1940, CAB 80/17.
11. 'British Administration in the Far East', Memo by Chancellor of the Duchy of Lancaster, WP 286 (41), 29 October 1941, CAB 66/20.
12. Minute by VCNS, 10 March 1941; Minute by Andrews for D of P, 6 March 1941, ADM 116/4877.
13. Notes of a Meeting between Bellairs and Furstner, 30 October 1940; Notes of a Meeting between Halifax and Furstner, 31 October 1940, ADM 199/1232.
14. ADA Mtg 4, 30 October 1940; Tel. C-in-C China Station to ADM, 30 October 1940, ADM 199/1232.
15. Tel. C-in-C China Station to ADM, WO and Air Ministry, 31 October 1940, ADM 199/1232.
16. Note on Anglo-American-Dutch Conversations by COS Committee, 10 November 1940, WO 106/3292; Report of the Singapore

Conference 22–31 October 1940, ADM 1/11183.

17. Tel. Govt Commonwealth of Australia to WO, 13 February 1941, WO 106/2477.

18. Ltr Hart to Stark, 13 November 1940, Hart Papers.

19. Ltr Stark to Hart, 12 November 1940, in US Congress (1946), *Pearl Harbor Attack: Hearings of the Joint Committee on the Investigation of the Pearl Harbor Attack* (PHA) 79 Congress, 1st session, Washington, pt 14, pp. 972–3.

20. Minute Alexander to Churchill, 16 February 1941, PREM 3/326.

21. Tel. C-in-C China Station to COS, 5 December 1940, WO 106/2477; FE Mtg 3, 16 January 1941, CAB 96/2.

22. 'Report of Conversations between the Chief of Staff and Netherlands East Indies Authorities at Batavia 10–14 January 1941', Memo by Purnell, 18 January 1941, Box 117, Series VII, Records Relating to Anglo-American-Dutch Cooperation, Records of the Strategic Plans Division.

23. Waldo Heinrichs (1988), *Threshold of War: F.D.R. and American Entry into World War II*, New York, p. 35.

24. Tel. C-in-C China Station to WO, 27 February 1941, WO 106/2517; Minute by Dening, 16 April 1941, FO 371/27775.

25. 'Report by JPS', JP 157 (41), 26 February 1941, CAB 84/27.

26. 'February Conference Report', 12 April 1941, FO 371/27775; Ltr Hart to Stark, 4 March 1941, Hart Papers.

27. Tel. C-in-C China Station to ADM, 24 February 1941, ADM 116/4877.

28. Tel. C-in-C China Station to ADM, 27 February 1941, ADM 116/4877; Crace Diary entry 22 and 24–25 February 1941, Crace Papers.

29. Tel. Commonwealth Govt to DO, 27 March 1941, FO 371/27775; Tel. ACNS to ADM, 9 February 1941; Memo D of P to VCNS, 5 February 1941, ADM 1/11352; Ltr Robert Brooke-Popham to Ismay, 28 February 1941, Brooke-Popham Papers.

30. Tel. WO to C-in-C FE, 7 April 1941, WO 106/2518.

31. Tel. C-in-C FE to WO, 11 April 1941, WO 106/2518; Tel. C-in-C FE to WO, 27 April 1941; Tel. NZ Govt to DO, 10 April 1941, FO 371/27776.

32. Ltr Robert Brooke-Popham to Ismay, 16 May 1941, Brooke-Popham Papers.

33. Memo CINCAF to CNO, 29 April 1941, Box 118, Series VII, Records Relating to Anglo-American-Dutch Cooperation, Records of the Strategic Plan Division.

34. Tel. C-in-C FE to WO, 27 April 1941, WO 106/2518.

35. 'Summary of Report of Singapore Conference', 27 April 1941, WO

106/2518.

36. Tel. ADM to C-in-C China Station, 4 April 1941, ADM 116/4877. See also Tel. ADM to Naval Attaché Washington, 19 May 1941, CAB 122/8.

37. 'Far Eastern Arrangements', Memo by Air Staff, 27 July 1941, AIR 8/945; 'Plenaps', 27 April 1941, AIR 23/1873.

38. Report by C-in-C China Station, 28 June 1942, ADM 199/411.

39. 'Summary of Report of Singapore Conference', 27 April 1941, WO 106/2518; Tel. C-in-C FE to WO, 27 April 1941, WO 106/2518.

40. Commentary by JPC on ADB, JP 371 (41), 13 May 1941, CAB 84/31.

41. Tel. WO to C-in-C FE, 17 May 1941, WO 106/2518.

42. Extract of Minutes DO Committee, 51 Mtg, 17 December 1940, ADM 199/1232.

43. Tel. ADM to C-in-C FE, 27 December 1940, ADM 199/1477.

44. US-UK Conversation Minutes, 5 February 1941, US Serial 09212–8, Microfilm Roll 5, Strategic Planning in the US Navy: Its Evolution and Execution1891–1945, Scholarly Resources Inc.

45. Tel. Danckwerts to C-in-C FE, 20 April 1941, ADM 199/1477; Ltr Danckwerts to First Sea Lord, 17 April 1941, CAB 122/294; COS Paper 308 (41), 4 May 1941, CAB 80/28.

46. Minutes of MTG between Army and Navy Committees, 19 February 1941; Minutes of the ABC Conference, Microfilm Roll 5, Strategic Planning in the U.S. Navy: Its Evolution and Execution 1891–1945, Scholarly Resources Inc.; Memo Army Committee to COS, 20 February 1941, WPD 4402. See also Arthur Marder (1981), *Old Friends, New Enemies: The Royal Navy and the Imperial Japanese Navy Strategic Illusions, 1936–1941*, Oxford, p. 189.

47. Ltr Richardson to Stark, 13 April 1940; Memo for the Secretary of the Navy, 12 September 1940, PHA pt 1, p. 260; pt 14, p. 958. For a description of Richardson's position on the question of the US Fleet's Pacific strategy see George C. Dyer (ed.) (1973), *On the Treadmill to Pearl Harbor: The Memoirs of Admiral J.O Richardson*, Washington. Copies of most of Richardson's correspondence with Stark can be found in Kimmel's Private Papers, Microfilm Roll 1.

48. Memo CINCUS and prospective CINCPAC to CNO, 28 January 1941, Secret Serial A 16/0140, Kimmel Papers.

49. Fleet Problem 21–1940, Microfilm Roll 31, M 964, Naval Fleet Problem Records; Ltr 'Poco' Smith to Hart, 28 April 1940, Hart Papers.

50. 'Are We Ready II', 1 July 1940; 'Are We Ready III', 14 June 1941,

Microfilm Roll 5, Strategic Planning in the U.S. Navy: Its Evolution and Execution 1891–1945, Scholarly Resources Inc.

51. Memo CINCPAC to CNO, 5 June 1941, CINCPAC Correspondence, Kimmel Papers.

52. Ltr CINCPAC to GB, 9 June 1941; Memo Cmdt 14th ND to CINCPAC, 1 August 1941, CINCPAC Correspondence, Kimmel Papers.

53. PHA, pt 4, p. 17; pt 16, p. 329.

54. 'Initial Deployment of the Pacific Fleet under Plan Dog', Memo CINCPAC to CNO, May 1941, CINCPAC Correspondance, Kimmel Papers; Ltr CINCPAC to CNO, 25 July 1941, Box 147 F, Series IX, Plans Strategic Studies and Related Correspondence.

55. Memo McCrea to CNO, 19 November 1940, Box 90, A 16–1, Series V; Memo DWPD to D Fleet Maintenance Division, 23 May 1940, Box 95, AA-AZ Auxiliaries, Series V, Subject Files, Records of the Strategic Plans Division.

56. US Pacific Fleet Annual Report 1941, Microfilm Roll 3, M 971, Annual Reports of US Fleets.

57. PHA, pt 23, p. 1220; Memo CNO to Sec. Nav., 1 December 1941, Box 83, Series IV, Serial File, Records of the Strategic Plans Division.

58. Memo DWPD to D Fleet Maintenance Division, 23 May 1940, Box 95, AA-AZ Auxiliaries, Series V, Subject Files; Memo CNO to Sec. Nav., 1 December 1941, Box 83, Series IV, Serial File, Records of the Strategic Plans Division.

59. Kimmel's vague response to the overtures by Danckwerts can now be understood. US Pacific Fleet Annual Report 1941, Microfilm Roll 3, M 971, Annual Reports of US Fleets.

60. Report by Captain Omar D. Conger, 11 July 1941, Box 48, CINCUS Flag Files, RG 313; Husband E. Kimmel (1955), *Admiral Kimmel's Story,* Chicago, p. 28.

61. 'Survey of Conditions in the Pacific Fleet', Ltr CINCPAC to CNO, 26 May 1941, Box 449, CINCPAC Flag Files, RG 313/106. For details on the condition of the Pacific Fleet see Gordon W. Prange (1981), *At Dawn We Slept: The Untold Story of Pearl Harbor,* London.

62. Ltr CINCPAC to CNO, 25 July 1941, Box 147 F, Series IX, Plans Strategic Studies and Related Correspondence, Records of the Strategic Plans Division; Memo CINCPAC to CNO, May 1941; Ltr CINCPAC to CNO, 26 May 1941, CINCPAC Correspondence, Kimmel Papers.

63. Ltr Stark to Kimmel, 25 November 1941, CINCPAC Correspondence, Kimmel Papers. In a most interesting diversion from the

mainstream argument about the defensive nature of the Pacific Fleet's war planning, Edward Miller has argued that Kimmel was offensively oriented, and that he planned a giant Jutland-like clash of battle fleets in the mid-Pacific. The key to this would seem to lie in the use that was to be made of the carriers. Miller feels these were to be concentrated into a strike force which would first raid then retire on the battleline lying in wait for an ambush. Miller may well be correct, but my own research in this area indicates that under Plan O-1 the carriers were to be divided among the various task forces to provide aerial protection over the fleet, and that the fleet itself was not to be concentrated but dispersed. See Edward M. Miller (1991),*War Plan Orange: The U.S. Strategy to Defeat Japan 1897–1945,* Annapolis, pp. 302–6, particularly p. 307.

64. 'Advanced Fleet Base in the Caroline Islands', Memo CNO to CINCPAC, 27 October 1941, Box 101, FA-FT, Series V, Subject Files, Records of the Strategic Plan Division.

65. Ltr Stark to Kimmel, 23 September 1941, CINCPAC Correspondence, Kimmel Papers.

66. Ltr CNO to Sec. Nav., 24 January 1941, Box 92, A16-3/ND14, Series V, Subject Files: 'Estimate of Patrol Plane Requirements for the Navy', Memo by Rear-Admiral Horne, May 1938, Box 97, VB-VZ Airplanes, Series V, Subject Files, Records of the Strategic Plans Division.

67. Ltr CNO to D Naval Districts, 31 December 1940; Ltr DND to CNO, 13 January 1941; Memo DWPD to DND, 16 June 1941, Box 92, A 16–3/ND 14, Series V, Subject Files, Records of the Strategic Plans Division.

68. Memo CINCUS to CNO, 25 January 1941, Box 147J, Series IX, Plans Strategic Studies and Related Correspondence, Records of the Strategic Plans Division; Memo WPD to COS, 14 March 1941, WPD 3444; Ltr Marshall to Short, 7 February 1941, WPD 4449–1; Memo CINCUS to CNO, 7 January 1941, A16–1/ND 14, Classified Records of the Secretary of the Navy 1939–41, RG 80.

69. 'Report on Air Raid Drill 1400 Hrs', Memo Cmdt 14th ND to CINCPAC, 25 March 1941; 'Base Defense Drills: Conduct Of', Memo Cmdr Battle Force to Cmdt 14th ND, 1 September 1941, CINCPAC Correspondence, Kimmel Papers.

70. 'Security of Fleet at Base and in Operating Areas', Memo CINCPAC to Pacific Fleet, 14 October 1941, CINCPAC Correspondence, Kimmel Papers.

71. For details see Stephen Roskill (1954), *The War at Sea*, London, vol. I, p. 616; JRM Butler (1957), *Grand Strategy, September*

1939–June 1941, London, vol. 2, chapters 20 and 22; Basil Collier (1957), *The Defence of the United Kingdom,* London, pp. 278, 504–5.

72. Heinrichs, *Threshold,* p. 48.
73. This followed the delivery of a stiffly worded note from Japan to the UnitedStates. Among other things, Japan demanded the US not sign any alliances with Great Britain and immediately recognize the puppet state in Manchukuo. Heinrichs, *Threshold,* p. 73.
74. Robert J. Quinlan, 'The United States Fleet: Diplomacy, Strategy and the Allocations of Ships (1940–41)', in Harold Stein (ed.) (1963), *American Civil Military Decisions: A Book of Case Studies,* Birmingham, AL, pp. 178–85.
75. 'Survey of Conditions in the Pacific Fleet', Memo CINCPAC to CNO, 26 May 1941, Stark Correspondence, Kimmel Papers.
76. Minute Ismay to Hollis, 8 August 1941, CAB 120/20; Ltr Danckwerts to Phillips, 23 June 1941, CAB 122/4.
77. Marder, *Old Friend's,* p. 209.
78. Tel. Danckwerts to COS, 26 July 1941, CAB 105/36.
79. Leutze, *Bargaining,* p. 253.
80. Tel. ADM to Naval Attaché Washington, 19 May 1941, CAB 122/8. See also footnote 116.
81. Notes of an Interview between Danckwerts and Turner, 23 June 1941, CAB 122/94.
82. Ltr Danckwerts to Turner, 17 June 1941, Box 118, Series VII, Records relating to Anglo-American-Dutch Cooperation, Records of the Strategic Plans Division.
83. Ltr CNO and COS to SPENAVO, 27 July 1941, enclosed in CAB 122/8.
84. Memo Glover to DWPD, 5 September 1941, Microfilm Roll 6, Strategic Planning in the US Navy: Its Evolution and Execution 1891–1945, Scholarly Resources Inc.
85. 'Report on A.D.B-American Comments', Memo by JPC, Annex to COS 283 Mtg, 11 August 1941, CAB 79/13; Tel. C-in-C Far East to WO, 27 April 1941, FO 371/27776.
86. 'Report on A.D.B-American Comments', 23 July 1941, Annex to COS 283 Mtg., 11 August 1941, CAB 79/13.
87. 'Report of Conversations between COS and Netherlands East Indies Authorities at Batavia 10–14 January 1941' by Purnell, 18 January 1941, Box 117, Series V11, Records relating to Anglo-American-Dutch Cooperation, Records of the Strategic Plans Division; Ltr Hart to Stark, 25 February 1941; Ltr Stark to Hart, 3 April 1941; Ltr Hart to Stark, 3 June 1941, Hart Papers.
88. Hart Diary, entry 15 September 1941.

89. Tel. BAD to ADM, 9 August 1941; Note on JP 648 (41) by COS Committee, 9 August 1941; Tel. C-in-C Far East to WO, 13 August 1941, WO 106/2518.

90. 'Report on ADB-American Comments', Memo by JPC, Annex to COS 283 Mtg, 11 August 1941, CAB 79/13.

91. Mtg of Staffs, 11 August 1941, CAB 99/18; see for details Theodore A. Wilson (1969), *The First Summit: Roosevelt and Churchill at Placentia Bay 1941,* London, chapter 7; David Reynolds (1981), *The Creation of the Anglo-American Alliance 1937–41: A Study in Competitive Co-operation*, London, pp. 213–15.

92. Notes on the Roosevelt-Churchill Conference by Arnold, undated, 1941, Box 271; see also Conference File by Arnold, Arnold Papers. The production of the P-40 had risen from 19 per month in February to 68 per month in June, but some 28 per month were being sent to Russia as part of Lend-Lease. The production of B-17s had risen from 6 per month at the end of 1940 to 25 per month in June. See Heinrichs, *Threshold,* pp. 143, 148.

93. Ltr Secretary of State for Air to Lord President of the Council, 23 September 1941, Sinclair Papers, AIR 19/275; see also Tel. WO to C-in-C Far East, 18 September 1941, AIR 8/945; COS Paper 569, 14 September 1941, CAB 80/30.

94. Notes on the Roosevelt-Churchill Conference by Arnold, undated, 1941, Box 22271, Arnold Papers; Ltr DO to Holmes, 4 September 1941, FO 371/27893.

95. Ltr Hollis to Ismay, 16 August 1941, CAB 120/121.

96. This has been the opinion of Professor Marder. See Marder, *Old Friends*, pp. 215–18.

97. Tel. Menzies to Churchill, 11 August 1941, PREM 3/156/1.

98. General Review for March 1941, Paper 14, Annex 1, ADM 1/738; For the origins of this see COS 13 Mtg, 8 January 1941, WO 106/2409; Draft Reply COS to C-in-C Far East, 25 July 1941, WO 106/2518.

99. JP Paper 565 (41), 20 July 1941, CAB 84/32; Memo Churchill to Ismay, 10 April 1941; 'Directive by the Prime Minister and the Minister for Defence', 28 April 1941, PREM 3/156/6; DO 30 (41) 2, 15 May 1941, CAB 69/2; Marder, *Old Friends*, p. 219; Speech by Churchill at the Lord Mayor's Dinner, 10 November 1941, PREM 3/156/1.

100. 'Japan: Measures to Counter further Southward Moves', Memo by JPC JP Paper 664 (41), 12 August 1941, CAB 79/133, discussed COS 284 Mtg, 12 August 1941, Cab 79/86. See also Tel. PM to FO, 12 August 1941, enclosed.

101. Minute by Churchill, 16 July 1941, PREM 4/252/1–4; COS 288

Mtg, 15 August 1941, cited in AIR 8/945; Tel. WO to C-in-C Far East, 22 August 1941, WO 106/2518; Tel. PM to PM Australia and PM New Zealand, 31 August 1941, PREM 3/163/2.

102. Tel. PM to PM Australia and PM New Zealand, 31 August 1941, PREM 3/163/2.

103. Tel. Govt NZ to DO, 14 August 1941, CAB 79/14.

104. Minute by Eden, 13 August 1941, FO 371/27847.

105. See David Day (22 June 1983), 'The Empire Man Strikes Out: Robert Menzies in London, 1941 – A Summary', Institute of Commonwealth Studies Paper. See also David Day (1986), *Menzies and Churchill at War*, Sydney, pp. 217–22.

106. Tel. UK High Commissioner in Australia to DO, 13 August 1941, CAB 120/20.

107. General Review for March 1941, Paper 14, Annex 1, ADM 1/738. See also references in Tel. Halifax to FO, 8 March 1941; Tel. Churchill to Roosevelt, 23 March 1941, PREM 3/324/8.

108. 'Far Eastern Defence Arrangements', Memo by JPS, 27 July 1941, discussed at COS 286 Mtg, 13 August 1941, enclosed in AIR 8/945.

109. Tel. ADM to C-in-C China, 4 April 1941, ADM 1/11855; Confidential Annex to CAB 48 (I), 8 May 1941; 'Gleam 42', Tel. Danckwerts to ADM, 8 May 1941, CAB 65/2.

110. Minute by Goodenough (DNC), 13 June 1941, ADM 116/4877.

111. Ltr CNO to Rear-Admiral Horne, 27 March 1941, Box 97, Series V, Subject Files, Records of the Strategic Plans Division.

112. 'Dispositions, 1 July 1941', Minute by the First Sea Lord, 14 June 1941, ADM 116/4877. For contrasting views on the whole question of Far Eastern naval reinforcement see Marder, *Old Friends*, chapter 8; James Neidpath (1980), *The Singapore Naval Base and the Defence of Britain's Eastern Empire 1919–41,* Oxford.

113. Tel. Danckwerts to COS, 29 April 1941; Minute by Goodenough (DNC), 13 June 1941, ADM 116/4877.

114. 'Use of Gibraltar as a Naval Base,' Memo CINCATL to CNO, 26 July 1941, Classified Records of the Secretary of the Navy, 1939–41, File EF 13/S 67–EF 13–4, Box 191, RG 80; Tel. CNO and COS to SPENAVO, dated 3 July 1941 but received 27 July 1941, CAB 122/8.

115. Tel. CNO and COS to SPENAVO, dated 3 July 1941 but received 27 July 1941, CAB 122/8.

116. Note on JP 648 (41) by COS Committee, 9 August 1941, WO 106/2518; JP Paper 565 (41), 20 July 1941; JP Paper 599 (41), 27 July 1941, CAB 84/33.

117. WM 82 (41), 11 August 1941, CAB 65/19.

118. WM 84 (41), 19 August 1941, CAB 65/19.
119. COS Paper 578 (41), 18 September 1941, AIR 9/144.
120. Ltr Danckwerts to Turner, 19 August 1941, CAB 122/4; Mtg in the First Lord's Office, 20 August 1941, ADM 199/1149; COS 288 Mtg, 15 August 1941, cited in AIR 8/945.
121. Supplement to the New Construction Programme by the First Lord, WP Paper 280 (41), 20 November 1941, CAB 66/20.
122. Capital Ship and Aircraft Dispositions, 28 August 1941, ADM 205/10; Minute by D of P, 25 August 1941, ADM 205/10.
123. Supplement to the New Construction Programme by the First Lord, WP Paper 280 (41), 20 November 1941, CAB 66/20.
124. Memo First Sea Lord to PM, 28 August 1941, PREM 3/163/3.
125. For details see Patrick Abbazia (1975), *Mr Roosevelt's Navy: The Private War of the U.S. Atlantic Fleet 1939–42*, Annapolis, chapter 20.
126. Ltr Pound to Cunningham, 3 September 1941, vol. V 52561, Cunningham Papers; WM 92 (41), 11 September 1941, CAB 65/19.
127. Tel. CNS Australian Navy Board to Naval Attaché Washington, 23 September 1941, CAB 122/8.
128. Tel. ADM to C-in-C China Station, 28 June 1941, ADM 199/1477.
129. 'General Strategy: Review', Memo by the COS (undated) Annex 1 to 'Report of Staff Discussions Aug 9–12', CAB 99/18.
130. Tel. ADM to BAD, 22 September 1941; Aide-Memoire for Use by the British Representative at Naval Planning Conference Singapore, September 1941, ADM 116/4877.
131. Ltr Churchill to First Sea Lord, 21 March 1941, PREM 3/324/31.
132. Aide-Memoire for Use by the British Representative at Naval Planning Conference Singapore, September 1941, ADM 116/4877.
133. Tel. BAD to ADM, 2 October 1941, CAB 122/8.
134. Tel. BAD to ADM, 12 October 1941, CAB 122/8.
135. Ltr Turner to Danckwerts, 1 October 1941, Box 117, Series VII, Records Relating to Anglo-American-Dutch Cooperation, Records of the Strategic Plans Division. See also George C. Dyer (1972), *The Amphibians Came to Conquer: The Story of Admiral Richmond Kelly Turner*, Washington, p. 176.
136. Plenary Session 4, 10 February 1941, Minutes of the US-UK Conversations, Serial 011512–6, Microfilm Roll 5, Strategic Planning in the US Navy, Its Evolution and Execution, 1891–1945, Scholarly Resources Inc.
137. 'Air Force Study', Memo Arnold to ACOS WPD, 14 March 1939, GHQ Army Air Corps, 321–9, RG 18.

138. Memo Grunert to ACOS WPD, 2 May 1941, WPD 4402–18; Rad. Grunert to WPD, 10 July 1940; Ltr Grunert to COS, 22 July 1940, WPD 3251–37; Ltr Hart to Stark, 13 November 1940, Classified Records of the Secretary of the Navy, 1939–41, A–3 (VZ), RG 80.
139. 'War Department Policy: Defence of the Philippine Islands', Memo by WPD, 10 October 1940, WPD 3251–37.
140. Memo by WPD undated 1939, WPD 4129–3.
141. For background on this see Brief of Interview between Hart and Quezon, 28–30 March 1940, Hart Papers.
142. Ltr Ickes to Knox, 18 November 1940; Memo Hull to FDR, 4 November 1940; Ltr Ickes to FDR, 24 October 1940; Memo Ickes to FDR, 10 April 1941, JB 305, Serial 672, RG 225; Tentative Draft Executive Order by Gerow, 4 September 1940; Ltr Stimson to Smith, 31 October 1940, WPD 3251–45. For more information about American-Philippine relations see Theodore Friend (1965), *Between Two Empires: The Ordeal of the Philippines 1929–46*, New Haven, pp. 160–8.
143. Memo CINCAF to CINCUS, 18 January 1941, Box 147 J, Series IX, Plans Strategic Studies and Related Correspondence, Records of the Strategic Plans Division.
144. Memo Emmons to GAC, 23 April 1940, AAC Records 373, RG 18.
145. Memo WPD to COS, 1 January 1941, WPD 3251–39.
146. Ltr Marshall to Short, 7 February 1941, WPD 4449–1; Memo Marshall to Gerow, 26 February 1941, OPD Exec File 10, Item 10; Memo Spaatz to COS, 23 May 1941, GHQ Air Force 321.9, RG 18.
147. Rad. Grunert to COS, 31 May 1941, WPD 3251–45; 'Implementation of Aviation Objectives', Memo Spaatz to OCAS, 24 September 1941, GHQ Air Force.
148. Programme of Expenditure 12 June 1941, AG 093–5, RG 94.
149. Memo FDR to Sec. War, 4 May 1941, Classified Records of the Secretary of the Navy, A 1–3 (VZ), RG 80.
150. Ltr Stark to Cooke, 31 July 1941; Memo Cmdr Subs Asiatic Fleet to CINCUS and CNO, 1 April 1942, Hart Papers.
151. Memo Brett to ACOS WPD, 11 February 1941, WPD 3251–37.
152. Ltr CNO to CINCAF, 16 May 1941, Box 97, SS-Submarines, Series III, Miscellaneous Files, Records of the Strategic Plans Division.
153. Irvine H. Anderson (1975), *The Standard-Vacuum Oil Company and United States East Asian Policy, 1933–41,* Princeton, pp. 168–92; Jonathon G. Utley (1976), 'Upstairs, downstairs at Foggy Bottom: Oil Exports and Japan 1940–41,' *Prologue*, vol. 8, pp.

17–28.

154. Memo Gerow WPD to COS, 16 June 1941, WPD 3602–21; Memo Gerow WPD to COS, 17 June 1941, WPD 3251–52.

155. Forrest C. Pogue (1966), *George C. Marshall: Ordeal and Hope*, New York, vol. 2, pp. 182–3; Rad. Marshall to Douglas Mac-Arthur, 26 July 1941, OCS 18136–35.

156. Ltr Stark to Cooke, 31 July 1941, Hart Papers; Diary of Chief of Air Staff, Entry for 26 July 1941, 337, RG 18; Memo Gerow to COS, 14 July 1941, WPD 3251–50.

157. Memo Brett to ACOS WPD, 5 June 1941, War Plans AWPD, 381–D, RG18.

158. New York *Times*, 10 January, 12 January 1931; D. Clayton James (1970), *The Years of MacArthur, 1880–1941*, London, vol. 1, pp. 369–71; Draft Agreement between General MacArthur and Admiral Pratt, 1 October 1931, AG 580.

159. Memo ACOS to WPD, 29 December 1933, AG 112.05, RG 94.

160. For more information about the development of American air-power see Wesley F. Craven and James L. Cate (eds) (1948), *Army Air Forces in World War II: Plans and Early Operations, January 1939 to August 1942,* Chicago, vol. 1, pp. 21–8; General 'Hap' Arnold (1949), *Global Mission*, New York, pp. 176–7; Robert W. Krauskopf (1958), 'The Army and the Strategic Bomber 1930–39', *Military Affairs*, vol. 22, pp. 83–94, 208–15.

161. PHA, pt 32, pp. 219–20; Entry 26 November 1941, Hart Diary. See also MacArthur folder Hart Papers.

162. COS Paper 504 (41), 20 August 1941, Annex 1, CAB 99/18.

163. Summary of Report of Singapore Conference, 28 April 1941, WO 106/251; Tel. Eastfar to Mil. Mission 16 June 1941, CAB 122/20.

164. The process of air reinforcement can be followed by looking at the following: Ltr Spaatz to Stark, 5 August 1941; Ltr CO Fort Shafter to CAAF, 5 September 1941; Ltr Beel to Clement, 4 October 1941; Rad Air Board Melbourne to CAS 15 October 1941; 'Movement of Air Echelon the Philippine Department', Memo AWPD to CGAFCC, 18 September 1941, Flights: Hawaii and the Philippines, 373, RG 18.

165. Tel. BAD to ADM, 2 September 1941, CAB 122/20; Note of a Visit by Lt.-Col. Vogel to War Dept, 14 September 1941, CAB122/30. It was anticipated that by January 1 1942 there would be 70 B-17s in the Philippines, with another 35 Liberator bombers reaching the islands by February. By March it was expected numbers would reach 165 bombers. This action was not defensive but aggressive; the B-17C could lift half a full bomb load to 900 miles, while the B-17E had a combat radius of action that enabled

it to reach southern Kyushu with a 4,000 lb bomb load. Heinrichs, *Threshold*, pp. 175, 196.

166. MM 18Mtg (41), 19 September 1941, CAB 122/128; JP Paper 693 (41), 25 September 1941, CAB 84/34.

167. Referred to in the previous chapter.

168. COS 348 Mtg, 9 October 1941, CAB 79/14.

169. Record of a meeting held in VCNS Office, 30 September 1941, ADM 116/4877.

170. Aide Memoire for use by the Brittish Representatives at the Singapore Conference, undated, 1941, ADM 116/4877.

171. Minute by First Lord of the Admiralty, 15 October 1941, ADM 116/4877; Tel. ADM to C-in-C Mediterranean, 10 October 1941, PREM 3/163/2.

172. Minute by Churchill, 12 October 1941, PREM 3/163/2.

173. Considerable controversy has raged between Professor Marder and Stephen Roskill about the rift that developed between Churchill and Pound concerning the use of deterrent forces. It has been charged that 'if the Admiralty had been more strongly represented at the top some of the worst naval disasters of the war (notably the dispatch of the *Prince of Wales* and *Repulse* to Singapore without air cover in the autumn of 1941 and the scattering of the Arctic convoy PQ 17 in July 1942 might well have been averted)'. For an outline of the Marder-Roskill debate see Stephen Roskill (1977), *Churchill and the Admirals*, London, Appendix pp. 283–9; see also Steven Roskill (1976), *Naval Policy Between the Wars: The Period of Reluctant Rearmament 1930–39*, London, vol. 2, p. 467; Marder, *Old Friends*, pp. 231–41. Those who have joined the historical debate have assumed that Pound succumbed to Churchill's pressure. Middlebrook and Mahoney refer to Pound's 'surrender'; Paul Haggie notes that 'Churchill had worn Pound down', and although Marder vigorously defends the character of the First Sea Lord, even he is forced to admit that 'Pound did not always win out in his many rough and tumbles with Churchill – Force Z is a conspicuous instance where he did not'. See Martin Middlebrook and Patrick Mahoney (1977), *Battleship: The Loss of the Prince of Wales and Repulse*, London, p. 35; Paul Haggie (1981), *Brittania At Bay: The Defence of the British Empire Against Japan 1931–41*, Oxford, p. 205; Marder, *Old Friends*, p. 235.

174. 'Reinforcement of British Naval Forces in the Far East', Memo by D of P, 11 September 1937, ADM 1/9909.

175. Minute Ronald to Troup, 30 June 1938, ADM 116/4087.

176. Tel. Crosby to Halifax, 7 November 1938; Tel. Craigie to Halifax,

14 December 1938, FO 371/23544.

177. Tel. Clark Kerr to FO, 6 January 1939, FO 371/23545; 'Memorandum Respecting the Proposal to Station a British Battle Squadron Permanently at Singapore' by Fitzmaurice, 27 January 1939, ADM 1/9909; SAC 1st Mtg, 1 March 1939, CAB 16/209; Paul Hasluck (1952), *The Government and the People 1939–41, Australia in the War of 1939–45,* Canberra, series 4, vol. I, pp. 296, 298; Memo by Butler, 23 November 1940, FE Committee 10 Mtg, 28 November 1940, CAB 96/1.

178. 'The Situation if the United States enters the War and Japan remains Neutral', Memo by D of P, 6 March 1941; Minute by Moore, 6 March 1941, ADM 116/4877.

179. Minute by First Sea Lord, 13 March 1941, ADM 116/4877.

180. Tel. ADM to C-in-C China Station, 28 April 1941; Tel. ADM to C-in-C China Station, 11 May 1941; Tel. ADM to C-in-C China Station, 3 October 1941; Tel. ADM to All Stations, 21 October 1941, ADM 116/4877. See also Marder, *Old Friends,* pp. 393–4.

181. Minute Pound to Churchill, 28 August 1941, PREM 3/163/3. Jon Sumida has pointed out that *Rodney* and *Renown* had been reconstructed with new hangers, catapults and aircraft, and had been fitted with the AFTC Mk VII fire control systems which the most modern and up to date available, while *Nelson* used the older AFTC Mk 1 fire control system which was still capable of highly accurate gun control solutions. Each of these ships would be able to act as a master ship for gun salvo concentration on a single target as favoured by the Admiralty. See Jon Sumida (November 1992), '"The Best Laid Plans": The Development of British Battle Fleet Tactics, 1919–1942', *International History Review,* vol. 14, no. 4, pp. 685, 695.

182. The Admiralty's Tactical School had hypothesized that the Japanese would divide their battle line into fast and slow divisions. Ibid., p. 692.

183. 'Forecast of British Naval Strength on December 31 1942 for Transmission to Germany', Memo by Admiralty, DP (P) 35, 19 October 1938, CAB 16/183 A. Interestingly enough, Sumida feels that by the beginning of the Second World War the best admirals favoured fighting actions of manoeuvre in semi-independent divisions consisting of between four and six ships operating at ranges between 10,000 and 15,000 yards. Sumida, 'The Best Laid Plans', pp. 688, 697.

184. 'Far Eastern Policy', Memo by Secretary of State for Foreign Affairs, WP Paper 230 (41), 30 September 1941, CAB 66/19.

185. Tel. C-in-C Far East and C-in-C China Station to COS, JP Paper

16 (41), Annex 1, 1 October 1941, CAB 84/35; Tel. PMA to PM, 17 October 1941, PREM 3/163/3.

186. Minute Churchill to Pound, 29 September 1941, ADM 205/10 and PREM 3/163/3.

187. Ibid.; DO 65 Mtg, 17 October 1941 CAB 69/7; see also DO 66 Mtg, 20 October 1941, CAB 69/8.

188. Tel. ADM to All Stations, 21 October 1941; Tel. ADM to BAD, 22 October 1941, ADM 116/4877.

189. Minute Churchill to Pound, 1 November 1941; Minute Pound to Churchill, 2 November 1941, ADM 205/10.

190. Minute by D of P, 23 October 1941, ADM 116/4877.

191. Tel. PM to PM Australia, 24 October 1941; Tel. PM to President, 1 November 1941; Tel. PM to Premier Stalin, 2 November 1941; Tel. PM to High Commissioner in Canada, 5 November 1941, PREM 3/163/3.

192. Draft Tel. PM to PM Australia, 23 October 1941, PREM 3/163/3.

193. Minute Pound to Churchill, 24 October 1941, ADM 205/10.

194. Bailey and Ryan, *Hitler*, pp. 179–87; 'Estimate of forces in the Eastern Theatre for War with Japan', Memo by D of P, Appendix I: Notes on the Tabular Figures, 27 September 1941, PREM 3/163/3.

195. Tel. ADM to C-in-C China Station, 27 September 1941, ADM 116/4877.

196. Tel. ADM to BAD, 4 November 1941, ADM 116/4877.

197. Tel. PM to High Commissioner Canada, 5 November 1941, PREM 3/163/3.

198. Aide-Memoire for British Representatives at the Naval Planning Conference at Singapore-Revised, 29 September 1941, ADM 116/4877.

199. Minute by Harwood, 29 October 1941, ADM 116/4877.

200. DO 65 Mtg, 17 October 1941, CAB 69/7.

201. DO 66 Mtg, 20 October 1941, CAB 69/8.

202. Tel. ADM to BAD, 22 September 1941, ADM 116/4877.

203. WM 112 (41) 1, 12 November 1941, CAB 65/24.

204. Tel. Pound to Stark, 17 November 1941, ADM 205/9.

205. Robert Rhodes James (ed.) (1974), *Complete Speeches of Winston Churchill, 1897–1963: 1935–42,* New York, vol. 6, pp. 6504, 6475. See too references in DO 71 Mtg, 13 December 1941, CAB 69/2.

206. John G. Winant (1947), *A Letter from Grosvenor Square: Account of a Stewardship*, London, p. 197.

207. Most British authors have argued that a definite political and military pledge was made, while many American authors –

including those responsible for much of the testimony during the Pearl Harbor Attack Hearings – have taken the view that no such definite pronouncement was ever made. For a representative sample of the two positions see Haggie, *Brittannia*, p. 206; Reynolds, *The Creation*, p. 246; Prange, *At Dawn*, pp. 846–8, and PHA, pt 10, pp. 5081–9.

208. Tel. Halifax to FO, 1 December 1941, FO 371/27914. For the background to this telegram see Tel. Halifax to FO, 29 November 1941; Tel. Halifax to FO, 30 November 1941; Tel. FO to Halifax, 28 November 1941, FO 371/27914.

209. Tel. Halifax to FO, 3 December 1941, FO 371/27914.

210. Some, like Raymond Esthus, have argued that the President made a commitment to military intervention, others have defined 'armed support' simply as another form of undeclared war. The Pearl Harbor Attack Hearings argue that 'armed support' did not commit the United States to war with Japan on behalf of the British, the Dutch, the Thais or anyone else. See Raymond Esthus (1963), 'President Roosevelt's Commitment to Britain to Intervene in a Pacific War', *Mississippi Valley Historical Review*, vol. 50, pp. 28–38; PHA, pt 16, p. 1412.

211. Tel. C-in-C Far East to WO, 27 November 1941, enclosed in FO 371/27914.

212. Tel. FO to Halifax, 28 November 1941; Tel. Halifax to FO, 1 December 1941, FO 371/27914.

213. Tel. JSM to WO, 30 September 1941, CAB 122/4; 'Aircraft Requirements for the defense of the Western Hemisphere and American Interests in Asia', Memo Spaatz to CAS, 26 August 1941, War Plans, 381 E, RG 18.

214. Tel. FO to Washington, 3 December 1941; Tel. Washington to FO, 4 December 1941; Minute by Sterndale Bennett, 4 December 1941; Tel. Halifax to FO, 5 December 1941, FO 371/27914.

215. See particularly PHA, pt 5, pp. 2190–1, pt 14, p. 1407, pt 4, p. 2048. Though Roosevelt had read Mahan he was no supporter of his doctrines. In March 1923 he had submitted an article to *Asia Magazine* arguing that improvements in aircraft performance and radius of action meant neither the US nor the Japanese could attack each other with impunity. As President Roosevelt was vitally concerned with 'making substantial saving through eliminating or deferring all expenditures which are not absolutely necessary'. In 1937 he had planned to put into commission 500 private yachts during the first thirty days of war by commandeering, and he even initiated a design for a hybrid, part seaplane tender, part picket boat, and part destroyer, allotting some

$15 million for the development of this 'experimental design'. As we have already seen his preoccupation with limiting war in the Pacific via patrol lines had plagued the Navy Department down to 1941. Franklin Delano Roosevelt (1923), 'Shall We Trust Japan?' *Asia Magazine*, pp. 475–8; Memo Roosevelt to all heads of Executive Departments, 7 April 1937, Box 190, RG 51; Memo Roosevelt to Edison, 10 February 1938, Official File, Box 4, Roosevelt Papers.

216. WM 109, Conclusions, 5 November 1941; WM 112, Conclusions, 12 November 1941, CAB 65/24.
217. Tel. OPNAV to SPENAVO, 25 October 1941, copy in ADM 116/4877.
218. Ltr CNO to Pound, 7 November 1941, ADM 116/4877.
219. Tel. Pound to SO Force G, 9 November 1941, ADM 116/4877; Minute PM to First Sea Lord, 11 November 1941, PREM 3/163/2.
220. Tel. Pound to SO Force G, 12 November 1941, ADM 116/4877.
221. Tel. BAD to ADM, 13 November 1941, CAB 105/36.
222. Memo CNO and COS to President, 5 November 1941, Box 67, Series III, Miscellaneous Files, Records of the Strategic Plans Division.
223. Compare this view with that of Hart. See Hart's comments in Hart Diary, Entry 28 October 1941, Hart Papers; Dispatch Hart to Stark, 27 October 1941, Sealed Top Secret Incoming OPNAV.
224. Mailgram Stark to Hart, 9 November 1941, Sealed Top Secret Outgoing OPNAV. See also Asiatic Fleet-Miscellaneous Correspondence.
225. Memo Ingersoll to Joint Board, 3 November 1941, Box 67, Series III, Miscellaneous Files, Records of the Strategic Plans Division.
226. Ltr CNO to Pound, 7 November 1941, ADM 116/4877.
227. Tel. BAD to ADM, 13 November 1941, CAB 105/36.
228. Tel. SO Force G to ADM, 28 November 1941, ADM 116/4877.
229. Tel. BAD to ADM, 13 November 1941, CAB 105/36. For the background of this see Tel. Halifax to C-in-C Far East, 22 April 1941, CAB 122/8.
230. Tel. First Sea Lord to SO Force G, 1 December 1941; Tel. First Sea Lord to SO Force G, 3 December 1941, PREM 3/163/3; Tel. C-in-C Eastern Fleet to ADM, 8 December 1941, ADM 199/2234.
231. WM 122 (41) 3, 1 December 1941, CAB 65/24.
232. Entry for 5 December 1941, Admiralty War Diary, ADM 199/2234; Vice-Admiral Durnford, 'A Shellback Remembers', pt 14, p. 206, unpublished manuscript, Durnford Papers.

233. Report of the Conference in Manila, 6 December 1941, Hart Papers.
234. Ibid.; Tel. CINCAF to OPNAV, 7 December 1941; Tel. CINCAF to CNO, 7 December 1941, cited in PHA, pt 10, pp. 5082–3; pt 14, pp. 1933–5.
235. Tel. First Sea Lord to SO Force G, 3 December 1941, PREM 3/163/3.
236. Tel. WO to C-in-C Far East, 5 December 1941; Tel. C-in-C Eastern Fleet to ADM, 7 December 1941, CAB 105/20. See also Report of the Conference in Manila, 6 December 1941, Hart Papers.
237. Tel. Creighton to CINCAF, 6 December 1941, cited in PHA, pt 14, p. 1412; Tel. CINCAF to CNO, 7 December 1941, PHA, pt 10, pp. 5082–3; Tel. C-in-C Eastern Fleet to ADM, 6 December 1941, CAB 105/20.
238. Marder, *Old Friends*, p. 398; 'Narrative of Events, Asiatic Fleet, Leading up to War and From 8 December 1941 to 15 February 1942' by Admiral Hart, undated, World War II Action Reports. See also Kemp Tolley (1966), 'Divided We Fell', *United States Naval Institute Proceedings*, vol. 32, p. 41.

Conclusions

It was only natural that the Admiralty and the US Navy Department should have chosen similar Far Eastern naval strategies during the inter-war period. After all, both were motivated by the view that competition between nation-states for colonial possessions and maritime trade was the natural order of things. Under such a premise, merchant shipping would have to be preserved and protected by a 'Blue Water' navy, in which the battleship was the primary component and fleet action the main arbiter of success. As Vincent Davis has argued, such a theory was a useful tool. Whether it be directed consciously as with Mahan, or indirectly if not unconsciously as in the British Navy, where little of the requisite naval doctrine appears to have been set down, it provided a justification for the growth of the navy if not its very existence, as well as a rationale for allocating and assigning defence expenditure when the budget was formulated.[1] Yet by the same token, this dogma was not simply mouthed but sincerely believed by naval staff on both sides.

Each felt preservation of their territorial possessions and their economic and moral commitments required a two-power naval standard, for at the end of the First World War each faced what they believed would be separate enemies in separate oceans. For the Admiralty, France and Japan were the two main potential opponents; for the US Navy Department it was Britain and Japan. However, in the atmosphere of moral rectitude that pervaded both nations in the 1920s, there was little prospect for substantial increases in naval expenditure. Indeed, the reverse was true: finances for all the services were pared almost to the bone, while the Washington Treaty reduced Britain and the United States both quantitatively and qualitatively to little more than a one-power naval standard. Motivated by the same principles, facing the same enemy with the same methods to hand, it was only logical that in the Pacific, both the Admiralty and the US Navy Department should have chosen similar means to achieve similar ends.

In the absence of sufficient seapower to permanently guard their outlying possessions in the Pacific in peacetime, both were forced to rely on the concept of a 'fleet in being', that is, on the implied threat of a fleet presence. If this deterrent strategy did not succeed and war broke out, the necessary seapower would have to be concentrated and transferred to the far Pacific to the point where it would do the most good. Until this concentration took place the advantage would lie with Japan, which both Britain and the United States expected initially to easily conquer Southeast Asia. Thus while the secondary objective of their respective naval war plans was to minimize the damage and to rescue and relieve their Far Eastern possessions, the primary objective was the defeat of Japan. Japanese home waters would have to be penetrated, its naval forces destroyed by battlefleet action and surrender brought on by economic strangulation. Such a strategy of course also guaranteed the navy a key position; the other services would be in either a subordinate or subservient role.

Thus although they were operating from opposite sides of the Pacific, the Admiralty's and the Navy Department's strategic responses to the problem of war with Japan were very similar. As the Washington Naval Treaty ensured numerical superiority over Japan until after 1936, carrying out such a strategy seemed to depend less on the quantity of capital ships and rather more on ancillary elements such as fuelling anchorages, supply bases, repair facilities and dockyards. Rather more attention was devoted to how to get the fleet into a position where it could operate; less attention was paid to what the fleet was to do once it got there. Each estimated that they required at least one main base and one advanced base en route. As to their choice of bases and fuelling anchorages, they preferred to use their own territorial possessions. War with Japan was divided into three phases: in Phase I the fleet would be concentrated and transferred to the main repair base; in Phase II each fleet would continue the offensive to its advanced operating base; in Phase III an offensive would be launched directly into Japanese home waters using other advanced bases as necessary. The Admiralty's main choices were Singapore as repair base and Hong Kong as advanced base; for the Navy Department the choice was Hawaii and possibly Cavite in Manila Bay. Failing that they preferred each other's territory. The British expressed considerable interest in the possible use of Manila, while the Americans were interested in taking over British possessions in the South Pacific.

At first glance such comparisons might appear to be incorrect, but that is only because the focal point for historical attention with regard to British Far Eastern strategy has always been Singapore, ostensibly the *sine qua non* of British defence policy. But although the Admiralty's attention in the 1920s was devoted to ways and means to get the fleet to Singapore, historians have tended to ignore the fact that by the 1930s the Royal Navy's focus had shifted north of the Malay Barrier and was concerned with getting the fleet to Hong Kong, and involved the planning and construction of an advanced naval base there. As far as the

Admiralty was concerned, the overall objective was always the rescue and relief of both bases as a springboard for further action. This does not denigrate the value of Singapore to the Admiralty, but it does raise the perceived value of Hong Kong to equal level. While it was felt that the Eastern Fleet could not operate north of the Malay Barrier without Singapore, it is equally true to say that British naval forces could not operate in Japanese waters without Hong Kong. For that reason, the views of the British and US Naval Plans Divisions and their respective war plans, the Far Eastern Naval War Memorandum and the original tenets of War Plan 'Orange', were exactly equivalent.

It was over this question, namely the question of advanced naval bases, that both British and US naval staff found themselves in an invidious position. Against naval recommendations, both governments had accepted a status quo agreement on all fortification and naval construction west of 110 degrees longitude, excluding Singapore and Hawaii but including the most likely sites for advanced bases like Hong Kong, Hainan, Kam Ranh Bay, Cavite, Dumanquilas Bay and Guam. Until 1936 when the Treaty expired, any attempt to improve existing facilities or to create additional facilities north of the Malay Barrier and west of Hawaii would contravene Article 19.

Even large-scale expenditure of the kind required to bring bases like Singapore and Pearl Harbor up to fleet standard could simply not be afforded, while the aggressive intent of these war plans was fundamentally at odds with the prevailing mood of international public opinion, if not anathema to a post-war world in the midst of economic and domestic recovery from four long years of bloody conflict of the most hideous kind. Representing the conservative element within the naval hierarchy, such views were bound to be opposed by their respective governments on political, economic and moral grounds. Instead of immediately abandoning such plans and re-adjusting their strategies accordingly, each planning agency sought to convince their respective administrations to either relinquish or redefine the fortification clause. They saw the limitations agreements and its accompanying philosophical assumptions concerning universal peace as a temporary aberration. Sooner or later, they believed the need for adequate defence would take precedence, the spirit of collaboration and compromise would collapse, and when the financial restrictions were lifted, satisfactory defence preparations could be made.

In the meantime, their objective was to ensure that in a period of parsimony sufficient resources were laid aside to provide a springboard for later developments; 'loopholes' in the non-fortification clause had to be found and exploited; camouflage, or at least disguising the true intent, while still constructing certain facilities became part of policy.

Naval support for the refurbishment of coastal defences, secret arrangements with private companies like Standard Oil or the Dohenny group or the attempt by the US Navy Department and the Admiralty to secure subsidies for private dock construction were typical examples. To achieve this meant going behind the back of the other services, the civilian leadership and Cabinet. Although the degree of influence exercised by each planning agency waxed and waned during the inter-war period, both naval command structures were never entirely without that influence.

But it must not be assumed that the Far Eastern Naval War Memorandum and War Plan 'Orange' were mirror images of the same plan. Though similar, there were differences in approach between the two strategies, differences which began as differences in degree but which, by the late 1930s, had become differences in kind. Some of these were inherent; others resulted from the limited success achieved by each plans division in influencing the naval command structure and the civilian government. From the beginning the Admiralty had enormous advantages over the US Navy Department. They were the senior service of their service hierarchy: all the traditions of past performance were theirs to exercise and command against the Cabinet and the Chiefs of Staff. British administrations were less aware of the activities of the Admiralty's Naval Plans Division than was the case in the United States. The Royal Navy never suffered an annual inquisition in which every nuance of performance, every penny of expenditure and every expectation and intent was raked over in microscopic detail by civilian committees eager to pounce on the slightest misplaced decimal point. Because of the nature of the British bureaucratic structure the Admiralty were better able to hide the redistribution of finance, to camouflage the construction of facilities under the guise of local defence preparations from the Committee of Imperial Defence, the Treasury, and the Prime Minister.

Thanks to their full participation in the decision-making processes – the US Navy Department by comparison was given few if any political guidelines – the Admiralty was always well aware that a commitment to the Far East would always be made by the British Government. Far more time was spent in the Committee of Imperial Defence arguing about the scale of Hong Kong's defences, than on whether the base should even be defended. For the US Navy Department, however, there was always uncertainty about the administration's future intentions. This led to a certain puzzlement about, if not actual questioning of government policy. They could never be sure under what circumstances the United States might go to war or even what kind of war would be fought if it did. Admiral Richardson's entreaty to inform the Pacific

Fleet's command 'why we are here and what we are supposed to be doing' bears a startling resemblance to service attitudes encountered nearly thirty years later during America's Vietnam interlude.[2] And as the 1930s proceeded, because of the Tydings-McDuffie Act, implementing the 'fast track' approach of the original War Plan 'Orange' appeared a dubious proposition. The United States might at any moment be deprived of access to the Philippines and to any remaining bases in the islands. It seemed more rational and reasonable to plan a step-by-step and gradual advance back to the Philippines via the Japanese Mandates, or if Japanese strength at the beginning of the conflict was at its height, to fall back and protect the vital Alaska-Hawaii-Panama triangle. As a result there was far less consensus of interest and far less unity of purpose behind War Plan 'Orange' – even within the Navy Department – compared with support behind the Far Eastern Naval War Memorandum within the Admiralty.

Part of the problem in executing War Plan 'Orange' also stemmed from the late start by the United States as a naval power. The Admiralty had all the benefits of a long naval history: a secure line of communications, a well-established set of fuelling anchorages and bases and the largest merchant marine in the world. The United States had none of these benefits. Indeed as late as 1918, the US Navy had the ships but did not have a single home base adequate for fleet needs. The United States was in the position Britain might have been in if it had tried to act as a major seapower without Chatham Dockyard, Rosyth or Scapa Flow.

Thus the construction of bases on the west coast took precedence in American naval minds. The issue was complicated by the fact that there was a far greater range of choice of location, and the battle for resources that resulted from the competition between the mainland and the Pacific bases further confused the whole issue. For example, Pearl Harbor was never the first choice as fleet repair base; it achieved that distinction more by default than by design, and it was nowhere near complete on the outbreak of war. For a time Guam and Dumanquilas Bay appeared better propositions than Manila, and facilities at Cavite were always competing to some degree with those at Subic Bay

Which of the two plans – the Far Eastern Naval War Memorandum or War Plan 'Orange' – was the more naive is difficult to assess. After all, both the Admiralty and the US Navy Department failed to achieve their goals in the end. It was perhaps more naive to have regarded the 'fast track' War Plan 'Orange' as feasible when the requisite fleet bases to support a trans-oceanic offensive were not even present. Nevertheless the US Navy – unlike the Admiralty – did not underestimate either the enemy or the task ahead. They at least came to realize that war against

Japan would involve a substantial proportion of US resources in an island hopping campaign of lengthy duration. In the end the Admiralty was better placed to transfer a fleet quickly to the Far East; the US Navy was more capable of maintaining a fleet in Eastern waters over a period of time. One could react in an emergency; the other sought to fight a longer-term conflict.

Disregarding national self-interest and given the limited financial and material resources of both nations, the best theoretical solution to their Far Eastern defence problems was to have combined forces and facilities to offset the weaknesses of one with the strengths of the other. However, both the Admiralty's and the US Navy's Naval Plans Divisions preferred to evolve their comparable Far Eastern strategies in complete isolation from each other: War Plan 'Orange' and the Far Eastern Naval War Memorandum were intended to be executed without the assistance of allies. This was because no real foundation for cooperation was ever established between each navy concerning the Pacific during the inter-war period. The points of contact between the two sides were few and far between; those points that did exist were more fraught with the spirit of competition than conciliation. At the end of the First World War the United States had displaced Britain as the world's leading economic power, but this was a position the British were distinctly unwilling to cede without a fight, and the ramifications of this carried over into Anglo-American naval relations. In the Pacific, any burgeoning relationship was coloured by the competition for air routes between the two countries, a competition that was but a natural outgrowth of the battles that had already taken place in the 1920s and early 1930s for access to markets and merchant shipping rights.

To defeat Japan, what was really required was a combined strategic approach and an effective joint operating plan, one that would operate both at the strategic and at the tactical level. To achieve that, however, the parameters of collaboration would have to be clearly defined while the command structures needed to be unified. It is interesting to note just how sadly deficient both the British and US navies were in these areas even as late as mid-1941. Despite the obvious decline in the international situation in the period 1937–1941 meetings between the naval staffs from both countries were few and infrequent. Because of Roosevelt's need to prevent the Congressional isolationist bloc from learning of the discussions, those that did take place were conducted under conditions of enforced secrecy and, at the President's insistence, without political commitment or territorial guarantees, which rendered most of the discussions that took place purely hypothetical and to some extent unrealistic. If war broke out in the Pacific, the Admiralty could place no trust in either the United States or its Navy.

Conclusions

Prompted by the outbreak of the Sino-Japanese War and the *Panay* Incident, the first strategic meeting between the two occurred in January 1938. The idea of a joint naval demonstration by both navies in Eastern waters was discussed but quickly dropped. Nearly a year then passed in which all contact between the two was confined for the most part to the technical arena, and there was another gap of over a year between the Hampton discussions and the arrival of the Ghormley mission in London. It is thus difficult to see, as James R. Leutze and others do, a continuity of contact, or the development of any kind of 'special relationship' in the Pacific. Between 1937 and mid-1940 there was little collaboration either planned or desired beyond the most basic understanding of mutual intentions if war broke out. In a sense this was quite deliberate, for neither truly believed that they needed the other to defeat Japan. By mid-1940 that situation had changed. Britain's entry into the war and the diversion of vital resources to the Mediterranean led to the abandonment of the Eastern Fleet strategy; increasingly the defence of Far Eastern waters came to depend on the assistance the United States might provide as Britain sought to establish dominion over the strategic planning process.

The overconfident belief that the US Navy Department would be willing to underwrite the defence of British Far Eastern possessions was based on a totally erroneous judgement made at the Hampton meetings in mid-1939. Admiral Leahy had indeed promised that the US Fleet would rescue and relieve Singapore, but his warning that this was purely his own opinion and not official policy was somehow lost in translation, perhaps because it suited the British position so perfectly. At times in 1940 it did seem as if the Roosevelt administration was going to take a stronger line both politically and military in the Far East: the imposition of an embargo on certain Japanese imports and the permanent basing of the US Fleet at Hawaii were but two examples. But in reality, US Far Eastern policy was just as ill coordinated and as disingenuous as it had been throughout the 1930s.

US military support for British Far Eastern strategy was equally uncertain. US naval strategy swung violently between hemispheric defence and modified versions of War Plan 'Orange', cut to suit America's limited resources. By 1940 the US Navy was in the process of creating a two-power naval standard, so the full blown trans-Pacific offensive remained in the background. However, War Plan 'Orange' was less a war plan than a fervent hope, less a plan of attack than an impractical long-range vision that would be carried out after the outbreak of war when there was no longer any financial restraint. The Rainbow Plans also reflected that same disarray. Not until late November did any kind of definite strategy emerge, when Admiral

Stark's Plan 'Dog' Memorandum established the Atlantic as the primary theatre. Over the short term hemispheric defence would secure US possessions; over the medium-term the US would commit to a full-scale offensive in the Atlantic and a much reduced advance by US naval forces into the Mandates in the Pacific, designed primarily to divert Japanese strength away from the Malay Barrier. Over the long term, a lengthy campaign into the Mandates would be required. The degree of collaboration to be expected from the US Navy was thus distinctly limited.

In 1940 the Admiralty approached possible talks more from a military than from a political point of view. As the chief if not the most experienced negotiating arm, the Foreign Office found its advice being ignored; indeed it was being all but deliberately being excluded from the discussions. The Royal Navy saw the Bailey Committee Meetings, the Anglo-American Standardisation of Arms Committee and the Ghormley Mission as a means to an end, a springboard for full-scale staff talks, while the British government hoped to make use of US naval forces at Singapore as a peacetime deterrent. Both sought to convince the United States of the 'rightness' of their position and to establish dominion over the negotiating process. However, the confidence the British exhibited in their trans-Atlantic neighbour was hardly justified. US foreign policy was directed more towards keeping the war away from the Americas, avoiding entangling alliances and political commitments, assessing Britain's chances of survival and the means to that end, and gathering intelligence and technological information. There was little real interest in political and military assistance to the Far East or the underwriting of the defence of British territorial possessions; indeed it was difficult for the United States to make definite decisions about the extent of its own interests and commitments in the Pacific. Thus the second half of 1940 was characterized by mounting British pressure for a full staff conference, while the Americans steeled themselves to resist British blandishments and keep them at arms length.

The surprising announcement that a full staff conference would be held in Washington was very much a Presidential decision. The British had expected that the signing of the Tripartite Pact and the US November elections would lead to a fundamental change in attitude on the part of the United States towards staff conversations, but in fact the main motivating factor behind the President's sudden reversal of form was Japan's occupation of northern IndoChina. Yet neither the US Navy nor the State Department saw any need for such a meeting. Although naval staff accepted the President's directive, they insisted that no meeting take place unless the British deferred completely to the American viewpoint. Any agreement with Britain would, of necessity, be only of the most general kind. There was little hope that the US Navy would be willing to jeopardize American interests and possessions to protect the British Empire; a view that extended to peacetime use by US naval forces of Singapore or the despatch of naval patrols across the region.

Thanks to a multitude of delays and misunderstandings by the time the British naval delegation and other service representatives arrived in Washington in late 1941, an already suspicious and Anglophobic Navy Department was full of the vision of a 'perfidious Albion'. Compounding those errors was the fact that the Admiralty had lied – quite deliberately so – about the real state of Singapore's facilities, a lie they continued to repeat right through the ABC-1 meetings. There was little that was surprising in the positions put forward by both sides at these meetings. To a great extent their mutual standpoints were dictated by the events of 1940 and their pre-war plans.

For Winston Churchill, the choice was clear: political considerations dominated his mind, and those considerations dictated that US entry into the war be bought at any cost. For the Admiralty, however, the choice was a great deal more complicated. Military and strategic considerations and British self-interest and future needs were the paramount concerns. They assumed that British naval tradition and past wartime experience would give them the edge at the negotiating table. In any case, US naval strategy was felt to have advanced little since pre-war days. Any planning for collaborative action was assumed to be still in the formative stage and therefore malleable. In event of problems the Admiralty placed its faith in sweet reason and rationality, in the ability to 'educate' the Americans round to their way of thinking; indeed as the title to this book suggests, it was a battle for domination, to see who would be master in the strategic arena. The alternative was inevitable decline as a power in the Pacific.

Like the Americans, the British saw the Atlantic and the Mediterranean as the vital theatres. The primary objective in any war with all three members of the Axis would be the defeat of Germany and Italy. Only after that had been accomplished would the defeat of Japan be pursued. In the meantime Japan would be contained north of the Dutch East Indies by at least nine US capital ships acting in concert with Allied naval forces operating from Singapore, still the *sine qua non* of the Pacific. In other words, the British spoke of the strategic and tactical employment of a combined fleet. For the Admiralty, protection of the Malay Barrier, the defence of Singapore and the rescue and relief of her Far Eastern possessions were the important concerns. The British saw the Pacific theatre as a US responsibility, the degree of support to be expected from the Royal Navy would be limited to secondary naval forces. However, at the same time, they were also anxious to obtain substantial US commitment in the Atlantic.

It is difficult to see how the Admiralty could have been more wrong in its assessments. It was unrealistic of the Royal Navy to have assumed that the United States would be prepared to accept strategic responsibility for the Pacific, as well as take on the burden of defence in the Atlantic, without reward in the form of control over the way in which the war would be fought commensurate with the degree of commitment. US Far Eastern strategy was only half-formulated, but out of the muddle of the Rainbow Plans – and despite the absence of political directives – certain fundamentals about the war and how the United States intended to fight had emerged by the time the 'Plan Dog' Memorandum was written. As far as the Americans were concerned, US interests in the Far East were of much less value to the United States than Allied interests were to the Allies. For that reason the Allied powers would have to accept the burden of defence for their own Far Eastern possessions. In any case, American planners were quite prepared to cede most of the region to Japan; the area could be re-conquered later or returned as part of the post-war settlement. The British spoke of combining forces and merging command structures; the Americans wished to compartmentalize the conflict by the creation of separate and distinct areas of responsibility. Collaboration would be in a strategic rather than a tactical sense, a feature that had been maintained since the Ingersoll conversations of 1938. Even when operating in British areas of control, US ships would maintain their own command hierarchy, and tactical support from US naval forces would depend on the degree of cooperation that individual commanders might provide.

The British came away from the ABC-1 Conference distinctly unhappy. Initially the US would agree to protect British and American interests only as far west as Guam north of the equator, and as far west as Fiji south of the equator. It would be up to the British themselves to defend their own territorial possessions through the resurrection of the previously defunct Eastern Fleet strategy. Presuming that war had broken out and that Britain and the United States were allies ranged against Japan – a presumption that was by no means politically guaranteed – the US agreed to assist the early release of British capital ships for the defence of the Malay Barrier by assuming partial responsibility in the Atlantic. Support for Far Eastern defence would be limited to attacks by the recently created Pacific Fleet against the Marshalls and the Carolines to divert Japanese naval strength away from the Malay Barrier, to raids on Japan's lines of communications and to whatever assistance might be provided by the US Asiatic Fleet after the Philippines became untenable, based on Singapore or Sorabaya.

However, the strategy was unworkable without the proper political and territorial guarantees, and the President's main interest was to ensure that these would not be made. As far as he was concerned the discussions were purely hypothetical: hence his stress on the use of the word 'associated' rather than 'allied'. This situation was similar to events in 1917.

The basic purpose of the ABC-1 Conference had been 'to determine the best methods by which the Armed Forces of the United States and the British Commonwealth, with its present allies, could defeat Germany and the powers allied with her, should the United States be compelled to resort to war.'[3] But the meeting also determined who would be the dominant partner in event of a wartime alliance in the Pacific, and the British lost that battle even before they entered into the discussions. The United States could survive without Britain; Britain could not survive without the United States. However hard her negotiators sought to avoid the issue, they had to take account of the imbalance that now existed in the Pacific. Commitment to the Atlantic was seen as the key to the survival of both countries; war against Germany and Italy was the priority, while a defensive would be maintained against Japan. Later Britain was to do substantially better in negotiating by convincing the United States to commit its forces to the North African campaign.

The Americans initially agreed to take on partial responsibility for the Atlantic theatre, but only under wartime conditions and if an ally of Britain. However, prompted by the deteriorating situation in the Middle East and the performance of German U-boats in British sea lanes, the United States government decided to accelerate the transfer of US naval forces. They began to assume such responsibilities in peacetime beginning in May 1941. Under the early Hemisphere Defence Plans, action by the US Navy was limited to patrol activity up to and including 26 degrees west, but this had an immediate 'concertina' effect on British naval plans. By mid-September, thanks to the adoption of the modified Hemisphere Plan 4, the Admiralty was able to modify the timetable of those early preparations.

There has been considerable historical controversy about the kind of British naval forces required in Eastern waters, when the decision was made to despatch those forces to the Far East and why such a decision was made. Authors have tended to concentrate the bulk of their attention on the quarrel between the Prime Minister and the Admiralty in the latter half of the year, and it has generally been presumed that British Far Eastern strategy had a degree of independence it never really possessed. In fact the defence policy of the 'associated powers' has been badly served by the historical literature.[4] What has not been recognized

Conclusions

has been the degree to which the Admiralty was being forced to pander to US desires. Various authors – Marder and Neidpath amongst others – have argued that the decision to despatch naval forces was taken sometime between August and the end of October 1941. However, the genesis of that decision owed less to Imperial connections and the Japanese occupation of southern IndoChina and rather more to US intransigence in February 1941. This forced a resurrection of the defunct Eastern Fleet strategy.

It was the United States that now dictated British naval strategy in the Far East. Throughout 1941 it was the US that decided the class and kind of naval forces the Admiralty intended to send, even down to the particular type of ship and the timing of their arrival. The faster the transfer of US forces to the Atlantic, the more responsibility they assumed; the more responsibility they assumed, the more likely the formation of the Eastern Fleet in peacetime or as early as possible after the outbreak of war. Such was the strain on British resources that the Admiralty would have difficulty in assembling the fleet unless deficiencies in cruisers and destroyers were made up from Dominion and US sources. Singapore's survival and the formation of the Eastern Fleet therefore depended on the direct assistance of the US Asiatic Fleet at as early a date as possible, but the strength of this combined force would not be sufficient to face the full might of the Imperial Japanese Navy. Unless the US Pacific Fleet could be counted on to launch a large-scale offensive into the Mandates to divert the bulk of Japanese naval strength away from the Malay Barrier, the operations of any combined fleet would be crippled. This, in one sense, was why the British advised the US administration not to reduce the strength of the Pacific Fleet below a minimum level of at least six capital ships.

Answers to such questions could only be provided by a joint operating plan to coordinate naval activities between both countries at the field command level. However, thanks to a myriad of errors and delays, poor communications and inadequate briefings, the five main Far Eastern Conferences held between October and May 1941 failed to gain unanimity on many issues. For example, the Admiralty failed to secure agreement regarding the diversion of cruisers and destroyers from Dominion home waters, and no real provision was made for the early release of the Asiatic Fleet until the eleventh hour. Although British authorities approved both ABC-1 and the ADB Agreement, no such assent was forthcoming from the United States. ABC-1 continued to be hypothetical and conditional. Many of the political provisions contained in ADB were anathema to the US Government, while militarily the US staff planners objected to the creation of the Eastern Theatre, partly because it contravened ABC-1, and partly because it was a blatant attempt to gain control over all the naval forces in the region. Their chief criticism of the document, however, concerned the British decision to disperse their naval forces on trade protection duties rather than concentrating those forces on the defence of the Malay Barrier. By late September 1941, British attempts to find a compromise using the existing ADB Agreement had failed. The creation of two cruiser strike forces at Singapore and Darwin fell far short of US expectations concerning a forward British offensive role. US planners were not only prepared to withdraw permission allowing the Asiatic Fleet to operate under British strategic direction in time of war, but had also already secretly done so, in order to force the British to take a predominant part in defence of the Malay Barrier.

To secure US wartime cooperation the Admiralty simply had to take notice of American predilections. Even the defence role assigned to the Eastern Fleet depended on US sanctions. The American defence posture now aimed at a more forward role in the Far East for US forces, one that called for the Philippines to be not merely defended but held. Historians have argued that this 'revolution' in strategy took place in July 1941 when the United States assumed responsibility for the defence of the islands directly, but in fact these changes were more an outgrowth of the discussions in late 1940 about political guarantees of support and possible peacetime reinforcement for the islands. Initially the paucity of resources limited any reinforcement to aircraft and submarines, but later, ground forces, anti-aircraft guns and tanks were added to the list. The emphasis placed upon airpower resulted in part from US strategic considerations, and in part from the desire of the Army Air Corps to assume the primary role in any war in the Pacific in order to revenge itself on the Navy for the privations suffered during the inter-war period. For the administration it was the cost-effectiveness of airpower that was its most attractive feature, a policy very much in keeping with Roosevelt's overall defence posture during the 1930s. Cost was always the President's paramount concern.

Britain's response to American gestures by returning its Far Eastern naval strategy back to traditional pre-war principles was logical, in stages and graduated. According to the Far Eastern Naval War Memorandum and British pre-war planning schedules, war in the Far East was to be conducted in two phases. Phase I would see concentration and despatch of an Eastern Fleet to Singapore, the main fleet repair base in Eastern waters. Phase II would see an advance to Hong Kong, the primary choice as advanced fleet base. Phase III, calling for an advance into Japanese home waters, had been dropped after 1935 except as a distant economic blockade. Even when British resources were stretched to capacity during the dark days of 1940, naval plans had continued to be based on the Memoranda with US capital ships taking the place of British naval forces. Manila was the substitute as an advanced base, an idea perfectly in keeping with pre-war tradition that had seen Cavite as a supplement to or a substitute for Hong Kong.

In February 1941, forced by American intransigence to resurrect the Eastern Fleet strategy, the Admiralty still saw a two-phase Far Eastern war as the main strategic imperative. However, only the period between the outbreak of war and the relief of Singapore was now covered. Since protection of British sea communications in the Indian Ocean and preservation of the route of passage to Singapore were the primary concerns during Phase I, they repeated the formula of 1940 when Britain had sought to limit both the strain on its resources and the extent of its assistance to the United States in the Pacific. Phase I concentrated one battlecruiser, an aircraft carrier and assorted cruisers and destroyers on Trincomalee. Creation of an Eastern Fleet and the rescue and relief of Singapore would be left until Phase II. Thanks to the American adoption of Hemisphere Defence Plan I, however, the Admiralty was able to contemplate basing a battlecruiser and a carrier in the Indian Ocean before the end of the year, as well as four of the 'R' class on the Cape. Phase I was to be fulfilled in peacetime, and since concentration of the Eastern Fleet could now take place sooner, the distinction between Phase I and Phase II had become blurred. By mid-September the Americans had adopted Hemisphere Defence Plan 4. Despite delays in shipping and refitting schedules, the Admiralty accelerated its own programme. *Hermes* was on station in the Indian Ocean by 10 September, and *Repulse* joined her early in November. By the New Year the Admiralty hoped to have six capital ships in the East Indies. Once again the length of time required to fulfil Phase II had been reduced. Two cruiser forces were also to be based in Eastern waters, one at Singapore and the other at Darwin. This the Admiralty hoped would provide the basis for a joint operating plan, but US planners rejected both ADB-1 and ADB-2, and the rationale was British unwillingness to take a more forward role in the defence of the Malay Barrier.

Prompted by the United States's more offensive stance, the need to secure US cooperation and the adoption of Hemisphere Plan 5, the Admiralty began its own strategic reassessment late in September. Under the new scheme, a capital ship force would be based on Singapore before the end of the year. Phase I and Phase II became all but academic, for only cruisers and destroyers would need to be added to create the full Eastern Fleet. Unfortunately, that was a perennial problem for the Admiralty. Given the new direction in American strategy, it was felt Japan might not want to adopt a forward stance in the South China Sea, so consideration was given to basing the fleet in the Philippines either just after, or more preferably before, the opening of hostilities. Manila would become the advanced operating base and Singapore the main repair base.

British Far Eastern strategy had come full circle, for this had much in common with traditional pre-war principles and the Far Eastern Naval War Memoranda. There is no doubt as to the brilliance of this move. At one stroke all the problems that had previously bedeviled Anglo-American naval relations in the Far East would be solved. A joint operating plan, political and military guarantees of support and American wartime cooperation were far more likely under conditions where the British were demonstrably committed to protection of US territorial possessions. If the islands were not merely defended but held, the US Pacific Fleet would be inevitably drawn to the Philippines. Substantial British naval support made that a more likely prospect and surface naval reinforcement was the one element lacking in the new Philippine defence programme. No longer would there be any need to secure the cooperation of the Asiatic Fleet from the outbreak of war, while the cruisers and destroyers that Admiral Hart could provide would make the creation of an Eastern Fleet a far easier proposition

Airpower too was an important consideration in the operation of any fleet. Malaya, and particularly Singapore, was badly served by the Royal Air Force. Historians have made much of the fact that no carrier accompanied the Eastern Fleet: *Indomitable*, earmarked for the task, had run aground in the West Indies. But in fact under this scheme, where the fleet was sheltering under the US aerial umbrella and use was made of more modern aircraft than possessed by British field commands, the loss was of little significance. As to the role of this fleet in the South China Sea, what the Admiralty had in mind was an early return to a traditional pre-war Phase II scenario, one which would see the rescue and relief of Hong Kong.

Though doubts still prevailed, the Americans were quite prepared to discuss the new strategy. The main sticking point was Britain's Prime Minister. He and the American President had much in common; both were concerned with cost effectiveness. Churchill was opposed to the despatch of any fleet even as far as the Indian Ocean, let alone Manila. He saw Germany as the most dangerous opponent, and was opposed to the squandering of resources and their diversion from what he perceived as the main theatre of operations; he favoured a political gesture, in the form of a deterrent force, designed more to prevent the outbreak of war than fight it. However, the Admiralty had always opposed such suggestions. To their mind, in peace or in war, if naval forces were sent to the Far East they must be prepared to fight. Only a fleet could fulfil that role. Caught trying to sneak the new measures past the watchful eye of the Prime Minister, the Admiralty resorted to 'double talk', tricks and illusions to camouflage their true intent, and they succeeded. By the time the Prime Minister learned the truth, the Admiralty's overture had reached the United States. Rather than seeing the ebbing of Admiralty influence over Far Eastern strategy, the Defence Committee Meetings in October 1941 saw the Royal Navy emerge in triumph with its strategy intact.

Success now ultimately rested on political and military guarantees of US support, on the formulation of a joint operating plan between the associated powers and on the availability of cruisers and destroyers for the enterprise. Though controversy has surrounded use of the term, a 'pledge' does appear to have been made by President Roosevelt by early December, though the scope of US 'armed support' would have been distinctly limited. Armed with this, Admiral Phillips proceeded to the Philippines in early December. After nearly a year and a half of wrangling, out of the discussions with Admiral Hart and General MacArthur the basis of a joint operating plan which might have seen an Eastern Fleet operating from Manila some time between March and April 1942 finally emerged. By 8 December the Admiralty had also secured sanction from Washington. Agreement had, to a large extent, already been reached about the formation of cruiser strike forces along the Malay Barrier. All that remained was agreement by the Dominions and the Dutch to the diversion of their destroyers from home waters. However, Allied timing was sadly misplaced. Delays in refittings and alterations to shipping schedules meant that the Japanese were able to strike at the eleventh hour with Allied strategy in a state of confused transition. Indeed, one could not have imagined a more inopportune moment from the Anglo-American point of view for an attack to take place. All plans were thrown into complete disarray. It was a case of too little too late.

If the Admiralty's 'new approach' had been fully implemented, and if the US reinforcement schedule had kept pace, could this have prevented the Japanese from overrunning Southeast Asia? Hypotheticals in history are difficult to answer, but if the scheme had been in place while Japanese plans were being formulated, there seems little doubt that it would have exerted a positive deterrent effect. A broad front offensive over six separate areas carried with it a considerable degree of risk, particularly as Japan did not possess sufficient military, naval and transport strength for the control of the whole intended area of conquest. The US Pacific Fleet was the only force in the Pacific that could contest the Japanese attack; that was the main strategic imperative behind the decision to attack Pearl Harbor. A second major naval force located on the flank of Japan's intended path of advance might well have reduced the number of likely targets, and perhaps even have led to cancellation of the whole southern offensive.

However, if Japanese plans had continued unabated and if Japan had retained the anticipated absolute superiority in the air, then in the end it is unlikely that the presence of the Eastern Fleet would have made any substantial difference. The Eastern Fleet would have sat uneasily amid the US command structure. What must be remembered too is that the operation of British naval forces north of the Malay Barrier was still dependent on large scale offensive action by the US Pacific Fleet. The Admiralty were unaware of the real state and intentions of Kimmel's command, or that the Japanese would retain the bulk of their battlefleet in reserve; had they known, the Royal Navy would have undoubtedly reassessed its own position. The Eastern Fleet would have stood little chance in open conflict with the full Imperial Japanese battleline. The presence of a fleet would probably have diverted even greater quantities of Japanese airpower to the Philippines. Ultimately Japan's quantitative and qualitative superiority would have forced withdrawal of the Eastern Fleet from Manila back to Trincomalee, or culminated in a disaster greater than the sinking of *Repulse* and *Prince of Wales*. It was the timing of the 'new approach' that was the most important consideration and on which success depended.

It was here that Allied plans went awry. It is all very well to argue that if only the United States had exhibited less intransigence, or if only it had reacted before the event rather than after – as in the case of the Japanese occupation of IndoChina – then an accelerated programme might have been implemented. Such an argument ignores the basis of Anglo-American naval relations in the Pacific and the delicate balance of US production schedules. It was incredibly arrogant of the British to have assumed that the United States would be prepared to leave the west coast of the United States and Hawaii undefended in order to underwrite British Far Eastern possessions. It was incredibly arrogant of the Americans to presume that the British would be prepared to cede Far Eastern territory while the United States herself was still committed to its own Far Eastern interests in Guam and the Philippines. Compromise is always difficult to achieve when self interest is the primary concern and where competition is the main determinant. Historians have often criticized the German military mind for its preoccupation with Clausewitz and its obsessive interest in the Schlieffen ideology of battles of annihilation, but clearly Germany is not the only country that can be accused of obsessiveness. Both the Admiralty and the US Navy Department in the end found it just as difficult to escape the all-encompassing embrace of traditional strategic principles.

Notes

1. Vincent Davis (1967), *The Admirals Lobby*, Chapel Hill, NC, pp. 123–5.
2. George C. Dyer (ed.) (1973), *On the Treadmill to Pearl Harbor: The Memoirs of Admiral J.O. Richardson*, Washington, p. 319.
3. Arthur Marder (1981), *Old Friends, New Enemies: The Royal Navy and the Imperial Japanese Navy, Strategic Illusions, 1936–41*, Oxford, p. 189.
4. James R. Leutze spend the first fifteen chapters of his book looking into Anglo-American relations up to 1941, but sums up the nine months preceding Pearl Harbor in only thirteen pages. Many authors leap from the ABC-1 Conference to the Prime Minister's conference with British naval authorities in August in one move. James R. Leutze (1977), *Bargaining for Supremacy: Anglo-American Naval Collaboration, 1937–41*, Chapel Hill, NC, Paul Haggie (1981), *Britannia At Bay: The Defence of the British Empire Against Japan 1939–41*, Oxford: W. David McIntyre (1979), *The Rise and Fall of the Singapore Naval Base*, London: Ian Hamill (1981), *The Strategic Illusion: The Singapore Strategy and the Defence of Australia and New Zealand*, Singapore: James Neidpath (1981), *The Singapore Naval Base and the Defence of Britain's Eastern Empire, 1919–41*, Oxford.

Bibliography

1. Unpublished sources

A. Great Britain

i. Public Records Office

Admiralty

ADM 1	Admiralty and Secretariat Files
ADM 116	Admiralty and Secretariat Cases
ADM 125	Station Records: China Station
ADM 167	Board Minutes and Memoranda
ADM 199	War History Cases and Papers
ADM 205	Papers of the First Sea Lord

Air

AIR 1	Air Historical Branch Records Series 1
AIR 2	Air Ministry: Far Eastern Papers
AIR 5	Air Historical Branch Records Series 11
AIR 8	Chief of Air Staff Records
AIR 20	Air Ministry: Unregistered Papers
AIR 23	Air Ministry: Overseas Command Records
AVIA 2	Air Ministry: Civil Aviation Files

Cabinet

CAB 2	Minutes of the Committee of Imperial Defence
CAB 4	Memoranda of the Committee of Imperial Defence: Miscellaneous Files
CAB 5	Memoranda of the Committee of Imperial Defence: Colonial Defence
CAB 7 and 8	Minutes and Memoranda of the Colonial and Overseas Defence Committee
CAB 16	Proceedings and Memoranda of the Cabinet ad-hoc Committees

CAB 21   Cabinet Registered Files
CAB 23   Minutes of the Cabinet to 1939
CAB 24   Memoranda of the Cabinet, Cabinet Papers G, GT and CP
          Series to 1939
CAB 27   Minutes of the Cabinet Committees: Central Series to 1939
CAB 29   International Conference Records to 1939
CAB 32   Imperial Conference Records to 1939
CAB 53   Minutes of the Chiefs of Staff Sub Committee
CAB 55   Memoranda of the Joint Planning Committee
CAB 63   Hankey Papers and Files
CAB 64   Files of the Minister for Coordination of Defence
CAB 65   Minutes of the War Cabinet
CAB 66   Memoranda of the War Cabinet: (WP) and (CP) Series
CAB 69   Minutes of the War Cabinet Defence Committee (Ops)
CAB 79   Minutes of the War Cabinet Chiefs of Staff Committee
CAB 80   Memoranda of the War Cabinet Chiefs of Staff
          Committee
CAB 82   Minutes of the Deputy Chiefs of Staff Committee
CAB 84   Minutes of the War Cabinet Joint Planning Committee
CAB 96   Minutes of the War Cabinet Far Eastern Sub-Committee
CAB 99   Commonwealth and International Conference Files
CAB 105   War Cabinet Telegrams 1941–45
CAB 122   British Joint Staff Mission: Washington Office Files

Foreign Office

FO 115   General Correspondence: Embassy and Consular
FO 371   Political: General Correspondence

Prime Ministers Office

PREM 1   Correspondence and Papers to 1940
PREM 3   Operational Papers
PREM 4   Confidential Papers

Treasury

T 161   Papers on Finance

War Office

WO 32   Registered Files: General Service
WO 106   Directory of Military Operations and Intelligence

B. United States

i. National Archives

RG 18	Army Air Corps Records, Central Decimal File 096
RG 26	Coast Guard Correspondence, Series 601
RG 38	Records of the Office of the Chief of Naval Operations
RG 48	Records of the Office of the Secretary of the Interior, 9-0-7, Territories and Island Possessions
RG 59	General Records of the Department of State
RG 72	Records of the Bureau of Aeronautics
RG 80	General Records of the Department of the Navy, 1897–1926, 1926–46.
RG 94	Office of the Adjutant General Central Files 1926–39.
RG 126	Records of the Office of Territories: Central Classified Files 1907–51
RG 165	War Department and Special Staff Files
RG 225	Joint Board Files
RG 332	HQ United States Army Forces Far East/Philippines
RG 381	HQ Army Air Corps War Plans
RG 319	Records of the Office of the Chief of Staff; Deputy Chief of Staff Papers; Army Operations, OPD Executive Files 1940–1941
RG 395	Records of US Army Overseas Operations and Commands 1898–1942
RG 407	Office of the Adjutant General: Central Decimal Files
M 964	Records Relating to US Navy Fleet Problems 1–23, 1923–1941
M 971	Annual Reports of Fleets and Task Forces of the US Navy 1920–1941
M 975	US Naval Attaché Reports

ii. Federal Records Center Suitland

RG 313	Administration Files Naval Operating Forces
RG 350	Records of the Bureau of Insular Affairs; Records of the Philippine Army Command 1935–1941

iii. Operational Naval Archives, Washington Navy Yard

Action and Operational Reports of Naval Commands 1941–53.
Central and Security Classified Records of the Offices of the Secretary of the Navy/Chief of Naval Operations 1940–47.

The Files of Naval Operating Commands 1941–63.

Records of the General Board of the Navy, Subject Files 404, 420–2, 422 and 438–1.

Records of the Navy Secretariat Joint Army-Navy Board 1903–47.

Records Relating to the Asiatic Fleet and Asiatic Defense Campaign 1933–44.

Commander Naval Forces Europe Files (Com. Nav. Eu.) 1938–46.

Records of the War Plans (later Strategic Plans) Division, Office of the Chief of Naval Operations 1917–55:

Series I	Lectures and Speeches 1912–41
Series II	Naval War College: Instructional Material
Series III	Miscellaneous Files
Series IV	Series Files 1938–47
Series V	Subject Files: Incoming and Outgoing Correspondence 1936–47
Series VII	Records Relating to Anglo-American-Dutch Cooperation 1938–44
Series IX	Plans, Strategic Studies and related Correspondence 1939–46
Series XII	Records of the Pacific Alaskan and Far Eastern Section 1940–46

Strategic and Operational Planning Documents 1939–50.

War Diaries of Naval Commands 1941–53.

iv. Naval War College, Newport, Rhode Island

Naval War College: Instructional Material
US Military History Research Collection

2. Private Papers

A. Great Britain

i. Birmingham University Library

Neville Chamberlain Papers
Earl of Avon Papers

ii. Churchill College Cambridge

Admiral Sir Plunkett-Ernle-Drax Papers
Sir Thomas Inskip Papers

Sir Alexander Cadogan Papers
A.V. Alexander Papers
Admiral Sir John Godfrey Papers
Sir James Somerville Papers
Viscount Templewood (Sir Samuel Hoare) Papers
Admiral Sir A.B. Cunningham Papers
Admiral Sir John Edelston Papers
Captain Arthur W. Clarke Papers

iii. Imperial War Museum, London

Admiral Sir Harold Burrough Papers
Admiral Sir John Godfrey Papers
Vice Admiral Sir Ballin Robertshaw Papers
Admiral Sir William Whitworth Papers
Admiral Sir Algenon Willis Papers
Sir Geoffrey Shakespeare Correspondence
Vice-Admiral A.G. Talbot Papers
Admiral Sir John Crace Papers
Vice-Admiral J.W. Durnford Papers
Vice-Admiral Harold Hickling Papers
Admiral Sir William Parry Papers

iv. British Museum London

Admiral Sir A.B. Cunningham Papers
Diaries of Sir Stanley V. Goodall

v. Kings College Archives London

Air Marshall Sir Robert Brooke-Popham Papers
C.A. Vlieland's Manuscript
Lord Alanbrooke Papers

vi. National Maritime Museum London

Baron Chatfield Papers
Admiral Sir William George Tennant Papers

B. United States

i. Library of Congress Manuscript Division

Rear-Admiral Mark L. Bristol Papers
Secretary of the Navy Josephus Daniels 1913-1921
Norman Davis Papers
Fleet Admiral William D. Leahy Papers
Secretary of the Navy Franklin Knox 1940-1944
Secretary of the Navy Dwight Wibur 1924-1929
Admiral Harry E. Yarnell Papers

ii. Library of Congress Historical Division

Admiral Claude C. Bloch Papers
Vice-Admiral Harold C. Bower Papers
Admiral Albert Gleaves Papers
Vice-Admiral John W. Greenslade Papers
Admiral Frederick J. Horne Papers
Admiral Royal E. Ingersoll Papers
Admiral Hilary P. Jones Papers
Admiral Husband E. Kimmell Papers
Admiral Alan G. Kirk Papers
Rear-Admiral Stephen B. Luce Papers
Rear-Admiral Charles B. McVay Papers
Admiral William V. Pratt Papers
Admiral William H. Standley Papers
Admiral Montgomery M. Taylor Papers

iii. Operational Naval Archives: Washington Navy Yard

Admiral Thomas C. Hart Papers
Admiral Alan G. Kirk Papers
Fleet Admiral William D. Leahy Papers
Admiral William V. Pratt Papers
Admiral R. Kelly Turner Papers
Admiral Harry E. Yarnell Papers

iv. Nimitz Library Annapolis

Admiral Husband E. Kimmel Papers

v. Franklin Delano Roosevelt Library, Hyde Park, New York

Franklin Delano Roosevelt Papers
President's Personal Files (PPF)
President's Secretary's Files (PSF)

3. Printed Sources

A. Official

i. Australia

Neale, R.G. (ed.) (1975–1978), *Documents on Australian Foreign Policy 1937–1941*, vols 1 and 2, Canberra.

ii. Great Britain

Woodward, E.L. and Butler, R. (eds) (1949–1955), *Documents on British Foreign Policy 1919–1939*, 1st, 2nd and 3rd series, London.
(1919–1941), *House of Commons Debates*, 5th series, London.
(1919–1941), *House of Lords Debates*, 5th series, London.

iii. United States

(1922–1941), *Annual Reports of the Chief of Army Engineers*, Washington.
(1920–1935), *Annual Reports of the Governor-General of the Philippines*, Washington.
(1935–1941), *Annual Reports of the Philippine High Commissioner,* Washington.
(1922–1941), *Annual Reports of the Secretary of the Navy*, Washington.
(1922–1941), *Annual Reports of the Secretary of War*, Washington.

US Congress,*Congressional Hearings* 1922–1941
——, *Congressional Record* 1922–1941
——, *House Committee on Appropriations* 1934–1939
——, *House Committee on Interstate and Foreign Commerce.*
——, *House Committee on Insular Affairs* 1934–1937
——, *House Committee on Naval Affairs* 1922–1941
——, *House Select Committee on Enquiring into Operations of the United States Air Services* 1937–1941
——, *Pearl Harbor Attack: Joint Committee on the Investigation of the Pearl Harbor Attack,* 79 Congress, 1st session, 1946

———, *Report on the Need for Additional Naval Bases to Defend the Coasts of the United States, Its Territories and Possessions*, 76 Congress, 1st session, 1939.

———, *Senate Appropriations Committee* 1922–1941

———, *Senate Committee on Foreign Relations* 1922–1941

———, *Senate Committee on Naval Affairs* 1922–1941

———, *Senate Committee on Territories and Insular Possessions*

Department of State (1955–1963), *Foreign Relations of the United States*, vols 1930–1941, Washington.

Scholarly Resources Inc., *Strategic Planning in the U.S. Navy; Its Evolution and Execution 1891–1945*, microfilm rolls 1–9, Wilmington, DW.

USGPO (1945), *Pearl Harbor Navy Yard: History in Four Volumes,* Shore Establishment File, Operational Archives Naval History Division, Washington.

USGPO (1976), *Public Papers of the President of the United States – Herbert Hoover*, Washington.

B. Semi-official and Memoir Sources

i. Books

Arnold, H.H. (1949), *Global Mission*, New York.

Arpee, E. (1953), *From Frigates to Flatops,* Princeton, NJ.

Avon Lord (1967), *Facing the Dictators*, London.

———, (1965), *The Reckoning*, London.

Ballantine, D.S. (1949), *U.S. Naval Logistics in the Second World War*, New Jersey.

Blum, J.M. (ed.) (1959, 1965), *From the Morgenthau Diaries,* vol. 1, *Years of Crisis, 1928–1938,* vol. 2, *Years of Urgency 1938–1941,* Boston.

Bryant, A. (1957), *The Turn of the Tide, 1939–1943: A Study Based on the Diaries and Autobiographical Notes of Field Marshal the Viscount Alanbrooke,* London.

Butler, J.R.M. (1957), *Grand Strategy* vol. II, *September 1939–June 1941,* London.

Casey, H.J. (1951), *Engineers of the Southwest Pacific 1941–1945 Airfield and Base Development*, vol. 6, Washington.

Churchill, W.S. (1948), *The Grand Alliance*, London.

———, (1948–1954), *The Second World War*, 6 vols, London.

Cline, R.S. (1951), *Washington Command Post: The Operations Division*, Washington.

Collier, B. (1957), *The Defence of the United Kingdom*, London.

Bibliography

Collins, Sir J. (1965), *As Luck Would Have It*, Melbourne.

Conn, S and Fairchild, B. (1960), *The Framework of Hemisphic Defense*, Washington.

Coontz, R.E. (1930), *From the Mississippi to the Sea*, New York.

Cosmas, G.A. (ed.) (1969), *A Brief History of Marine Corps Aviation 1912–1940*, Washington.

Craven, W.F. and Cate, W. (1948), *The Army Air Forces in World War II: Plans and Early Operations, January 1939 to August 1942*, vol. I, Chicago.

Department of State (1943), *Peace and War*, Washington.

Dilks, D. (ed.) (1971), *The Diaries of Sir Alexander Cadogan, O.M., 1938–1945*, London.

Dixon, J.E. (1980), *The American Military in the Far East*, Washington.

Dyer, G.C. (ed.) (1972), *The Amphibians Came to Conquer: The Story of Admiral Richmond Kelly Turner*, Washington.

——, (1973), *On the Treadmill to Pearl Harbor: The Memoirs of Admiral James O. Richardson*, Washington.

Farley, J.A. (1948), *Jim Farley's Story: The Roosevelt Years*, New York.

Furer, J. (1959), *Administration of the Navy Department in World War II*, Washington.

Gibbs, N.H. (1976), *Grand Strategy*, vol. I, *Rearmament Policy*, London.

Gill, G.H. (1957), *Royal Australian Navy, 1939–1942*, Canberra.

Hankey, M. (1946), *Diplomacy by Conference*, New York.

Harvey, J. (ed.) (1978), *The Diplomatic Diaries of Oliver Harvey*, London.

Hasluck, P. (1952), *The Government and the People 1939–1941: Australia in the War of 1939–1945*, series 4, vol. 1, Canberra.

Haynes, G.P. (1953), *History of the Joint Chiefs of Staff in the War Against Japan* vol. 1: *Pearl Harbor through Trident*, Washington.

Hinsley, F.H., Ransom, C.F.G. and Thomas, E.E. (1979), *British Intelligence in the Second World War: Its Influence on Strategy and Operations*, vols 1–2, New York.

Knight, R. C. and Hooker, N. (1956), *The Moffat Papers 1919–1943*, Cambridge, MA.

Hull, C. (1958), *The Memoirs of Cordell Hull*, 2 vols, New York.

Ickes, H.L. (1954), *The Secret Diary of Harold L. Ickes*, 3 vols, New York.

King, E.J. and Whitehall, W.M (1952), *Fleet Admiral King: A Naval Record*, New York.

Langer, W.L. and Gleason, S.E. (1952), *The Challenge to Isolation 1937–1940*, London.

Leahy, W.D. (1950), *I Was There*, New York.

Leutze, J.R. (1971), *The London Journal of General Raymond E. Lee*, Boston.

Loewenheim, F., Langley, H.D. and Jonas, M. (eds) (1975), *Roosevelt and Churchill: Their Secret Wartime Correspondence,* New York.

MacArthur, D. (1965), *Reminiscences*, New York.

——, (1936), *Report on the National Defense of the Philippines*, Manila.

Matloff, M. and Snell, E.M. (1953), *Strategic Planning for Coalition Warfare 1941–1942*, Washington.

Morison, S. Eliot (1947–1948), *The History of United States Naval Operations in World War II*, 15 vols, Boston.

Morton, L. (1953), *The Fall of the Philippines*, Washington.

——, (1962), *The War in the Pacific: Strategy and Command*, Washington.

Nicholson, N. (ed.) (1967), *The Diaries and Letters of Nigel Nicholson* vol. 2: *The War Years 1939–1945*, New York.

Nixon, E.B. (ed.) (1969), *Franklin D. Roosevelt and Foreign Affairs,* 3 vols, Cambridge.

Quezon, M. (1946), *The Good Fight*, New York.

Rhodes, James R. (ed.) (1974), *Complete Speeches of Winston Churchill 1897–1963,* vol. 6, *1935–1942*, New York.

Rosenman, S.I. (1950), *The Public Papers and Addresses of Franklin D. Roosevelt,* vols 8–10, New York.

Roskill, S. (1954), *The War at Sea*, vol. 1, London.

Stimson, H.L. and Bundy, McGeorge (1947), *On Active Service in Peace and War*, New York.

Thomson, H.C. and Mayo, L. (1960), *The Ordnance Department*, Washington.

Watson, M.S. (1950), *Chief of Staff, Prewar Plans and Preparations*, Washington.

Williams, K. (1945), *Army Air Forces in the War against Japan 1941–1942*, Washington.

Wiley, H.A. (1934), *An Admiral from Texas*, New York.

Winant, J.G. (1947), *A Letter from Grosvenor Square: Account of a Stewardship*, London.

Kirby Woodburn, S. (1957), *The Fall of Singapore*, London.

Woodward, E.L. (1970), *British Foreign Policy in the Second World War,* vol. 1, London.

Zacharias, E.M. (1946), *Secret Mission: The Story of an Intelligence Officer*, New York.

Bibliography

ii. Articles

Public Opinion Quarterly, 1937–1941
United States Naval Institute Proceedings, 1922–1941

iii. Newspapers

New York Times, 1934–1941
Saturday Evening Post, 1934–1941

C. *Secondary Sources*

i. Books

Abbazia, P. (1975), *Mr. Roosevelt's Navy: The Private War of the U.S. Atlantic Fleet 1939–1942,* Annapolis, MD.
Agar, H. (1972), *Britain Alone: June 1940–June 1941,* London.
Alden, J.D. (1979), *The Fleet Submarine in the U.S. Navy,* Annapolis MD.
Allan, H.C. (1954), *Great Britain and the United States: A History of Anglo-American Relations 1783–1952,* London.
Allen, L. (1977), *Singapore 1941–1942: The Politics and Strategy of the Second World War,* London.
Anderson, I.H. Jr (1975), *The Standard-Vacuum Oil Company and the United States East Asian Policy, 1933–1941,* Princeton, NJ.
Bachison, M.R. (1978), *Battleships in the U.S. Navy,* Newark, NJ.
Badagon, U.S. (1975), *Military History of the Philippines,* Manila.
Bailey, T.A. and Ryan, P.B. (1979), *Hitler versus Roosevelt: The Undeclared War,* London.
Barnes, H.E. (ed.) (1953), *Perpetual War for Perpetual Peace,* Boise, ID.
Barnett, C. (1972), *The Collapse of British Power,* London.
Barron, J. (1973), *Leadership in Crisis: F.D.R. and the Path to Intervention,* Port Washington, WS.
Bataan, A.I. (1944), *The Judgement Seat: The Saga of the Philippine Command of the United States Army Forces, May 1941 to May 1942,* New York.
Bates, J.L. (1963), *The Origins of Teapot Dome: Progressives, Parties and Petroleum,* New York.
Baylis, J. (1981), *Anglo-American Defence Relations 1939–1979: The Special Relationship,* London.
Beck, J.B. (1974), *MacArthur and Wainright: Sacrifice of the Philippines,* Albuquerque, NM.

Belotte, J.H. and Belotte,W.H. (1967), *Corregidor: The Saga of a Fortress,* New York.

Bergamini, D. (1971), *Japan's Imperial Conspiracy,* New York.

Bechloss, M.R. (1980), *Kennedy and Roosevelt: The Uneasy Alliance,* New York.

Bond, B. (1980), *British Military Policy Between the Two World Wars,* Oxford.

Borg, D. (1964), *The United States and the Far Eastern Crisis 1933–1938,* Harvard.

Borg, D. and Okamoto, S. (eds) (1973), *Pearl Harbor As History: Japanese-American Relations, 1931–1941,* New York.

Braisted W.R. (1958), *The United States Navy in the Pacific 1897–1909,* Austin, TX.

——, (1971), *The United States Navy in the Pacific 1909–1922,* Austin, TX.

Brown, D.K. (1983), *A Century of Naval Construction,* Greenwich.

Buckley, T.H. (1976), *The United States and the Washington Conference 1921–1922,* Knoxville, TN.

Burns, R.D. (1968), *Disarmament in Perspective,* vol. 3, *Limitation on Seapower,* Los Angeles.

Butow, R.J.C. (1961), *Tojo and the Coming of War,* Stanford, CA.

Bywater, H.C. (1934), *Sea Power in the Pacific,* Boston.

Callaghan, R. (1977), *The Worst Disaster: The Fall of Singapore,* Princeton, NJ.

Challener, R.D. (1973), *Admirals, Generals and American Foreign Policy,* Princeton, NJ.

Clifford, K.J. (1983), *Amphibious Warfare Development in Britain and America 1920–1940,* New York.

Cole, B.D. (1983), *Gunboats and Marines: The United States Navy in China 1925–1928,* Deleware, OH.

Coletta, P.E. (ed.) (1980), *American Secretaries of the Navy:* vol. 2, *1913–72,* Annapolis, MD.

——, (1979), *Bradley A. Fiske and the American Navy,* Garden City, KS.

Cowling, M. (1975), *The Impact of Hitler: British Politics and British Strategy 1933–40,* London.

Dallek, R. (1979), *Franklin D. Roosevelt and American Foreign Policy 1932–1945,* New York.

Davis, V. (1967), *The Admirals Lobby,* Chapel Hill, NC.

Day, D. (1986), *Menzies and Churchill at War,* Sydney.

Dingman, R. (1976), *Power in the Pacific,* Chicago.

Dorward, J. (1983), *Conflict of Duty: U.S. Navy's Intelligence Dilemma 1919–1945,* Annapolis, MD.

Bibliography

Drummond, I.S. (1974), *Imperial Economic Policy, 1917–1939: Studies in Expansion and Protection*, London.

Dubque, J.H. and Glockner, R.F (1951), *The Development of the Heavy Bomber 1918–1944*, Washington, DC.

Dupuy, E. (1956), *The Compact History of the U.S. Army*, New York.

Eayrs, J. (1965), *In Defence of Canada*, vol. 2, Toronto.

Edmonds, W.D. (1951), *They Fought With What They Had: The Story of the Army Air Forces in the South West Pacific 1941–1942*, Boston.

Feis, H. (1964), *The Road to Pearl Harbor*, New York.

Friedman, N. (1978), *Battleship Design and Development 1905–1945*, Greenwich.

Friend, T. (1965), *Between Two Empires: The Ordeal of the Philippines 1929–1946*, New Haven, CN.

Fry, J.H. and Ide, H.C. (1946), *A History of Petroleum: Administration for War 1941–45*, vol. 3, Washington.

Furer, J. (1959), *Administration of the Navy Department in World War 2*, Washington.

Garcia, E.V., II (1968), *U.S. Military Bases and Philippine-American Relations,* Quezon City.

Gentleman, D. (1987), *The Special Relationship*, London.

Gilbert, M. (ed.) (1966), *A Century of Conflict, 1850–1950: Essays for A.J.P. Taylor*, London.

Gooch, J. (1981), *The Prospect of War: Studies in British Defence Policy*, London.

Goodhard, P. (1965), *Fifty Ships That Saved the World: The Foundation of the Anglo-American Alliance*, London.

Hagan, K.J. (1978), *Peace and War: Interpretations of American Naval History 1775–1978*, New York.

Haggie, P. (1981), *Britannia at Bay: The Defence of the British Empire Against Japan 1937–1941*, Oxford.

Hall, C. (1987), *Britain, America, and Arms Control 1921–1937*, New York.

Hamill, I. (1981), *The Strategic Illusion: The Singapore Strategy and the Defence of Australia,* Singapore.

Heinl, R.D., Jr (1962), *Soldiers of the Sea: The United States Marine Corps 1775–1962*, Annapolis, MD.

Herzog, J.H. (1973), *Closing the Open Door: American-Japanese Diplomatic Negotiations, 1936–1941*, Annapolis, MD.

Hogan, M. (1977), *Informal Entente: The Private Structure of Cooperation in Anglo-American Economic Diplomacy, 1918–1928*, Colombia, MO.

Hough, F.O. (1969), *Pearl Harbor to Guadalcanal: History of United States Marine Corps Operations in World War 2,* vol. 1, Washington.

Hough, R. (1964), *The Hunting of Force Z*, London.

——, (1965), *Dreadnought: A History of the Modern Battleship*, London.

Howard, J. (1968), *Mr. Justice Murphy: A Political Biography*, Princeton, NJ.

Howard, M. (1974), *The Continental Commitment: The Dilemma of British Defence Policy in the Era of Two World Wars*, London.

Hoyt, E.P. (1976), *The Lonely Ships*, New York.

Hunt, F. (1954), *The Untold Story of Douglas MacArthur*, New York.

Iriye, A. (1967), *Across the Pacific: An Inner History of American-East Asian Relations*, New York.

——, (1987), *The Origins of the Second World War in the Pacific*, London.

Clayton, J.D. (1970), *The Years of MacArthur,* vol. I, *1880–1941*, London.

——, (1975), *The Years of MacArthur,* vol. 2, *1941–1945*, Boston, MA.

Jordan G. (ed.) (1977), *Naval Warfare in the Twentieth Century: Essays in Honour of A.J. Marder*, London.

Karsten, P. (1972), *The Naval Aristocracy: The Golden Age for Annapolis and the Emergence of Modern American Navalism*, Annapolis, MD.

Kennett, L. (1985), *The U.S. Goes to War: Pearl Harbor-1942*, New York.

Kilmarx, R.A. (ed.) (1979), *America's Maritime Legacy: A History of the U.S. Merchant Marine and Shipbuilding Industry Since Colonial Times,* Boulder, CO.

Kimball, W.F. (1980), *American Diplomacy in the Twentieth Century*, St. Louis, MO.

——, (1969), *The Most Unsordid Act: Lend-Lease, 1939–1941*, Baltimore, MD.

Knott, R.C. (1979), *The American Flying Boat: An Illustrated History*, Annapolis, MD.

Kosskoff, D.E. (1974), *Joseph P. Kennedy: A Life and Times,* Princeton, NJ.

Kottman, R.N. (1968), *Reciprocity and the North Atlantic Triangle 1932–1938*, New York.

Lane, J.C. (1978), *Armed Progressive: General Leonard Wood*, London.

Langer, W.L. and Gleason, S.E (1952), *The Challenge to Isolation, 1937–1940*, New York.

——, (1953), *The Undeclared War, 1940–1941*, New York.

Lash, J.P. (1976), *Roosevelt and Churchill, 1939–1941: The Partnership that Saved the West*, New York.

Bibliography

Lee, B.A. (1973), *Britain and the Sino-Japanese War 1937–1939*, London.

Leigh, M. (1976), *Mobilizing Consent: Public Opinion and American Foreign Policy 1937–1947*, Westport, CN.

Lewis, M. (1948), *The Navy of Britain: A Historical Portrait*, London.

Leutze, J.R. (1981), *A Different Kind of Victory: A Biography of Admiral Thomas C. Hart*, Annapolis, MD.

——, (1977), *Bargaining for Supremacy: Anglo-American Naval Collaboration, 1937–1941*, Chapel Hill, NC.

——, (1981), *A Different Kind of Victory: A Biography of Admiral Thomas C. Hart*, Annapolis, MD.

Lind, A.W. (1946), *Hawaii's Japanese*, Newark, NJ.

Lissington, M.P. (1972), *New Zealand and the United States, 1840–1944*, Wellington.

Livezey, E. (1947), *Mahan On Seapower*, Norman, OK.

Long, G. (1969), *MacArthur As Military Commander*, London.

Louis, W.R. (1971), *British Strategy in the Far East 1919–1939*, Oxford.

——, (1977), *Imperialism At Bay, 1941–1945: The United States and the Decolonisation of the British Empire*, Oxford.

Love, R.W., Jr (ed.) (1980), *The Chiefs of Naval Operations*, Annapolis, MD.

Lundstrom, J.B. (1976), *The First South Pacific Campaign: Pacific Fleet Strategy, December 1941–June 1942*, Annapolis, MD.

Macleod, I. (1961), *Neville Chamberlain*, London.

MacDonald, C.A. (1977), *The Roosevelt Administration and British Appeasement 1936–1939*, Oxford.

Marder, A.J. (1974), *From the Dardanelles to Oran: Studies of the Royal Navy in War and Peace 1915–1940*, London.

——, (1981), *Old Friends, New Enemies: The Royal Navy and the Imperial Japanese Navy, Strategic Illusions 1936–1941*, Oxford.

May, E.R. (ed.) (1984), *Knowing One's Enemies: Intelligence Assessment Before the Two World Wars*, Princeton, NJ.

McCoy, D.R. (1967), *Calvin Coolidge: The Quiet President*, New York.

McFarland, K.D. (1975), *Secretary of War Harry H. Woodring and the Problems of Readiness, Rearmament and Neutrality 1936–1940*, Lawrence, KN.

McGibbon, I.C. (1981), *Blue Water Rationale: The Naval Defence of New Zealand 1914–1942*, Wellington.

McInnes, C. and Sheffield, G.D. (1988), *Warfare in the Twentieth Century*, London.

McIntyre, W.D. (1979), *The Rise and Fall of the Singapore Naval Base*, London.

McKercher, B.J. (1984), *The Second Baldwin Government and the United States 1924–1929: Attitudes and Diplomacy*, Cambridge.

Melhorn, C.M. (1974), *Two Block Fox: The Rise of the Aircraft Carrier 1911–1929*, Annapolis, MD.

Middlebrook, M. and Mahoney, P. (1977), *Battleship: The Loss of the Prince of Wales and Repulse*, London.

Middlemas, K. (1972), *The Diplomacy of Illusion: The British Government and Germany 1937–1939*, London.

Miller, E.S. (1991), *War Plan Orange: The U.S. Strategy to Defeat Japan, 1897–1945*, Annapolis, MD.

Mondey, D. (1980), *The U.S.A.A.F. at War in the Pacific*, New York.

Morgan, H.W. (1965), *America's Road to Empire*, New York.

Morison, E.R. (1942), *Admiral Sims and the Modern American Navy*, Boston.

Morley, J.W. (ed.) (1980), *The Fateful Choice: Japan's Advance into Southeast Asia 1939–1941*, New York.

Neidpath, J. (1981), *The Singapore Naval Base and the Defence of Britain's Eastern Empire 1919–1941*, Oxford.

Nish, I. (1972), *Alliance in Decline: A Study in Anglo-Japanese Relations 1908–1923*, London.

——, (1966), *The Anglo-Japanese Alliance, The Diplomacy of Two Island Empires 1894–1907*, London.

——, (1977), *Japanese Foreign Policy, 1869–1942: Kasuwigaseki to Miyakezaka*, London.

Noggle, B. (1962), *Teapot Dome: Oil and Politics in the 1920s*, Baton Rouge, LO.

O'Connor, R.G. (1962), *Perilous Equilibrium: The U.S. and the London Naval Conference of 1930*, Lawrence, KN.

Offner, A.A. (1975), *The Origins of the Second World War: American Foreign Policy and World Politics 1917–1941*, New York.

Ovendale, R. (1975), *'Appeasement' and the English Speaking World: Britain the United States, the Dominions, and the Policy of 'Appeasement' 1937–1939*, Cardiff.

Parnish, T. (1985), *The Ultra Americans: The U.S. Role in Breaking the Nazi Codes*, New York.

Pawlowski, G.L. (1971), *Flat Tops and Fledglings: A History of American Aircraft Carriers*, New York.

Pelz, S.E. (1974), *Race to Pearl Harbor: The Failure of the Second London Naval Conference and the Onset of World War 2*, Cambridge, MA.

Peden, G.C. (1979), *British Rearmament and the Treasury 1932–1939*, Edinburgh.

Perers, A.R. (1987), *Anthony Eden at the Foreign Office 1933–1938*, New York.

Petillo, C. (1981), *Douglas MacArthur: The Philippine Years,* Bloomington, IL.

Pogue, F.C. (1966), *George C. Marshall,* vol. 2, *Ordeal and Hope*, New York.

Pomeroy, E.S. (1951), *Pacific Outpost: American Strategy in Guam and Micronesia*, Stanford, CA.

Porten, E.P. von der (1969), *The German Navy in World War II*, London.

Prange, G.R. (1982), *At Dawn We Slept: The Untold Story of Pearl Harbor,* London.

——, 1985), *Pearl Harbor: The Verdict of History*, New York.

Pratt, L. (1975), *East of Malta, West of Suez: Britain's Mediterranean Crisis, 1936–39*, Cambridge.

Pritchard, R. (1987), *Far Eastern Influences upon British Strategy Towards the Great Powers 1937–1939*, London.

Reynolds, D. (1981), *The Creation of the Anglo-American Alliance: A Study in Competitive Co-operation*, London.

——, (1982), *Lord Lothian and Anglo-American Relations, 1939–1940,* Philadelphia.

Rodger, N.A.M. (1979), *The Admiralty*, Norwich.

Roskill, S. (1977), *Churchill and the Admirals*, London.

——, (1968–1975), *Naval Policy Between the Wars,* vol. 1, *The Period of Anglo-American Antagonism 1919–1929,* vol. 2, *The Period of Reluctant Rearmament 1930–1939,* London.

Russett, B.M. (1972), *No Clear and Present Danger: A Skeptical View of the U.S. Entry into World War II*, New York.

Schmidt, G. (1986), *The Politics and Economics of Rearmament: British Foreign Policy in the 1930s*, New York.

Schroeder, P.W. (1958), *The Axis Alliance and Japanese-American Relations, 1941*, New York.

Sherwood, R. (1948), *Roosevelt and Hopkins: An Intimate History*, New York.

Smith, P.C. (1977), *The Great Ships Pass*, London.

Stein, H. (ed.) (1963), *American Civil Military Decisions: A Book of Case Studies*, Birmingham, AL.

Stevenson, W. (1977), *A Man Called Intrepid: The Secret War*, New York.

Swanborough, G and Bowers, P.M. (1968), *United States Navy Aircraft Since 1911*, London.

Tate, M. (1948), *The United States and the Limitations of Armaments*, Cambridge, MA.

Taylor, G.E. (1964), *The Philippines and the United States: Problems of Partnership,* New York.

Thorne C. (1978), *Allies of a Kind: The United States, Great Britain and the War Against Japan 1941–1945,* London.

——, (1978), *The Approach of War,* London.

Till, G. (1979), *Air Power and the Royal Navy 1914–1945: A Historical Survey,* London.

Tolly, K. (1971), *Yangtse Patrol: The U.S. Navy in China,* Annapolis, MD.

Trefousse, H.L. (1982), *Pearl Harbor: The Continuing Controversy,* New York.

Trotter, A. (1975), *Britain and East Asia 1933–1937,* London.

Tuchman, B. (1971), *Stillwell and the American Experience in China,* New York.

Tuleja, T. (1963), *Statesmen and Admirals,* New York.

Turnbull, A. D. and Lord, C.L. (1972), *History of United States Naval Aviation,* New York.

Utley, J. (1984), *Going to War with Japan, 1937–1941,* Knoxville, TN.

Vlahos, M. (1981), *The Blue Sword: The Naval War College and the American Mission,* Annapolis, MD.

Watt, D. Cameron (1965), *Personalities and Policies: Studies in the Formulation of British Foreign Policy in the Twentieth Century,* London.

——, (1984), *Succeeding John Bull: America in Britain's Place 1900–1975,* Cambridge.

——, (1975), *Too Serious A Business: European Armed Forces and the Approach to the Second World War,* London.

Weigley, R.F. (1967), *History of the United States Army,* New York.

Weinberg, G.L. (1980), *The Foreign Policy of Hitler's Germany,* vol. 2, *Starting World War II, 1937–1939,* Chicago.

Wheeler, G.E. (1974), *Admiral William Veazie Pratt U.S. Navy: A Sailor's Life,* Washington.

——, (1963), *Prelude to Pearl Harbor: The United States Navy and the Far East 1921–31,* Missouri.

White, D.H. (ed.) (1976), *Proceedings of the Conference on War and Diplomacy,* Charleston, SC.

Wilson, T. (1969), *The First Summit: Roosevelt and Churchill at Placentia Bay 1941,* London.

Wiltz, J.E. (1963), *In Search of Peace: The Senate Munitions Enquiry 1934–1936,* Baton Rouge, LA.

Wohstetter, R. (1962), *Pearl Harbor: Warning and Decision,* Stanford, CA.

Young, K. (1966), *Churchill and Beaverbrook, A Study in Friendship and Politics,* London.

Bibliography

ii. Articles

Alden, J.D. (1967), 'ARD-1 The Pioneer', *United States Naval Institute Proceedings,* vol. 93, no. 7, pp. 71–8.

Anderson, I.H., Jr (1975), 'The 1941 De Facto Embargo on Oil to Japan: A Bureaucratic Reflex,' *Pacific Historical Review*, vol. 64, pp. 201–31.

Andrade, E. (1969), 'The United States Navy and the Washington Conference', *The Historian*, vol. 31, pp. 345–63.

——, (1971), 'Submarine Policy of the United States Navy 1919–41', *Military Affairs,* vol. 35, pp. 50–6.

——, (1968) 'The United States Navy and the Washington Conference', *The Historian,* vol. 31, pp. 345–63.

——, (1968), 'The Ship That Never Was: The Flying Deck Cruiser', *Military Affairs,* vol. 32, no. 3, pp. 132–40.

Armstrong, W.J. (1978), 'Aircraft Go to Sea: A Brief History of Aviation in the U.S. Navy', *Aerospace History*, vol. 25, no. 2, pp. 79–91.

Barclay, G. St J. (1975), 'Singapore Strategy: The Role of the United States in Imperial Defence,' *Military Affairs,* vol. 39, no. 2, pp. 54–9.

Bartsch, W. (1979), 'Corregidor', *After the Battle,* no. 23, pp. 1–29.

Borg, D. (1957), 'Notes on Roosevelt's Quarantine Speech', *Political Science Quarterly,* vol. 72, pp. 405–33.

Braisted, W.R. (1954), 'The Philippine Base Problem 1898–1909', *Mississippi Valley Historical Review,* vol. 41, pp. 21–40.

Brune, L.H. (1978), 'Considerations of Force in Cordell Hull's Diplomacy, July 26 to November 26, 1941', *Diplomatic History,* vol. 2, pp. 389–405.

Burns, R.D. (1968), 'Inspection of the Mandates 1919–1941', *Pacific Historical Review,* vol. 37, no. 3, pt 1, pp. 435–62.

——, (1968), 'Inspection of the Mandates', *Pacific Historical Review,* vol. 37, no. 4, pt 2, pp. 445–62.

Butow, R.J.C. (1960), 'The Hull Nomura Conversations: A Fundamental Misconception', *American Historical Review,* vol. 65, pp. 822–36.

Campbell, J. P. (1964), 'Marines, Aviators, and the Battleship Mentality 1923–33', *RUSI Journal,* vol. 109, no. 1, pp. 45–50.

Carlton, D. (1968), 'Great Britain and the Coolidge Naval Disarmament Conference of 1927,' *Political Science Quarterly,* vol. 83, no. 4, pp. 573–98.

Carpenter, R.H. (1986), 'Admiral Mahan, "Narrative Fidelity" and the Japanese Attack on Pearl Harbor', *Quarterly Journal of Speech,* vol.

72, no. 3, pp. 290–350.

Clifford, N. (1963), 'Britain, America and the Far East 1937–1940: a Failure in Cooperation', *Journal of British Studies*, vol. 3, pp. 137–54.

Cook, C.O., Jr (1978), 'The Strange Case of Rainbow 5', *United States Naval Institute Proceedings,* vol. 104, pp. 67–73.

Costigiola, F.C. (1977), 'Anglo-American Finance Rivalry in the 1920s,' *Journal of Economic History,* vol. 37, no. 4, pp. 911–34.

Day, D. (1983), 'The Empire Man Strikes Out: Robert Menzies in London, 1941 – A Summary', *Institute of Commonwealth Studies Paper,* pp. 1–13.

Douglas, N.M. (1974), 'The Open Secret: The US Navy in the Battle of the Atlantic, April–December 1941', *Naval War College Review,* vol. 26, no. 4, pp. 63–83.

Doyle, M.K. (1980), 'The US Navy and War Plan Orange, 1933–1940: Making Necessity a Virtue', *Naval War College Review,* no. 3, pp. 49–63.

Dubay, W. (1970), 'The Geneva Naval Conference of 1927: A Study of Battleship Diplomacy', *Southern Quarterly,* vol. 8, no. 2, pp. 177–99.

Dunbabin, J.P.D., Jr (1975), 'British Rearmament in the Thirties: A Chronology and Review', *History Journal,* vol. 18, pp. 587–609.

Eastman, J.N., Jr (1978), 'The Development of the Big Bomber', *Aerospace Historian,* vol. 25, no. 4, pp. 211–19.

Edgerton, R.K. (1977), 'General Douglas MacArthur and the American Military Impact in the Philippines', *Philippine Studies,* vol. 25, no. 4, pp. 420–40.

Edwards, P.G. (1974), 'R.G. Menzies' Appeal to the United States May –June 1940', *Australian Outlook,* vol. 28, no. 1, pp. 64–70.

Esthus, R. (1964), 'President Roosevelt's Commitment to Britain to Intervene in a Pacific War', *Mississippi Valley Historical Review,* vol. 50, pp. 28–39.

Friend, T. (1963), 'The Philippine Sugar Industry and the Politics of Independence 1929–1935', *Journal of Asian Studies,* vol. 22, no. 2, pp. 179–82.

Futrell, F.F. (1965), 'Air Hostilities in the Philippines, 8 December 1941', *Air University Review,* vol. 16, no. 2, pp. 33–45.

Gibbs, N.H. (1977), 'The Naval Conferences of the Interwar Years: A Study in Anglo-American Relations', *Naval War College Review,* vol. 30, no. 1, pp. 50–63.

Goldberg, M.D. (1973), 'Anglo-American Economic Competition 1920–1930', *Economy and History,* vol. 16, pp. 15–36.

Haglund, D.G. (1980), 'George C. Marshall and the Question of

Military Aid to England May–June 1940', *Journal of Contemporary History,* vol. 15, pp. 745–60.

Haight, M.J., Jr (1971), 'Franklin D. Roosevelt and a Naval Quarantine of Japan', *Pacific Historical Review,* vol. 40, pp. 203–26.

——, (1980), 'F.D.R.'s "Big Stick", *United States Naval Institute Proceedings,* vol. 106, no. 7, pp. 68–73.

Haines, G.K. (1978), 'The Roosevelt Administration Interprets the Monroe Doctrine', *Australian Journal of Politics and History,* vol. 24, pp. 332–45.

——, (1977), 'Under the Eagle's Wing: The Franklin Roosevelt Administration Forges an American Hemisphere', *Diplomatic History,* vol. 1, pp. 373–88.

Hall, H. III (1976), 'The Foreign Policy Making Process in Britain 1934–1935 and the Origins of the Anglo-German Naval Agreement', *Historical Journal,* vol. 19, pp. 477–99.

Harrington, D. F. (1979), 'A Careless Hope: American Air Power and Japan 1941', *Pacific Historical Review,* vol. 48, pp. 217–38.

Hellyer, G. (1982), 'The Australian Government, Japan, and the Approach of War', *Defence Force Journal,* pp. 25–36.

Holmes, W.J. (1978), 'Pearl Harbor Aftermath', *United States Naval Institute Proceedings,* vol. 104, no. 12, pp. 68–75.

Hoopes, T. (1958), 'Overseas Bases in American Strategy', *Foreign Affairs,* vol. 37, no. 1, pp. 69–82.

Hone, T.C. (1982), 'Spending Patterns of the United States Navy 1921–1941', *Armed Forces and Society,* vol. 8, no. 3, pp. 443–62.

Howard, W. (1964), 'Frank Murphy and the Philippine Commonwealth', *Pacific Historical Review,* vol. 33, pp. 45–67.

Jacobs, A.E. (1986), 'The Loss of Repulse and Prince of Wales Dec. 10, 1941', *Warship International,* vol. 23, no. 1, pp. 12–38.

Johnson, W.S. (1972), 'Naval Diplomacy and the Failure of Balanced Security in the Far East – 1921–1935', *Naval War College Review,* vol. 24, no. 6, pp. 67–88.

Krauskopf, R.W. (1958), 'The Army and the Strategic Bomber 1930–1939', *Military Affairs,* vol. 22, pp. 208–15.

Lademan, J.U., Jr (1973), 'U.S.S. Gold Star: Flagship of the Guam Navy', *United States Naval Institute Proceedings,* vol. 99, no. 12, pp. 67–79.

La Plante, J.B. (1973), 'The Evolution of Pacific Policy and Strategic Planning: June 1940 – July 1941', *Naval War College Review,* vol. 25, no. 5, pp. 57–72.

Livermore, S. (1944), 'American Naval Base Policy in the Pacific', *Pacific Historical Review,* vol. 13, pp. 113–35.

Lotchin, R.W. (1979), 'The Metropolitan-Military Complex in

Comparative Perspective: San Francisco, Los Angeles and San Diego, 1919–1941', *Journal of the West,* vol. 18, no. 3, pp. 19–30.

Lowe, P. (1974), 'Great Britain and the Coming of the Pacific War 1939–1941, *Transactions of the Royal Historical Society,* vol. 24, pp. 43–62.

Maddox, R.J. (1974), 'Bandits Over Clark Field', *American History Illustrated,* vol. 9, no. 3, pp. 20–7.

Maurer, J.H. (1981), 'Fuel and the Battle Fleet: Coal, Oil and American Naval Strategy', *Naval War College Review,* vol. 34, no. 6, pp. 60–77.

——, (1962), 'A Delicate Mission: Aerial Reconnaissance on Japanese Islands Before World War II', *Military Affairs,* vol. 26, pp. 66–75.

McCarthy, J.M. (1971), 'Singapore and Australian Defence, 1921–1942', *Australian Outlook,* vol. 25, pp. 165–80.

McKercher, B.J.C. (1986), 'A Sane and Sensible Diplomacy: Austin Chamberlain, Japan and the Naval Balance of Power in the Pacific Ocean 1924–1929', *Canadian Journal of History,* vol. 22, no. 2, pp. 187–213.

Megaw, R. (1973), 'Undiplomatic Channels: Australian Representation in the United States 1918–1939', *Historical Society Australia and New Zealand,* vol. 15, no. 60, pp. 610–30.

Meter, R. Van (1977), 'The Washington Conference of 1921–22: A New Look', *Pacific Historical Review,* vol. 46, pp. 603–24.

Moore, H. (1933), 'The American State in the Philippines', *Foreign Affairs,* vol. 11, no. 3, pp. 517–20.

Morton, L. (1949), 'American and Allied Strategy in the Far East', *Military Affairs,* vol. 39, pp. 22–39.

——, (1959) 'War Plan "Orange": Evolution of a Strategy', *World Politics,* vol. 2, no. 2, pp. 221–50.

——, (1948), 'The Philippine Army 1935–1939: Eisenhower's Memorandum to Quezon', *Military Affairs,* vol.12, pp. 103–7.

Neumann, W.D. (1953), 'Franklin Delano Roosevelt and Japan 1913–1933', *Pacific Historical Review,* vol. 22, pp. 713–19.

Norton, D.M. (1974), 'The Open Secret: The U.S. Navy in the Battle of the Atlantic April–December 1941', *Naval War College Review,* vol. 26, no. 4, pp. 63–83.

O'Connor, R.G. (1959), 'The "Yardstick" and Naval Disarmament in the 1920s', *Mississippi Valley Historical Review,* vol. 45, pp. 441–63.

Orange, V. (1980), 'Pearl Harbor, 7 December 1941', *Historical News,* vol. 40, pp. 1–8.

Parker, R.A.C. (1975), 'Economics, Rearmament and Foreign Policy: The United Kingdom Before 1939 – A Preliminary Survey', *Journal of Contemporary History,* vol. 10, pp. 637–47.

Patterson, J.T. (1966), 'A Conservative Coalition forms in Congress, 1933–1939', *Journal of American History,* vol. 52, pp. 757–72.

Peden, G.C. (1979), 'Sir Warren Fisher and British Rearmament Against Germany', *English Historical Review,* vol. 94, no. 370, pp. 29–47.

Pomeroy, E.S. (1948), 'American Policy Respecting the Marshalls, Carolines and Marianas, 1898–1941', *Pacific Historical Review,* vol. 17, pp. 43–53.

Pratt, L.R. (1971), 'The Anglo-American Naval Conversations on the Far East of January 1938', *International Affairs,* vol. 47, pp. 745–63.

Pritchard, R.J. (1973–1974), 'The Far East as an Influence on the Chamberlain's Pre-War European Policies', *Millenium,* vol. 2, pp. 7–23.

Rader, F.J. (1979), 'The Works Progress Administration and Hawaiian Preparedness 1935–1940', *Military Affairs* vol. 43, no. 1, pp. 12–17.

Reynolds, C.G. (1980), 'MacArthur As Maritime Strategist', *Naval War College Review,* vol. 33, no. 2, pp. 79–91.

——, (1976), 'Admiral Ernest J. King and the Strategy for Victory in the Pacific', *Naval War College Review,* vol. 28, no. 3, pp. 57–64.

Reynolds, D. (1980), 'Competitive Co-operation: Anglo-American Relations in World War II', *Historical Journal,* vol. 23, pp. 233–45.

Richards, D.K. (1944), 'The Beginnings of Pearl Harbor, July 1909 to December 7, 1941', *United States Naval Institute Proceedings,* vol. 70, no. 5, pp. 536–45.

Roberts, J.R. (1981), 'Penultimate Battleships: The Lion Class 1937–1946', *Warship,* no. 19 and 20, pts. 1 and 2, pp. 167–83, 236–50.

Roberts, S.S. (1977), 'The Decline of the Overseas Station Fleets: The United States Asiatic Fleet and the Shanghai Crisis of 1932', *American Neptune,* vol. 37, no. 3, pp. 185–202.

Rosenberg, D.A. (1975), 'Officer Development in the Interwar Navy: Arleigh Burke – The Making of a Naval Professional, 1919–1940', *Pacific Historical Review,* vol. 44, pp. 503–26.

Schaffer, R. (1973), 'General Stanley D. Embick: Military Dissenter', *Military Affairs,* vol. 37, no. 3, pp. 89–95.

Schaller, M. (1976), 'American Air Strategy in China, 1939–1941: The Origins of Clandestine Air Warfare', *American Quarterly,* vol. 28, pp. 3–19.

Smith, M. (1977), 'The Royal Air Force, Air Power, and British Foreign Policy 1932–1937', *Journal of Contemporary History,* vol. 12, no. 1, pp. 313–37.

——, (1978) 'Rearmament and Deterrence in Britain in the 1930s, *Journal of Strategic Studies,* vol. 1, no. 3, pp. 313–37.

Sumida, Jon (1992), '"The Best Laid Plans": The Development of British Battle Fleet Tactics, 1919–1942', *International History*

Review, vol. 14, no. 4, pp. 684–700.

Symonds, C.L. (1980), 'William Veazie Pratt as C.N.O. 1930–1933', *Naval War College Review,* vol. 33, no. 2, pp. 17–33.

Tarling N. (1977), 'Quezon and the British Commonwealth', *Australian Journal of Politics and History,* vol. 23, no. 2, pp. 182–206.

Taussig, J.K., Jr (1972), 'I Remember Pearl Harbor', *United States Naval Institute Proceedings,* vol. 98, no. 12, pp. 18–24.

Thomas, W.R. (1966), 'Pacific Blockade: A Lost Opportunity of the 1930s', *Naval War College Review,* vol. 19, no. 1, pp. 36–42.

Tolley, K. (1966), 'Divided We Fell', *United States Naval Institute Proceedings,* vol. 92, no. 10, pp. 37–51.

Trimble, W.F. (1979), 'Admiral Hilary P. Jones and the 1927 General Naval Conference', *Military Affairs,* vol. 53, no. 1, pp. 1–4.

Utley, J.G. (1976), 'Upstairs, Downstairs at Foggy Bottom: Oil Exports and Japan 1940–41', *Prologue,* vol. 8, pp. 17–28.

Vlahos, M. (1980), 'The Naval War College and the Origins of War Planning against Japan', *Naval War College Review,* vol. 33, no. 4, pp. 23–41.

Walter, J.C. (1980), 'Congressman Carl Vinson and F.D.R.: Naval Preparedness and the Coming of World War II', *Georgia Historical Quarterly,* vol. 114, no. 3, pp. 295–305.

Watt, D. Cameron (1973), 'Roosevelt and Neville Chamberlain: Two Appeasers', *International Journal,* vol. 28, pp. 185–204.

——, (1956), 'The Anglo-German Treaty of 1935: An Interim Judgement', *Journal of Modern History,* vol. 28, pp. 155–75.

Wheeler, G. (1959), 'The U.S. Navy and the War in the Pacific 1919–41', *World Affairs Quarterly,* vol. 30, no. 2, pp. 199–225.

——, (1957), 'The United States Navy and the Japanese Enemy 1919–1931', *Military Affairs,* vol. 21, pp. 61–74.

——, (1959), 'Republican Philippine Policy 1921–1933', *Pacific Historical Review,* vol. 27, pp. 377–90.

——, (1964), 'The Movement to Reverse Philippine Independence', *Pacific Historical Review,* vol. 33, pp. 167–81.

——, (1959), 'Republican Philippine Policy, 1921–1933', *Pacific Historical Review,* vol. 28, pp. 377–90.

Wilson, E.E. (1950), 'The Navy's First Carrier Task Force', *United States Naval Institute Proceedings,* vol. 76, no. 2, pp. 159–69.

Wise, J.E., Jr (1964), 'Ford Island', *United States Naval Institute Proceedings,* vol. 90, no. 10, pp. 77–91.

Wrench, D.J. (1980), 'The Influence of Neville Chamberlain on Foreign and Defence Policy 1932–1935', *RUSI Journal,* vol. 125, pp. 49–57.

4. Unpublished Sources

Agbi, O.S. (1975), 'British Imperial Defence and Foreign Policy in Asia and the Pacific and the Impact of Anglo-Japanese Relations 1937–1941', unpublished PhD thesis, Birmingham University.

Bright, C.C. (1970), 'Britain's Search for Security 1930–1936: The Diplomacy of Naval Disarmament and Imperial Defense', unpublished PhD thesis, Yale University.

Carpenter, S. (1976), 'Towards the Development of Philippine National Security Capability 1920–1940: With Special Reference to the Commonwealth Period, 1935–1940', unpublished PhD thesis, New York University.

Crace, R.J. (1974), 'Anglo-American Relations Regarding the Far East 1937–1941', unpublished PhD thesis, Fordham University.

Doyle, M.K. (1977), 'The U.S. Navy's Strategy, Defense and Foreign Policy 1932–41', unpublished PhD thesis, Washington University.

Fagan, G.V. (1954), 'Anglo-American Naval Relations, 1927–1937', unpublished PhD thesis, University of Pennsylvania.

Gilman, E. (1976), 'Economic Aspects of Anglo-American Relations in the Era of Roosevelt and Chamberlain, 1937–1940', unpublished PhD thesis, University of London.

Haggie, P. (1974), 'The Royal Navy and the Far Eastern Problem 1931–1941', unpublished PhD thesis, Manchester University.

Herzog, J. (1964), 'The Role of the United States Navy in the Evolution and Execution of American Foreign Policy relative to Japan 1936–1941', unpublished PhD thesis, Brown University.

Kittredge, T.B. (undated), 'Anglo-American Naval Relations 1937–1942', unpublished manuscript, Office of Naval History.

Lippincott, J. (1976), 'The Strategy of Appeasement: The Formation of British Defence Policy 1934–1939', unpublished PhD thesis, Oxford University.

Melhorn, C.M. (1973), 'Lever for Rearmament: The Rise of the Carrier', unpublished PhD thesis, University of California.

Metcalf, O.R. (1977), 'British Defence Policy, Strategy and Diplomacy 1931–1936', unpublished PhD thesis, Cambridge University.

Murfet, M.H. (1980), 'Anglo-American Relations in the Period of the Chamberlain Premiership May 1937–May 1940: The Relationship between Naval Strategy and Foreign Policy', unpublished PhD thesis, Oxford University.

Oyos, L. (1958), 'The Navy and United States Far Eastern Policy 1930–1939', unpublished PhD thesis, Nebraska University.

Snowbarger, W.E. (1950), 'The Development of Pearl Harbor', unpublished PhD thesis, University of California.

Index

Index

Index

Index

Singapore Conferences 210–16
Slessor, John 192
Sourabaya 194
Spratley Island 33
Standard Oi l61
Stanford, M. 62
Stanhope, Lord 141, 145
Starbuck Island 122
Stark, Harold 173–5, 179, 180, 182, 191, 211, 220, 221, 222, 235, 255, 258, 262
Staveren Van, Captain 212
Strong, George 176, 182
Suva 127, 180
Suvarov Island 72, 128
Swanson, Claude 83
Swatow 32, 130, 150

Tahiti 69
Taongi 69
Taranto 186
Tawi-Tawi Bay 67, 68, 72
Taylor, Harold 61
'Teapot Dome' 75
Temeraire HMS 166
Terror HMS 19, 23
Thailand 193, 194, 212, 256, 257, 262
Thi Tu Island 30, 33
Thomas, F. P. 210
Tirpitz 249, 252, 253
Torres Straits 72, 136, 188
Trincomalee 234, 236
Tripartite pact 207, 287
Tromp 261
Truk 69, 72

Turner, Richmond 181, 184, 192, 194, 216, 225, 234, 236, 238, 257
Tuscaloosa USS 231
Tutuila 72, 120, 218
Tydings-McDuffie Act 26, 83

Upham, F. B. 79

Valdero de Manila 63
Venezuela 90
Vinson Acts 65, 137
Vinson, Claude 85–6

Walsh, David 84
Wake Island 65, 72, 91, 128, 218, 219
War Plan 'Orange' 58–67
  'changes 73–4, 81, 86
  repudiation of 87–9, 92–3, 119, 171, 178, 182, 218, 245, 281, 283, 284, 285
Warspite HMS 14, 166, 167
Washington, Admiral 64
Washington Island 69, 74
Washington Treaty 13–14, 61, 96, 120, 128, 280, 281
Washington USS 234
Welles, Sumner 175
Wemyss, Rosslyn 117
Willson, Russell 138
Wilson, Woodrow 116
Winant, John 256
Wolea Island 69

Yarnell, Harry 88,89, 132
Yorktown USS 13, 223